IFRS 9 and CECL Credit Risk Modelling and Validation

A Practical Guide with Examples Worked in R and SAS

IFRS 9 and CECL Credit Risk Modelling and Validation

A Practical Guide with Examples Worked in R and SAS

Tiziano Bellini

ACADEMIC PRESS
An imprint of Elsevier

Academic Press is an imprint of Elsevier
125 London Wall, London EC2Y 5AS, United Kingdom
525 B Street, Suite 1650, San Diego, CA 92101, United States
50 Hampshire Street, 5th Floor, Cambridge, MA 02139, United States
The Boulevard, Langford Lane, Kidlington, Oxford OX5 1GB, United Kingdom

Library of Congress Cataloging-in-Publication Data
A catalog record for this book is available from the Library of Congress

British Library Cataloguing-in-Publication Data
A catalogue record for this book is available from the British Library

ISBN: 978-0-12-814940-9

For information on all Academic Press publications
visit our website at https://www.elsevier.com/books-and-journals

Working together
to grow libraries in
developing countries

www.elsevier.com • www.bookaid.org

Publisher: Candice Janco
Acquisition Editor: Scott Bentley
Editorial Project Manager: Susan Ikeda
Production Project Manager: Bharatwaj Varatharajan
Designer: Mark Rogers

Typeset by VTeX

A mio papà,
ad un eroe silenzioso,
alla sua encomiabile moralità.

Contents

Tiziano Bellini's Biography

Tiziano Bellini received his PhD degree in statistics from the University of Milan after being a visiting PhD student at the London School of Economics and Political Science. He is a Qualified Chartered Accountant and Registered Auditor. He gained wide risk management experience across Europe (including in London) and in New York. He is currently Director at BlackRock Financial Market Advisory (FMA) in London. Previously he worked at Barclays Investment Bank, EY Financial Advisory Services in London, HSBC's headquarters, Prometeia in Bologna, and other leading Italian companies. He is a guest lecturer at Imperial College in London, and at the London School of Economics and Political Science. Formerly, he served as a lecturer at the University of Bologna and the University of Parma. Tiziano is the author of *Stress Testing and Risk Integration in Banks, A Statistical Framework and Practical Software Guide (in Matlab and R)* edited by Academic Press. He has published in the *European Journal of Operational Research*, *Computational Statistics and Data Analysis*, and other top-reviewed journals. He has given numerous training courses, seminars, and conference presentations on statistics, risk management, and quantitative methods in Europe, Asia, and Africa.

Preface

A series of concerns have been expressed since the adoption of the incurred losses paradigm by both the International Accounting Standard Board (IASB) and the Financial Accounting Standard Board (FASB). The recent (2007–2009) financial crisis uncovered this issue by inducing a review of accounting standards which culminated with the International Financial Reporting Standard number 9 (IFRS 9) and Current Expected Credit Loss (CECL).

This book provides a comprehensive guide on credit risk modelling and validation for IFRS 9 and CECL expected credit loss (ECL) estimates. It is aimed at graduate, master students and practitioners. As a distinctive practical imprint, software examples in R and SAS accompany the reader through the journey. The choice of these tools is driven by their wide use both in banks and academia.

Despite the non-prescriptive nature of accounting standards, common practice suggests to rely on the so-called probability of default (PD), loss given default (LGD), and exposure at default (EAD) framework. Other non-complex methods based on loss-rate, vintage, cash flows are considered as a corollary. In practice, banks estimate their ECLs as the present value of the above three parameters' product over a one-year or lifetime horizon. Based on this, a distinction arises between CECL and IFRS 9. If the former follows a lifetime perspective for all credits, the latter classifies accounts in three main buckets: stage 1 (one-year ECL), stage 2 (lifetime ECL), stage 3 (impaired credits). The key innovation introduced by the new accounting standards subsumes a shift towards a forward-looking and lifetime perspective. Therefore a link between macroeconomic variables (MVs), behavioural variables (BVs), and the above three parameters is crucial for our dissertation. Such a framework is also a natural candidate for stress testing projections.

From an organizational standpoint, Chapter 1 serves the purpose to introduce IFRS 9 and CECL. It points out their similarities and differences. Then the focus is on the link connecting expected credit loss estimates and capital requirements. A book overview is provided as a guide for the reader willing to grasp a high-level picture of the entire ECL modelling and validation journey.

Chapter 2 focuses on one-year PD modelling. Two main reasons suggest our treating one-year and lifetime separately. Firstly, banks have been developing one-year PD models over the last two decades for Basel II regulatory requirements. Secondly, a building-block-structure split in one-year and lifetime PD facilitates the learning process. As a starting point, this chapter focuses on how default events are defined for accounting purposes and how to build a consistent PD database. Moving towards modelling features, firstly, generalized linear models (GLMs) are explored as a paradigm for one-year PD estimates. Secondly, machine learning (ML) algorithms are studied. Classification and regression trees (CARTs), bagging, random forest, and boosting are investigated both to challenge existing models, and explore new PD modelling solutions. In line with the most recent literature, the choice of these approaches is driven both by their effectiveness and easy implementation. If a wide data availability encourages the use of data driven methods, low default portfolios and data scarcity are other challenges one may need to face. Bespoke methods are scrutinized to address issues related to limited number of defaults, and ad hoc procedures are explored to deal with lack of deep historical data.

One of the key innovation introduced by the new accounting standards refers to lifetime losses. Even though this concept is not new in risk management, its implementation in the financial industry is extremely contemporary as discussed in Chapter 3. Account-level information is usually required to develop a comprehensive modelling framework. Based on data availability, one may consider few alternative methods. As a first way to tackle the challenge, generalized linear models (GLMs) are explored. As a second step, survival modelling is introduced by means of three main techniques. The pioneering Kaplan–Meier (KP) frame paves the way to lifetime PD modelling by means of Cox Proportional Hazard (CPH) and accelerated failure time (AFT) models. Thirdly, machine learning (ML) procedures are scrutinized. Bagging, random forest and boosting are directly applied on panel data to capture the relationship with both BVs and MVs over time. Then, as an alternative, random survival forest is explored by embedding survival modelling into a ML structure. Fourthly, transition matrices are studied by considering both bespoke approaches, based on transition matrix adjustments over a multi-period horizon and multi state Markov models.

Chapter 4 focuses on loss given default (LGD) representing the portion of a non-recovered credit in case of default. As a starting point to develop an LGD model, one needs to rely on a suitable database. Its goal is to collect all information needed to assess recoveries throughout the so-called "workout process" until an account is fully cured or written-off. From a modelling standpoint, firstly a micro-structure LGD modelling is introduced to provide a comprehensive view of the post-default recovery process. The focus is on two key components: probability of cure and severity. As a next step, the focus is on regression techniques. Tobit, beta and other methods are first studied as silos approaches, and then combined in mixture models to improve both goodness-of-fit and model predictive power. Thirdly, machine learning (ML) modelling is explored. Classification and regression trees are natural candidates to fit LGDs. Bagging, random forest and boosting are also studied as a valid enhancement of the most traditional ML methods. Some hints are provided on how to apply Cox proportional hazard (CPH), and accelerated failure time (AFT) models to LGDs. Scarce data issues and low default portfolios are then investigated by pointing out the need for simpler approaches. Qualitative assessments play a key role in such a setting.

Chapter 5 is devoted to exposure at default (EAD) analysis. A key distinction operates between committed products (for example, loans) and uncommitted facilities (for instance, overdrafts). Loan-type products usually cover a multi-year horizon. Consequently, economic conditions may cause a deviation from the originally agreed repayment scheme. Full prepayments and overpayments (partial prepayments) are first investigated by means of generalized linear models (GLMs) and machine learning (ML). Hints on survival analysis are also provided to estimate and project prepayment outcomes. Growing attention is devoted both by researchers and practitioners to competing risks. As a second step of our investigation, the focus is on a framework to jointly model full prepayments, defaults, and overpayments. On the one hand, we model these events by means of a multinomial regression. In this case, when the outcome is not binary (for example, overpayment) a second step is needed. Tobit and beta regressions are used to capture overpayment specific features. On the other hand, full prepayments and overpayments are jointly investigated by means of ML models. As a third focus area, uncommitted facilities are inspected by means of a bespoke framework. One needs to deal with additional challenges, comprising accounts with zero or negative utilization at reporting date and positive exposure at default. All states of the world relevant for ECL computation are scrutinized from different angles.

Finally, Chapter 6 brings together all ECL ingredients studied throughout the book. Given the role of scenarios, multivariate time series are investigated by means of vector auto-regression (VAR) and vector error-correction (VEC) models. Information regarding global vector auto-regression (GVAR) modelling is also provided. Case studies allow us to grasp how to compute ECL in practice. Emphasis is placed on IFRS 9 and CECL comparison. Finally, full ECL validation is scrutinized. Indeed, the presumed independence between risk parameters and lack of concentration effects is challenged by means of historical validation and forward-looking portfolio analysis.

Tiziano Bellini
London, August 2018

Acknowledgements

When I graduated in Business and Economics at the University of Parma, my dream was to become a professional accountant. It was hard to invest the earliest years of my career by working both in banking, and in professional services to get the degree of *Dottore Commercialista e Revisore Contabile* (Qualified Chartered Accountant and Registered Auditor). Curiosity led me to study numbers from a different angle throughout the doctorate in statistics at the University of Milan, and at the London School of Economics and Political Science. The experience gained on expected credit losses operating in the financial industry across Europe (including in London) and New York combined my two souls as accountant and statistician. My wish is to provide the reader of this book a useful guide through the lenses of a practitioner inclined to academic research.

I need to thank Emeritus Professor Giuseppe Galassi who introduced me to accounting research. I am grateful to Professor Marco Riani and Professor Luigi Grossi, who accompanied my initial steps into statistics and data analysis.

I express my deepest gratitude to Nikola Perovic and Omar Khan for their enormous help in software development. Special thanks are addressed to Manuele Iorio and Professor Tony Bellotti for their careful reading of early drafts. This book also benefits from a number of genuine discussions with Flavio Cocco and Carlo Toffano, who mentored me through my risk management profession. I am also immensely grateful for all comments received from four anonymous reviewers. The book highly profits from their challenges and advice.

I thank Scott Bentley for supporting and endorsing this project as Academic Press Editor. I am beholden to Billie Fernandez and Susan Ikeda for their patience and affectionate help all along the publication process.

My greatest thank is to my family. I would have never been able to face this challenge without my mom's and my sister's encouragement. I dedicate this book to my dad. His morals and courage inspired all my life. This book was a surprise I wanted to offer him. I was too late...

INTRODUCTION TO EXPECTED CREDIT LOSS MODELLING AND VALIDATION

As a response to incurred losses criticisms, both the International Accounting Standard Board (IASB) and Financial Accounting Standard Board (FASB) worked to redesign accounting standards towards an expected credit loss paradigm. The aim was to anticipate loss recognition by avoiding issues experienced—in particular—during the 2007–2009 financial crisis.

Starting from an initial joint effort for a unique solution, IASB and FASB agreed on common principles, but then issued two separated standards. IASB's International Financial Reporting Standard number 9 (IFRS 9), issued in 2014, relies on a three-bucket classification, where one-year or lifetime expected credit losses are computed. On the contrary, FASB's Current Expected Credit Loss (CECL) accounting standard update 2016–13 (topic 326: credit losses) follows a lifetime perspective as a general rule.

IFRS 9 and CECL are separately introduced in Sections 1.2 and 1.3 to point out their similarities and differences. Then the focus is on the link connecting expected credit loss estimates and capital requirements, as detailed in Section 1.4. As a final step, a book overview is provided in Section 1.5 as a guide for the reader willing to grasp on overview of the entire expected credit loss modelling and validation journey.

KEY ABBREVIATIONS AND SYMBOLS

CECL	Current expected credit loss
$EAD_{i,s,t}$	Exposure at default for account i in sub-portfolio s at time t
ECL	Expected credit loss
FASB	Financial Accounting Standard Board
IASB	International Accounting Standard Board
IFRS	International financial reporting standard
$LGD_{i,s,t}$	Loss given default for account i in sub-portfolio s at time t
$PD_{i,s,t}$	Probability of default for account i in sub-portfolio s at time t
PIT	Point-in-time
RWA	Risk weighted asset
TTC	Through the cycle
UL	Unexpected loss

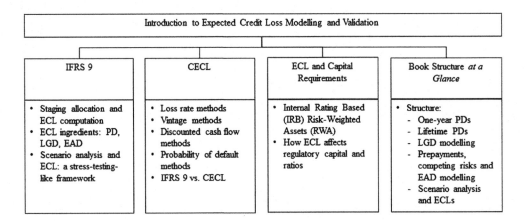

FIGURE 1.1

ECL engine: topics explored throughout the chapter.

1.1 INTRODUCTION

Since the adoption of the incurred losses archetype by both IASB and FASB, a series of concerns have been expressed about the inappropriateness of delaying the recognition of credit losses and balance sheet financial assets overstatement. The recent (2007–2009) financial crisis uncovered this issue to its broader extent by forcing a profound review of accounting standards, culminating with the International Financial Reporting Standard number 9 (IFRS 9) (IASB, 2014) and Current Expected Credit Loss (CECL) (FASB, 2016). IFRS 9 goes live in 2018 by considering not only expected credit loss (ECL) rules, but also classification mechanics and hedge accounting. Hereafter, our focus is limited to ECLs. On the other hand, FASB's new impairment standard will be effective for SEC filers for years beginning on or after December 15, 2019 (with early adoption permitted one year earlier), and one year later for other entities.

The key innovation introduced by new accounting standards subsumes a shift from a backward-incurred-losses perspective towards a forward-looking ECL representation. This change implies a deep review in terms of business interpretation, computational skills and IT infrastructures. Furthermore, a deeper senior management involvement is at the very heart of new accounting standards practical implementation. A holistic perspective is required in such a complex framework involving widespread competences to be aligned on a common goal.

Figure 1.1 summarises the key areas touched in this chapter as an introduction to the main topics discussed throughout the book.

- **IFRS 9.** Despite the non-prescriptive nature of the accounting principle, common practice suggests relying on the so-called probability of default (PD), loss given default (LGD) and exposure at default (EAD) framework. Banks estimate ECL as the present value of the above three parameters' product over a one-year or lifetime horizon, depending upon experiencing a significant increase in credit risk since origination. Section 1.2 starts by describing the key principles informing the staging allocation process. Three main buckets are considered: stage 1 (one-year ECL), stage 2 (lifetime

ECL), stage 3 (impaired credits). The focus, then, moves on ECL key ingredients, that is, PD, LGD, EAD. A forward-looking perspective inspires IFRS 9 by emphasising the role of economic scenarios as a key ingredient for ECL computation. Based on this, an easy parallel can be drawn between ECL and stress testing.

- **CECL.** Few methodologies are mentioned under FASB (2016) to compute ECLs. In this regard, Section 1.3 provides an overview of approaches one may adopt to align with CECL requirements. Loss-rate, vintage and cash flow methods are inspected by means of illustrative examples. These non-complex approaches are not further investigated throughout the book. Indeed, the focus of the book is on more complex methods based on PD, LGD and EAD to leverage similarities with IFRS 9.
- **ECL and capital requirements.** Section 1.4 highlights some of the key connections linking accounting standards and regulatory capital requirements. Firstly, internal risk-based (IRB) weighted assets are introduced. Secondly, expected credit losses are scrutinised in the context of regulatory capital quantification. IFRS 9 and CECL impact on common equity Tier 1, Tier 2 and total capital ratios is pointed out by means of a few illustrative examples.
- **Book structure at a glance.** Both IFRS 9 and CECL require an outstanding effort in terms of data, modelling and infrastructure. A deep integration is required to coherently estimate ECLs. For this reason Section 1.5 provides a guide for the reader through the journey. An introduction to each chapter is provided together with a narrative highlighting the key choices made in presenting each topic.

1.2 **IFRS 9**

The recent (2007–2009) financial crisis urged a response not only from a capital perspective, but also from an accounting point of view. Indeed, BIS (2011) introduced new constraints to banking activity and enforced existing rules. Capital ratios were strengthened by defining a consistent set of rules. Leverage ratio was introduced as a measure to prevent banks expanding their assets without limit. Liquidity ratios (that is, liquidity coverage ratio and net stable funding ratio) constituted a response to liquidity problems experienced during the crisis. Finally, stress testing was used as a key tool to assess potential risks on a wider perspective by encompassing economic, liquidity and capital perspectives all at once.

From an accounting perspective, IASB introduced the new principle, IFRS 9 (IASB, 2014). Its most important innovation refers to credit losses estimation. In terms of scope, the new model applies to:

- **Instruments measured at amortised cost.** Assets are measured at the amount recognised at initial recognition minus principal repayments, plus or minus the cumulative amortisation of any difference between that initial amount and the maturity amount, and any loss allowance. Interest income is calculated using the effective interest method and is recognised in profit and loss.
- **Instruments measured at fair value through other comprehensive income (FVOCI).** Loans and receivables, interest revenue, impairment gains and losses, and a portion of foreign exchange gains and losses are recognised in profit and loss on the same basis as for amortised cost assets. Changes in fair value are not recognised in profit and loss, but in other comprehensive income (OCI).

A necessary condition for classifying a loan or receivable at amortised cost or FVOCI is whether the asset is part of a group or portfolio that is being managed within a business model, whose objective is to collect contractual cash flows (that is, amortised cost), or to both collect contractual cash flows and to sell (that is, FVOCI). Otherwise, the asset is measured at fair values profit and loss, and ECL model does not apply to instruments measured at fair value profit and loss (for example, trading book assets).

Figure 1.2 summarises the key topics investigated throughout Section 1.2.

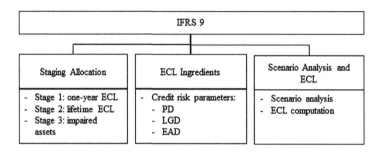

FIGURE 1.2

Workflow diagram for Section 1.2.

Section 1.2.1 introduces the staging allocation process. Indeed, IASB (2014) relies on the concept of significant increase in credit risk to distinguish between stage 1 and stage 2 credits. For stage 1, one-year ECL holds, whereas for stage 2 lifetime ECL needs to be computed. Stage 3 refers to impaired credits and lifetime ECL applies. Section 1.2.2 provides an overview of the key ingredients commonly used to compute ECL. Indeed, apart from simplified approaches, probability of default (PD), loss given default (LGD) and exposure at default (EAD) are key elements for ECL estimate.

1.2.1 STAGING ALLOCATION

IFRS 9 standard (IASB, 2014) outlines a three-stage model for impairment based on the following:

- **Stage 1.** This bucket includes financial instruments that have not had a significant increase in credit risk since initial recognition or that have low credit risk at the reporting date. For these assets, one-year ECL is recognised and interest revenue is calculated on the gross carrying amount of the asset (that is, without deduction for credit allowance). One-year ECL is the expected loss that results from default events that are possible within one year after the reporting date.
- **Stage 2.** Financial instruments that experienced a significant increase in credit risk since initial recognition, but that do not have objective evidence of impairment are allocated to stage 2. For these assets, lifetime ECL is recognised. Interest revenue is still calculated on the gross carrying amount of the asset. Lifetime ECL refers to all possible default events over the expected life of the financial instrument.
- **Stage 3.** Assets that have objective evidence of impairment at reporting date are allocated to stage 3. For these assets, lifetime ECL is recognised and interest revenue is calculated on the net carrying amount (that is, net of credit allowance).

In line with the above, the definition of significant increase in credit risk plays a key role throughout the entire IFRS 9 process. Indeed, this is the trigger causing ECL to be computed over a one-year instead of lifetime horizon. Reasonable and supportable information—available without undue cost or effort—including past and forward-looking information, are at the very root of the decision. Few presumptions inform this process as listed below:

• **Low credit risk.** No significant increase in credit risk is presumed in the case of low credit risk at the reporting date. As an example, one may consider an externally rated investment grade instrument. A bank can use internal methods to identify whether an instrument has a low credit risk.
• **Presumption 30 days past due.** There is a rebuttable presumption that the credit risk has increased significantly, when contractual payments are more than 30 days past due.

A bank compares the risk of a default occurring over the expected life of the financial instrument, such as at the reporting date with the risk of default and at the date of initial recognition. In line with IASB (2014), the assessment of significant increase in credit risk relies on a relative comparison. Nevertheless, an absolute comparison (example, absolute threshold) is viable when it provides a consistent outcome, as under a relative approach. Factors to consider in determining the occurrence of a significant increase in credit risk include, but are not limited to, the following:

• **Quantitative indicators.** Probability of default is the most common indicator adopted in practice to assess credit risk increase. A residual lifetime PD should be used. It implies that the same remaining period is considered for both PD at origination and reporting date. As a practical expedient, a one-year PD can be used if changes in one-year PD are a reasonable approximation to changes in the lifetime PD.
• **Qualitative indicators.** IFRS 9 provides some examples, including: credit spread, credit default swap price, market information related to the borrower, significant change in the credit rating, internal credit rating downgrade and significant change in the value of the collateral. Qualitative factors should be considered separately, when they have not already been included in the quantitative assessment.

Judgement is applied in determining what threshold would be considered a significant increase in credit risk. The risk of recognising expected losses too late should be balanced against defining a narrow band to avoid instruments frequently moving in and out of the different stages without this reflecting a significant change in credit risk. What is a significant change varies, based on a series of circumstances. The same absolute change in the risk of default will be more significant for an instrument with a lower initial credit risk, compared to an instrument with a higher initial risk of default. As an example, if origination PD is 0.10% and reporting date PD is 0.20%, a relative increase of 100.00% occurred. However, it accounts for a relatively small change, 0.10%. On the contrary, if the PD at initial recognition was 1.00% and this increased by the same absolute amount of 0.10% to 1.10%, this is an increase of only 10%. Therefore staging mechanics need specific balance to account for both relative and absolute features.

It is evident that a key issue in measuring expected losses is to specify when a default occurs. IFRS 9 does not provide a specific definition. Nevertheless, an entity must apply a definition that is consistent with internal credit risk management purposes. There is a rebuttable presumption that a default does not occur later than 90 days past due.

The following section provides a high-level description of the key ECL ingredients: PD, LGD, and EAD.

1.2.2 ECL INGREDIENTS

In line with IFRS 9 principles, ECL must reflect an unbiased evaluation of a range of possible outcomes and their probabilities of occurrence. Reasonable and supportable information needs to be used without undue cost or effort at the reporting date about past events, current conditions and forecasts of future economic conditions. Estimates also need to reflect the time value of money by means of relevant discounting.

Based on what was described in the previous section, default definition plays a crucial role. Such a concept, together with data to use for its practical implementation, will be investigated throughout all chapters of the book. In what follows, a high-level description of the main ingredients to use for ECL estimate is provided. It allows us to familiarise with their characteristics and understand the reason why adequate models are necessary.

- **Probability of default (PD).** Default events can be interpreted as realisations of a random variable. PD represents the expectation of these occurrences over a given time frame. When applied to a financial instrument, PD provides the likelihood that a borrower will be unable to meet debt obligations within a certain period. One of the key innovations introduced by IFRS 9 is extending to a lifetime time frame credit risk estimates. The distinction between one-year and lifetime ECL, referred to as stage 1 and 2, respectively, needs to be reflected in terms of one-year and lifetime PDs. In this regard, starting from a lifetime perspective, PDs may be broken down into sub-period within the remaining life term. One-year PD relates to a one-year interval.

  It is worth noting that from a credit risk management organisational standpoint, regulatory capital relies on one-year estimates (BIS, 2006). As a consequence, banks fancy the idea to use a common framework for both capital requirements and accounting purposes. A stress-testing-like framework may serve as a viaticum for one-year through-the-cycle (TTC) PDs towards point-in-time (PIT) forward-looking lifetime estimates, as detailed in Chapters 2 and 3 of the book.

- **Loss given default (LGD).** LGD represents the portion of a non-recovered credit in case of default. Two extremes can easily be identified. On the one hand, a full recovery is associated with 0% LGD. On the contrary, a zero recovery scenario leads to a 100% LGD. A series of partial recoveries may also occur in practice, so that LGD is usually bounded between 0% and 100%. Due to its nature, LGD is estimated over the entire workout process. In other words, one needs to consider all recoveries occurred after default without imposing time restrictions. In this connection, LGD may be regarded as a lifetime metric. On the other hand, accurately investigating whether and how macroeconomic conditions affect LGDs is necessary. Indeed, a forward-looking perspective is required for IFRS 9 and CECL estimates, as detailed in Chapter 4.

- **Exposure at default (EAD).** Chapter 5 of the book focuses on the balance expected credit loss (ECL) is computed on. A key distinction arises between loan-type products (for example, mortgages) and uncommitted facilities (such as overdrafts). In the former case, a multiyear horizon usually applies. As a consequence, deviations from the originally agreed repayment scheme may take place. Full prepayments and overpayments (partial prepayments) require adequate modelling. With regards to uncommitted facilities, firstly one needs to highlight the distinction between contractual and behavioural maturity. Then defaulted drawn amount is the target variable under scrutiny.

As an additional step, a competing risk framework is considered against the more traditional credit risk silos representation. Indeed, growing attention has been addressed both by practitioners and researchers to integrate risk estimates by capturing their interdependencies. Our focus is on prepayments, defaults and overpayments.

All above ingredients are jointly used to compute ECL, based on staging allocation rules introduced and scenarios, as summarised in the following section.

1.2.3 SCENARIO ANALYSIS AND ECL

IASB (2014) requires a scenario-weighting scheme (that is, probability-weighted). In some cases a simple modelling may be sufficient as per B5.5.42. In other situations, the identification of scenarios that specify the amount and timing of the cash flows for particular outcomes, and their estimated probability, is required. In those situations, the expected credit losses shall reflect at least two outcomes (see paragraph 5.5.18). One may infer an upper limit to the number of scenarios from Section BC5.265. Consequently, the requirement of a simulation-based approach over thousands of scenarios can be disregarded.

A connecting framework is needed to link account information, macroeconomic scenarios, and credit risk satellite models (for example, PD, LGD, EAD). This is also the typical high-level frame used for stress testing. Indeed, in both cases (that is, ECL and stress testing) credit risk models are linked to macroeconomic scenarios to forecast a set of metrics. In the case of ECL, the focus is on IFRS 9 scope (that is, credits), whereas stress testing also involves the entire asset and liability structure of a bank.

One may summarise the process as follows:

- **Data.** At reporting date, a set of information is needed as a starting point to assess ECL; information regarding both performing and defaulted portfolios is needed.
- **Macroeconomic scenarios.** Given ECL forward-looking nature, scenarios are required both for IFRS 9 and CECL. In more detail, IFRS 9 explicitly required a multiscenario framework; on the other hand, CECL is not prescriptive. Nevertheless, CECL may be organised by relying on a multiple-scenario scheme, as per IFRS 9.
- **Satellite models.** Credit risk models, such as PD, LGD and EAD, in conjunction with a set of other frames (for example, effective interest rate), rely on account-level, portfolio-level data, and scenarios. Projections are drawn over a lifetime horizon both for IFRS 9 and CECL. As part of the lifetime curve, IFRS 9 requires one-year parameters to estimate stage 1 ECL.
- **IFRS 9 staging allocation.** Staging rules apply to each financial instrument, based on criteria aligned with IASB (2014) requirements.
- **ECL computation for each scenario.** The output of credit risk satellite models feed the ECL engine. If CECL relies on lifetime perspective for all accounts, IFRS 9 requires a distinction between one-year and lifetime ECLs, based on the staging allocation process described above.
- **Weighting scheme and final ECL estimation.** As a final step of the process, ECL is obtained as a weighted average of ECLs estimated under alternative scenarios. For CECL, if only one scenario is used, ECL is estimated as part of the previous step: *ECL computation for each scenario*.

Example 1.2.1 helps us to grasp interconnections between credit risk parameters, scenarios, staging allocation, and ECL estimation.

EXAMPLE 1.2.1 STAGING ALLOCATION AND ECL

Let us focus on a given borrower with only one loan. Two illustrative staging threshold are considered, that is, 6.00% and 5.00%. Three scenarios (A, B, and C) are defined, as summarised in Table 1.1. All credit risk parameters (that is, PD, LGD, and EAD) are affected by scenarios. The account is allocated to one stage, based on the weighted average lifetime PD. In our case, the average lifetime PD is 5.55% (that is, $2.00\% \cdot 30.00\% + 5.50\% \cdot 50.00\% + 11.00\% \cdot 20.00\%$).

- **Hypothesis threshold 6.00%.** Since $5.55\% < 6.00\%$, the account is allocated to stage 1. Therefore ECL is $19.28 thousand (that is, one-year estimate).
- **Hypothesis threshold 5.00%.** If the staging threshold is set at 5.00%, the account is allocated to stage 2, and the ECL is $28.84 thousand (that is, lifetime estimate).

Table 1.1 Staging allocation: ingredients and ECL outcomes ($ Thousands)

Scenario	Weight	One-year PD	Lifetime PD	LGD	EAD	One-year ECL	Lifetime ECL	One-year ECL weighted	Lifetime ECL weighted
A	30.00%	1.00%	2.00%	40.00%	900.00	3.60	7.20	1.08	2.16
B	50.00%	4.00%	5.50%	50.00%	980.00	19.60	26.95	9.80	13.48
C	20.00%	7.00%	11.00%	60.00%	1,000.00	42.00	66.00	8.40	13.20
Average PD			5.55 %						
ECL								19.28	28.84

The following section focuses on CECL (FASB, 2016).

1.3 CECL

In line with the general principle informing post 2007–2009 financial crisis account reform, CECL (FASB, 2016) goes in parallel with IFRS 9 by moving from an incurred perspective towards an expected loss frame. One needs to include forward-looking information and recognise the expected lifetime losses upon origination or acquisition. Off-balance sheet commitments, which are not unconditionally cancellable also require ECL computation. In a broad sense, CECL applies to financial assets measured at amortised cost by including, among others, financing receivables, held to maturity (HTM) securities, receivables from repurchase agreements and securities lending transactions, and reinsurance receivables. It excludes, among others, assets measured at fair value through net income, loans made to participants by defined contribution employee benefit plans and policy loan receivables of an insurance company.

In terms of methodologies, the standard is not prescriptive. In particular, it is open to methods based on loss-rate, probability of default (that is, PD, LGD, EAD), discounted cash flows, roll-rate, or use an ageing schedule. When developing ECL methods, one needs to consider the following:

- **Historical loss information.** Internal and external past information are at the very heart of ECL estimate. This is the starting point for the assessment. Portfolio segmentation and pooling are also crucial to identify common risk characteristics.
- **Current conditions.** Estimates need to include current conditions. This is in line with the point-in-time principle also inspiring IFRS 9 computation.
- **Reasonable and supportable forecasts.** The forward-looking perspective urged by IFRS 9 is also at the root of CECL. Therefore economic forecasts need to be embedded into ECL estimates.
- **Reversion to history.** Banks need to revert to historical loss information when unable to make reasonable and supportable forecasts. This reversion needs to be performed systematically by starting from inputs, or applied at an aggregated level. It implies that banks need to:
  - Define a sustainable and supportable horizon for mean reversion.
  - Estimate a long-term expected loss.

Figure 1.3 summarises the key topics investigated throughout Section 1.3.

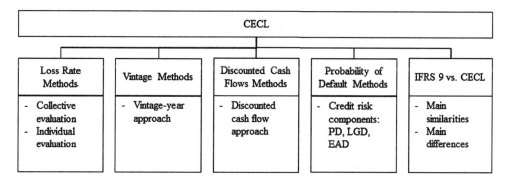

FIGURE 1.3

Workflow diagram for Section 1.3.

Section 1.3.1 provides an overview of loss-rate methods. Cumulative credit losses are inspected from two standpoints: collective and individual. Section 1.3.2 describes how to measure ECLs based on the origination date and historical performance of assets with similar vintage characteristics. Section 1.3.3 summarises the key features of cash flows methods. Section 1.3.4 points out the key elements to consider when a probability of default method is adopted. In line with IFRS 9, PD, LGD and EAD are the key ingredients to compute ECL. As a practical choice, the book focuses on the most complex modelling methods. For this reason, loss-rate, vintage, cash flow, and others will not be further investigated in the following chapters. Attention will be driven by PD, LGD and EAD modelling. Finally, Section 1.3.5 pinpoints the key similarities and differences between IFRS 9 and CECL frameworks.

1.3.1 LOSS-RATE METHODS

Loss-rate methods can take various forms. In all cases, they are based on historical rates of loss. As a starting point, one may consider the percentage of receivables that have historically gone bad, and then make any necessary adjustments based on relevant information around current or future conditions.

Example 1.3.1 refers to FASB (2016) Example 1 by pointing out the difference between incurred loss and ECL estimates.

EXAMPLE 1.3.1 LOSS RATE ANALYSIS

Table 1.2 provides all information needed to estimate losses under the incurred loss method. For each year a one-year emerging period is considered as incurred losses estimate (that is, the *Annual Loss column*). A constant 0.30% represents the loss-rate percentage. An extra 0.50% adjustment is applied to obtain a total 0.80% incurred loss percentage. The latter is then applied to year 2020 exposure (that is, $3,000.00 thousand) to compute $24.00 thousand incurred loss.

Table 1.2 Loss-rate: incurred loss method ($ Thousands)			
Time (Year)	Amortised cost	Annual loss	Loss-rate %
2010	1,500.00	4.50	0.30%
2011	1,610.00	4.80	0.30%
2012	1,730.00	5.20	0.30%
2013	1,850.00	5.50	0.30%
2014	1,980.00	6.00	0.30%
2015	2,120.00	6.40	0.30%
2016	2,270.00	6.80	0.30%
2017	2,430.00	7.30	0.30%
2018	2,610.00	7.80	0.30%
2019	2,800.00	8.40	0.30%
2020	3,000.00	9.00	0.30%
Total		71.70	
Average rate			0.30%
Adjustment factor			0.50%
Total loss-rate			0.80%
Total incurred loss	3,000.00	24.00	0.80%

Moving from FASB (2016) Example 1, one may estimate ECL as summarised in Table 1.3. A ten-year historical incurred losses track is put in place. In our case, the starting point is the amortised cost balance of $1,500.00 thousand as per 2010. Losses are tracked throughout the period 2010–2020. Total incurred losses is $22.50 thousand corresponding to 1.50% of the initial balance. Some adjustments are introduced to take into account expectations on economic condition evolution. The overall expected loss percentage is 1.65%. Based on 2020 exposure of $3,000.00 thousand, ECL accounts for $49.50 thousand.

Table 1.3 Loss-rate: incurred loss method ($ Thousands)			
Time (Year)	Amortised cost	Loss	Loss-rate %
2010	1,500.00		
2011		3.60	
2012		3.40	
2013		3.20	
2014		3.00	
2015		2.80	
2016		2.50	
2017		2.30	
2018		1.70	
2019			
2020			
Total	1,500.00	22.50	
10Y cumulative loss-rate			1.50%
Adjustment current conditions			0.00%
Adjustment real estate values			0.10%
Adjustment unemployment			0.05%
Adjustment other factors			0.00%
Total ECL %			1.65 %
Total ECL	3,000.00	49.50	1.65%

The key advantages of a loss-rate method refer to its simplicity, relative easy historical data access (that is, accounting incurred losses), and intuitive interpretation of economic adjustments. Loss-rate method major drawback relates to difficulties in supporting adjustments from a quantitative perspective.

The following section provides some hints about vintage methods.

1.3.2 VINTAGE METHODS

Vintage analysis is essentially a special case of the loss-rate model referred to as closed pools. Loans are grouped by similar risk profiles and by origination period (for example, year, quarter), so that once a period has passed, no loans are added to the pool, making it a closed pool. Under a vintage analysis, one may isolate loss components and perform ad hoc analyses, such as investigating trends in the portfolio.

Example 1.3.2 originates from FASB (2016) Example 3. The focus is on vintage-year losses.

EXAMPLE 1.3.2 VINTAGE ANALYSIS

Let us consider a bank originating amortising loans with four-year term. Loss-rates are tracked, as detailed in Table 1.4. A full representation of incurred losses applies to loans originated until 20X4. For the following vintages, one needs to define an expected credit loss rule.

Table 1.4 Vintage (historical) loss-rates

Origination (Year)	Originated balance	Year 1%	Year 2%	Year 3%	Year 4%	Incurred %
20X1	20,000.00	0.25%	0.60%	0.65%	0.15%	1.65%
20X2	21,000.00	0.20%	0.60%	0.70%	0.25%	1.75%
20X3	22,500.00	0.20%	0.55%	0.75%	0.15%	1.65%
20X4	23,000.00	0.25%	0.55%	0.75%	0.15%	1.70%
20X5	24,000.00	0.25%	0.60%	0.75%		1.75%
20X6	24,500.00	0.25%	0.60%			1.60%
20X7	25,000.00	0.40%				1.00%
20X8	25,000.00					0.25%

One may consider an average loss percentage for each year after origination as expected loss. As an alternative, a percentile of the distribution can represent a more robust metric. Table 1.5 relies on median vintage loss percentage. ECL is then computed by applying remaining expected loss percentages to vintage original balances, as detailed in the last two columns of Table 1.5 (that is, remaining expected loss %, and ECL).

Table 1.5 Vintage (historical and expected) loss-rates, and ECL

Origination (Year)	Originated balance	Year 1%	Year 2%	Year 3%	Year 4%	Incurred %	Remaining expected loss %	ECL
20X1	20,000.00	0.25%	0.60%	0.65%	0.15%	1.65%		
20X2	21,000.00	0.20%	0.60%	0.70%	0.25%	1.75%		
20X3	22,500.00	0.20%	0.55%	0.75%	0.15%	1.65%		
20X4	23,000.00	0.25%	0.55%	0.75%	0.15%	1.70%		
20X5	24,000.00	0.25%	0.60%	0.75%	0.15%	1.75%	0.15%	36.00
20X6	24,500.00	0.25%	0.60%	0.75%	0.15%	1.60%	0.90%	220.50
20X7	25,000.00	0.40%	0.60%	0.75%	0.15%	1.00%	1.50%	375.00
20X8	25,000.00	0.25%	0.60%	0.75%	0.15%	0.25%	1.75%	437.50
ECL								1,069.00

Vintage analysis allows us to isolate changes, such as those in the economic environment, collateral value and underwriting. On the other hand, it usually requires extensive data based on the level of disaggregation adopted for the investigation. Economic forecast improves as more data become available. In this regard, careful evaluation of the impact of external conditions (for example, macroeconomic fluctuations) is necessary. A granular segmentation may help ECL computation. Nevertheless, excessive granularity may cause unexpected jumps due to account specificities connected to name and sector concentration.

The following section focuses on discounted cash flow methods.

1.3.3 DISCOUNTED CASH FLOW METHODS

Banks may use a discounted cash flow (DCF) model to estimate expected future cash flows, and record appropriate loan loss reserves, as detailed below.

- **FASB (2016) 326-20-30-4.** *If an entity estimates expected credit losses using methods that project future principal and interest cash flows (that is, a discounted cash flow method), the entity shall discount expected cash flows at the financial asset's effective interest rate. When a discounted cash flow method is applied, the allowance for credit losses shall reflect the difference between the amortised cost basis and the present value of the expected cash flows. If the loan's financial asset's contractual interest rate varies based on subsequent changes in an independent factor, such as an index or rate, for example, the prime rate, the London Interbank Offered Rate (LIBOR), or the U.S. Treasury bill weekly average, that loan's financial asset's effective interest rate (used to discount expected cash flows, as described in this paragraph) shall be calculated based on the factor as it changes over the life of the financial asset. Projections of changes in the factor shall not be made for purposes of determining the effective interest rate or estimating expected future cash flows.*

Notwithstanding the lifetime nature of the CECL estimate, FASB (2016) does not explicitly utilise this concept to avoid banks believing that they must specifically identify the exact timing of uncollected cash flows.

Under CECL, there is no explicit requirement to consider probability weighted outcomes, as prescribed by IFRS 9. However, banks will not necessarily use their best estimate as per the incurred loss approach. Indeed, they always need to consider a risk of loss. Multiple scenarios are not required. Nevertheless, one may rely on them to estimate ECLs. Let us assume that a bank originates one-year commercial loans to a firm as detailed in Table 1.6. All contractual payments under the loans (that is, principal of $1,000.00 and interest of $100.00) are due in one year time. Table 1.6 summarises banks' view on possible repayment scenarios. ECL $58.00 is computed as a weighted average, based on scenario probabilities.

Table 1.6 Discounted cash flow, multiple scenario analysis				
Scenario	Payment	Credit loss	Scenario probability	ECL
1	1,100.00	0.00	80.00%	0.00
2	900.00	200.00	18.00%	36.00
3	0.00	1,100.00	2.00%	22.00
Total			100.00%	58.00

Note that this methodology does not represent a best, nor worst case scenario. On the contrary, it reflects the risk of loss. It does not need to rely solely on a single outcome (that is, FASB (2016) 326-30-35-7), nor is bank required to reconcile the estimation technique it uses with a discounted cash flow model (that is, FASB (2016) 326-20-30-3). The application of discounted cash flow methods in banks with lengthy repayment terms, and no prepayment data, may not be practical or worthwhile. On the contrary, this approach may be viable when detailed information on asset cash flows is available, and the portfolio is made up by homogeneous products with short duration.

The section below summarises how probability of default methods are used for CECL. This approach relies on the same credit risk components (that is, PD, LGD and EAD) discussed in Section 1.2.2; they constitute the primary focus of the book.

1.3.4 PROBABILITY OF DEFAULT METHODS

In line with IASB (2014), the probability of default method (that is, PD, LGD, and EAD) indicated by FASB (2016), aligns with IFRS 9 main approach to compute ECL, based on the following product[1]:

$$ECL = \mathbb{E}(PD \cdot LGD \cdot EAD), \qquad (1.1)$$

where, in case of independence, the following applies:

$$ECL = \mathbb{E}(PD) \cdot \mathbb{E}(LGD) \cdot \mathbb{E}(EAD). \qquad (1.2)$$

This assumption plays a key role. Indeed, it subsumes absence of contagion and does not account for the role of concentration (that is, name and sector) threatening banks' resilience under adverse scenarios (Duffie and Singleton, 2003). A more extensive discussion on these assumptions is provided in Chapter 6. In this context, it is worth emphasising that scenarios affect PD, LGD, and EAD throughout the residual maturity of each account. Therefore one may apply the following equation both for CECL and IFRS 9 lifetime ECL:

$$ECL_{pt}^{life}(\mathbf{x}_t^*) = \sum_{i=1}^{n_{pt}} \left[\sum_{t=1}^{T_i} PV_t\Big(PD_{i,t} \cdot LGD_{i,t} EAD_{i,t}|\mathbf{x}_t^*\Big) \right], \qquad (1.3)$$

where the superscript $life$ stands for lifetime, whereas the subscript pt indicates the portfolio on which the analysis is conducted (that is, a portfolio is made-up by n_{pt} accounts). $PV_t(\cdot)$ represents the present value operator, which may assume different characteristics under CECL and IFRS 9. Computations are conducted at account level i over a lifetime horizon T_i. Finally, the forward-looking perspective is captured by conditioning both credit risk parameters and present value estimate on macroeconomic scenario $\mathbf{x}_t^*$. As previously noted, IASB (2014) explicitly requires multiple scenarios, whereas FASB (2016) does not prescribe the adoption of multiple scenarios.

The following section points out the main similarities and difference between IFRS 9 and CECL.

1.3.5 IFRS 9 VS. CECL

FASB (2016) highlights a few notable similarities and differences between the CECL model and IFRS 9. Table 1.7 focuses on similarities, whereas Table 1.8 points out differences between these two standards.

The following section builds a bridge between expected credit losses computed for accounting purposes and capital requirements.

1.4 ECL AND CAPITAL REQUIREMENTS

In the recent past, emphasis has been posed on credit risk modelling for internal rating based (IRB) models used for capital requirements. Indeed, banks are allowed to use their internally estimated prob-

---

[1] A present value estimation is assumed to be embedded in credit risk parameter estimates.

Table 1.7 Main similarities of IFRS 9 and CECL (see FASB (2016) BC131)

#	Description
i.	Both the CECL model and IFRS 9 are considered to be expected credit loss models. The CECL model requires that the full amount of expected credit losses be recorded for all financial assets measured at amortised cost, whereas IFRS 9 requires that an allowance for credit losses equal to the one-year expected credit losses, as defined in IFRS 9, be recognised, until there is a significant increase in credit risk, when lifetime expected credit losses are recognised.
ii.	Under IFRS 9, the full amount of expected credit losses is measured for financial assets that have experienced a significant increase in credit risk since initial recognition. For these assets, there may be similar measurements of expected credit losses under IFRS 9 and CECL because, under both, an entity will measure credit losses over the expected life, subject to key differences highlighted in Table 1.8.

Table 1.8 Main differences between IFRS 9 and CECL (see FASB (2016) BC131)

#	Description
i.	The amendments in FASB (2016) have different requirements, based on the measurement attribute. Specifically, different considerations and indicators for impairment exist for available-for-sale debt securities. IFRS 9 requires one credit loss approach for all financial assets (described as fair value through other comprehensive income assets under IFRS 9), regardless of the measurement attribute.
ii.	The FASB acknowledges the time value of money implicitly present in credit loss methodologies using amortised cost information, whereas IFRS 9 requires an explicit consideration of the time value of money.
iii.	The CECL model requires collective evaluation of credit losses when similar risk characteristics exist. IFRS 9 states that the measurement of expected credit losses shall reflect a probability-weighted amount, but particular measurement techniques are not prescribed. Therefore IFRS 9 allows collective evaluation of credit losses based on shared risk characteristics. However, unlike the CECL model, the probability weighted outcomes must be considered.
iv.	GAAP treats a concession provided to a troubled borrower to be a continuation of the original lending agreement. Differences exist for modifications of financial assets, and the concept of a troubled debt restructuring does not exist in IFRS 9.
v.	Differences exist for purchased financial assets. IFRS 9 also includes requirements for originated credit impaired financial assets and purchased credit impaired financial assets. GAAP does not contain provisions for originated impaired financial assets, and there are differences in the scope and measurement of expected credit losses for purchased financial assets.
vi.	GAAP continues to permit the application of non-accrual practices, whereas IFRS 9 continues to preclude the use of non-accrual practices. IFRS 9 requires a net-interest approach to be applied to the "Stage 3" assets, which represent individual assets that are credit impaired, whereas a gross interest approach is used otherwise.
vii.	The discount rate utilised when a discounted cash flow approach is used under the CECL model is required to be the effective interest rate. IFRS 9 provides that an entity also is permitted to use an approximation of the effective discount rate when discounting expected credit losses.
viii.	The CECL model requires expected credit losses for unfunded commitments to reflect the full contractual period over which an entity is exposed to credit risk via a present obligation to extend credit. The CECL model does not require an allowance for expected credit losses beyond the contractual term, or beyond the point in which a loan commitment may be unconditionally cancelled by the issuer. In contrast, for a financial asset that contains both a loan and an undrawn commitment component, IFRS 9 states that an entity should measure expected credit losses over the period that an entity is exposed to credit risk, and expected credit losses are not mitigated by credit risk management actions, even if that period extends beyond the maximum contractual period.
ix.	The CECL model requires the amortised cost basis of financing receivables and net investment in leases to be disclosed by credit quality indicator, disaggregated by year of origination. This information is intended to help users understand the credit quality trends within the portfolio from period to period. IFRS 9 requires an entity to disclose a reconciliation of the financial assets relating to the allowance for credit losses from the opening balance to the closing balance, and requires explanations of how significant changes in the gross carrying amounts of financial assets during the period contributed to the changes in the allowance for credit losses.

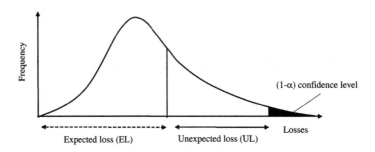

FIGURE 1.4

Credit loss distribution. Expected loss (EL) versus unexpected loss (UL). The notation EL is used instead of ECL to align with the frame described in Sections 1.4.1 and 1.4.2. In particular, Section 1.4.2 highlights the difference between ECL and EL computed according to Basel II capital requirements.

ability of default (PD), loss given default (LGD), and exposure at default (EAD) for computing their risk weighted assets (RWAs).

The idea behind this framework is to require banks to hold enough capital to face both expected and unexpected losses. Given that expected losses are already accounted as part of the capital measure (that is, ECL), the focus of regulatory capital requirements is on unexpected losses (ULs), as summarised in Figure 1.4. This curve highlights a typical asymmetric profile, where small credit losses have higher chance than greater losses. UL is obtained as a difference between a given quantile of the distribution (that is, credit value at risk $VaR_{credit,(1-\alpha)}$) and EL. Risk weighted assets (RWAs) are computed as a function of UL. It is clear that a change on ECL may have an impact on UL.

BIS (2006) aimed to ensure banks enough capital to face ULs. For this purpose, the following threshold was introduced as a trigger for capital enforcement:

$$Regulatory \quad Capital \geq 8\%(RWA_{market} + RWA_{credit} + RWA_{operational}), \quad (1.4)$$

where $(RWA_{market} + RWA_{credit} + RWA_{operational})$ is the sum of market, credit and operational RWAs, while regulatory capital represents bank's own funds.

It is important to question the use of RWA instead of assets (as it is common practice in finance) in Equation (1.4). The main reason is to take into account the impact of risks. In other words, assuming that a risky asset has a 100% weight, a $ 100.00 investment on such asset involves a minimum regulatory capital of $ 8.00. On the other hand, a risk-free asset having a 0% weight, does not need any capital exceeding expected losses requirement (already included within own funds by means of provisions).

Figure 1.5 helps understanding the relationship between assets, liabilities and regulatory capital. Assets are classified according to their risk profile in order to compute the RWA. The latter may be lower or greater than the total asset value (for this reason the RWA box has some thin layers on top). Regulatory capital components, on the other hand, are ranked in line with their capability to absorb losses (Bellini, 2017). Therefore common equity is made-up by instruments like common shares, retained earnings, and so on. Debt-like instruments with some degree of subordination are included as additional Tier 1 and Tier 2 components. It is worth noting that ECL estimates affect regulatory capital

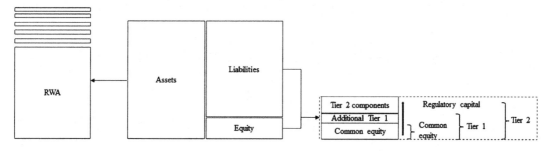

FIGURE 1.5

Regulatory framework at a glance.

Table 1.9 Basel Committee on Banking Supervision (BCBS) minimum capital requirements roadmap. Dates referred to as 1 January				
	2016	**2017**	**2018**	**2019**
Minimum common equity capital ratio	4.50%	4.50%	4.50%	4.50%
Capital conservation buffer	0.625%	1.25%	1.875%	2.50%
Minimum common equity plus capital conservation buffer	5.125%	5.75%	6.375%	7.00%
Minimum Tier 1 Capital	6.00%	6.00%	6.00%	6.00%
Minimum total capital	8.00%	8.00%	8.00%	8.00%
Minimum total capital plus conservation buffer	8.625%	9.25%	9.875%	10.50%

by means of provisions. RWA is also affected as a difference between VAR_{credit} and ECL as detailed in Figure 1.4.

In line with this representation, a risk-based capital ratio is represented as follows:

$$Capital \quad Ratio = \frac{Regulatory\ Capital}{RWA}, \tag{1.5}$$

where highest ratios ensure a more comprehensive risk coverage. Basel III (BIS, 2011) revised the definition of capital and specified new minimum capital requirements in line with Table 1.9. By January 2019, the total minimum total capital requirement (Tier 1 and Tier 2) will increase from its original 8% level to 10.50%. This is due to a 2.50% capital conservation buffer to absorb losses during periods of financial and economic stress.

The main goal of this section is to highlight the link between accounting ECL and capital ratios.

As per Figure 1.6, Section 1.4.1 describes how to compute capital requirements based on IRB modelling. On the other hand, Section 1.4.2 points out the role of ECL as element connecting accounting and regulatory capital requirement frameworks.

1.4.1 INTERNAL RATING-BASED CREDIT RISK-WEIGHTED ASSETS

Minimum capital requirements for banks adopting an IRB approach for credit risk rely on unexpected losses, as represented in Figure 1.4. A Merton-like approach inspires the framework. More specifically,

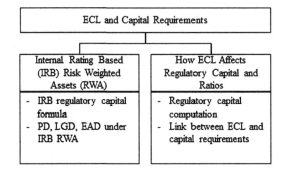

FIGURE 1.6

Workflow diagram for Section 1.4.

the so-called asymptotic single risk factor (ASRF) model infers the default distribution, based on firm's asset value returns. A single common factor ($\varkappa_t$), and an idiosyncratic noise component ($\epsilon_{i,s,t}$), drive the normalised asset return ($\xi_{i,s,t}$) over time t as follows:

$$\xi_{i,s,t} = \sqrt{\rho_{i,s}}\,\varkappa_t + \sqrt{1-\rho_{i,s}}\,\epsilon_{i,s,t}, \tag{1.6}$$

where $\sqrt{\rho_{i,s}}$ is the correlation between asset returns and the common factor (Duffie and Singleton, 2003). $\varkappa_t$ and $\epsilon_{i,s,t}$ are independent and identically distributed $N(0, 1)$. Therefore $\xi_{i,s,t}$ has a standardised normal distribution.

A binary default random variable is the starting point of the model used for IRB as detailed below:

$$1_{i,s}^{def,IRB} = \begin{cases} 1 & \text{for} \quad \xi_{i,s,t} \leq \Phi^{-1}(PD_{i,s,t}), \\ 0 & \text{for} \quad \xi_{i,s,t} > \Phi^{-1}(PD_{i,s,t}), \end{cases} \tag{1.7}$$

where Φ is the cdf of a standard normal distribution, whereas $PD_{i,s,t}$ indicates the probability of default for account i belonging to sub-portfolio s.[2] The following equation summarises the probability of default conditioned to a specific scenario x_{scen}:

$$\begin{aligned}
P\left(1_{i,s}^{def,IRB} = 1 | \varkappa_{scen}\right) &= P\left(\xi_{i,s,t} \leq \Phi^{-1}(PD_{i,s,t}) | \varkappa_{scen}\right) = \\
&= P\left(\sqrt{\rho_{i,s}}\,\varkappa_t + \sqrt{1-\rho_{i,s}}\,\epsilon_{i,s,t} \leq \Phi^{-1}(PD_{i,s,t}) | \varkappa_{scen}\right) = \\
&= P\left(\epsilon_{i,s,t} \leq \frac{\Phi^{-1}(PD_{i,s,t}) - \sqrt{\rho_{i,s}}\,\varkappa_t}{\sqrt{1-\rho_{i,s}}} | \varkappa_{scen}\right) = \\
&= \Phi\left(\frac{\Phi^{-1}(PD_{i,s,t}) - \sqrt{\rho_{i,s}}\,\varkappa_t}{\sqrt{1-\rho_{i,s}}} | \varkappa_{scen}\right) = \\
&= \Phi\left(\frac{\Phi^{-1}(PD_{i,s,t}) - \sqrt{\rho_{i,s}}\,\varkappa_{scen}}{\sqrt{1-\rho_{i,s}}}\right).
\end{aligned} \tag{1.8}$$

---

[2] The assumption one customer, one account is made to simplify the notation.

Vasicek (2002) and Gordy (2003) extended Merton (1974) single asset model to a portfolio model by relying on an infinitely granular portfolio, where each debtor is independent from others. The ASRF assumption informs the IRB formula used to assess capital requirements (BIS, 2006).

The IRB formula is derived as follows:

$$CLoss_{h,(1-\alpha)} = \sum_{s=1}^{S} \sum_{i=1}^{n_s} EAD_{i,s,t} LGD_{i,s,t} \Phi \left(\frac{\Phi^{-1}(PD_{i,s,t}) - \sqrt{\rho_{i,s}}\Phi^{-1}(1-\alpha)}{\sqrt{1-\rho_{i,s}}} \right), \qquad (1.9)$$

where n_s represents the number of accounts in a sub-portfolio s, while S is the total number of sub-portfolios. The unexpected loss ($UL_{h,(1-\alpha)}$) is the difference between $CLoss_{h,(1-\alpha)}$ and EL as detailed below:

$$UL_{h,(1-\alpha)} = \sum_{s=1}^{S} \sum_{i=1}^{n_s} EAD_{i,s,t} LGD_{i,s,t} \Phi \left(\frac{\Phi^{-1}(PD_{i,s,t}) - \sqrt{\rho_{i,s}}\Phi^{-1}(1-\alpha)}{\sqrt{1-\rho_{i,s}}} - PD_{i,s,t} \right). \quad (1.10)$$

Regulatory RWAs are computed by applying the reciprocal of 8% on Equation (1.10) together with an additional 1.06 overall adjustment, as listed below:

$$RWA = 12.5$$
$$\cdot 1.06 \sum_{i=1}^{n} EAD_{i,s,t} LGD_{i,s,t} \Phi \left(\frac{\Phi^{-1}(PD_{i,s,t}) + \sqrt{\rho}\Phi^{-1}(0.999)}{\sqrt{1-\rho}} - PD_{i,s,t} \right) adj(M),$$
$$(1.11)$$

where $adj(M)$ represents an account specific maturity adjustment. The percentile 0.999 corresponds to $(1-\alpha)$ in Equation (1.10), and the parameter ρ is defined according to the segment (such as large corporate and small medium enterprise).[3]

It is worth noting that Equation (1.11) is used for the non-defaulted portfolio only. Additionally, a distinction holds between foundation and advanced IRB approaches. According to the foundation approach, a bank is authorised to use internally estimated PDs, whereas all other parameters are given. In contrast, an advanced IRB bank relies on internally estimated PDs, LGDs and EADs.

Example 1.4.1 outlines how the IRB formula works in practice.

EXAMPLE 1.4.1 RWA IRB APPROACH

Let us consider a portfolio with six accounts with $1.00 million exposure each. Three of them belong to the small medium enterprise (SME) segment (their turnover is Euro 10 million), whereas others are classified in the corporate portfolio. For both segments, accounts have default probabilities of 0.50%, 2.00%, and 3.00% applied together with a fixed 40% LGD. The maturity is 5 years for all accounts. All other elements being equal, SME RWA is lower due

---

[3]It is worth noting that in BIS (2006), the correlation parameter is indicated with R and different formulas apply according to the segment. For example, for corporate, sovereign and bank exposures, $R = 0.12 \times (1 - e^{-50 \times PD})/(1 - e^{-50}) + 0.24 \times [1 - (1 - e^{-50 \times PD})/(1 - e^{-50})]$.

to the presumed low risk related to small companies. Weights resulting from the IRB regulatory formula are less than 100% only for account 1 and 4 (that is, PD equal to 0.5%). (See Table 1.10.) Figure 1.7 shows that the IRB weighting scheme supports high-quality credits and penalises the low-quality ones.

Table 1.10 Bank Rho credit RWA ($ millions)			
ID	Segment	PD	RWA
1	SME	0.50%	0.75
2	SME	2.00%	1.10
3	SME	3.00%	1.18
4	Corporate	0.50%	0.93
5	Corporate	2.00%	1.38
6	Corporate	3.00%	1.50
Total			6.85

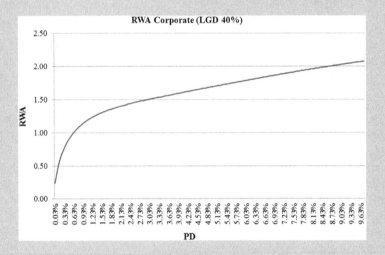

FIGURE 1.7

IRB RWA curve for corporate exposure (given a $LGD = 40\%$).

It is worth noting that IRB parameters rely on a through-the-cycle (TTC) philosophy. Indeed, a need for stable capitalisation informs Basel II to avoid procyclicality fluctuations undermining financial sector resilience. In contrast, accounting standards align with a point-in-time mindset, as summarised in Figure 1.8 with regards to PDs. This concept is further studied in Chapters 2 and 3. In this regard, CECL additionally requires reversion to long-term expected loss rates, as detailed in Section 1.3.

The following section summarises the link connecting accounting expected credit losses and regulatory capital requirements.

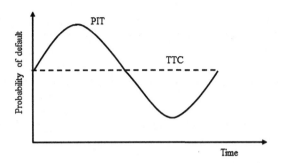

Point-in-time (solid line) vs. through-the-cycle (dotted line) probabilities of default.

1.4.2 HOW ECL AFFECTS REGULATORY CAPITAL AND RATIOS

Risk weighted assets (RWAs) described in the previous section represented the denominator of Equation (1.5). As anticipated, ECL affects both RWA and regulatory capital. Let us now focus on the numerator to facilitate a comprehensive understanding of ECL impact on capital ratios. Regulatory capital is estimated by adjusting financial reporting figures, as listed below:

- **Tier 1 – common equity**. Common equity consists of a combination of shares and retained earnings. It is the primary and most restrictive form of regulatory capital. To qualify as Tier 1, capital has to be subordinated, perpetual in nature, loss-bearing and fully paid-up with no funding having come from the bank. On top of common equity, all major adjustments are applied, as described below.
- **Tier 1 – additional capital**. This additional layer of the Tier 1 capital consists of instruments paying discretionary dividends, having neither a maturity date nor an incentive to redeem. Innovative hybrid capital instruments are phased out because of their fixed distribution percentage, non-loss absorption capabilities, and incentive to redeem through features like step-up clauses.
- **Tier 2 capital**. Tier 2 capital contains instruments that are capable of bearing a loss, not only in case of default, but also in the event that a bank is unable to support itself in the private market. Their contractual structure needs to allow banks to write them down, or convert them into shares.

Following 2007–2009 crisis, a deep reform modified regulatory capital definitions and ratios. Table 1.11 aims to outline some of the differences between Basel II and Basel III components (BIS, 2011). This is an illustrative and non-exhaustive exemplification.

Table 1.11 Comparison between Basel II and Basel III regulatory capital treatment of some (major) capital components

Capital category	Basel II	Basel III
Common shares	Tier 1 – common equity	Tier 1 – common equity
Retained earnings	Tier 1 – common equity	Tier 1 – common equity
Innovative capital instruments	Tier 1 – additional	Excluded and grandfathered
Non-innovative capital instruments	Tier 1 – additional	Included in Tier 1 – additional, subject to conditions
Subordinate debt	Tier 2	Included in Tier 2, subject to conditions

As anticipated above, misalignments may arise between accounting and regulatory capital requirements. In this regard, one needs to apply regulatory adjustments. As an example, goodwill and intangibles are usually recognised under the current accounting standards. Nevertheless, these elements need to be excluded from the regulatory capital. With regards to the key topic of this book, the (negative) difference between accounting provisions and the IRB expected loss (that is, estimated on internal rating parameters) is deducted from the regulatory capital. Table 1.12 shows some illustrative examples of adjustments.

Table 1.12 Regulatory capital adjustments (illustrative examples)	
Adjustment	**Description**
Goodwill and intangible assets	To be deducted from Tier 1 common equity
Shortfall provisions	To be deducted from Tier 1 common equity
Unrealised gains and losses	To be taken into account in Tier 1 common equity

A two-step process applies to compute capital requirements. Firstly, accounting components are qualified in terms of regulatory categories (that is, Tier 1 common equity, Tier 1 additional capital and Tier 2). Secondly, deductions are computed. These two phases are listed below.

1. **Identification of regulatory categories**. As part of the first step, balance sheet components are examined and qualified as Tier 1 or Tier 2 as follows:

   - **Shareholder's equity**:
     - **Common shares**. Common stockholder's equity is included in accounting capital and consists of voting shares. This is the most desirable capital element from a supervisory perspective. Indeed, shares absorb bank losses commensurate with their accounting value. They provide a savings association with the maximum amount of financial flexibility necessary during a crisis.
     - **Preferred shares**. Preferred shares typically entitle a holder to a fixed dividend, which is received before any common stockholders may receive dividends. As a general rule, they qualify for inclusion in Tier 1 capital if losses are absorbed, while the issuer operates as a going concern. Clauses, covenants and restrictions that make these shares more debit-like may cause them not to be acceptable for Tier 1 capital.
     - **Retained earnings**. Cumulated earnings due to realised profit non-distributed among shareholders are usually assimilated to common shares, and included within the Tier 1 capital.
   - **Subordinated debts**. Few characteristics are required for a debt to be qualified as subordinated and be classified as Tier 2 capital. A limited repayment right usually identifies a subordinated debt in the event of default. In more detail, these financial instruments are usually limited to non-payment amount. The only remedies afforded to the investor is to petition for the winding-up of the bank. In this latter case, investors are allowed to claim in the winding-up. Additionally, the maturity needs to be higher than a certain period (for example, five years), and the amortisation process is required to be aligned with regulatory schemes.
   - **Non-controlling interests**. Non-controlling interests are created when a depository institution owns a controlling interest, but not 100% of a subsidiary. Remaining interest is owned by third parties, referred to as non-controlling shareholders. The non-controlling interest should absorb

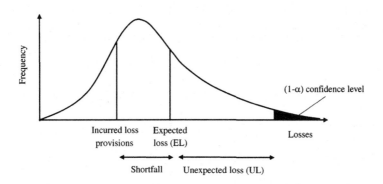

FIGURE 1.9

Provision shortfall mechanics.

losses in the subsidiary, commensurate with the subsidiary's capital needs. It should not represent an essentially risk-free or low-risk investment for the holders of the subsidiary capital instrument.

2. **Computation of deductions**. With regards to the topic covered in this book, shortfall provisions play a very important role. It has also been a subject of intense debate within the financial industry due to potential provision increases related to IFRS 9 and CECL, as listed below:

- **Provision shortfall**. According to BIS (2004), *in order to determine provision excesses or short-falls, banks will need to compare the IRB measurement of expected losses $EAD \times PD \times LGD$ with the total amount of provisions that they have made, including both general, specific, portfolio-specific general provisions and eligible credit revaluation reserves discussed above. As previously mentioned, provisions or write-offs for equity exposures will not be included in this calculation. For any individual bank, this comparison will produce a shortfall if the expected loss amount exceeds the total provision amount, or an excess if the total provision amount exceeds the expected loss amount.*
  The idea behind this deduction can be outlined through Figure 1.9. Regulatory capital faces un-expected losses. Indeed, expected losses are supposed to be captured by provisions and deducted from equity. Therefore the difference (shortfall) between expected losses and provisions (that is, $EL > provisions$) is deducted from capital.
  Example 1.4.2, following, details how to compute provision shortfall.

EXAMPLE 1.4.2 PROVISION SHORTFALL

A bank has a $ 8.50 billion Tier 1 capital and a $5.50 billion Tier 2 capital. Its total capital accounts for $14.00 billion. From a provisioning standpoint, the next table summarises: expected loss (due to Basel IRB parameters) and provisions. A shortfall originates from the difference between these two components. (See Table 1.13.)

Table 1.13 Provision shortfall computed as difference between Basel II expected loss and accounting provisions ($ billions)

Portfolio	EL (Basel II)	Provisions	Shortfall
Performing	10.00	9.00	1.00
Non-performing	25.00	22.00	3.00
Total	35.00	31.00	4.00

With regards to non-performing, one needs to further consider expected loss best estimate (that is, EL_{BE}). In this example, we assume EL_{BE} to be aligned with EL. According to the above, an overall $4.00 billion shortfall needs to be deducted (for the sake of simplicity, no phasing-in is considered). Therefore Tier 1 reduces to $4.50 billion. Likewise, the total capital drops from $14.00 to $10.00 billion.

As an additional step of the journey, one may investigate the impact of shortfall on capital ratios. Example 1.4.3 provides some additional hints on capital requirement mechanics.

EXAMPLE 1.4.3 CREDIT RISK AND CAPITAL RATIOS: THE ROLE OF EL_{BE}

The bank introduced in Example 1.4.2 has a $8.50 billion Tier 1 capital and a $5.50 billion Tier 2 capital. Likewise Example 1.4.2, EL_{BE} is assumed to be aligned with EL. Therefore an overall $4.00 billions capital deduction is recorded, as detailed in the next table. As a result, the Tier 1 capital reduces to $4.50 billion, and the total capital becomes $10.00 billion. (See Table 1.14.)

Table 1.14 Shortfall when $EL = EL_{BE}$ ($ billions)

Portfolio	EL (Basel II)	Provisioning	EL_{BE}	Shortfall RWA	Shortfall capital
Performing	10.00	9.00			1.00
Non-performing	25.00	22.00	25.00		3.00
Total	35.00	31.00			4.00

Let us additionally assume that Basel I credit and market RWAs sum-up to $100.00 billion. By applying the 80% regulatory threshold, a floor is set-up at $80.00 billion. Moreover, the sum of (advanced modelling) market, credit and operational risk RWA is $75.00 billion. In this context, the floor being higher than the sum of RWA silos, a $5.00 billion add-on is needed.

Risk-based capital ratios when $EL = EL_{BE}$ are computed as follows:

- Tier 1 capital ratio $\frac{4.50}{80} = 5.625\%$.
- Tier 2 capital ratio $\frac{10}{80} = 12.50\%$.

Let us now modify our assumption on EL_{BE}, as detailed in Table 1.15.

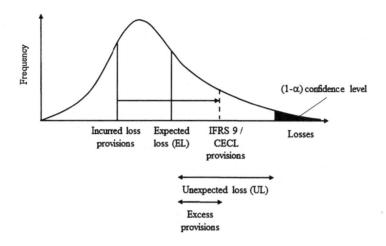

FIGURE 1.10

Unexpected losses and provisions after the adoption of IFRS 9 and CECL.

Table 1.15 Shortfall when $EL > EL_{BE}$

Portfolio	EL (Basel II)	Provisioning	EL_{BE}	Shortfall RWA	Shortfall capital
Performing	10.00	9.00			1.00
Defaulted	25.00	22.00	22.00	37.50	
Total	35.00	31.00		37.50	1.00

Capital deductions account for $1.00 billion. This situation causes a Tier 1 reduction to $7.50 billion and a total capital drop to $13.00 billion. The difference between EL and EL_{BE} (that is, $3.00 billion) increases the RWA by $3 \times 12.50 = $37.50 billion. Therefore the sum of RWAs is $75.00 + 37.50 = $112.50 billion. In this case, the floor is crossed. No additional add-on is required.

Finally, risk-based capital ratios when $EL > EL_{BE}$ are listed below.

- Tier 1 capital ratio $\frac{7.50}{112.50} = 6.67\%$.
- Tier 2 capital ratio $\frac{10.00}{80.00} = 11.55\%$.

It is evident that EL_{BE} plays a key role in the overall capital assessment.

Figure 1.10 points out the potential impact of ECLs due to IFRS 9 and CECL adoption. It clearly highlights that, instead of experiencing a shortfall, one may expect ECL to exceed Basel II expected loss (that is, excess provisions).

The following section provides an overview of the book both from an organisational perspective and from a toolkit point of view.

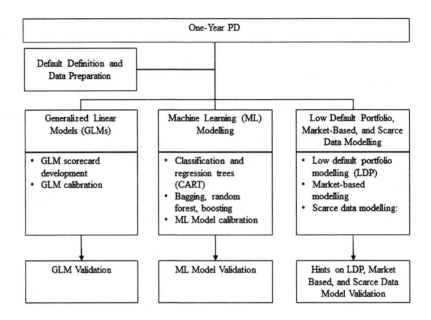

FIGURE 1.11

Chapter 2 workflow diagram.

1.5 BOOK STRUCTURE AT A GLANCE

This book aims to provide not only a theoretical framework, but a series of tools for credit risk model development and validation. Worked examples in R and SAS constitute the backbone of each chapter, as detailed in the following:

- **Chapter 2: one-year PD.** Figure 1.11 summarises the key areas explored in this chapter. The chapter starts by describing the key elements one needs to grasp to develop a comprehensive database for PD model development. In this regard, default definition plays a crucial role. Generalised linear models (GLMs) are then introduced as a paradigm for PD model development. A comprehensive scorecards development analysis is performed followed by its calibration based on the most recent historical period under investigation (that is, point-in-time estimation). As an alternative and challenger approach, machine learning (ML) procedures are explored to estimate one-year PDs. The focus is on classification and regression trees (CARTs), bagging, random forest and boosting. Data scarcity remains a key challenge. This is due either to lending business, as in the case of low default portfolios (for example, insurance or banking industries), or bank specific difficulties to collect data. Bespoke techniques are investigated to deal with both these issues.
- **Chapter 3: lifetime PD.** Figure 1.12 summarises how this chapter tackles lifetime modelling challenges. Few alternative approaches are studied. As a starting point, a framework based on generalised linear modelling (GLM) is explored. It originates from stress testing practice, and it can be considered as a natural extension of one-year PD modelling. Indeed, a four-step process is involved based on one-year PIT PD, link function, PD shift and lifetime PD computation. Two alternative ap-

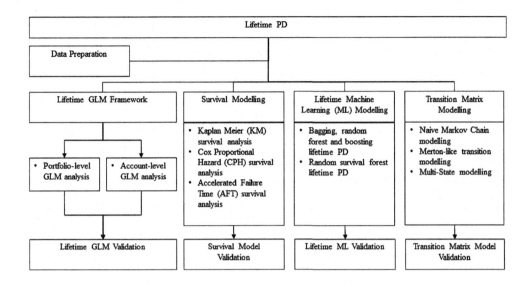

FIGURE 1.12

Chapter 3 workflow diagram.

proaches are studied: portfolio-level GLM and account-level GLM. In the first case, an aggregated link function connecting PDs, and macroeconomic variables (MVs) informs estimates. In contrast, the second approach relies on account-level panel data. The idea is to fit a regression by means of both behavioural variables (BVs) and MVs. Survival analysis is then introduced as an alternative way to capture lifetime PD features. Kaplan–Meier (KM) approach is used to introduce the basic ideas of survival analysis. It suddenly leaves the floor to Cox proportional hazard (CPH) and accelerated failure time (AFT) techniques. Indeed, both latter frames are capable to embed BVs and MVs to allow for a forward-looking perspective. Machine learning (ML) techniques are also used for lifetime modelling. The focus is on bagging, random forest, boosting and random survival forests. As a final approach, transition matrices are explored to build the term structure of lifetime PDs. The analysis is conducted starting from a simple Markov chain framework, which is then enriched by means of structural modelling. Finally, multi-state modelling is explored.

- **Chapter 4: LGD modelling.** Figure 1.13 summarises the path to model LGDs. Historical data are at the very heart of LGD modelling. Model sophistication and robustness are strictly linked to the quality of workout process data. As a first step, one needs to describe LGD database key elements. From a modelling standpoint, micro-structure LGD is the first approach to be scrutinised. A key distinction is made between probability of cure and severity. The first component can be considered as a binary variable (that is, cure against non-cure) and is modelled by means of generalised linear model (GLM), and classification trees (that is, machine learning). Severity, on the contrary, represents the portion of defaulted balance not recovered. Regression and machine learning techniques are used for their fit. In all cases, a forward-looking perspective is captured by embedding MVs or developing a separate (two-step) process, where economic conditions are integrated as part of a consistent process. As an alternative to micro-structure LGD modelling, regression methods are studied

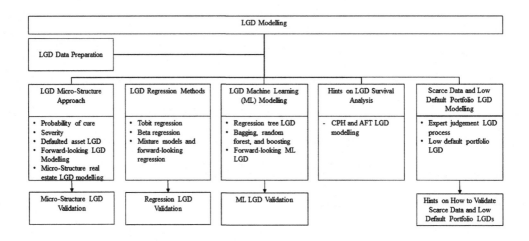

FIGURE 1.13

Chapter 4 workflow diagram.

to capture all workout outcomes in one go. Tobit, beta regression and other similar techniques are explored to fit an outcome defined as percentage of loss over defaulted balance.

One may think of LGD as an average loss for accounts sharing similar characteristics. Machine learning methods (for example, classification and regression trees, bagging, random forest and boosting) are natural candidates for LGD estimates. Despite its appealing statistical structure, survival analysis has not been widely used for LGD modelling. Hints are then provided on survival LGD model. One of the major issues one needs to face to develop an LGD model is data gathering. Poor data quality usually characterises the workout process. Despite write-off data availability, gaps between recoveries and defaults occur. For this reason specific focus is devoted on procedures to embrace both scarce data, and low default portfolios LGD modelling.

- **Chapter 5: prepayments, competing risks and EAD modelling.** Figure 1.14 summarises Chapter 5's structure. A full prepayment is the most extreme deviation from the repayment schedule. Indeed, the loan is repaid in full at some point before maturity. As a first approach, one may tackle this problem by focusing on generalised linear models (GLMs). Machine learning techniques are also inspected, whereas hints are provided on survival analysis. Contrary to PDs and LGDs, full prepayment modelling relies on non-defaulted accounts. Indeed, the goal is to investigate loan balance evolution based on live accounts to assess the outstanding balance at each reporting date. As a consequence, one may consider prepayments and defaults as competing risks. Overpayments (that is, excess payments on the scheduled profile) are also included as part of the study. In this regard, our first focus is on multinomial regression to analyse full prepayments and defaults. Then, a two-step procedure is investigated to explore prepayments and overpayments. Indeed, one does not only need the probability of these events to occur, but in case of overpayments, the amount paid needs to be modelled. Tobit and beta regression are used for this scope. Finally, EAD modelling concentrates on uncommitted products (for example, overdraft, revolving facilities) to investigate balance (example, credit line utilisation) until the event of default.

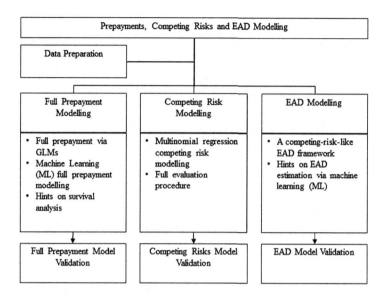

FIGURE 1.14

Chapter 5 workflow diagram.

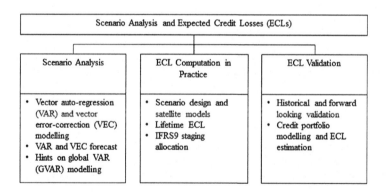

FIGURE 1.15

Chapter 6 workflow diagram.

- **Chapter 6: scenario analysis and expected credit losses.** Figure 1.15 summarises how scenarios, ECL and its overarching validation are investigated throughout the chapter. Multivariate time series analysis is introduced to generate scenarios. Details on how to perform vector auto-regression (VAR) and vector error-correction (VEC) are provided. As a next step, one needs to bring together all credit risk models investigated throughout the book in conjunction with scenarios to compute ECL. Finally, the focus is funnelled on the overall ECL validation. Indeed, a silos risk parameter validation does not ensure a consistent ECL output. Two main perspectives are considered. On the one hand, historical credit losses are considered as a paradigm for ECL validation. On the other hand, a credit portfolio modelling view is followed.

1.6 SUMMARY

The key elements of IFRS 9 and CECL accounting principles were presented to inform our expected credit loss journey. Both accounting principles moved from an incurred loss mindset towards an expected loss perspective. Few major differences were pointed out. As an example, IFRS 9 requires a staging allocation process. Financial instruments not experiencing a significant increase in credit risk are classified in stage 1 and are subject to one-year expected credit loss. Lifetime ECL applies to both stage 2 and stage 3. In contrast, CECL relies on a lifetime perspective without making distinctions among credit pools. A forward-looking perspective combines IFRS 9 and CECL. In terms of methodologies, even if IFRS 9 did not prescribe any specific approach, the vast majority of financial institutions adopted a PD, LGD, EAD method. FASB's standard was not prescriptive; it left the door open to methods based on loss-rate, probability of default (that is, PD, LGD, EAD), discounted cash flows, roll-rate, or based on ageing schedule. Examples of loss-rate, vintage, discounted cash flows methods were inspected to point out their main features. Nevertheless, it was highlighted that the focus of the book is on methods relying on PD, LGD, EAD, being also references for IFRS 9. A link between expected credit losses and capital requirements was inspected to figure out linkages between these two areas. Finally, book structure was scrutinised to guide the reader through the journey. An introduction to each chapter was provided together with a narrative highlighting the key choices made in presenting each topic.

REFERENCES

Bellini, T., 2017. Stress Testing and Risk Integration in Banks: A Statistical Framework and Practical Software Guide in Matlab and R. Academic Press, San Diego.

BIS, 2004. Modifications to the Capital Treatment for Expected and Unexpected Credit Losses in the New Basel Accord. Bank for International Settlements, Basel, Switzerland.

BIS, 2006. Basel II International Convergence of Capital Measurement and Capital Standards: A Revised Framework. BIS, Basel.

BIS, 2011. Basel III: A Global Regulatory Framework for More Resilient Banks and Banking Systems. Bank for International Settlements, Basel, Switzerland.

Duffie, D., Singleton, K.J., 2003. Credit Risk Pricing, Measurement and Management. Princeton University Press, Princeton.

FASB, 2016. Accounting Standards Updata No. 2016–13, Financial Instruments-Credit Losses (Topic 326). June 16, 2016. Financial Accounting Series. Financial Accounting Standards Board.

Gordy, M., 2003. A risk-factor foundation for risk-based capital rules. Journal of Financial Intermediation 12, 199–232.

IASB, 2014. IFRS 9 Financial Instruments. July 2014. Technical report. International Accounting Standards Board.

Merton, R., 1974. On the pricing of corporate debt: the risk structure of interest rates. Journal of Finance 29 (2), 449–470.

Vasicek, O., 2002. Loan portfolio value. Risk 15 (2), 160–162.

ONE-YEAR PD

2

One-year probability of default (PD) can be seen as a snapshot of lifetime PD. Two main reasons suggest treating one-year and lifetime separately. Firstly, banks have been developing one-year PD models over the last two decades for Basel II regulatory requirements. Secondly, a building-block-structure split in one-year and lifetime PD facilitates the learning process.

As a starting point, this chapter focuses on how default events are defined for accounting purposes. As a following step, the process to build a consistent PD database is investigated.

Generalised linear models (GLMs) are explored as a paradigm for one-year PD estimates. Indeed, this approach is the most commonly adopted in the banking industry. A two-step scheme, based on scorecard development and its calibration, allows us to estimate point-in-time (PIT) PDs.

In recent years, growing attention has been devoted to big data. Machine learning (ML) algorithms play a key role in this field. Classification and regression trees (CARTs), bagging, random forest, and boosting are studied both to challenge existing models, and explore new PD modelling solutions.

If a wide data availability encourages the use of data driven methods, low default portfolios and data scarcity are other challenges one may need to face. Indeed, a limited number of defaults requires bespoke methods. Likewise, lack of deep historical data forces banks to develop ad hoc approaches for one-year PD models.

Examples and case studies are explored throughout the chapter by means of R software. A laboratory section provides details on how to perform the implementation by means of SAS language.

KEY ABBREVIATIONS AND SYMBOLS

DTD	Distance to default
GLM	Generalised linear model
IV	Information value
ML	Machine learning
SC_i	Score for account i
V_t	Asset company value at time t
χ_i	Vector of behavioural variables (BVs) for account i
y_i	Response variable (default vs. non-default) for account i
WOE	Weight of evidence

2.1 INTRODUCTION

IFRS 9 and CECL accounting requirements lead banks to develop models by focusing on: point-in-time (PIT), unbiased and forward-looking lifetime estimates. These requirements puzzle banks relying

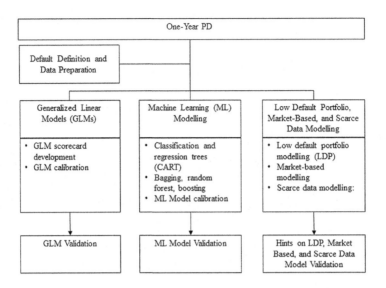

FIGURE 2.1

Chapter's workflow diagram.

on the Basel II regulatory capital framework (BIS, 2006). Indeed, a one-year through-the-cycle (TTC) perspective informs Basel II capital requirement framework. Therefore new methodologies and information technology (IT) infrastructures are compulsory to align with new accounting requirements.

This chapter provides the foundation for PD model development and validation. A lifetime perspective is at the very heart of FASB (2016) accounting principle. On the other hand, IASB (2014) relies on one-year or lifetime expected losses, based on a significant increase in credit risk criteria. One may focus on one-year PDs as a snapshot of the lifetime PD term structure. Then, taking into account banks' appetite to rely on a framework already put in place for Basel II and stress testing purposes, a split between one-year and lifetime PDs is considered beneficial for the entire learning journey.

The intended outcome of this chapter does not directly feed ECL formula. Additional components are needed to align with accounting requirements. Nevertheless, it provides a solid background for our development process. In more detail, general concepts, such as default definition and database architecture are crucial throughout the book. From a modelling perspective, generalised linear models (GLMs) constitute the first pillar to scrutinise binary outcomes, such as default against non-default. Machine learning (ML) is the second pillar of our challenging credit risk modelling framework.

Figure 2.1 summarises the key areas explored in this chapter as detailed below:

- **Default definition and data preparation.** Section 2.2 describes the key elements one needs to grasp to develop a comprehensive database for PD model development. In this regard, default definition plays a crucial role. A detailed interpretation of accounting rules is provided to align PD estimation with standard requirements.
- **Generalised linear models (GLMs).** Section 2.3 introduces generalised linear models (GLMs) as a paradigm for PD model development. A comprehensive scorecards development analysis is

performed, followed by its calibration on the most recent historical period under investigation (that is, PIT estimation). Appendices provide additional details both on GLM statistical framework and discriminatory power metrics used throughout the book.

- **Machine learning (ML) modelling.** Big data play a major role in our economy. Techniques dealing with them are in high demand for credit risk purposes. For this reason, Section 2.4 investigates machine learning (ML) procedures by means of classification and regression trees (CARTs), bagging, random forest, and boosting. These methods provide a consistent challenge to existing models (for example, GLMs), and allow us to explore alternative ways of analysing data and estimate one-year PDs.

- **Low default portfolio, market-based, and scarce data modelling.** If wide data availability boosts ML utilisation, data scarcity remains a key challenge. This is due either to lending business characteristics, as in the case of low default portfolios (example, insurance or banking industries), or banks' difficulties to collect data. Section 2.5 explores how to tackle these issues by means of bespoke approaches, such as Pluto and Tasche (2005), distance to default, and more qualitative methods based on expert judgements.

A separate section at the end of each methodological dissertation focuses on model validation. Indeed, this is a key step for model development and is also part of independent processes performed, among others, by internal and external model validation, internal and external audit.

Examples and case studies are examined by means of R software throughout the chapter. Finally, Section 2.6 provides SAS programming details on the chapter's key examples.

2.2 DEFAULT DEFINITION AND DATA PREPARATION

Probability of default refers to the ability of a borrower to repay debt obligations. The higher this ability, the less likely the borrower will default.

Basel II, IFRS 9, CECL do not necessarily align in terms of default event definition. For this reason Section 2.2.1 compares few alternatives by means of practical examples. Then, the focus is on the process to collect and provide data for model development, as detailed in Section 2.2.2.

2.2.1 DEFAULT DEFINITION

Following Basel II principles *"A default is considered to have occurred when: the banking institution considers that an obligor is unlikely to repay in full its credit obligations to the banking group, without recourse by the banking institution to actions such as realising security; or the obligor has breached its contractual repayment schedule and is past due for more than 90 days on any material credit obligation to the banking group"* (BIS, 2006).

From an IFRS 9 perspective, Section B5.5.37 of IASB (2014) does not directly define default, but requires entities to align with internal credit risk management. A rebuttable presumption holds. Default does not occur later than a financial asset is 90 days past due.

From a FASB (2016) standpoint, *"Estimating expected credit losses is highly judgmental and generally will require an entity to make specific judgments. Those judgments may include any of the following: a. The definition of default for default-based statistics ..."*

All in all, an effort is required by regulators to align capital requirement and accounting definitions. Additionally, banks need to improve transparency and intelligibility of financial reports. As a matter of fact, quantitative and qualitative elements are considered as default triggers. In terms of illustrative examples, one may consider the following:

- **Quantitative indicators.** 90 days past due (DPD) or 3 months in arrears (MIA) are common default triggers. A counter is put in place to account for delays or arrears balance.
- **Qualitative indicators.** The following elements are commonly used in practice as default triggers:
  - Bankruptcy. This event may be triggered with regards to a bank's specific exposure, or due to exposures towards other institutions.
  - Maturity or term expiry. Default is caused by an outstanding balance due after the maturity date.
  - Others. Other indicators, such as forbearances, play a major role as a default trigger.

From a modelling perspective, a default flag is defined as binary variable. It conventionally assumes the value 0 if no default occurs, and 1 in the case of default, as detailed in Example 2.2.1 (following).

EXAMPLE 2.2.1 INSTANT CURE AND PROBATIONARY PERIOD DEFAULT DEFINITION

Let us consider a mortgage with a $100,000.00 residual balance, and monthly instalments of $5,000.00. This account pays $5,000.00 in January, misses February, March, pays $5,000.00 in April, misses May, then pays $5,000.00 in June, $20,000.00 in July, and $5,000.00 every month until the end of the year. Default is triggered as 3 months in arrears (MIA). Table 2.1 summarises payments, missing payments, overpayments (that is, excess payments compared to the original schedule), and shows how the default flag is created under two alternatives:

- **Instant cure.** In this case, an account returns to the up-to-date status (that is, non-default) immediately after the cause of default is removed.
- **Probationary period.** Contrary to the instant cure setting, when a probationary period (for example, 6 months) is adopted, one needs to wait until the end of this period before returning to the up-to-date status. It is worth noting that a probationary period mitigates potential jumps in and out of default status. Therefore it reduces the risk of the account's multiple defaults.

Table 2.1 Default flag based on instant cure and 6-month probationary period ($ Thousands)

	Jan	Feb	Mar	Apr	May	Jun	Jul	Aug	Sep	Oct	Nov	Dec
a. Actual payments	5.00	0.00	0.00	5.00	0.00	5.00	20.00	5.00	5.00	5.00	5.00	5.00
b. Missing payments	0.00	5.00	5.00	0.00	5.00	0.00	−15.00	0.00	0.00	0.00	0.00	0.00
c. Cumulative missing payments	0.00	5.00	10.00	10.00	15.00	15.00	0.00	0.00	0.00	0.00	0.00	0.00
d. Default flag: Istant cure	0	0	0	0	1	1	0	0	0	0	0	0
e. Default flag: 6M probationary period	0	0	0	0	1	1	1	1	1	1	1	1

In line with Table 2.1, the following applies:

- **Instant cure.** Row d. of Table 2.1 summarises a monthly default flag mechanism. Default occurs in May and this status remains until June (that is, default flag is 1). In July, a $20,000.00 payment covers the previous gap and aligns the account with scheduled payments. The account under analysis moves to the up-to-date status (that is, default flag is 0) in July.
- **Probationary period.** In line with row e. of Table 2.1, the 6-month probationary period causes the default flag to persist from May until the end of the year (that is, default flag turns to 0 after 6 months from default cause removal).

One of the key challenges necessary to be addressed is how to build a database for one-year PD modelling. The next section provides some hints on how to tackle this issue.

2.2.2 DATA PREPARATION

Example 2.2.2 (following) pinpoints some of the key elements required to build a PD database, including a one-year PD database. Regarding this, two key steps characterise the model development process: scorecard estimation and model calibration. A comprehensive description of these steps is provided in the next sections.

EXAMPLE 2.2.2 INGREDIENTS TO BUILD A PD DATABASE

Let us consider a database spanning over a 5-year time horizon.

One needs to specify whether an accounted defaulted over a given time horizon. Figure 2.2 highlights contiguous one-year intervals. Years are denoted as Y1, Y2, Y3, Y4, Y5. In this regard, Y1 represents the first of a 5-year time series (that is, it does not represent the year when an account firstly entered into the portfolio).

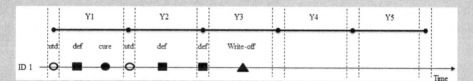

FIGURE 2.2

Account specific multi-period information to define default flags.

The scope of a one-year PD modelling is to assess the probability that a non-defaulted account (at the beginning of the period) will default within a one-year horizon. Therefore the analysis starts from non-defaulted accounts and investigates their evolution through time, as detailed below:

- **Y1.** The following applies:
  - Account ID 1 is up-to-date at the beginning of the period.
  - It defaults after 4 months (within year 1).
  - It cures 4 months after its default (within year 1).

- It is flagged as default in year 1, regardless of the instant cure, or probationary period definition.
- **Y2.** In this case, the adoption of a probationary period plays an important role, as detailed below:
  - **Instant cure.** At the beginning of Y2, ID 1 is up-to-date in the case of an instant cure. Then, ID 1 is candidate to be part of Y2 PD sample.
    - It defaults in year 2 and does not cure.
    - It is written-off in Y3.
  - **Probationary period.** If, for example, a 6-month probationary period is used, ID 1 is not part Y2 PD sample. Indeed, an account needs to be in the non-default status at the beginning of the period for it to belong to a PD development sample.

Figure 2.3 extends the above-described mechanism to other accounts (that is, ID 2, ID 3). It allows us to understand which accounts can be considered as part of the PD development sample.

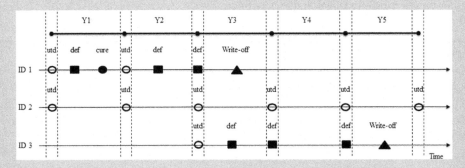

FIGURE 2.3

How to build a PD database starting from account specific multi-period information.

Figure 2.3 highlights the following:

- ID 1 can be part of the PD development sample for Y1 and Y2 (if an instant cure rule applies).
- ID 2 can be part of any sample (that is, Y1, Y2, ..., Y5).
- ID 3 can be part of Y3 sample only.

Example 2.2.2 points out some key decisions one needs to make when developing a PD database. Nevertheless, other questions need to be addressed. As an example, shall we consider ID 2 throughout the entire 5-year horizon, or is it preferable to avoid an account entering many times in our development sample? Based on this, the following holds:

- **Time horizon.** A distinction arises between scorecard development and calibration. BIS (2006) requires at least a 5-year dataset for PD modelling. On the other hand, no specific accounting requirement informs PD modelling. Nevertheless, banks are required to define, and operate consistently with, their risk management practices. From an accounting perspective, a PIT estimate requires to calibrate the model over the most recent horizon (for example, the latest available year).

- **Duplicated cases.** As an additional step, one needs to decide whether to include the same account over different periods (for example, ID 2 in Example 2.2.2). Some practitioners point out the importance of retaining as much information as possible. Others pinpoint a potential bias introduced by considering the same account many times.
- **Time horizon sampling.** Sampling schemes usually apply over a multi-year horizon. As an example, one may decide to sample more often from the recent periods than the remote ones.

All above decisions are influenced by data availability. For low default portfolios, and in case of data scarcity, Section 2.5 describes few approaches one may follow. The next section enters into the details of PD modelling by means of GLMs.

2.3 GENERALISED LINEAR MODELS (GLMS)

In the last decades, quantitative methods provided an enormous aid to reduce the subjectivity of judgemental methods. Indeed, the ability to handle voluminous data is crucial to detect complex relationships as required in modern credit risk modelling. One question arises: which method is the best? No ultimate answer can be provided. The focus of this section is on generalised linear models (GLMs). Firstly, we start from GLMs because of their practicality and widespread popularity in the financial industry. Secondly, GLMs provide a useful framework for other methods.

It is worth noting that PIT PDs estimated in this section do not directly feed ECL formula. A forward-looking perspective is needed to align with accounting rules, as detailed in Chapter 3.

Figure 2.4 summarises the key steps for GLMs modelling.

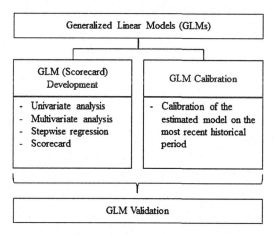

FIGURE 2.4

Workflow diagram for Section 2.3.

A two-step process is explored as listed below:

- **GLM development (Scorecard).** Section 2.3.1 explores how to develop a credit scorecard by means of GLMs (for example, logit regression). The main goal of a scorecard is to rank accounts based on default likelihood.

- **GLM calibration.** Section 2.3.2 describes how to rescale a scorecard to derive PDs. As an additional step, one may aggregate accounts in rating classes. This process is particularly relevant for lifetime PD modelling. Indeed, Chapter 3 describes how to estimate a term structure of PDs by means of rating transition matrices (Jafry and Schuermann, 2004).

Finally, Section 2.3.3 focuses on validation. A comprehensive process embracing data, methodology and statistical testing is investigated by means of examples worked in R software.

2.3.1 GLM (SCORECARD) DEVELOPMENT

Default flag, as investigated in Section 2.2.1, is one of the key ingredients for a PD framework. Indeed, one uses a set of explanatory variables to fit a binary response representing defaults, as detailed below:

$$y_i = \begin{cases} 1 & default, \\ 0 & non\text{-}default, \end{cases} \tag{2.1}$$

where i indicates a account within the portfolio under investigation.[1]

One may consider alternative functional forms. The following logistic relationship is commonly adopted in practice:

$$SC_i = \frac{1}{1 + e^{-(\beta_0 + \beta_1 \chi_{i,1} + \dots + \beta_k \chi_{i,k})}}, \tag{2.2}$$

where $\chi_i = (\chi_{i,1}, \dots, \chi_{i,k})'$ is the $k \times 1$ vector of explanatory behavioural variables (BVs).

The following linear relationship can easily be derived from the above equation:

$$\ln\left(\frac{SC_i}{1 - SC_i}\right) = \beta_0 + \beta_1 \chi_{i,1} + \dots + \beta_k \chi_{i,k}, \tag{2.3}$$

where $\ln\left(\frac{SC_i}{1-SC_i}\right)$ is the commonly denominated logit.

Readers interested in a more comprehensive, non-complex introduction to GLM may refer to Appendix A, where a comparison between linear models and logit regression is provided. Examples worked on a simple portfolio help grasping both theoretical and practical fundamental insights. Furthermore, Appendix B describes key metrics for assessing the model's discriminatory power. The focus is on: receiver operating characteristic (ROC) curve, area under the curve (AUC), Gini index, information value (IV), and weight of evidence (WOE). These metrics are used throughout the whole book as a key model development and validation tool.

Remark. It is worth noting that other link functions can also be considered (for example, probit, log-log) as part of generalised linear modelling. Nevertheless, logit link is the most commonly used in practice. For this reason it will be considered as a reference function throughout the book.

---

[1]Hereafter, the notation is simplified to familiarise with the key concepts of the chapter. A richer formalisation will be required for lifetime modelling in the following chapters.

Moving from Equation (2.2), one needs to identify an effective set of explanatory variables to fit y_i. In this regard, both statistical significance and economic soundness are at the very heart of the model development process, as listed below:

i. **Default definition and data preparation.** In line with Section 2.2, default flag identification and data preparation constitute the starting point for the entire model development process.

ii. **Univariate analysis.** A set of explanatory variables is tested by running univariate regressions. The analysis is usually performed on a transformation. A common technique is to rely on weight of evidence (WOE), as detailed in Appendix B. In other words, the domain of an explanatory variable is spit into intervals. It allows us to simplify characteristics representation and avoid issues related to outlying units. This approach is also quite useful when categorical and non-numeric variables are part of the data set under investigation. The goal of univariate analysis is to identify variables with high individual discriminatory power, based on a given criterion or a combination of criteria. In practice, the following metrics are currently adopted: area under the curve (AUC), Gini index and information value (IV), as described in Appendix B. As an example, one may use IV critical values to inform the process of including or excluding variables from the so-called long list (that is, list of candidate variables for the final model). In practice a model with $IV < 0.10$ is usually qualified as weak; medium discriminatory power is commonly associated with $0.1 < IV < 0.4$, whereas $IV > 0.4$ denotes strong prediction. Therefore one may exclude from the long list all variables with $IV < 0.10$.[2]

iii. **Multivariate analysis.** Moving from the above detailed long list, the next step is to investigate the combination of variables to fit y_i. Correlation analysis, sense checks and expert judgement pave the way for the so-called short list (that is, shortened list of candidate variables for the final model).

iv. **Stepwise regression.** The shortlist is further scrutinised by means of selection processes based on statistical criteria. Two directions can be followed to run a stepwise regression: forward or backward. The difference relies on whether the initialisation process starts with:

- No predictors. In this case, a forward stepwise regression is performed by progressively adding explanatory variables until all of them are included.
- All variables in the shortlist. In a backward stepwise regression variables are progressively discarded until the minimum subset size is reached.

At each step, the procedure is looking at the models that provide the biggest improvement in terms of a given metric. Two, among others, are the most widely used criteria to perform this selection:

- Akaike Information Criterion (AIC):

$$AIC = -2 \cdot log Likelihood + 2 \cdot m, \qquad (2.4)$$

where $log Likelihood$ represents the logarithm of the likelihood, and m is the number of variables entering the model. The latter component aims to penalise the inclusion of additional variables.

---

[2]One may tailor the threshold based on data availability and modelling appetite.

- Bayesian Information Criterion (BIC):

$$BIC = -2 \cdot logLikelihood + m \cdot log(n),\qquad(2.5)$$

where n stands for the number of observations in the set.

The goal is to take into account the $logLikelihood$ value, and penalise it by considering the number of variables that entered the model. For two models with the same $logLikelihod$, the one with less variables is the best.

v. Expert judgement. As a key step of the process, business experts participate in the checking of both relevance and consistency of variables included in the model. Indeed, their experience can hardly be replicated through a statistical model. Experts participate throughout the entire process by including the assessment of model overlays.

Example 2.3.1 summarises the key GLM model development steps by means of a comprehensive database.

EXAMPLE 2.3.1 SCORECARD DEVELOPMENT

Let us consider a retail loan portfolio database. The goal is to show how to build a scorecard through the following steps:

1. Default flag definition and data preparation,
2. Univariate analysis,
3. Multivariate analysis, and
4. Stepwise regression.

```
# 1. Default flag definition and data preparation
# 1.1. Import data
oneypd<- read.csv('chap2oneypd.csv') [,2:45]
library(dplyr)
# 1.1.1.  Data overview: data content and format
dplyr::glimpse(oneypd)
# $ id                   <int> 6670001, 9131199...
# $ vintage_year         <int> 2005, 2006...
# $ monthly_installment  <dbl> 746.70, 887.40...
# $ loan_balance         <dbl> 131304.44, 115486.51...
# $ bureau_score         <int> 541, 441...
# ...
# 1.1.2. Date format
library(vars)
oneypd <- dplyr::mutate_at(oneypd, vars(contains('date')),
funs(as.Date))
class(oneypd$origination_date)
# 1.1.3. Round arrears count fields
oneypd$max_arrears_12m<- round(oneypd$max_arrears_12m,4)
oneypd$arrears_months<- round(oneypd$arrears_months,4)
```

The scheme described in Section 2.2.1 is applied to define a one-year default flag. In more detail, default flag relies on the following events: arrears, bankruptcy and term expiry. Firstly, default is caused when arrears exceed 3 months (that is, 3 months in arrears (MIA) or 90 days past due). Secondly, a default flag is triggered when bankruptcy takes place. Thirdly, term expiry indicates that a facility passed its original maturity with a positive residual debt. The process is implemented as follows:

```
# 1.2. Default flag definition
oneypd<- dplyr::mutate(oneypd,
default_event = if_else(oneypd$arrears_event == 1 |
oneypd$term_expiry_event == 1 |
oneypd$bankrupt_event == 1, 1,0))
```

As a next step, a stratified sampling scheme is followed to split the database into train and test sets. The first represents 70% of the population, until the latter encompasses the residual 30%.

```
# 1.3. Database split in train and test samples
# Recode default event variables for more convenient use
# 0-default, 1-non-default
oneypd$default_flag<-
dplyr::if_else(oneypd$default_event == 1,0,1)
# Perform a stratified sampling: 70% train and 30% test
library(caret)
set.seed(2122)
train.index <- caret::createDataPartition(oneypd$default_event,
p = .7, list = FALSE)
train <- oneypd[ train.index,]
test  <- oneypd[-train.index,]
```

A binning process is performed based on WOE. For the sake of simplicity, the corresponding code is not shown here. Nevertheless, the reader can easily implement it by means of R functions, such as *smbinning*. Table 2.2 summarises the binning scheme adopted in the final steps of the analysis (that is, intervals are expressed in terms of WOE). As a following step, one needs to specify a criterion to select the most predictive variables. For our purposes, we consider as a weak predictor the variable with IV lower than 0.1, medium if IV is between 0.1 and 0.4, and strong if IV is greater than 0.4.

```
# 2. Univariate analysis
# Information Value (IV) assessment
library(smbinning)
iv_analysis<- smbinning.sumiv(df=train,y="default_flag")
# Plot IV summary table
```

```
par(mfrow=c(1,1))
smbinning.sumiv.plot(iv_analysis,cex=1)
```

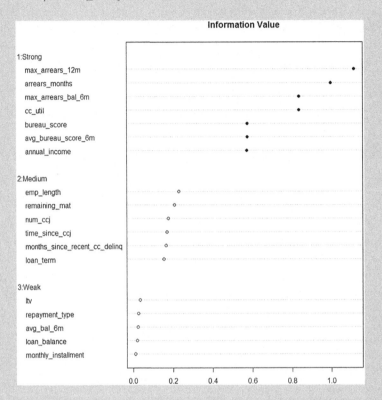

FIGURE 2.5

IV analysis: weak, medium, and strong predictors.

According to Figure 2.5, a set of 7 variables shows a strong power in predicting default. Other 6 variables have a medium IV, and 5 variables show weak discriminatory power. A business check highlights that some variables encompass similar information. In particular arrears_months shares a similar content with max_arrears_12m (that is, maximum number months in arrears during the last 12 months). Likewise, avg_bureau_score_6m (that is, average bureau score over the previous 6-month period) is pretty close to bureau_score. For this reason they are not considered in the next step of the process. As part of an expert judgement evaluation, emp_length (that is, the length of employment), num_ccj (number of County Court Judgements), and months_since_recent_cc_delinq (number of months since the most recent delinquent status) are chosen among the variables with medium IV. All these variables constitute the long list to examine through a multivariate assessment, as detailed below. Table 2.2 summarises the binning scheme adopted. It is worth noting that bureau score variable is used notwithstanding in some cases one may prefer not to rely on variables already encompassing a combination of relevant information.

Table 2.2 Binning scheme adopted for multivariate analysis

Variable	Attribute	Bin_1	Bin_2	Bin_3	Bin_4	Bin_5	Bin_6
bureau_score	Interval	NA	<= 308	(308,404]	(404,483]	> 483	
	WOE	−0.091	−0.7994	−0.0545	0.7722	1.0375	
woe_cc_util	Interval	NA	<= 0.55	(0.55,0.70]	(0.70,0.85]	> 0.85	
	WOE	0	1.8323	−0.4867	−1.1623	−2.3562	
woe_num_ccj	Interval	NA	<= 0	> 0	> 1		
	WOE	−0.091	0.1877	−0.9166	−1.1322		
max_arrears_12	Interval	NA	<= 0	(0,1]	(1,1.4]	> 1.4	
	WOE	0	0.7027	−0.8291	−1.1908	−2.2223	
max_arrears_bal_6m	Interval	NA	<= 0	(0,300]	(300,600]	(600,900]	> 900
	WOE	0	0.5771	−0.7818	−1.2958	−1.5753	−2.211
emp_length	Interval	NA	< 2	(2,4]	(4,7]	> 7	
	WOE	0	−0.7514	−0.3695	0.1783	0.5827	
months_since_recent_cc_delinq	Interval	NA	< 6	(6,11]	> 11		
	WOE	0	−0.4176	−0.1942	1.3166		
annual_income	Interval	NA	< 35064	(35064,41999]	(41999,50111]	(50111,65050]	> 65050
	WOE	0	−1.8243	−0.8272	−0.3294	0.2379	0.6234

```
# 3. Multivariate analysis
# Compute Spearman rank correlation based on variables' WOE
# based on Table 2.2 binning scheme
woe_vars<- train %>%
dplyr::select(starts_with("woe"))
woe_corr<- cor(as.matrix(woe_vars), method = 'spearman')
# Graphical inspection
library(corrplot)
corrplot(woe_corr, method = 'number')
```

Figure 2.6 points out two highly correlated pairs. In more detail, woe_max_arrears_12m, and woe_max_arrears_bal_6m (WOE maximum arrears balance in the previous 6 months) have a 0.87 correlation. Moreover, woe_emp_length, and woe_annual_income (WOE of annual income) have a 0.51 correlation. If we set a 0.60 threshold, only one variable is discarded. On the other hand, if this threshold is set at 0.50, another variable does not enter the stepwise regression process.

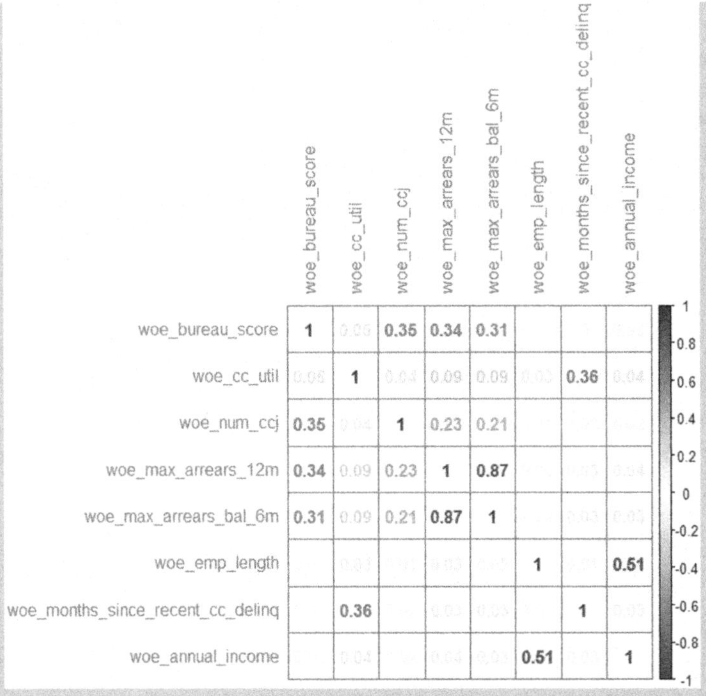

	woe_bureau_score	woe_cc_util	woe_num_ccj	woe_max_arrears_12m	woe_max_arrears_bal_6m	woe_emp_length	woe_months_since_recent_cc_delinq	woe_annual_income
woe_bureau_score	1	0.09	0.35	0.34	0.31			
woe_cc_util	0.06	1	0.04	0.09	0.09	0.02	0.36	0.04
woe_num_ccj	0.35	0.04	1	0.23	0.21			
woe_max_arrears_12m	0.34	0.09	0.23	1	0.87	0.03	0.04	
woe_max_arrears_bal_6m	0.31	0.09	0.21	0.87	1	0.03	0.05	
woe_emp_length	0.03					1		0.51
woe_months_since_recent_cc_delinq		0.36		0.03	0.03		1	
woe_annual_income	0.04		0.04	0.04		0.51		1

FIGURE 2.6

Pairs correlation analysis.

As a final step of the journey, a stepwise is performed, based on the short list of variables retained after a correlation and business check investigation, described above.

```
# 4. Stepwise regression
# 4.1 Discard highly correlated variable
woe_vars_clean<-  woe_vars %>%
dplyr::select( -woe_max_arrears_bal_6m)
#Support functions and databases
library(MASS)
attach(train)
# 4.2 Stepwise model fitting
logit_full<- glm(default_event~ woe_bureau_score+
woe_annual_income+woe_emp_length+woe_max_arrears_12m
+woe_months_since_recent_cc_delinq+woe_num_ccj+woe_cc_util,
family = binomial(link = 'logit'), data = train)
logit_stepwise<- stepAIC(logit_full, k=qchisq(0.05, 1,
lower.tail=F), direction = 'both')
detach(train)
```

```
summary(logit_stepwise)
#                           Estimate Std.Error z value Pr(>|z|)
# (Intercept)               -2.87285  0.04808 -59.756 < 0.0 ***
# woe_bureau_score          -0.49111  0.06228  -7.886   0.0 ***
# woe_annual_income         -0.97559  0.04965 -19.648 < 0.0 ***
# woe_max_arrears_12m       -0.82580  0.03723 -22.179 < 0.0 ***
# woe_months_since_recent   -0.28424  0.08320  -3.416   0.0 ***
# woe_cc_util               -0.93828  0.03414 -27.479 < 0.0 ***
# ---
# Signif. codes:  0 '***' 0.001 '**' 0.01 '*' 0.05 '.' 0.1 ' ' 1
```

Example 2.3.1 summarised the key elements of the scorecard building process. The next step is to calibrate the model on a given target default rate, as detailed in the following section.

2.3.2 GLM CALIBRATION

A score reflects an account's relative creditworthiness compared with others in a portfolio. On the other hand, ECL computation requires PDs. The following steps are usually performed to move from scorecards to PDs:

i. **Score normalisation.** As a first step, one may be interested in normalising scores within a given interval. Example 2.3.2 highlights how to perform this process.

EXAMPLE 2.3.2 FROM SCORE TO POINTS

Let us consider the model developed in Example 2.3.1. Our aim is to define a new scale with anchor set at 660 points and log-odds doubling each 40 points. A 72:1 odds ratio is identified in line with credit bureau common practice. The following steps are performed:

1. Define a scaling function, and
2. Score the entire dataset.

```
# 1. Define a scaling function
scaled_score <- function(logit, odds, offset = 500, pdo = 20)
{
b = pdo/log(2)
a = offset - b*log(odds)
round(a + b*log((1-logit)/logit))
}
# 2. Score the entire dataset
library(dplyr)
# 2.1 Use fitted model to score both test and train datasets
predict_logit_test <- predict(logit_stepwise, newdata = test, type = 'response')
predict_logit_train - predict(logit_stepwise, newdata = train, type = 'response')
# 2.2 Merge predictions with train/test data
```

```
test$predict_logit <- predict(logit_stepwise, newdata = test, type = 'response')
train$predict_logit <- predict(logit_stepwise, newdata = train, type = 'response')
train$sample = 'train'
test$sample = 'test'
data_whole <- rbind(train, test)
data_score <- data_whole %>%
dplyr::select(id, default_event, default_flag, woe_bureau_score,
woe_annual_income, woe_max_arrears_12m,
woe_months_since_recent_cc_delinq,
woe_cc_util, sample, predict_logit)
# 2.3 Define scoring parameters in line with objectives
data_score$score<-
scaled_score(data_score$predict_logit, 72, 660, 40)
```

Figure 2.7 shows the distribution of accounts among scores. As expected, the vast majority of them is concentrated on the highest score bands, corresponding to lowest credit risk.

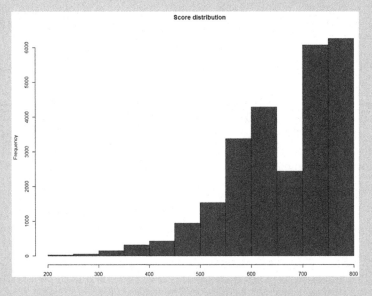

FIGURE 2.7

Score distribution.

ii. **Calibration.** In our case, the aim of a PIT calibration is to centre average portfolio PD to its most recent default rate. One may perform the calibration by means of alternative functions. When sufficient (default) data is available, a logistic regression is commonly used. In this regard, let us assume that a scorecard was built upon a multi-year horizon, and the goal is to obtain a one-year PIT calibration. This is what IASB (2014) requires for computing one-year PD for accounts allocated in stage 1. One may fit the following logistic regression:

$$\Psi_{s,t}^* = \underset{(\alpha,\beta)}{\arg\max} \sum_{i=1}^{n} \frac{1}{1 + e^{-(\alpha + \beta \cdot \widehat{SC}_i)}}, \tag{2.6}$$

where $\Psi_{s,t}^*$ is the target creditworthiness index (for example, over a one-year horizon) for portfolio s at time t.

Example 2.3.3 highlights the key steps to perform as part of the above calibration process.

EXAMPLE 2.3.3 PD CALIBRATION

We aim to calibrate the scorecard investigated in Examples 2.3.1 and 2.3.2, by relying on Equation (2.6). For the sake of simplicity, the same data is used to perform the calibration, by means of the following steps:

- Upload data, and
- Fit logistic regression.

```
# 1. Upload data
attach(data_score)
# 2. Fit logistic regression
pd_model<- glm(default_event~ score,
family = binomial(link = 'logit'), data = data_score)
summary(pd_model)
#                 Estimate Std. Error z value     Pr(>|z|)
# (Intercept)  7.1357807  0.1855217   38.46 <0.0000 ***
# score       -0.0173218  0.0003519  -49.23 <0.0000 ***
# ---
# Signif. codes:  0 '***' 0.001 '**' 0.01 '*' 0.05 '.' 0.1 ' ' 1
# 2.1 Use model coefficients to obtain PDs
data_score$pd<- predict(pd_model, newdata = data_score,
type = 'response')
```

Generally speaking, absence of sufficient internal data may lead to using external information (example, ratings). A linear or log-linear regression can be used for PD calibration. Finally, if neither sufficient internal data, nor external information is available, one needs to consider ad-hoc procedures, as detailed in Section 2.5.

iii. **Rating class assignment.** The very last step of the calibration is to map PDs into rating classes. This is an explicit requirement for IRB purposes. Indeed, risk weighted assets (RWAs) rely on ratings. In contrast, for IFRS 9 and CECL this is not strictly needed. Indeed, one may directly use PDs to compute expected credit losses. From an implementation point of view, once a rating grid is defined, a simple mapping process is performed to assign each account to the corresponding rating band. Transition matrices are often used for lifetime PD estimation, as detailed in Chapter 3.

The next section describes how to conduct model validation by focusing on the GLM framework investigated throughout this section.

2.3.3 GLM VALIDATION

The validation process is examined by focusing on: data, methodology and statistical testing, as follows:

a. Data. As a first step of the process, data validation can be organised by means of representativeness analysis, assessment of variable appropriateness, and data completeness, as listed below:

- **Data representativeness.** One of the first issues one faces in developing a one-year PD model is to use internal or external sources. Furthermore, one may refer to internal or external information, and demonstrate that data used for modelling truly represent the phenomenon under investigation.
- **Variable appropriateness.** A check is required to show that all variables used for modelling are relevant and appropriate for the scope of one-year PD modelling. Indeed, variables representing facts and events not relevant for the analysis (for example, dismissed business, products not in scope) should be disregarded.
- **Data completeness.** No specific requirements are provided by IASB (2014) and FASB (2016) on data to use for modelling purposes. Contrary to BIS (2006), which requires at least five-year data to develop Basel II models, no details are provided on historical depth. However, one needs to consider a database wide enough to include information over the most relevant past history to support PIT estimates. Furthermore, Chapter 3 will highlight the need to cover at least two economic cycles by including a downturn.

b. Methodology. The key advantages of GLM can be summarised in terms of its simplicity and easy interpretation of its results. At the same time, it provides a rigorous and robust statistical framework to develop, and calibrate, PD models. In all cases, key assumptions need to be revised by taking into account data availability and compared against other methods, such as machine learning or other approaches investigated in the next sections.

c. Statistical testing. The following checks are commonly performed to assess model's statistical appropriateness:

- **Discriminatory power.** The major aim of discrimination power inspection is to verify whether a model correctly distinguishes between defaulters and non-defaulters. Two of the most commonly used metrics are Gini index and ROC curve. The analysis is applied both on train and test samples. One may also check it through time.
  Example 2.3.4 illustrates how to conduct the analysis starting from Example 2.3.1.

EXAMPLE 2.3.4 MODEL DISCRIMINATORY POWER VALIDATION

Let us consider the model developed in Example 2.3.1. Discriminatory power is inspected by means of the following:

1. Gini index, and
2. ROC curve.

```
# 1. Gini index
library(optiRum)
gini_train<- optiRum::giniCoef(train$predict_logit,
train$default_event)
```

```
print(gini_train)
# 0.8335868
```

Both train and test Gini indices (that is, 0.833 and 0.823) pinpoint a strong discriminatory power. (See Figure 2.8.)

```
# 2. ROC curve
library(pROC)
plot(roc(train$default_event,train$predict_logit,
direction="<"),
col="blue", lwd=3, main="ROC Curve")
```

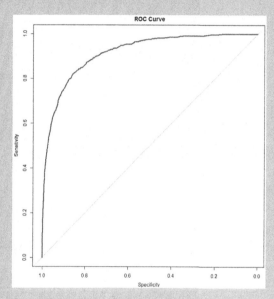

FIGURE 2.8

ROC analysis.

- **Calibration.** Controls are needed to verify model's alignment to actual defaults. A quick summary of the major checks is usually performed to ensure an effective calibration are listed below:
  - Comparison of actual and fitted PDs (by score band). The calibration process summarised in 2.3.2, ensures an effective alignment of the average portfolio PDs. Tolerance bands can be defined by distinguishing between absolute level and relative threshold. Example 2.3.5 compares actual and fitted PDs by focusing on score bands.

EXAMPLE 2.3.5 COMPARISON OF ACTUAL VERSUS FITTED PDS (BY SCORE BAND)

Let us focus on the calibration process described in Example 2.3.3. The validation is performed by means of the following steps:

1. Create score bands, and
2. Compare actual against fitted PDs.

```
# 1. Create a validation database
# 1.1. Create score bands
library(smbinning)
score_cust<- smbinning.custom(data_score, y = 'default_flag',
x= 'score', cuts= c(517,576,605,632,667,716,746,773))
# 1.2. Group by bands
data_score<- smbinning.gen(data_score, score_cust,
chrname = 'score_band')
# 2. Compare actual against fitted PDs
# 2.1. Compute mean values
data_pd<- data_score %>%
dplyr::select(score, score_band, pd, default_event) %>%
dplyr::group_by(score_band) %>%
dplyr::summarise(mean_dr = round(mean(default_event),4),
mean_pd = round(mean(pd),4))
# 2.2. Compute rmse
rmse<-sqrt(mean((data_pd$mean_dr - data_pd$mean_pd)^2))
# 0.002732317
```

Figure 2.9 shows the average actual and fitted PDs per score band. Visual inspection confirms the closeness of these metrics for each score band under analysis.

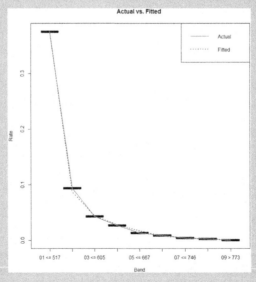

FIGURE 2.9

Actual versus fitted PDs per score band.

- When the focus is on rating classes, one may consider aggregated measures at portfolio level to verify how close PDs and observed DRs are. One may also enter into each rating class to compare the default rate observed for each class the average (or median) PD of the class. One may, for example, refer to Vasicek test or binomial test, as discussed in BIS (2005).
- **Out-of-sample and out-of-time stability.** The aim of stability checks is to verify whether changes occurred by making a model no longer appropriate. Firstly, one needs to check whether the population on which the model is currently used is to similar to the development population. If differences occur, one needs to verify the stability of the individual variables in the model. The following metrics are commonly adopted to check model stability:
  - Stability Index. A comparison is made between model development and actual current population. The difference between populations is measured by means of a Stability Index (SI) computed as follows:

$$SI = \sum_{j=1}^{J}(R_j - O_j)\ln\frac{R_j}{O_j},\tag{2.7}$$

    whereby j indicates the class under analysis, R_j represents the percentage of the reference population in class j, and O_j is the percentage of the observed population in class j. One may point out the similarity with information value (IV), described in equation (2.27). High values of SI indicate more substantial shifts in the population. As a rule of thumb, when $SI \leq 0.1$, no significant shift occurred. In case of $0.1 < SI \leq 0.25$, then, a minor shift occurred, whereas in the case of $SI > 0.25$, a major shift took place. Expert intuition is also important to mitigate the rigidity of this classification.
  - Other statistics can also be used for the purpose of verifying PD stability (Lantz and Nebenzahl, 1996). Furthermore, qualitative checks are usually recommended to have a full picture of how a model behaves under different circumstances.
- **Cross-validation.** In cross validation, the data set is split into g folds. A model is then developed on $g-1$ training folds and tested on the remaining validation fold. This is repeated for all possible validation folds resulting in g performance estimates, and model performance metrics (for example, AUC, Gini index) can then be averaged.

Example 2.3.6 illustrates how to conduct a cross-validation starting from Example 2.3.1.

EXAMPLE 2.3.6 CROSS-VALIDATION

Let us consider the model developed in Example 2.3.1. The following steps are performed:

1. Prepare cross-validation dataset, and
2. Perform cross-validation loop.

```
# 1. Prepare the cross-validation dataset
data_subset<- data_whole %>%
dplyr::select(id, default_event, default_flag, woe_bureau_score,
woe_annual_income, woe_max_arrears_12m,
```

```
woe_months_since_recent_cc_delinq, woe_cc_util, sample)
# 2. Perform the cross-validation loop
# 2.1 Initialise loop arguments and vectors
j<-1 #initialise counter
m<- 20 #number of folds
n = floor(nrow(data_subset)/m) #size of each fold
auc_vector<- rep(NA,m)
gini_vector<- rep(NA, m)
ks_vector<- rep(NA, m)
# 2.2 Run the loop
attach(data_subset)
for (j in 1:m)
{
s1 = ((j-1)*n+1) #start of the subset (fold)
s2 = (j*n) # end of the subset (fold)
data_cv_subset = s1:s2 #range of the subset (fold)
train_set <- data_subset[-data_cv_subset, ]
test_set <- data_subset[data_cv_subset, ]
# Model Fitting
model <- glm(default_event~ woe_bureau_score+
woe_annual_income+woe_max_arrears_12m+
woe_months_since_recent_cc_delinq+woe_cc_util,
family=binomial(link = 'logit'), data = train_set)
# Predict results
predict_cv <- predict(model, newdata = test_set,
type = 'response')
pred_obj<- ROCR::prediction(predict_cv, test_set[,2])
perf_obj<- ROCR::performance(pred_obj, 'tpr', 'fpr')
# Calculate performance metrics for each fold/run:
test_auc<- ROCR::performance(pred_obj, 'auc')
auc_vector[j] <- test_auc@y.values[[1]]
gini_vector[j]<- optiRum::giniCoef(predict_cv,
test_set[,2])
}
```

Figure 2.10 highlights low volatility of both AUC and Gini index throughout the validation exercise. This volatility is further reduced by increasing the number of folds in the
cross-validation process.

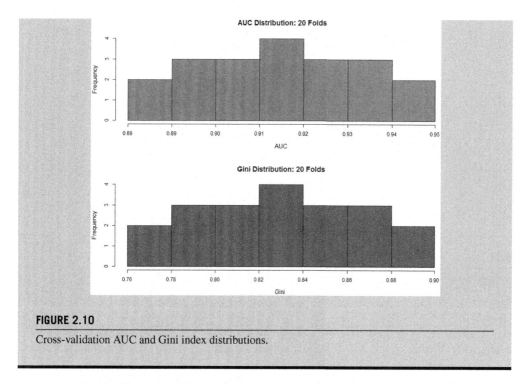

FIGURE 2.10

Cross-validation AUC and Gini index distributions.

- **Reproducibility.** One of the most relevant issues one encounters while reproducing a PD model has to do with the data. Indeed, an effective data documentation together with meticulous storage are part of the reproducibility process. Furthermore, one needs to ensure that the overall process and the software used for development and implementation are well-described. Eventually, one needs to perform a replication study on the same data used for model development.

The next section focuses on machine learning techniques one may effectively adopt for one-year PD modelling. The focus is on classification methods, such as classification and regression trees (CART), bagging, random forest, and boosting.

2.4 MACHINE LEARNING (ML) MODELLING

In recent years, growing attention has been devoted to machine learning procedures (Bellotti and Crook, 2009). Machine learning (ML) in computer science literature refers to a set of algorithms specifically designed to tackle computationally intensive pattern-recognition problems based on extremely large datasets. These techniques include tree-based classifiers and are ideally suited for credit-risk analysis. The extraordinary speed-up in computing, coupled with significant algorithmic theoretical advances, has created a renaissance in computational credit risk modelling.

It is worth noting that, as per GLMs, even ML models inspected throughout this section do not directly feed ECL. In this regard, a forward-looking framework is needed, as detailed in Chapter 3.

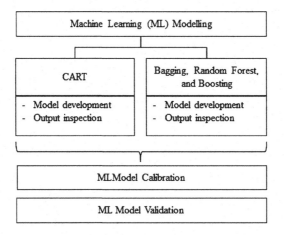

FIGURE 2.11

Workflow diagram for Section 2.4.

In what follows, the focus is on classification and regression trees (CART), bagging, random forest and boosting, as detailed in Figure 2.11. For a state-of-art summary of classification algorithms applied in credit scoring, one may refer to Lessmann et al. (2015).

Section 2.4.1 focuses on CART. Once the key decision-tree concepts have been introduced, Section 2.4.2 provides an overview of bagging, random forest and boosting. Model calibration is investigated in Section 2.4.3. Finally, Section 2.4.4 concentrates on validation.

2.4.1 CLASSIFICATION AND REGRESSION TREES (CART)

Decision trees are mostly used in classification problems. They work for both categorical and numerical variables. Their objective is to split the population into homogeneous sets, based on the most significant input (explanatory) variables. The following two types of trees are commonly used in practice:

- **Regression tree.** The target variable is usually continuous.
- **Classification tree.** The target variable is categorical (for example, default or non-default).

Figure 2.12 summarises the structure of a tree by means of the following terminology:

- **Root node.** It represents the starting point of the top-down population splitting into two or more homogeneous sets.
- **Splitting.** It is a process of dividing a node into two or more sub-nodes.
- **Decision node.** When a sub-node splits into further sub-nodes, then it is called decision node.
- **Terminal node (leaf).** Node that is not further split and represents a leaf of the tree.
- **Pruning.** A tree may reach high deep, but in some cases it becomes necessary to reduce its dimension by removing decision nodes.

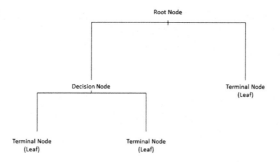

FIGURE 2.12

Tree structure.

The overarching idea underlying tree splitting is to divide the predictor space into partitions (that is, non-overlapping subsets). Different rules apply for regression and classification trees as detailed below:

- **Regression trees.** One may create partitions of the predictor space by means of high-dimensional rectangles (boxes). Based on this, it is common to summarise terminal nodes through the mean value of the numeric predictor. As a consequence, one may find rectangles $R_1, \ldots, R_J$ that minimise the residual sum of squares (RSS), as detailed below:

$$\sum_{j=1}^{J} \sum_{i \in R_j} (y_i - \hat{y}_{R_j})^2, \tag{2.8}$$

where j denotes the rectangle, y_i is the response variable for observation i, and $\hat{y}_{R_j}$ is the estimated average response for all observations $i \in j$ of the set under analysis. A top-down recursive binary splitting is used to obtain two new branches at each step of the tree-building process. Given the availability of a series of predictor variables (χ_j), we firstly select χ_j, such that the split into its sub-regions $\chi_j < s$, and $\chi_j \geq s$, leads to the greatest reduction in RSS, as detailed below:

$$\underset{(j,s)}{\arg\min} \sum_{i:\chi_i \in R_1(j,s)} (y_i - \hat{y}_{R_1})^2 + \sum_{i:\chi_i \in R_2(j,s)} (y_i - \hat{y}_{R_2})^2. \tag{2.9}$$

- **Classification trees.** For classification trees, one cannot use the measure described in Equation (2.8). A natural alternative to RSS is the classification error rate, defined as the fraction of observations in that region that do not belong to the most common class. On this basis, the following Gini impurity index is commonly used in practice:

$$G = \sum_{k=1}^{K} \hat{pr}_{m,k}(1 - \hat{pr}_{m,k}), \tag{2.10}$$

where $\hat{pr}_{m,k}$ is the proportion of training observations in the m-th region that are from the k-th class (for example, default or non-default class). The Gini impurity index assumes small values if all $\hat{pr}_{m,k}$ are near zero or one. Small values of the index denote that a node contains observations predominantly from one of the m classes of the target variable (for example, in the case of default, either defaulted or non-defaulted accounts). An alternative to the Gini impurity index is the cross-entropy, as detailed below:

$$D = -\sum_{k=1}^{K} \hat{pr}_{m,k} \log(\hat{pr}_{m,k}).$$
(2.11)

Since $0 \le \hat{pr}_{m,k} \le 1$, then $0 \le \hat{pr}_{m,k} \log(\hat{pr}_{m,k})$. Consequently, the cross-entropy still take on a value near zero if each $\hat{pr}_{m,k}$ is near zero or one.

Example 2.4.1 (following) introduces CART by means of the simple default dataset explored in Example 2.8.1 in Appendix A.

EXAMPLE 2.4.1 DECISION TREES FOR DEFAULT ANALYSIS

Let us consider the portfolio studied in Example 2.8.1, where 20 accounts are considered over a one-year horizon: 5 accounts defaulted (that is, default flag 1), whereas the remaining 15 did not (that is, default flag 0). We consider both regression and classification trees by focusing on the following steps:

1. Upload data and create categories "No", "Yes",
2. Fit classification tree, and
3. Fit regression tree.

```
# 1. Upload data and create categories "No", "Yes"
def <- read.csv("chap2ptfregression.csv")
library(tree)
defflag_char=ifelse(def$DEF==0,"No","Yes")
def_new=data.frame(def,defflag_char)
# 2. Fit classification tree
def_cla_tree=tree(defflag_char~. -DEF,data=def_new)
summary(def_cla_tree)
plot(def_cla_tree)
text(def_cla_tree,pretty=0)
# 3. Fit regression tree
def_reg_tree=tree(DEF~., data=def)
summary(def_reg_tree)
plot(def_reg_tree)
text(def_reg_tree,pretty=0)
```

Figure 2.13 summarises the key features of the fitted classification tree. The first split distinguishes observations with DDELAY < 43.5 against ≥ 43.5. Therefore when DDELAY ≥ 43.5, an additional split is made by considering UTI < 0.56 against ≥ 0.56. The final nodes are assigned one of the two categories (that is, no or yes), according to their respective prevalence among units belonging to these leaves.

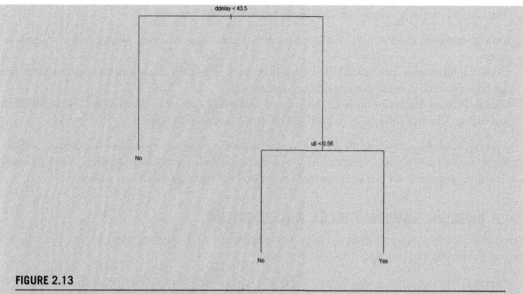

FIGURE 2.13

Classification tree.

Figure 2.14 focuses on the regression tree structure. In this case, the first split relies on UTI variable, whereas the second is based on DDELAY. Contrary to the classification tree, final nodes assume the mean value of their corresponding units (that is, a mean between zeros, representing non-defaulted accounts, and ones referring to defaulted accounts).

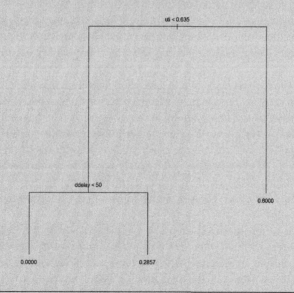

FIGURE 2.14

Regression tree.

The key advantages of using trees can be summarised as follows:

- **Easy to explain.** Trees can be displayed graphically and can be easily interpreted even by non-expert.
- **Handle quantitative and qualitative variables.** Both quantitative and qualitative characteristics can be used without need to create dummy variables.
- **Mirror human decision-making.** Trees are in many cases easier to grasp than regression, given that their mechanics are usually aligned with business decision making.

In terms of disadvantages, trees do not usually have the same level of predictive accuracy of other methods, such as regression. Nevertheless, some enhancement, for instance, bagging, random forest and boosting improve their predictive performance, as detailed in the following section.

2.4.2 BAGGING, RANDOM FOREST, AND BOOSTING

Few techniques have recently been developed to overcome CART main deficiencies. In what follows, the focus is on bagging, random forest and boosting.

- **Bagging.** Decision trees, introduced in Section 2.4.1, are characterised by high variance. Results are dramatically affected by splits applied on train and test data. The aim of bagging is to reduce this variance by means of aggregation procedures. One may think of increasing the accuracy of a prediction by reducing its variance by means of the following bagging procedure:
  - Training set generation. B bootstrapped training data sets are generated.
  - Model prediction. A separate model is built on each training set.
  - Average. As a final step, in case of quantitative outcome, the average of predictions is computed. In the case of classification trees, one may record the class predicted by each of the B trees and take a majority vote. The overall prediction is the most commonly occurring class among all B predictions.

One can easily estimate the test error of a bagged model without needing cross-validation. Indeed, one can show that on average, each bagged tree makes use of about two-thirds of the observations. The remaining one-third of the observations not used to fit a given bagged tree are referred to as the out-of-bag (OOB) observations. We can predict the response by means of the trees in which that observation was OOB. We can average these predicted responses (if regression is the goal), or can take a majority vote (if classification is the goal) in order to obtain the prediction for a specific observation. The resulting OOB error is a valid estimate of the test error for the bagged model, since the response for each observation is predicted using only the trees that did not fit using that observation.

Bagging can be seen as an improved accuracy estimate over a single tree. However, model interpretation may become difficult. One can obtain a summary of the importance of each predictor, using the residual sum of squared (RSS) in the case of regression trees, or the Gini index for bagging classification trees. In the first case, a large reduction of RSS due to the exclusion of a variable indicates a high important predictor. Similarly, in the case of classification tree, where Gini index is decreased by splits over a given predictor, and averaged over all B trees.

- **Random forest.** Random forest provides an improvement over bagged trees by introducing constraints to reduce correlation. Indeed, when building a forest, at each split in the tree, the algorithm is not allowed to consider the majority of the available predictors. Indeed, for each tree built upon the training random sample, each split considers only a subset of all predictors. As a consequence, many of the strong predictors cannot be used. The main difference between bagging and random forest is the choice of predictor subset, size m. If a random forest is built on all predictors, then results similar to bagging are obtained. On the other hand, if the number of variables is much lower than a reduction in both test and OOB errors, over bagging are recorded.
- **Boosting.** This procedure works similarly to bagging except that the trees are grown sequentially. Each tree is fitted using information from previously grown trees. Boosting does not involve bootstrap sampling. Instead each tree is fit on a modified version of the original data set.

  Given the current model, we fit a regression tree to the residuals from the model. That is, the response variable is not the original one, but residuals from a fitted tree. The procedure is slightly more complex in the case of classification trees. Nevertheless—even in this case—the process is deeply affected by: the number of trees, the shrinkage parameter, which controls the rate at which boosting learns, and the number of splits in each tree. Based on this, one should avoid over-fitting by maintaining a relatively low tree depth.

The next example (Example 2.4.2) summarises how to apply what is described above on the dataset, examined in Section 2.3.

EXAMPLE 2.4.2 RANDOM FOREST AND BOOSTING

Let us consider the portfolio studied in Example 2.3.1. The following steps are performed:

1. Upload and prepare data,
2. Perform random forest analysis, and
3. Perform boosting analysis.

```
# 1. Upload and prepare data
# 1.1. Upload data
library(dplyr)
oneypd_tree <- read.csv("chap2oneypd.csv")
dplyr::glimpse(oneypd_tree)
# Create default flag as per Example 2.3.1
# From "default_event" derive "default_indicator" as "Yes" "No"
# as per Example 2.4.1
# 1.2 Select a subset of variables
oneypd_tree_sel_orig <- oneypd_tree %>%
dplyr::select("default_indicator", "default_event","bureau_score",
"time_since_bankrupt", "num_ccj", "time_since_ccj", "ccj_amount",
"ltv", "mob", "max_arrears_12m", "max_arrears_bal_6m",
"avg_bal_6m", "annual_income", "loan_balance", "loan_term",
```

```
"cc_util", "emp_length", "months_since_recent_cc_delinq")
# 1.3 Filter out NAs
oneypd_tree_sel <- oneypd_tree_sel_orig %>%
na.omit(oneypd_tree_sel_orig)
# 1.4 Create stratified samples: 70% train and 30% test
library(caret)
set.seed(123)
train_index <- caret::createDataPartition(oneypd_tree_sel$default_event,
p = .7, list = FALSE)
train <- oneypd_tree_sel[ train_index,]
test  <- oneypd_tree_sel[-train_index,]
```

A database with a relevant number of observations is now ready for the analysis. Defaults represent approximately 5.3% of the total number of accounts, both in train and test samples.

```
# 2. Perform random forest analysis
# 2.1 Fit random forest
library(randomForest)
set.seed(123)
rf_oneypd <- randomForest(default_indicator~.-default_event,
data=oneypd_tree_sel[train_index,], mtry=4, ntree=100,
importance=TRUE, na.action=na.omit)
# Call:
# Type of random forest: classification
# Number of trees: 100
# No. of variables tried at each split: 4
# OOB estimate of  error rate: 4.05%
# 2.2 Variable importance analysis
importance(rf_oneypd)
varImpPlot(rf_oneypd)
```

Figure 2.15 points out the relevance of variables already highlighted through the logistic regression analysis in Section 2.3. The most relevant variables are: cc_util (current account utilisation), annual_income, max_arrears_12m (maximum arrears in the last 12 months), loan_term, max_arrears_bal_6m (maximum arrears balance in the last 6 months), and bureau_score.

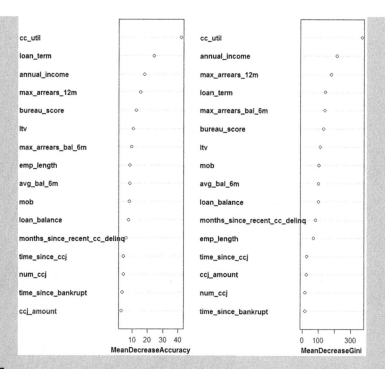

FIGURE 2.15

Variable importance: random forest.

As a final step of the investigation, boosting is performed, as detailed below.

```
# 3. Perform boosting analysis
library(gbm)
set.seed(1)
boost_oneypd=gbm(default_event~.-default_indicator,
data=oneypd_tree_sel[train_index,],distribution="gaussian",
n.trees=100,interaction.depth=4)
summary(boost_oneypd)
# var                rel.inf
# cc_util           46.4146077
# max_arrears_12m   39.5646338
# loan_term          6.6518817
# annual_income      6.1805305
# max_arrears_bal_6m 1.0547685
# mob                0.1335778
# bureau_score       0.0000000
par(mfrow=c(1,2))
plot(boost_oneypd,i="cc_util")
```

```
plot(boost_oneypd,i="max_arrears_12m")
# 3.1 Test sample analysis
yhat_boost_oneypd=predict(boost_oneypd,
newdata=oneypd_tree_sel[-train_index,],n.trees=100)
oneypd_test_boost=oneypd_tree_sel[-train_index,"default_event"]
mean((yhat_boost_oneypd-oneypd_test_boost)^2)
# 0.04486367
# 3.2 Inclusion of shrinkage
boost_oneypd_1=gbm(default_event~.-default_indicator,
data=oneypd_tree_sel[train_index,],distribution="gaussian",
n.trees=100,interaction.depth=4,shrinkage=0.2,verbose=F)
yhat_oneypd_1=predict(boost_oneypd_1,
newdata=oneypd_tree_sel[-train_index,], n.trees=100)
mean((yhat_oneypd_1-oneypd_test_boost)^2)
# 0.02833842
```

The out-of-sample analysis highlights a very low error rate. This error is additionally reduced when the model is shrunk. Indeed, in this case the mean squared error reduces from 4.48% to 2.83%.

The most important variables are in line with random forest and logit analyses. Additionally, Figure 2.16 highlights an approximate *S* shape for both the marginal variation of cc_util and max_arrears_12m. This is in line with a logistic shape used for the regression performed in Section 2.3.

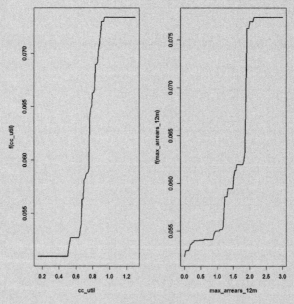

FIGURE 2.16

Incremental analysis: variables cc_util and max_arrears_12m.

2.4.3 ML MODEL CALIBRATION

The calibration process for machine learning does not substantially differ from what is described in Section 2.3.2. Platt (2000) scaling was originally introduced on this basis as a method for calibrating support-vector machines. It works by finding the parameters of a sigmoid function, maximising the likelihood of the calibration set, as detailed in Equation (2.6).

Isotonic regression was suggested as a calibration method that can be regarded as a general form of binning that does not require any specific number or size of bins to be predetermined (Zadrozny and Elkan, 2001).

Example 2.4.3 provides some hints on how to use Equation (2.6) for machine learning calibration purposes.

EXAMPLE 2.4.3 ML CALIBRATION

Let us consider the portfolio studied in Example 2.4.2. Equation (2.6) is applied to calibrate model outputs. The same process described in Example 2.3.3 is adopted by means of the following steps:

1. Create the data set, and
2. Fit calibration function.

```
# 1. Create the data set
pred_orig <- as.matrix(predict(rf_oneypd,newdata=oneypd_tree_sel,
type="prob"))
rf_pred <- as.matrix(pred_orig[,2])
rf_db_cal <- as.data.frame(cbind(oneypd_tree_sel$default_event,
rf_pred))
colnames(rf_db_cal) <- c("def", "pred")
# 2. Fit calibration function
pd_model<- glm(def~ pred, family = binomial(link = 'logit'),
data = rf_db_cal)
summary(pd_model)
#             Estimate Std. Error z value Pr(>|z|)
# (Intercept) -5.72909    0.09949  -57.58 <0.00000 ***
# pred        12.86705    0.27898   46.12 <0.00000 ***
# ---
# Signif. codes:  0 '***' 0.001 '**' 0.01 '*' 0.05 '.' 0.1 ' ' 1
```

The following section focuses on the validation process.

2.4.4 ML MODEL VALIDATION

The validation process described in Section 2.3.3 also applies to machine learning. A summary of ML specific validation checks are listed below:

a. **Data validation.** Activities listed in Section 2.3.3 also apply to machine learning. No specific additional checks are generally required for ML.

b. **Methodology validation.** Non-traditional methods like ML are usually subject to a series of challenges. Algorithms underlying random forest and boosting need to be carefully understood and shared with stakeholders. Methodological comparison is usually performed before adopting ML procedures.

c. **Statistical testing validation.** One should pay particular attention to the following:

- **Discriminatory power.** One needs to ascertain the capability of a model to correctly classify defaulted and non-defaulted accounts. Example 2.4.4 provides some hints on how to perform this investigation.

EXAMPLE 2.4.4 ML DISCRIMINATORY POWER ASSESSMENT

Let us consider random forest Example 2.4.2. What follows demonstrates how validation process is performed, based on the following steps:

1. ROC analysis (AUC assessment) (see Figure 2.17),
2. Kolmogorov–Smirnov (KS) analysis, and
3. Gini index.

```
# 1. ROC Analysis
library(ROCR)
predict_test_orig <- as.matrix(
predict(rf_oneypd,newdata=oneypd_tree_sel[-train_index,],type="prob"))
predict_test <- as.matrix(predict_test_orig[,2])
oneypd_test <- oneypd_tree_sel[-train_index,"default_indicator"]
actual_test <- as.matrix(ifelse(oneypd_test=="Yes",1,0))
pred_test<- ROCR::prediction(predict_test,actual_test)
perf_test<- ROCR::performance(pred_test, 'tpr', 'fpr')
# 1.1 Plot graphs
plot(perf_test, main='ROC curve test', colorize=T)
abline(0,1, lty =8, col = 'black')
# 1.2 Calculate AUC
auc_test<- ROCR::performance(pred_test, 'auc')
# 0.9410772

# 2. KS Analysis
ks_test<- max(attr(perf_test,'y.values')[[1]]-
attr(perf_test,'x.values')[[1]])
print(ks_test)
# 0.732483
# 3. Gini index
library(optiRum)
gini_test<- optiRum::giniCoef(predict_test,actual_test)
# 0.8821544
```

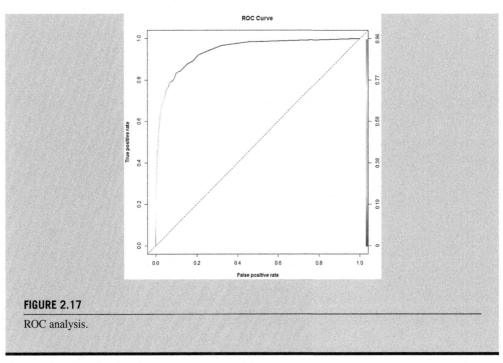

FIGURE 2.17

ROC analysis.

- **Calibration.** The process to validate calibrated PDs is very similar to what is examined in Section 2.3.3. Example 2.4.5 provides some hints on how to perform this analysis, based on Example 2.4.3.

EXAMPLE 2.4.5 CALIBRATED PD VALIDATION

Let us consider Example 2.4.3. A validation process for PD calibration is performed, based on the following steps:

1. Group accounts in bands, and
2. Compare average actual and fitted PDs.

```
# 1. Group accounts in bands
# 1.1. Predict base on model parameters
rf_db_cal$pd<- predict(pd_model, newdata = rf_db_cal,
type = 'response')
library(smbinning)
# 1.2. Create bands
score_cust<- smbinning.custom(rf_db_cal, y = 'def', x= 'pred',
cuts= c(0.2,0.4,0.6,0.8))
rf_db_cal<- smbinning.gen(rf_db_cal, score_cust, chrname ="band")
# 2. Compare average actual and fitted PDs
# 2.1 Calculate mean values
```

```
rf_db_cal_plot<- rf_db_cal %>%
dplyr::group_by(band) %>%
dplyr::summarise(mean_dr = round(mean(def),4),
mean_pd = round(mean(pd),4))
# 2.2 Compute rmse
rmse<-sqrt(mean((rf_db_cal_plot$mean_dr - rf_db_cal_plot$mean_pd)^2))
# 0.03232782
```

Root mean squared error together with graphical inspection of Figure 2.18 highlight how close actual and fitted PDs are.

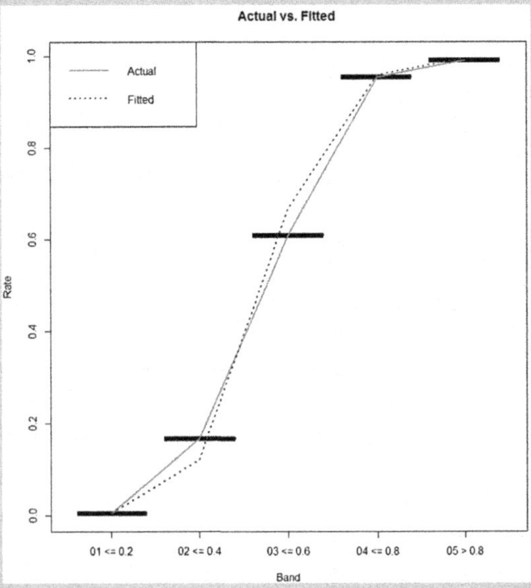

FIGURE 2.18

Actual versus fitted calibrated PDs.

One of the key challenges banks need to face is data availability. The next section attempts to tackle this issue together with problems due to low default portfolios.

2.5 LOW DEFAULT PORTFOLIO, MARKET-BASED, AND SCARCE DATA MODELLING

Widespread data availability is at the very root of statistical PD modelling. Given this foundation, a large amount of information may characterise some sectors, such as insurance or banking industries, but few default events are available for modelling purposes. Low default portfolio models have been developed to face this issue. Furthermore, one may consider market-based models, for instance,

KMV^{TM}. Finally, scarce data may prevent the development of a robust statistical framework. In this case, a more qualitative process is usually adopted by relying on expert judgement, external data, benchmarking and other related information. Figure 2.19 summarises the key areas investigated throughout this section.

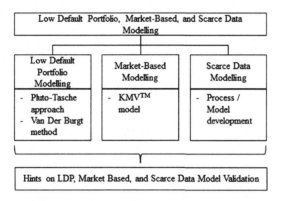

FIGURE 2.19

Workflow diagram for Section 2.5.

In more detail, Section 2.5.1 focuses on low default portfolio modelling based on approaches developed by Pluto and Tasche (2005), Van der Burgt (2008). Ideas informing the methodology proposed by Tasche (2013) are also taken into account. In all cases, the emphasis on model calibration is based on historical observation and target PDs. Shadow ratings may be used for ranking purposes, as briefly described in Section 2.5.3. Section 2.5.2 focuses on structural modelling to estimate publicly traded corporate PDs, by relying on the well-known Crosbie and Bohn (2003) approach, based on Merton (1974) structural frame. In this case, a two-step process applies. On the one hand, a ranking is defined by means of a distance-to-default (DTD) model. On the other hand, a calibration process is put in place as a result of mapping $DTDs$ on historical defaults. Finally, Section 2.5.3 describes activities one may put in place to overcome data scarcity.

2.5.1 LOW DEFAULT PORTFOLIO MODELLING

The use of statistical techniques in credit risk assessment heavily relies on data availability. An obstacle can be the low number of defaults, as in the case of sovereign and banks. Indeed, a mere statistical model may exhibit a high degree of volatility, due to the relatively low number of default events.

From a Basel II perspective, concerns on credit risk underestimation have repeatedly been risen. Given this situation, Pluto and Tasche (2005), Benjamin et al. (2006) propose methodologies to identify a PD upper confidence bound. Based on this, if we denote ψ the average portfolio PD, the probability that a random set of n observations from this portfolio contains at most k defaults (under the assumption of independence of default events) is as follows:

$$P(\#def \leq k) = \binom{n}{i} \sum_{i=0}^{k} \psi^i (1 - \psi)^{n-i}. \tag{2.12}$$

Hence, if γ denotes the probability that a random set of n observations contains more than k defaults, the following applies:

$$\gamma = 1 - \binom{n}{i} \sum_{i=0}^{k} \psi^i (1 - \psi)^{n-i}. \tag{2.13}$$

Les us assume that k defaults occur in a set of n observations, a conservative PD with confidence γ takes the value ψ as computed from the above formula, by substituting k, n and γ. Indeed, if ψ were the actual PD of the population, the data set would contain more than k defaults with probability γ.

It is worth noting that a binomial distribution can be expressed in terms of an appropriate beta function to estimate ψ as follows:

$$\psi = BetaInv(\gamma, k + 1, n - k). \tag{2.14}$$

Benjamin et al. (2006) enhanced the above-described framework by removing independence assumption and considering potential contagion effects. They also published a look-up table, from which a PD ID derived and compared with the weighted average PD of a portfolio. Furthermore, Van der Burgt (2008) introduced a method for calibrating low default portfolios by means of a closed-form function derived from the cumulative accuracy profile (CAP), also known as the power curve. The concave shape of the CAP curve can easily be modelled by means of a mathematical function. Assuming that the PD increases exponentially with the rating class, the derivative of the CAP function must be exponential, as detailed below:

$$y(z) = \frac{1 - e^{-\theta \cdot z}}{1 - e^{-\theta}}, \tag{2.15}$$

where y represents defaults as a function of the cumulative percentage of debtors (that is, z), whereas θ is the CAP concavity parameter.

The calibration is performed in a few steps. Firstly, one needs to construct the CAP from observations. Fitting is conducted by minimising root-mean-square (RMS) errors as listed below:

$$RMS_{CAP} = \sqrt{\frac{1}{n_{class}} \sum_{j=1}^{n_{class}} \left(y_j - \frac{1 - e^{-\theta \cdot z_j}}{1 - e^{-\theta}} \right)^2}, \tag{2.16}$$

where n_{class} indicates portfolio's number of rating classes. After deriving the concavity, the PDs can be derived from the CAP curve by means of the following equation:

$$PD_j = \frac{\theta \cdot \bar{DR}}{1 - e^{-\theta}} e^{-\theta z_j}, \tag{2.17}$$

where $\bar{DR}$ is the average default rate for the portfolio, whereas z_j represents the cumulative percentage of counterparties in rating class j.

Example 2.5.1 provides a guideline on how to calibrate low default portfolios based on Pluto and Tasche (2005), Van der Burgt (2008) and Tasche (2013).

EXAMPLE 2.5.1 LOW DEFAULT PORTFOLIO CALIBRATION

Let us consider a portfolio, where accounts are distributed among five classes, as detailed in Table 2.3.

Table 2.3 Low default portfolio account distribution

Rating	A	B	C	D	E
# Accounts	10	40	25	15	10
# Defaults	2	1	0	0	0

A calibration process is performed based on:

1. Pluto Tasche approach,
2. Van Der Burght CAP method, and
3. Tasche quasi maximum likelihood model.

```
# 1. Pluto Tasche approach
library(LDPD)
portfolio <- c(10,15,25,40,10)
defaults <- c(1,2,0,0,0)
set.seed(123)
pd_one_pt <- PTOnePeriodPD(portfolio, defaults,
conf.interval=0.90)
# CI=0.90  0.336  0.248  0.128  0.072 0.065
# 1.1. Alternative confidence intervals (CI)
# CI=0.75  0.247  0.195  0.100  0.056 0.050
# CI=0.50  0.162  0.144  0.072  0.040 0.036
# 2. Van Der Burght CAP method
pd_one_vdb <- VDBCalibratePD(portf.uncond=portfolio,
pd.uncond.old=0.03, pd.uncond.new=0.03, AR=0.90,
rating.type = 'RATING')
# AR=0.90  0.214  0.030  1.2e-03 7.7e-06 1.5e-07
# 2.1. Alternative AR
# AR=0.75  0.152  0.061  0.014  0.001  0.0002
# AR=0.50  0.089  0.058  0.029  0.009  0.0040
```

Both Pluto and Tasche (2005) and Van der Burgt (2008) approaches are very sensitive to their input parameters. As an example, if one reduces the confidence interval, then PDs reduce across all rating classes. In the latter case, we put PD target equal to original PD to allow us a comparison with the other method.

```
# 3. Tasche quasi maximum likelihood model
pd <- c(0.215, 0.03, 0.001, 0.0001, 0.0001)
```

```
qmm <- QMMRecalibrate(0.05, pd, portfolio, rating.type="RATING")
QMMPlot(qmm)
```

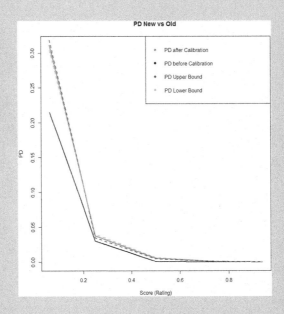

FIGURE 2.20

PD calibration based on quasi-maximum likelihood approach.

Tasche (2013) approach is adopted to show how PD levels change if we set a portfolio PD target different from the original rate. Figure 2.20 shows an uplift of the curve with significant jump on the worst rating classes (that is, D and E).

In the case of publicly traded instruments, one may rely on market-based modelling, as detailed in the next section, where Merton (1974) model is the reference framework to compute the so-called distance-to-default (DTD).

2.5.2 MARKET-BASED MODELLING

When the focus is on companies quoted in a stock exchange, one may attempt to develop PD models based on share prices. In line with Merton (1974), a firm's value can be represented by means of a stochastic process. The firm defaults when its asset value falls below its liability threshold. In this regard, one may assume that a firm is financed by equity S_t and a bond D_t, with maturity T, and principal DEB. Within this framework, firm's asset value V_t follows a geometric Brownian motion as listed below:

$$dV_t = \mu V_t dt + \sigma V_t dW_t, \tag{2.18}$$

where dV_t indicates firm's instantaneous value change, μ is a drift term, dt is time differential, σ denotes asset volatility, and W_t is a standard Brownian motion.

Due to limited liability, the equity value at maturity is $S_t = \max(V_t - DEB, 0)$. In line with the Black–Scholes option pricing formula, equity value at time $t \leq T$ can be written as follows:

$$S(V_t, \sigma) = V_t N(d_t) - e^{-r(T-t)} \cdot DEB \cdot N(d_t - \sigma\sqrt{T-t}), \tag{2.19}$$

where r is the instantaneous risk-free rate, and $N(\cdot)$ is the standard normal cumulative distribution function. Furthermore, the following applies:

$$d_t = \frac{\ln\left(\frac{V_t}{DEB}\right) + \left(r + \frac{\sigma^2}{2}\right)(T - t)}{\sigma\sqrt{T-t}}, \tag{2.20}$$

where $\ln\left(\frac{V_t}{DEB}\right)$ is the logarithm of the leverage ratio, whereas $\sigma\sqrt{T-t}$ is the volatility over the period $(T - t)$ (that is, constant volatility over the time horizon under analysis).

Moving from these assumptions, one may show that a firm's PD at time T evaluated at time t is $N(-DTD_t)$, where DTD stands for distance to default defined as follows:

$$DTD_t = \frac{\ln\left(\frac{V_t}{DEB}\right) + \left(\mu + \frac{\sigma^2}{2}\right)(T - t)}{\sigma\sqrt{T-t}}, \tag{2.21}$$

where μ is the average return rate. Then, $\left(\mu + \frac{\sigma^2}{2}\right)(T - t)$ stands for the expected return of the firm over the period $(T - t)$.

Let us grasp the economic intuition of all above equations by considering two firms with identical leverage ratios and volatilities, but the asset value of one is expected to increase at a faster rate than the other. One naturally expects the one with a higher expected return to be further away from default (that is, it has a larger DTD). If two firms have identical leverage ratios and expected returns, their volatilities will determine which one is further away from default. It is evident that the conclusion depends on the sign of the numerator. If the numerator is positive, meaning that the asset value will cover the debt obligation on average, a lower volatility should make the firm less likely to default, and that it, indeed, has a larger DTD. When the numerator is negative, the firm is on average not expected to meet its debt obligation in the future. A higher volatility will make DTD less negative, which is consistent with the intuition that the firm has a higher chance, due to a higher volatility, to get its future asset value to exceed the debt obligation.

A series of challenges needs to be faced to implement the above-described framework summarised in Equation (2.21). Firstly, asset values are not directly observable. Secondly, parameters governing the unobserved asset value process are unknown, and need to be estimated. Their estimation is extremely difficult, because asset values are not directly observed. The following three alternatives have been used in practice:

- **Market value proxy method.** When equity time series are available, one may think of adding the market value of equity and debt to derive asset estimates. Daily logarithmic asset returns are then used to compute the return sample mean μ and the standard deviation σ, as required in Equation (2.21).

- **Volatility restriction method.** The following two-equation system is used to estimate DTD:

$$S_t = S(V_t|\sigma), \tag{2.22}$$

$$\sigma_{S_t} = \sigma \frac{V_t}{S(V_t|\sigma)} N(d_t), \tag{2.23}$$

where $S(V_t|\sigma)$, $N(\cdot)$ and d_t have already been explored above. Equation (2.22) links the observed market capitalisation according to its theoretical value. On the other hand, Equation (2.23) links equity volatility with asset volatility by means of Ito's lemma. The system of two equations allows us to find the two unknowns: V_t and σ.

- KMV^{TM} **method.** Crosbie and Bohn (2003) described the actual KMV^{TM} method as an iterative procedure consisting of the following steps:

  - Step 1. Apply an initial value of σ to Equation (2.21) (by assuming $\mu = \frac{\sigma^2}{2}$) to obtain a time series of implied asset values and, hence, continuously compounded asset returns.
  - Step 2. Use the time series of continuously compounded asset returns to obtain updated estimates for μ and σ.
  - Step 3. Go back to Step 1 with the updated σ, unless convergence has been achieved.

  KMV^{TM} implementation fixes the maturity at one year, and sets the default point to the sum of the short term debt, and one half of the long-term debt.

Example 2.5.2 provides a practical guide to implement DTD model.

EXAMPLE 2.5.2 DTD ESTIMATION

Let us consider a firm with market capitalisation $10.00 billion, debt $5.00 billion, equity volatility 0.40 and risk-free interest rate 3.00%. DTD is illustrated by means of the following steps:

1. DTD estimate, and
2. DTD (simulated) time series analysis.

```
# 1. DTD estimate
library(ifrogs)
library(testthat)
# 1.1. Estimation of DTD
est_dtd <- dtd(mcap=10000000000, debt=5000000000, vol=0.4, r=0.03)
# 2. DTD (simulated) time series analysis
compute_time <- system.time(simulate <- lapply(1:1000,
function(i){
set.seed(i)
E <- rnorm(1, mean=55000, sd=200)
F <- rnorm(1, mean=25000, sd=400)
sE = rnorm(1, mean=0.25, sd=0.02)
ans <- dtd(mcap=E, vol=sE,
```

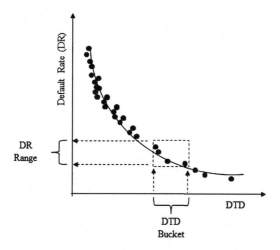

FIGURE 2.21

DDT mapping onto default frequency.

```
debt=F,  r=0.03)
simulate_dtd <- ans["dtd.v"]
simulate_v <- ans["asset.v"]
simulate_sv <-ans["sigma.v"]
return(c(E=E, sE=sE, F=F, simulate_dtd, simulate_v,
simulate_sv))
}))
simulate_results <- do.call(rbind, simulate)
head(simulate_results)
#  E         sE         F        dtd.v   asset.v   sigma.v
# [1,] 54874.71 0.2332874 25073.46 4.286558 79207.13 0.1616216
# [2,] 54820.62 0.2817569 25073.94 3.549159 79153.51 0.1951409
# [3,] 54807.61 0.2551758 24882.99 3.918867 78955.20 0.1771330
# [4,] 55043.35 0.2678229 24783.00 3.733811 79093.91 0.1863844
# [5,] 54831.83 0.2248902 25553.74 4.446615 79630.35 0.1548548
# [6,] 55053.92 0.2673732 24748.01 3.740091 79070.51 0.1861622
```

The output of a DTD model is not directly interpretable as a PD. For this reason, one needs to build a mapping procedure between $DTDs$ and actual defaults. Figure 2.21 illustrates how this process is organised.

One needs to group company observations in buckets with similar DTD. Each observation is tracked over a one-year horizon to flag all the observed defaults.

The empirical default rate is the ratio between the total number of defaults and the total number of observations at the beginning of the period under analysis (that is, one year).

This exercise is repeated for all DTD buckets to build a look-up table mapping DDTs to default rates. As an additional step, one may fit a smooth function through each bucket.

It is worth noting that, once again, the entire procedure is deeply affected by the definition of default adopted for the analysis. Indeed, bond missing payments, bankruptcy and debt restructuring are usually included as part of a broad default definition. It needs to align with the overarching definition used for IASB (2014) and FASB (2016).

The following section focuses on procedures to activate in case of data scarcity.

2.5.3 SCARCE DATA MODELLING

Scarce data umbrella embraces a plethora of different features. In what follows, we do not aim to provide an exhaustive recipe covering all potential issues one may encounter while modelling PDs. Our goal is to cover some of the most common issues by providing simple suggestions, as listed below:

- **Data enhancement.** This first category considers a series of techniques one may trigger to face issues related both to limited number of default and poor data history.
  - Data pooling. A combined data collection with other banks, or market participants, is particularly appealing in segments, such as worldwide project finance, where individual banks may not have enough data. A shared data set may provide a comprehensive picture of the phenomenon under analysis. This process may be less appealing for low default portfolios, with large overlap for different market participants (for example, sovereigns, banks).
  - Portfolio data aggregation. One may combine internal portfolios with similar risk characteristics to derive a more comprehensive base on which to develop PD models. This procedure is certainly easier than data pooling, given that it does not involve other institutions. The key challenge is to identify homogeneous portfolios.
  - Proxy default. When few defaulted observations are collected or the portfolio experiences a limited number of critical events, one may think of extending the definition to near-default events. As an example, one may consider 60 instead 90 days past due. Furthermore, the number of days in arrears can be used directly as the dependent variable for a linear or logistic regression. The key advantage is to facilitate a ranking model development. Once accounts are accurately ordered, a separate calibration process is put in place.
- **Benchmarking.** Internal and external benchmarks are usually a precious source of information to use as part of an overarching PD modelling frame, as listed below:
  - Shadow ratings. External ratings or market proxies are a valid benchmarking target. They usually cover some segments or few companies for specific portfolios of interest. Firstly, one may capture default likelihood through a regression framework, where the external rating target variable is explained by means of internal or external drivers. Secondly, one may extend benchmark analysis to assess PDs for obligors sharing similar characteristics with externally rated entities.
  - Expert judgement. An expert assessment usually relies on a limited set of information (for example, financial statement, behavioural dynamics and sector information) available at the time of the assessment. Few requirements usually inform the process:
    - The assessment is focused on expected default occurrence, while recovery is out of scope.
    - A sample of accounts needs to be evaluated by a group of experts. A two-step process usually applies. Firstly, the assessment is conducted separately, to ensure an independent evaluation. Secondly, a broad consensus is achieved within a forum.
    - The assessment is provided with reference to an intuitive common scale, for example: very low, low, medium, high, and very high risk. As an alternative, one may use ratings.

In all cases a validation process is required to ensure consistency and adequate communication of the decisions made, as briefly summarised in the next section.

2.5.4 HINTS ON LOW DEFAULT PORTFOLIO, MARKET-BASED, AND SCARCE DATA MODEL VALIDATION

In all cases investigated in this section, the typical three-area validation framework used for GLMs and ML modelling only partially applies. In more detail, data and methodology validation can be performed according to the same standards, so far described for other PD methods. On the other hand, statistical validation requires bespoke adjustments as listed below:

a. **Data validation.** Activities listed in Section 2.3.3 also apply to all cases above investigated. One needs to focus on portfolio peculiarities affecting low default portfolios (for example, multi-country exposures and multi-instrument issuances). With regards to scarce data, database architecture checks play a major role.

b. **Methodology validation.** As per other PD methods, a comprehensive comparison of alternative approaches is at the very heart of the process. Indeed, for low default portfolio, all investigated methodologies tackled the issue from different angles by providing not completely homogeneous outcomes. With regard to scarce data modelling, clear governance need to inform expert assessments. Validation needs to cover both process design and implementation nuances.

c. **Statistical testing validation.** From a quantitative point of view, one may clearly distinguish between statistical and expert judgement methods. In regard to calibration approaches studied in Section 2.5.1, historical fitting and accurate sensitivity analysis are required to point out model's capabilities to capture the phenomenon under scrutiny. Moving to market-based models, effort needs to be devoted both to check historical fitting of $DTDs$ and their corresponding calibrated PDs. Finally, ad-hoc procedures are required for scarce data modelling. Indeed, apart from the shadow-rating procedure that can be validated by means of some common metrics investigated in Section 2.3.3, tailored procedures are required for expert judgements. In the latter case, firstly, one needs to dive deep into governance rules. Secondly, historical evidence needs to challenge expert evaluations.

In all cases, an additional step is needed to produce PD estimates to use for ECL computation. Indeed, a forward-looking perspective is required, even for the IFRS 9 one-year assessment, referred to as stage 1 accounts. Chapter 3 provides a comprehensive overview on how to estimate and validate PDs for ECL evaluation.

The next section focuses on SAS implementation of the most relevant examples studied throughout the chapter.

2.6 SAS LABORATORY

Two main approaches are considered in what follows. On the one hand, GLM scorecard development is investigated. On the other hand, our focus is on machine learning. An overview of SAS implementation is provided by focusing on the main steps of the modelling workflow. Details explored in the previous sections by means of R can easily be replicated in SAS. In all cases, the same data scrutinised in previous sections constitute our reference for SAS implementation.

SAS laboratory 2.6.1 focuses on GLM.

SAS LABORATORY 2.6.1 GLM ANALYSIS

Let us consider Example 2.3.1. As a starting point, one needs to upload the same data file, then the following SAS code replicates the analysis by means of the next steps:

1. Create default flag,
2. Train and test samples,
3. Define binning and compute WOE,
4. Perform correlation analysis, and
5. Fit logit regression.

```
/* 1. Create default flag */
data default_flag;
set oneypd;
if arrears_event=1 or term_expiry_event=1 or bankrupt_Event=1
then default_flag=1;
else default_flag=0;
run;


/* 2. Train and test Samples */
proc sort data=default_flag;
by default_flag vintage_year;
run;
proc surveyselect data=default_flag
out=stratified_data method=srs rate=0.7 outall;
strata default_flag;run;


data train test;
set stratified_data;
if selected=1 then output train;
else output test;
run;


/* 3. Define binning and compute WOE */
proc hpbin data=train numbin=5;
bureau_score num_ccj max_arrears_12m
max_arrears_bal_6m cc_util annual_income
emp_length months_since_recent_cc_delinq;
ods output mapping=mapping;
run;
ods trace on;
ods output woe=WOE infovalue=IV;
```

```
proc hpbin data=train WOE bins_meta=mapping output=binned_dataset;
id _all_;
target default_flag/level=interval;
run;

proc sql;
create table appending_woe as select distinct

b.*,
c1.woe as woe_bureau_score,
c2.woe as woe_cc_util,
c3.woe as woe_num_ccj,
c4.woe as woe_max_arrears_12m,
c5.woe as woe_max_arrears_bal_6m,
c6.woe as woe_emp_length,
c7.woe as woe_months_since_recent_cc_delin,
c8.woe as woe_annual_income

from binned_dataset as b
left join woe as c1 on b.bin_bureau_Score=c1.bin and
c1.variable='bureau_score'
left join woe as c2 on b.bin_cc_util=c2.bin and
c2.variable='cc_util'
left join woe as c3 on b.bin_num_ccj=c3.bin and
c3.variable='num_ccj' left join woe as c4
on b.bin_max_arrears_12m=c4.bin and c4.variable='max_arrears_12m'
left join woe as c5 on b.bin_max_arrears_bal_6m=c5.bin and
c5.variable='max_arrears_bal_6m'
left join woe as c6 on b.bin_emp_length=c6.bin and
c6.variable='emp_length'
left join woe as c7 on b.bin_months_since_recent_cc_delin=c7.bin and
c7.variable='months_since_recent_cc_delinq'
left join woe as c8 on b.bin_annual_income=c8.bin and
c8.variable='annual_income';
quit;

/* 4. Perform correlation analysis */
proc corr data=appending_woe outs=spear_corr spearman;
var woe_:;
run;

/* 5. Fit logit regression */
ods output fitsummary=out_fit parameterEstimates=Params;
```

```
ods graphics on;
proc logistic data=appending_woe plots=roc ;
model default_flag(event='1') =
woe_bureau_score
woe_cc_util
woe_num_ccj
woe_max_arrears_12m
woe_emp_length
woe_months_since_recent_cc_delin
woe_annual_income
/selection=stepwise ;
quit;
ods graphics on;
proc hpsplit data=default_flag leafsize=50 maxdepth=8
plots=zoomedtree;
target default_flag / level=interval;
input bureau_Score cc_util annual_income emp_length
months_since_recent_cc_delinq /level=interval;
input num_ccj max_Arrears_12m /level=ordinal;
output growthsubtree=growth importance=factor_imp
nodestats=node_stats;
run;
quit;
```

SAS laboratory 2.6.2 provides some hints on machine learning implementation. In more detail, the focus is on both CART and random forest examples investigated throughout the chapter. Other procedures can easily be derived as an enrichment process of the code already provided.

SAS LABORATORY 2.6.2 ML ANALYSIS

Let us focus on Examples 2.4.1 and 2.4.2. Data imported and manipulated in SAS laboratory 2.6.1 constitute the starting point for machine learning analysis conducted by means of the following steps:

1. Fit CART,
2. Fit random forest,
3. Score random forest, and
4. Fit boosting.

```
/* 1. Run CART */
proc hpsplit data=default_flag leafsize=50
maxdepth=8 plots=zoomedtree;
target default_flag / level=interval;
input bureau_Score cc_util annual_income emp_length
```

```
months_since_recent_cc_delinq /level=interval;
input num_ccj max_Arrears_12m /level=ordinal;
output growthsubtree=growth importance=factor_imp
nodestats=node_stats;
run;
quit;


/* 2. Fit random forest */
proc hpforest data=default_flag criterion=Variance
maxtrees=100 vars_to_try=4 splitsize=200 leafsize=100
maxdepth=8 alpha=0.05;
target default_flag / level=interval;
input bureau_Score cc_util annual_income emp_length
months_since_recent_cc_delinq /level=interval;
input num_ccj max_Arrears_12m /level=ordinal;
ods output fitstatistics=fitstats;
save file = 'C:\random_forest_rules.bin';
run;
quit;


/* 3. Score random forest */
proc hp4score data=default_flag;
id _all_;
score file='C:\random_forest_rules.bin' out=randomforest_scored;
run;


/* 4. Fit boosting */
proc treeboost data=default_flag exhaustive=5000 iterations=100
leafsize=50 maxdepth=2 shrinkage=0.3;
target default_flag / level=interval;
input bureau_Score cc_util annual_income emp_length
months_since_recent_cc_delinq /level=interval;
input num_ccj max_Arrears_12m /level=ordinal;
score out=scored_GradientBoost;
importance out=imp;
quit;
```

2.7 SUMMARY

Default definition and database construction paved the way for one-year model development and validation. The key elements entering the definition of a default were investigated by distinguishing between quantitative and qualitative aspects.

Generalised linear models (GLMs) were introduced as a paradigm for one-year PD model development. Based on this, a distinction was made between scoring and PD estimates. Indeed, a score allowed us to rank accounts (customers), whereas a calibration process was defined to obtain PIT PDs. Discriminatory power indicators, such as Gini index, area under the curve (AUC) and information value (IV) were explored and used both for model selection and model validation.

As an alternative to GLMs, machine learning (ML) methods were studied to deal with large data sets. Classification and regression trees (CARTs) constituted our starting point. Then, the emphasis moved towards more sophisticated ML classification procedures, such as bagging, random forest and boosting.

As a final step of the one-year PD journey, we focused on low default portfolios, market-based models and data scarcity. Pluto and Tasche (2005) method, Van der Burgt (2008), and Tasche (2013) approaches were investigated to face the first challenge. A distance-to-default perspective was followed to estimate one-year PDs in the case of publicly traded companies. Finally, data enrichment and benchmarking were considered as the two main pillars to estimate PDs, when limited data are available.

For each methodology a specific validation process was investigated. Additionally, a series of examples worked in R allowed us to grasp details of both model development and validation. In the very last section, the SAS laboratory covered the most relevant cases examined throughout the chapter.

Data and complementary examples' software code are available at www.tizianobellini.com.

SUGGESTIONS FOR FURTHER READING

Loeffler and Posch (2011) describe how to estimate credit-risk parameter by means of Excel and VBA. Engelmann and Rauhmeier (2011) provide a comprehensive view of credit-risk parameter estimation with a Basel II perspective. Siddiqi (2016) presents a business–oriented process for the development and implementation of risk-prediction scorecards. One may find in Thomas et al. (2017) a comprehensive review of the objectives, methods, and practical implementation of credit and behavioural scoring. Lessmann et al. (2015) provides a state-of-art summary of credit score modelling. A comprehensive description of validation procedures can be found in BIS (2005). The reader interested in machine learning may find it useful refer to Hastie et al. (2009) for a theoretical introduction, whereas James et al. (2013) provide a more hands-on perspective by means of examples in R. Pluto and Tasche (2005), Van der Burgt (2008), and Tasche (2013) are the reference papers for low default portfolio modelling. With regard to market-based models, Crosbie and Bohn (2003) constitutes the key reference in the financial literature.

2.8 APPENDIX A. FROM LINEAR REGRESSION TO GLM

As a first attempt to fit a binary response, one may consider a linear regression, as detailed below:

$$SC_i^{linear} = \beta_0 + \beta_1 \chi_{i,1} + \ldots + \beta_k \chi_{i,k} + \epsilon_i, \tag{2.24}$$

where SC_i stands for account i score, whereas $\chi_i = (\chi_{i,1}, \ldots, \chi_{i,k})'$ is the $k \times 1$ vector of explanatory behavioural variables (BVs), and ϵ_i is an error term.

Example 2.8.1 provides a useful frame to familiarise with a binary variable fitting process.

EXAMPLE 2.8.1 LINEAR REGRESSION ANALYSIS

Let us consider a (simplified) portfolio with 20 accounts. Five of them default over a one-year horizon. Our goal is to develop a model to predict defaults over the next year by means of the following variables:

- **DEF.** Default flag (dependent variable) assuming 1 when default occurs, and 0 otherwise.
- **DDELAY.** This explanatory variable pinpoints the average number of late-payment days. Indeed, businesses payments do not usually occur instantaneously. High values of this variable may uncover customer's potential liquidity issues.
- **UTI.** This explanatory variable exhibits the credit line utilisation rate. High utilisation intensity subsumes financial tensions.

Table 2.4 provides the actual figures of the illustrative (simplified) database to use for modelling purposes.

Our goal is to regress DEF (that is, dependent variable), against DDELAY and UTI (that is, explanatory variables). Figure 2.22 summarises the relationship between DEF, DDELAY and UTI. In more detail, the left hand-side panel highlights a positive relationship between defaults and DDELAY. Indeed, highest DDELAY are associated with highest likelihood of default. A similar positive relationship emerges from the right hand-side panel, referred to as UTI.

Table 2.4 One-year scorecard modelling (simplified) database			
ID	DEF	DDELAY	UTI
1	0	52	0.62
2	1	52	0.57
3	0	60	0.55
4	0	45	0.32
5	1	90	0.48
6	0	37	0.44
7	0	48	0.55
8	0	70	0.60
9	0	45	0.55
10	0	60	0.51
11	1	68	0.78
12	0	58	0.48
13	0	37	0.50
14	1	45	0.65
15	0	42	0.42
16	0	41	0.63
17	0	33	0.61
18	0	35	0.64
19	0	37	0.67
20	1	95	0.78

The following R code provides some hints on how to implement the analysis by means of Equation (2.24). As a starting point, a univariate analysis, based on $DDELAY$, is performed by means of the following steps:

1. Upload data, and
2. Fit linear regression.

```
# 1. Upload data
def<- as.data.frame(read.csv("chap2ptfregression.csv"))
# 2. Fit linear regression
lm_DDELAY<- lm(formula=DEF~DDELAY,data = def)
summary(lm_DDELAY)
#             Estimate Std. Error t value Pr(>|t|)
# (Intercept) -0.550165  0.266763  -2.062  0.05391 .
# DDELAY        0.015241  0.004836   3.152  0.00552 **
# ---
# Signif. codes:  0 '***' 0.001 '**' 0.01 '*' 0.05 '.' 0.1 ' ' 1
# Residual standard error: 0.3664 on 18 degrees of freedom
# Multiple R-squared:  0.3556,  Adjusted R-squared:  0.3198
# F-statistic: 9.934 on 1 and 18 DF,  p-value: 0.005516
```

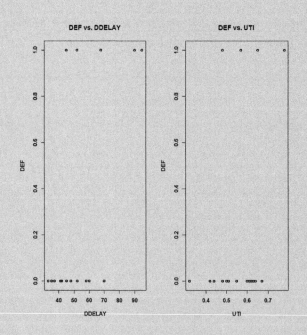

FIGURE 2.22

Default indicators vs. DDELAY, and UTI.

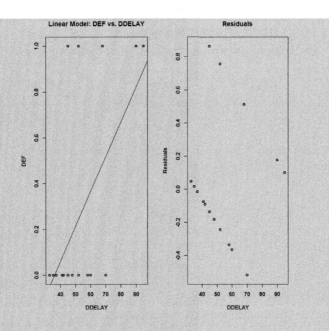

FIGURE 2.23

Linear regression: DEF vs. DDELAY.

The output of the above analysis can be written as follows:

$$\widehat{SC}_i^{linear} = -0.5501 + 0.0152 \cdot DDELAY_i.$$

In Figure 2.23, the left hand-side plot shows a poor linear model fitting, which is confirmed by residual distribution on the left hand-side panel.

Few key drawbacks clearly emerge from Example 2.8.1, as detailed below:

- **Fitting.** The dependent variable assumes only two values (that is, {0, 1}). However the linear model may predict values beyond the [0,1] interval.
- **Variance residuals.** The assumption of constant variance of residuals underlying linear regression does not hold.

In the case of a binary response variable, a curved function—instead of a linear relationship—may better represent the phenomenon. Based on this, one may consider the following logistic relationship:

$$SC_i^{logit} = \frac{1}{1 + e^{-(\beta_0 + \beta_1 \chi_{i,1} + \cdots + \beta_k \chi_{i,k})}}. \tag{2.25}$$

Starting from Equation (2.25), one may easily derive logit functions, as detailed in Equations (2.2) and (2.2) in Section 2.3.1.

Example 2.8.2 details how to implement Equation (2.25) on the database examined in Example 2.8.1.

EXAMPLE 2.8.2 LOGISTIC REGRESSION ANALYSIS

Let us consider the portfolio studied in Example 2.8.1. Equation (2.25) is fitted as detailed below:

```
# 1. Fit logistic regression
log_DDELAY<- glm(formula=DEF ~ DDELAY, data=def,
family=binomial(link=logit))
summary(log_DDELAY)
#                Estimate Std. Error z value Pr(>|z|)
# (Intercept)    -6.34063    2.69562   -2.352   0.0187 *
# DDELAY          0.09329    0.04574    2.040   0.0414 *
# ---
# Signif. codes:  0 '***' 0.001 '**' 0.01 '*' 0.05 '.' 0.1 ' ' 1
# (Dispersion parameter for binomial family taken to be 1)
# Null deviance: 22.493  on 19  degrees of freedom
# Residual deviance: 15.433  on 18  degrees of freedom
# AIC: 19.433
# Number of Fisher Scoring iterations: 5
```

The output of the above analysis can be written as follows:

$$\widehat{SC}_i^{logit} = \frac{1}{1 + e^{-(-6.340 + 0.093 \cdot DDELAY_i)}},$$

where Figure 2.24 shows how this equation fits the data.

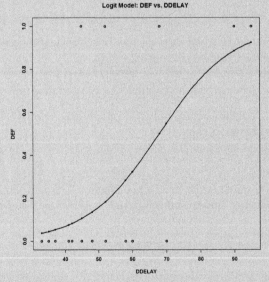

Logit Model: DEF vs. DDELAY

FIGURE 2.24

Logit regression: DEF vs. DDELAY.

Table 2.5 DEF against $\widehat{SC}^{logit}$

ID	DEF	$\widehat{SC}^{logit}$	DDELAY
1	0	0.18	52.00
2	1	0.18	52.00
3	0	0.32	60.00
4	0	0.11	45.00
5	1	0.89	90.00
6	0	0.05	37.00
7	0	0.13	48.00
8	0	0.55	70.00
9	0	0.11	45.00
10	0	0.32	60.00
11	1	0.50	68.00
12	0	0.28	58.00
13	0	0.05	37.00
14	1	0.11	45.00
15	0	0.08	42.00
16	0	0.08	41.00
17	0	0.04	33.00
18	0	0.04	35.00
19	0	0.05	37.00
20	1	0.93	95.00

We can summarise the key advantages of using logistic instead of a linear regression as follows:

- **Fitting.** The fitted score is bounded within the interval [0,1]. An s-shaped curve provides a better fit to actual outcome distribution compared to linear regression.
- **Variance.** The variance is not constant, but is a function of the fitted score.

2.9 APPENDIX B. DISCRIMINATORY POWER ASSESSMENT

One would intuitively compare fitted against actual results to assess a model discriminatory power. However, this direct comparison is not so easy in the case of binary outcomes. Indeed, the dependent variable assumes values {0, 1}, whereas predictions belong to the interval [0, 1].

Table 2.5 provides some hints on how to conduct the analysis based on the model fitted in Example 2.8.2. Its main goal is to compare the binary variable DEF_i against $\widehat{SC}_i^{logit}$.

In all cases, $0 < \widehat{SC}_i^{logit} < 1$. Additionally, the following holds:

- **Defaulted accounts.** For IDs 5 and 20 the model predicts values relatively close to 1; $\widehat{SC}_{11}^{logit}$ is 0.50, and $\widehat{SC}_{14}^{logit}$ is 0.11. For ID 2, $\widehat{SC}_2$ is 0.18.

Table 2.6 Predicted default for a 0.5 cut-off threshold			
ID	**DEF**	$\widehat{SC}^{logit}$	**Predicted DEF (Cut-off 0.5)**
1	0	0.18	0
2	1	0.18	0
3	0	0.32	0
4	0	0.11	0
5	1	0.89	1
6	0	0.05	0
7	0	0.13	0
8	0	0.55	1
9	0	0.11	0
10	0	0.32	0
11	1	0.50	1
12	0	0.28	0
13	0	0.05	0
14	1	0.11	0
15	0	0.08	0
16	0	0.08	0
17	0	0.04	0
18	0	0.04	0
19	0	0.05	0
20	1	0.93	1

- **Non-defaulted accounts.** $\widehat{SC}_8^{logit}$ is 0.55, whereas scores for all other accounts are below 0.50.

Our goal is to derive a discriminatory metric, based on the comparison of DEF_i and $\widehat{SC}_i^{logit}$. One may think of defining thresholds within the interval [0,1] and assign 0 when $\widehat{SC}_i^{logit} <$ threshold. On the contrary, assign 1 when $\widehat{SC}_i^{logit}$ exceeds the threshold.

Table 2.6 summarises this framework, when a 0.50 threshold is chosen:

- **True positive (TP).** For IDs 5, 11 and 20, predicted outcomes correspond to actuals.
- **False positive (FP).** In the case of ID 8, default is predicted for a non-defaulted case.
- **False negative (FN).** For IDs 2 and 14, non-default is predicted against actual default.
- **True negative (TN).** For all other IDs, the predicted 0 default flag corresponds to the actual outcome.

Table 2.7 summarises these results by means of a confusion matrix. A common way to represent a binary model discriminatory power is to rely on sensitivity and specificity, as listed below:

- **Sensitivity (true positive rate)** $= \frac{TP}{TP+FN}$. It is defined as the proportion of observed positives that were predicted to be positive. In line with Table 2.7, sensitivity is $\frac{3}{3+2} = 0.60$.

Table 2.7 Confusion matrix: 0.5 cut-off

		Actual	
		Default	**No-Default**
Predicted	Default	(TP) 3	(FP) 1
	No-Default	(FN) 2	(TN) 14

- **Specificity (true negative rate)** $= \frac{TN}{TN+FP}$. It is computed as the proportion of observed non-defaulted accounts that were correctly predicted as such over the predicted non-defaulted population. In line with Table 2.7, specificity is $\frac{14}{14+1} = 0.93$.
- **Accuracy** $= \frac{TP+TN}{TP+FP+TN+FN}$. It is the proportion of observed true positive and negatives over the sum of all possible cases. In line with Table 2.7, accuracy is $\frac{14+3}{3+1+14+2} = 0.85$.

All above ratios are useful tools to assess a model discriminatory power. Nevertheless, the following metrics are commonly used in credit-risk management practice:

- **Receiver operating characteristic (ROC) curve.** One may represent sensitivity and specificity on vertical and horizontal axis to derive the ROC curve, as detailed in Figure 2.25.
  One may easily compute the area underlying the curve (that is, AUC) to grasp the model's discriminatory power. It represents the probability that a randomly sampled defaulter gets a higher score than a randomly sampled non-defaulter. A perfect model would approximate AUC = 1, whereas a random model would correspond to the 45 degree line, detailed in Figure 2.25, with AUC = 0.5. As a rule of thumb, when AUC lies in the interval (0.80, 1), the model has very good discriminatory power, whereas in the case of AUC $\in$ (0.65, 0.80), the model has a fair discriminatory power.
- **Gini index.** The idea underlying this index is quite similar to ROC. Indeed, it originates from the Lorenz curve, and its relationship with AUC is as follows:

$$Gini_{index} = 2 \times AUC - 1. \tag{2.26}$$

- **Information value (IV).** One may define IV as follows:

$$IV = \sum_{j=1}^{J} \left(Distribution Good_j - Distribution Bad_j \right) \cdot \ln \left(\frac{Distribution Good_j}{Distribution Bad_j} \right), \tag{2.27}$$

where $Distribution Good_j$ refers to the proportion of class j non-defaulted accounts over the total number of non-defaulted accounts. While $Distribution Bad_j$ is the ratio of class j defaulted accounts over the total number of defaulted accounts. It is worth noting that the second component of Equation (2.27) is denoted as weight of evidence (WOE). Therefore the WOE is as follows:

$$WOE = \ln \left(\frac{Distribution Good_j}{Distribution Bad_j} \right). \tag{2.28}$$

Table 2.8 highlights how to put into practice Equations (2.27, 2.28) on data used in Example 2.8.2 by considering three classes (that is, $J = 3$).

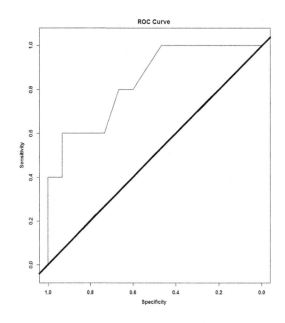

FIGURE 2.25

ROC curve for Example 2.8.2.

Table 2.8 IV computation for the 20 accounts portfolio analysis

DDELAY Group j	Total number of loans	Number of bad loans	Number of good loans	% Bad loans	Distib. bad (DB)	Distib. good (DG)	WOE	DG − DB	(DG − DB)× WOE
0–45	10	1	9	0.10	0.2	0.60	1.10	0.40	0.44
46–68	7	2	5	0.29	0.4	0.33	−0.18	−0.07	0.01
>60	3	2	1	0.67	0.4	0.07	−1.79	−0.33	0.60
Total	20	5	15						1.05

In practice, credit analysts often rely on IV thresholds. Weak prediction is associated with IV < 0.10, medium discriminatory power is commonly associated with $0.1 < IV < 0.4$, whereas $IV > 0.4$ denotes strong prediction.

EXERCISES

Exercise 2.1. Let us consider the same database used in Example 2.3.1. Develop an alternative scorecard by relying on the following:

- Select accounts belonging to the three main regions (that is, variable region).
- Do not include the variable bureau_score into the scorecard.
- Compute Gini index, AUC for the estimated scorecard.

Exercise 2.2. Based on the same data set, selected for Exercise 2.1, perform the following analyses:

- Fit both random forest and boosting models.
- Calibrate them based on the default rate of the most populated region (that is, the one with the highest number of accounts).
- Validate both models by considering both discriminatory power and accuracy.

Exercise 2.3. Utilising the same data used in Example 2.3.1, perform low default portfolio calibration by relying on the following:

- Select accounts belonging to the less populated region (that is, variable region).
- Define rating classes, based on bureau_score.
- Apply Pluto and Tasche (2005) and Van der Burgt (2008) procedures by considering a suitable target portfolio PD.

REFERENCES

Bellotti, T., Crook, J., 2009. Support vector machines for credit scoring and discovery of significant features. Expert Systems with Applications 36, 3302–3308.

Benjamin, N., Cathcart, A., Ryan, R., 2006. Low default portfolios: a proposal for conservative estimation of default probabilities. Financial services authority.

BIS, 2005. Studies on the Validation of Internal Rating Systems. Working paper no. 14. Bank for International Settlements, Basel, Switzerland.

BIS, 2006. Basel II International Convergence of Capital Measurement and Capital Standards: A Revised Framework. BIS, Basel.

Crosbie, P., Bohn, J., 2003. Modelling Default Risk. Moody's KMV technical document.

Engelmann, B., Rauhmeier, R., 2011. The Basel II Risk Parameters. Springer-Verlag, Berlin, Heidelberg.

FASB, 2016. Accounting standards updata no. 2016–13, financial instruments-credit losses (topic 326). June 16, 2016. Financial Accounting series. Financial Accounting Standards Board.

Hastie, T., Tibshirani, R., Friedman, J., 2009. Elements of Statistical Learning: Data Mining, Inference and Prediction. Springer, New York.

IASB, 2014. IFRS 9 Financial Instruments. Technical report, July 2014. International Accounting Standards Board.

Jafry, Y., Schuermann, T., 2004. Measurement, estimation and comparison of credit migration matrices. Journal of Banking and Finance 28 (11), 2603–2639.

James, G., Witten, D., Hastie, T., Tibshirani, R., 2013. An Introduction to Statistical Learning with Applications in R. Springer, New York.

Lantz, C., Nebenzahl, E., 1996. Behavior and interpretation of the κ statistic: resolution of the two paradoxes. Journal of Clinical Epidemiology 49 (4), 431–434.

Lessmann, S., Baesens, B., Seow, H.V., Thomas, L.C., 2015. Benchmarking state-of-the-art classification algorithms for credit scoring: an update of research. European Journal of Operational Research 247, 124–136.

Loeffler, G., Posch, P., 2011. Credit Risk Modeling Using Excel and VBA. Wiley, Chichester.

Merton, R., 1974. On the pricing of corporate debt: the risk structure of interest rates. Journal of Finance 29 (2), 449–470.

Platt, J., 2000. Probabilities for Support Vector Machines. In: Advances in Large Margin Classiers. MIT Press, pp. 61–74.

Pluto, K., Tasche, D., 2005. Thinking positively. Risk, 72–78.

Siddiqi, N., 2016. Intelligent Credit Scoring: Building and Implementing Better Credit Risk Scorecards. Wiley, Hoboken.

Tasche, D., 2013. The art of probability-of-default curve calibration. Journal of Credit Risk 9, 63–103.

Thomas, L., Crook, J., Edelman, D., 2017. Credit Scoring and Its Applications. Series: Mathematics in Industry. Society of Industrial and Applied Mathematics, Philadelphia.

Van der Burgt, M., 2008. Calibrating low-default portfolios, using the cumulative accuracy profile. Journal of Risk Model Validation 1 (4), 17–33.

Zadrozny, B., Elkan, C., 2001. Obtaining calibrated probability estimates from decision trees and naive Bayesian classifiers. In: Proc. 18th International Conference on Machine Learning, pp. 609–616.

LIFETIME PD

3

One of the key innovations introduced by the new accounting standards refer to lifetime losses. Though this concept is not new in risk management, its implementation in the financial industry is extremely contemporary.

Account-level information is usually required to develop a comprehensive modelling framework. Based on data availability, one may consider few alternative methods.

As a primal way to tackle the challenge, generalised linear models (GLMs) are explored. Two perspectives are followed. On the one hand, a portfolio-level analysis is conducted. Its main advantage is simplicity both in terms of data requirements and implementation. On the other hand, an account-level panel regression is performed to capture a wide range of details available only when granular information is used.

As a second step, survival modelling is introduced by means of three main approaches. The pioneering Kaplan–Meier (KP) frame paves the way to lifetime PD modelling by means of Cox proportional hazard (CPH) and accelerated failure time (AFT) models. All of them rely on account-level information.

Thirdly, machine learning (ML) procedures are scrutinised. Bagging, random forest and boosting are directly applied on panel data to capture the relationship with both behavioural and macroeconomic variables over time. Then, as an alternative, random survival forest is explored by embedding survival modelling into an ML structure.

As the last step of our journey, transition matrices are studied by considering both bespoke approaches, based on transition matrix adjustments over a multi-period horizon and multi state Markov models.

Examples and case studies are examined by means of R software. Then, the final section of the chapter provides SAS programming details on the most relevant exemplifications.

KEY ABBREVIATIONS AND SYMBOLS

DR_τ	Default rate over the time horizon τ
$h = \tau_1 + \ldots + \tau_J$	Time horizon corresponding to the sum of sub-periods τ_j
$PD_{i,s,h}$	PD for account i in sub-portfolio s over the time horizon h
$PD_{i,s,(t_\tau, t_h]}$	PD for account i in sub-portfolio s over the time horizon $(t_\tau, t_h]$
$\dot{PD}_{i,s,t,\Delta}$	Shifted PD for account i in sub-portfolio s based on scenario Δ
$S_{i,s,\tau}$	Survival probability for account i in sub-portfolio s over period τ
$\tau \leq h$	Short time horizon (that is, $\tau \leq h$); h is used only when a split in sub-period arises
$\Psi_{s,t}$	Creditworthiness index for sub-portfolio s at time t
$\lambda_{i,s,t\mid\mathbf{z}_{i,s,t}}^{CPH}$	CPH rate for account i in sub-portfolio s at time t; conditioned on BVs and MVs stuck in $\mathbf{z}_{(\cdot)}$

$\lambda^{AFT}_{i,s,t|\mathbf{z}_{i,s,t}}$ AFT hazard rate for account i in sub-portfolio s at time t; conditioned on BVs and MVs stuck in $\mathbf{z}_{(.)}$

$\boldsymbol{\chi}_{i,s,[t_{-n_i},t_{-n_i+v_i}]}$ Behavioural variable (BV) matrix for account i, in sub-portfolio s over the interval $[t_{-n_i},t_{-n_i+v_i}]$

$\mathbf{x}_{s,[t_{-N},t_{-1}]}$ Macroeconomic variable (MV) matrix for sub-portfolio s over the time interval $[t_{-N},t_{-1}]$

$\mathbf{y}_{i,s,[t_{-n_i},t_{-n_i+v_i}]}$ Default flag vector for account i in sub-portfolio s over a time interval $[t_{-n_i},t_{-n_i+v_i}]$

$\mathbf{z}_{i,s,[t_{-n_i},t_{-n_i+v_i}]}$ Matrix combining $\boldsymbol{\chi}_{i,s,[t_{-n_i},t_{-n_i+v_i}]}$ and $\mathbf{x}_{s,[t_{-N},t_{-1}]}$

3.1 INTRODUCTION

Accounting standards require banks to compute ECL, based on point-in-time (PIT), unbiased, forward-looking, and lifetime estimates. Chapter 2 focused on one-year PIT PD, the aim of this chapter is to embed a forward-looking perspective, and extend over a lifetime horizon PD estimates. Few alternative approaches can be followed. Figure 3.1 summarises how this chapter tackles the challenge.

- **Data preparation.** Section 3.2 provides an account-level (panel) data overview for lifetime PD analysis. On the one hand, default flag time series are introduced for each account under scrutiny. On the other hand, attention is given to explanatory indicators by considering both behavioural (BVs) and macroeconomic variables (MVs).

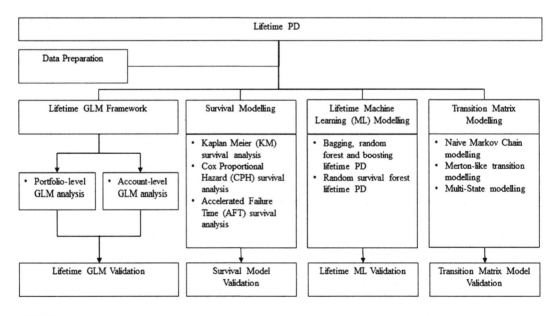

FIGURE 3.1

Chapter's workflow diagram.

- **Lifetime GLM framework.** Section 3.3 proposes a generalised linear model (GLM) framework based on four milestones: one-year PIT PD, link function, PD shift, and lifetime PD. Two alternative approaches are studied:
  - **Portfolio-level GLM analysis.** The key idea is to apply a macro link (portfolio-level) function on top of each account's one-year PD. Firstly, a macro link is fitted. Secondly, a shift mechanism is used to estimate forward-looking PDs. The last step is building a lifetime PD term structure.
  - **Account-level GLM analysis.** Panel GLM regression, based on both BVs and MVs, is used to capture account-level details, such as PD evolution, throughout a financial instrument life-cycle. Finally, PD shift and lifetime computation are performed at an account-level.
- **Survival modelling.** Section 3.4 proposes survival analysis for fitting at once lifetime PDs (that is, without using a multi-step procedure as in the above-described GLM framework). As starting point, the Kaplan and Meier (1958) approach is explored. Its key idea is to consider account information over a lifetime horizon. The need to link PDs with behavioural variables (BVs) and macroeconomic variables (MVs) leads us to investigate Cox (1972) methodology. Finally, AFT methods are explored by means of Weibull and exponential link functions.
- **Machine learning (ML) modelling.** Section 3.5 focuses on bagging, random forest and boosting methods. Account-level analysis is performed on panel data. The outcome is a forward-looking model on which a lifetime term structure is built. As an alternative, random survival modelling is explored by embedding survival analysis into a random forest framework.
- **Transition matrix modelling.** Section 3.6 focuses on transition matrices to build lifetime PDs. Firstly, inhomogeneous processes are studied to derive bespoke matrices embedding forward-looking adjustments. Secondly, the analysis focuses on a multi-state modelling.

For each modelling approach a model validation section details checks and controls needed to ensure a consistent ECL estimation.

Examples and case studies are examined by means of R code. Section 3.7 provides SAS details on the key examples investigated throughout the chapter.

3.2 DATA PREPARATION

Data play a key role in risk management. This is particularly true in the case of forward-looking and lifetime PDs. The focus of this section is on account-level information. Information based on the same account is collected through time to build a panel structure. On the other hand, when data are not granular enough to allow for a panel investigation, portfolio-level modelling is regarded as one of the alternatives to pursue.

Following is a brief introduction to account-level data sets, which paves the way to analyses conducted throughout the chapter. Section 3.2.1 focuses on default flag time series. Section 3.2.2 provides a formal representation of an account-level database to use for lifetime PD modelling.

3.2.1 DEFAULT FLAG CREATION

Chapter 2 described how quantitative and qualitative indicators may trigger a default event. The focus here is on multi-period analysis. In this regard, Figure 3.2 represents an account over the period between

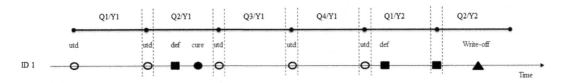

FIGURE 3.2

Default flag built on a quarterly time horizon.

quarter 1 of year 1 (that is, Q1/Y1), until quarter 2 of year 2 (that is, Q2/Y2). The example refers to quarterly data to align with the most common MV statistic data frequency. Starting from an up-to-date (that is, non-defaulted) situation at the beginning of the first quarter of year 1, a default event is triggered during the second quarter. During the same quarter the default is cured, based on instant cure definition. A new default event occurs during the first quarter of year 2.

Table 3.1 summarises quarterly default flag evolution for the account studied in Figure 3.2. A distinction operates between instant cure and 6-month probationary period. The choice between these two alternatives should be consistent with the approach adopted for one-year PD modelling.

	Table 3.1 Quarterly default flag		
		Default flag	
ID	**Reporting date**	**Instant cure**	**6-month probation**
1	Q1/Y1	0	0
1	Q2/Y1	1	1
1	Q3/Y1	0	1
1	Q4/Y1	0	1
1	Q1/Y2	1	1

A distinction arises between historical data used for model development and projections. Figure 3.3 summarises the notation adopted to differentiate between past and future. Based on this, $[t_{-n+j-1}, t_{-n+j}]^1$ represents interval τ_j. Both Figure 3.2 and Table 3.1 refer to quarterly intervals (that is, τ_j is a quarter).

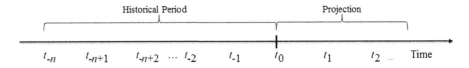

FIGURE 3.3

Time series structure and notation.

It is worth noting that accounts may appear in the portfolio at different points in time, and they can be censored as described below:

---

[1] Square brackets include extremes, and parentheses do not include extremes.

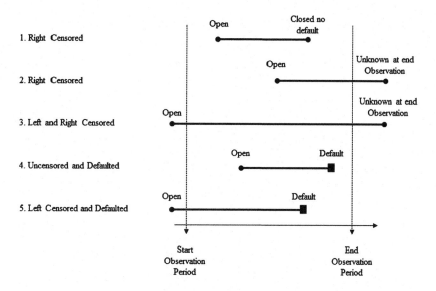

FIGURE 3.4

Censoring mechanics.

- **Right censored.** Under this category, one needs to consider both accounts that do not default during the period under analysis and expiring without default, or default after the end of the observation period (that is, unknown status at the end of observation period). See examples 1 and 2 in Figure 3.4.
- **Left and right censored.** In some cases accounts are opened before the observation period (that is, left censored) and are also right censored. See example 3 in Figure 3.4.
- **Defaulted.** This last class includes accounts that default during the observation period. See examples 4 and 5 in Figure 3.4.

The next section formalises panel data characteristics for lifetime PD modelling.

3.2.2 ACCOUNT-LEVEL (PANEL) DATABASE STRUCTURE

A panel database embeds account information through time by means of the following matrices:

- **Default flag time series.** Default flag time series is stack in a $(v_i + 1) \times 1$ vector as listed below:

$$
\mathbf{y}_{i,s,[t_{-n_i},t_{-n_i+v_i}]} = \begin{pmatrix} y_{i,s,t_{-n_i}} \\ \vdots \\ y_{i,s,t_{-n_i+v_i}} \end{pmatrix}, \tag{3.1}
$$

where $y_{i,s,t_{-k_i}} = 1$ if default occurs over the period $[t_{-k_i-1}, t_{-k_i}]$. Vice-versa $y_{i,s,t_{-k_i}} = 0$. For the sake of simplicity, in what follows censored accounts are treated as non-defaulted. Chapter 5 investigates additional phenomena, such as full prepayments and overpayments. In that case, additional outcomes are included as part of the outcome vector $\mathbf{y}_{(.)}$.

- **BV time series.** A $(v_i + 1) \times r$ matrix contains all behavioural information based on account i as detailed below:

$$\boldsymbol{\chi}_{i,s,[t_{-n_i},t_{-n_i}+v_i]} = \begin{pmatrix} \chi_{i,s,t_{-n_i},1} & \cdots & \chi_{i,s,t_{-n_i},r} \\ \vdots & \ddots & \vdots \\ \chi_{i,s,t_{-n_i}+v_i,1} & \cdots & \chi_{i,s,t_{-n_i}+v_i,r} \end{pmatrix}, \qquad (3.2)$$

where $\boldsymbol{\chi}_{i,s,[t_{-n_i},t_{-n_i}+v_i]}$ contains a wide range of information including, among others, time-on-book (TOB), time-to-maturity (TTM), and loan-to-value (LTV).
- **MV time series.** Macroeconomic data available at sub-portfolio-level (that is, s) are stuck in the following $N \times p$ matrix:

$$\mathbf{x}_{s,[t_{-N},t_{-1}]} = \begin{pmatrix} x_{s,t_{-N},1} & \cdots & x_{s,t_{-N},p} \\ \vdots & \ddots & \vdots \\ x_{s,t_{-1},1} & \cdots & x_{s,t_{-1},p} \end{pmatrix}, \qquad (3.3)$$

where t_{-N} indicates the oldest observation in the overall database (that is, usually $N \geq n$).
- **Matrix of BVs and MVs.** For each observation, the combination of $\boldsymbol{\chi}_{i,s}$ and $\mathbf{x}_s$ is represented through the $(v_i + 1) \times (r + p)$-dimensional matrix $\mathbf{z}_i$, as detailed below:

$$\mathbf{z}_{i,s,[t_{-n_i},t_{-n_i}+v_i]} = \begin{pmatrix} \chi_{i,s,t_{-n_i},1} & \cdots & \chi_{i,s,t_{-n_i},r} & x_{s,t_{-n_i},1} & \cdots & x_{s,t_{-n_i},p} \\ \vdots & \ddots & \vdots & \vdots & \ddots & \vdots \\ \chi_{i,s,t_{-n_i}+v_i,1} & \cdots & \chi_{i,s,t_{-n_i}+v_i,r} & x_{s,t_{-n_i}+v_i,1} & \cdots & x_{s,t_{-n_i}+v_i,p} \end{pmatrix}. \qquad (3.4)$$

Example 3.2.1 describes how to build and explore data organised by means of the matrices $\mathbf{y}_{(\cdot)}$, $\boldsymbol{\chi}_{(\cdot)}$ and $\mathbf{x}_{(\cdot)}$.

EXAMPLE 3.2.1 DATABASE MANAGEMENT FOR ACCOUNT-LEVEL MODELLING

Let us consider a database with account observations spread over the period 2003–2016. The next steps are performed as part of the database analysis:

1. Upload and check data, and
2. Create train and test samples.

```
# 1. Upload and check data
ltpd_panel<- read.csv('chap3ltpdpanel.csv')
library(dplyr)
# 1.1. Overview of data content and format
dplyr::glimpse(ltpd_panel)
library(vars)
ltpd_panel <- dplyr::mutate_at(ltpd_panel,
vars(contains('date')), funs((as.Date(.,format = '%m/%d/%Y'))))
# 1.2. Compute default rates
```

```
dr_data<- ltpd_panel %>%
dplyr::group_by(report_date, year) %>%
dplyr::summarise(dr_QoQ = mean(default_flag)) %>%
dplyr::select(report_date, year, dr_QoQ)
```

Starting from vectors $\mathbf{y}_{(\cdot)}$ one may compute the average portfolio DR_t (i.e., default rate). Figure 3.5 summarises the quarterly default rate evolution over the period 2003–2016.

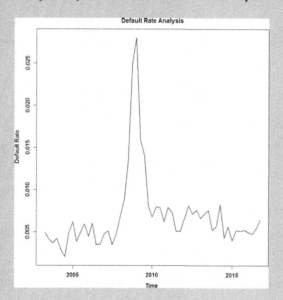

FIGURE 3.5

Quarterly DR time series.

As part of the model development process, one needs to split the data into train and test samples. In what follows a 70% against 30% split is considered.

```
# 2. Create train and test samples
ltpd_subset<- ltpd_panel %>%
dplyr::select(id, default_ind) %>%
dplyr::distinct()
# 2.1. Stratified sampling: train 70%, test 30%
set.seed(2122)
sample_id<- caret::createDataPartition(ltpd_subset$default_ind,
p=0.7, list=FALSE)
train_id<- ltpd_subset[sample_id,]
test_id<- ltpd_subset[-sample_id,]
# 2.2. Assign sample ID column and merge data
```

```
train_id$sample <- 'train'
test_id$sample <- 'test'
all_id<- rbind(train_id, test_id)
all_id<- all_id %>%
dplyr::select(id, sample)
# 2.3. Join with ltpd dataset
ltpd_panel<- dplyr::left_join(ltpd_panel,
all_id, by = 'id')
ltpd_panel$sample<- as.factor(ltpd_panel$sample)
```

The next section provides a lifetime PD framework based on GLMs.

3.3 LIFETIME GLM FRAMEWORK

A multi-step process, based on the one-year PIT estimates explored in Chapter 2, is at the very heart of our GLM framework. The idea is to estimate a link function capturing economic dynamics and apply a shift on top of one-year PDs to obtain forward-looking measures. As a final step, a lifetime term structure is derived as a cumulative process of forward-looking PDs. The key ingredients of the framework are listed below:

i. **One-year PIT PDs.** PDs studied in Chapter 2 constitute the first ingredient of the process. From a notation perspective, PD_{i,s,t_0} indicates starting point (t_0) probability of default for account i, belonging to sub-portfolio s.

ii. **Link function.** Two main approaches are considered to estimate a link function:

- **Portfolio-level GLM analysis.** A creditworthiness index based on sub-portfolio s (i.e., $\Psi_{s,t}$) is regressed against MVs. As an example, one may rely on default rate time series as creditworthiness index.
- **Account-level GLM analysis.** A distinction operates as follows:
  - Reduced set of variables. Account-level PDs are fitted against both BVs and MVs by means of a panel GLM regression. The focus is on easy-to-project BVs, such as time-on-book (TOB), time-to-maturity (TTM), loan-to-value (LTV).
  - Full set of variables. A full set of BVs (including all variables studied in Chapter 2 to build a scorecard) may enter the account-level panel regression described above. Nevertheless, two main drawbacks affect this approach. Firstly, idiosyncratic characteristics usually dominate the model by leaving little space for MVs. Secondly, BV projections require another very complex modelling framework.

  Remark. Due to its practical implementation issues, and given the similarity to the reduced set of variables approach, in what follows, the full set of variable method will not be further investigated.

iii. **PD shift.** A shift based on economic projections funnelled through the above link function is applied on top of PD_{i,s,t_0}. Proportional or logit shift are usually adopted in practice. This shift allows us to obtain forward-looking PDs.

iv. Lifetime PDs. Steps ii and iii can be replicated on a rolling basis (for example, quarterly or yearly) to obtain a sequence of forward-looking PDs feeding the following lifetime equation:

$$PD_{i,s,h} = S_{i,s,\tau} \cdot PD_{i,s,(t_\tau,t_h]}, \tag{3.5}$$

where $S_{i,s,\tau}$ represents the survival probability over the time horizon τ (that is, $\tau \leq h$), and $PD_{i,s,(t_\tau,t_h]}$ is the default probability along the time interval t_τ and t_h.[2] This notation is used to highlight that t indicates a point in time, whereas τ and h are intervals.

Figure 3.6 highlights the split between portfolio-level and account-level GLM modelling. Indeed, the same steps are performed in both cases, but different estimation techniques are applied.

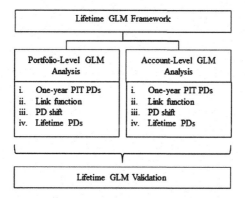

FIGURE 3.6

Workflow diagram for Section 3.3.

Section 3.3.1 focuses on the portfolio-level GLM analysis, whereas Section 3.3.2 enters into the details of account-level GLM panel time series modelling. Finally, Section 3.3.3 describes how to validate lifetime PD models.

3.3.1 PORTFOLIO-LEVEL GLM ANALYSIS

When data are not available at account-level, as detailed in Section 3.2 or micro-granularity is not needed, one may conduct the study at portfolio-level. The idea is to fit a creditworthiness index against MVs (Bellini, 2017). A PD shift, based on macroeconomic projections, is applied on top of one-year PIT PDs to derive forward-looking PDs. Finally, a lifetime term structure is computed for each account, based on Equation (3.5).

The four-step procedure described in Section 3.3 is implemented as follows[3]:

ii. Link function. The choice of a suitable creditworthiness index ($\Psi_{s,t}$) informs the entire procedure. As an example, one may rely on default rates (DRs) (that is, $\Psi_{s,t}$ corresponds to the default rate

---

[2]Square brackets include extremes, whereas parentheses do not include extremes.

[3]One-year PIT PD is considered as given (see Chapter 2).

for sub-portfolio s at time t). We define a DR as the ratio between the number of defaults occurred over a give time horizon ($Def_{s,\tau}$) and the number of live accounts at the beginning of the period (Acc_{s,t_0}), as listed below:

$$DR_{s,\tau} = \frac{Def_{s,\tau}}{Acc_{s,t_0}}, \tag{3.6}$$

where τ stands for a generic time horizon (example a quarter or year). In this regard, PD can be interpreted as the expectation of a default random variable defined as follows:

$$y_{i,s,t,\tau} = \begin{cases} 1 & default, \\ 0 & non\text{-}default, \end{cases} \tag{3.7}$$

where the subscript t refers to time of assessment. Then, DR is the actual occurrence of this random variable.

In terms of link function, one may link $\Psi_{s,t}$, or a suitable transformation,[4] to macroeconomic variables by means of a regression, as listed below:

$$\Psi_{s,t} = \eta_{s,0} + \eta_{s,1} x_{1,t} + \ldots + \eta_{s,p} x_{p,t} + \epsilon_{s,t}, \tag{3.8}$$

where the vector $\mathbf{x} = (x_1, \ldots, x_p)'$ stacks MVs,[5] whereas $\boldsymbol{\eta} = (\eta_{s,0}, \ldots, \eta_{s,p})'$ is the vector of coefficients and $\epsilon_{s,t}$ is an error term.

Example 3.3.1 performs the analysis by means of a linear regression.

EXAMPLE 3.3.1 DEFAULT RATE REGRESSION AGAINST MVS

Let us consider the UK corporate default rate time series along the period 2000 to 2013 as a creditworthiness index $\Psi_{s,t}$. A linear model is fitted on UK quarterly macroeconomic variables is summarised in Table 3.2.

Table 3.2 List of UK macroeconomic variables used to fit the credit-worthiness index $\Psi_{s,t}$

Descriptions	Symbols and analytical formulas
GDP growth rate	$GDP_t^{growth} = \frac{GDP_t - GDP_{t-1}}{GDP_{t-1}}$
Unemployment rate	UER_t
Consumer price index (CPI) growth rate	$CPI_t^{growth} = \frac{CPI_t - CPI_{t-1}}{CPI_{t-1}}$
House price index (HPI) growth rate	$HPI_t^{growth} = \frac{HPI_t - HPI_{t-1}}{HPI_{t-1}}$
Long term interest rate (IR)	IR_t

---

[4] The notation $\Psi_{s,t}$ does not change in case of transformed variable to avoid unnecessary complexity.

[5] As described in more detail in Chapter 6, one is usually required to deal with stationary time series. Based on this, KPSS test (Hamilton, 1994) figures out that if a time series is stationary around a mean or linear trend, or is non-stationary due to a unit root. The null hypothesis for the test is that the time series is stationary. The alternate hypothesis for the test is that data are not stationary.

The regression is performed by means of the following steps:

1. Upload data,
2. KPSS testing, and
3. Fit regression model.

```
# 1. Updload data
mac <- read.csv('chap3drts.csv', header = TRUE, sep = ";", dec = ".")
mac$Date <- as.Date(mac$Date,format = '%d/%m/%Y')
```

Figure 3.7 represents all time series under analysis. It is worth noting that the GDP^{growth} fall during the 2007–2009 crisis anticipates, by approximately one year, default rate jump.

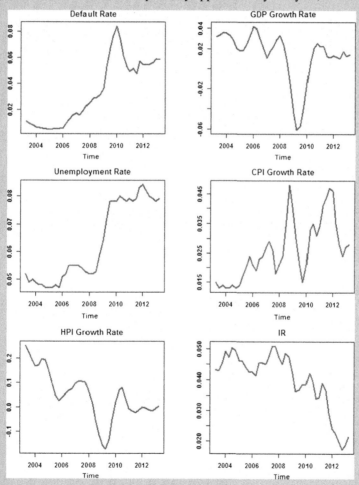

FIGURE 3.7

Time series under analysis (quarterly data).

```
# 2. KPSS testing
library(tseries)
kpss.test(mac[,'dr'], null = 'Level', lshort = TRUE)
# p-value <  0.01
kpss.test(mac[,'dr'], null = 'Trend', lshort = TRUE)
# p-value = 0.02023
```

Table 3.3 summarises the key KPSS outputs for all variables considered. For any of them, the null hypothesis of stationary level cannot be rejected at 5.00% level. For the vast majority, a 1.00% confidence level holds. With regard to trend stationary, only CPI^{growth} fails the test.

Table 3.3 KPSS test outputs

Variable	Level (p-value)	Trend (p-value)
DR	< 0.01	0.02
GDP^{growth}	0.04	0.02
UER	< 0.01	< 0.01
CPI^{growth}	< 0.01	> 0.10
HPI^{growth}	< 0.01	< 0.01
IR	< 0.01	< 0.01

After careful statistical investigation and inspection of Figure 3.7, a significant relationship between DR and GDP^{growth} with one year lag is detected. Indeed, DR does not immediately react to the economic downturn characterized by negative GDP^{growth} rates. A regression is run by means of $GDP^{growth}_{t,lag}$ and UER_t, as detailed below.

```
# 3. Fit regression model
# 3.1. Data preparation
dr_t   <- as.matrix(mac[5:nrow(mac),2])
gdp_tlag <- as.matrix(mac[1:(nrow(mac)-4),3])
uer_t  <- as.matrix(mac[5:nrow(mac),4])
xx   <- as.data.frame(cbind(dr_t,gdp_tlag,uer_t)/100)
colnames(xx) <- c('dr_tt','gdp_ttlag', 'uer_tt')
# 3.2. Fit model
fit <- lm(dr_tt~gdp_ttlag+uer_tt,data=xx)
summary(fit)
#              Estimate Std. Error t value Pr(>|t|)
# (Intercept)  -0.05204    0.00784  -6.638 1.29e-07 ***
# gdp_ttlag    -0.21199    0.06081  -3.486  0.00137 **
# uer_tt        1.40331    0.11205  12.524 2.73e-14 ***
# ---
# Signif. codes:  0 '***' 0.001 '**' 0.01 '*' 0.05 '.' 0.1 ' ' 1
# Residual standard error: 0.007805 on 34 degrees of freedom
```

```
# Multiple R-squared:  0.9046,  Adjusted R-squared:  0.899
# F-statistic: 161.2 on 2 and 34 DF,  p-value: < 2.2e-16
# 3.3. Predict
dr_fit <- predict(fit,xx)
```

Figure 3.8 compares actual default rate against model's fitted time series ($R^2 = 0.899$).

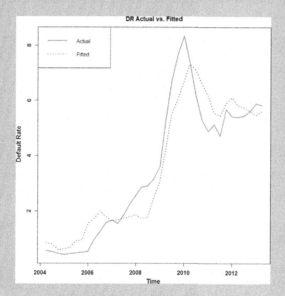

FIGURE 3.8

Actual versus fitted default rate time series.

The next step is to use the fitted macroeconomic link function to shift PIT PDs, as detailed below.

iii. **PD shift.** One needs to apply a variation on top of one-year PIT PD (that is, PD_{i,s,t_0}), based on macroeconomic projections feeding the link function investigated above. We can represent a shifted PD as follows:

$$\dot{PD}_{i,s,t,\Delta} = PD_{i,s,t_0} + f(\hat{\Psi}_{s,\Delta}, \Psi_{s,t_0}), \tag{3.9}$$

where $\dot{PD}_{(\cdot)}$ refers to a shifted PD, whereas $f(\hat{\Psi}_{s,\Delta}, \Psi_{s,t_0})$ is a generic shift represented as a function of the projected creditworthiness index $\hat{\Psi}_{s,\Delta}$, and its value in t_0, Ψ_{s,t_0}. A comprehensive study is detailed in Appendix A by emphasising the distinction between proportional and logit shift methods.

iv. **Lifetime PDs.** As a last step of the lifetime estimation process, let us split the time horizon h into non-overlapping, consecutive sub-intervals such that: $h = \tau_1 + \ldots + \tau_J$, where τ_j stands for a generic time interval (for example, a quarter or year). We can, therefore, rewrite Equation (3.5) as follows:

$$PD_{i,s,t,h} = \prod_{j=1}^{J-1}(1 - \dot{P}D_{i,s,t,\tau_j}) \cdot \dot{P}D_{i,s,t,\tau_J}, \tag{3.10}$$

where $\prod_{j=1}^{J-1}(1 - \dot{P}D_{i,s,t,\tau_j}) = S_{i,s,t,\tau_{J-1}}$ represents the survival probability up to τ_{J-1} estimated in t.

Example 3.3.2 highlights the key steps of lifetime PD modelling based on the portfolio introduced in Example 3.8.1 in Appendix A.

EXAMPLE 3.3.2 PORTFOLIO-LEVEL LIFETIME PDS

Let us consider a portfolio made by 5 accounts as listed in Table 3.4.

Table 3.4 Corporate and SME portfolio

ID	Segment	$PD_{i,s,t}$
1	Corporate	0.50%
2	Corporate	2.00%
3	Corporate	3.00%
4	SME	3.50%
5	SME	4.00%

Examples 3.8.1 and 3.8.2 in Appendix A show how to compute proportional and logit shift for τ_1 within the scenario forecast detailed in Table 3.5.

Table 3.5 Multi-period macroeconomic scenario

	τ_1	τ_2	τ_3	τ_4	τ_5
GDP_t^{growth}	−2.94%	1.05%	1.50%	1.75%	2.00%
UER_t	8.50%	9.00%	7.50%	7.00%	6.80%

Table 3.6 points out the PD evolution for each account belonging to the portfolio (based on the logit shift method detailed in Appendix A). These PDs, collectively, constitute the key ingredient of Equation (3.10).

Table 3.6 PD projections $\dot{P}D_{i,s,t,\tau_j}$

ID	τ_1	τ_2	τ_3	τ_4	τ_5
1	0.64%	0.63%	0.43%	0.36%	0.33%
2	2.55%	2.50%	1.71%	1.44%	1.33%
3	3.82%	3.74%	2.57%	2.17%	2.00%
4	4.45%	4.36%	3.00%	2.54%	2.34%
5	5.08%	4.98%	3.43%	2.91%	2.68%

As a last step of the lifetime PD estimation process, Table 3.7 applies Equation (3.10) to the portfolio under analysis.

Table 3.7 Multi-period marginal PDs

ID	τ_1	τ_2	τ_3	τ_4	τ_5
1	0.64%	0.62%	0.41%	0.34%	0.31%
2	2.55%	2.44%	1.63%	1.35%	1.22%
3	3.82%	3.60%	2.38%	1.96%	1.76%
4	4.45 %	4.17%	2.74%	2.25%	2.02%
5	5.08%	4.72%	3.09%	2.53%	2.26%

Once marginal PDs are estimated, one is able to compute the cumulative lifetime curve by adding marginal PDs over each period of interest. Table 3.8 shows the results for the portfolio under analysis.

Table 3.8 Multi-period lifetime cumulative PDs

ID	τ_1	τ_2	τ_3	τ_4	τ_5
1	0.64%	1.26%	1.69%	2.04%	2.36%
2	2.55%	4.99%	6.62%	7.97%	9.19%
3	3.82%	7.42%	9.80%	11.76%	13.52%
4	4.45%	8.62%	11.36%	13.61%	15.63%
5	5.08%	9.80%	12.90%	15.43%	17.69%

A different perspective is followed in the case of panel analysis. As detailed in the next section, MVs are part of the core probability of default estimation process in conjunction with account specific BVs.

3.3.2 ACCOUNT-LEVEL GLM ANALYSIS

When data are available at account-level, as detailed in Section 3.2, one may be interested to fit a link function by jointly capturing BVs and MVs characteristics. This is particularly relevant for retail products, such as mortgages, where PDs depend upon ageing (for example, time-on-book).

Modelling improvements due to account-level BVs information rely on the more sophisticated link function detailed below:

ii. **Link function.** As detailed in Section 3.2, one needs to build time series for each account. An account-level link function can be represented as follows:

$$\theta_{i,s,t} = \beta_0 + \beta_1\chi_{1,i,s,t} + \ldots + \beta_r\chi_{r,i,s,t} + \beta_{r+1}x_{1,s,t} + \ldots + \beta_{r+p}x_{p,s,t} + \epsilon_{i,s,t}, \qquad (3.11)$$

where $\theta_{i,s,t}$ is a suitable transformation of $y_{i,s,t}$, whereas $\chi_{i,s,t} = (\chi_{1,i,s,t} \ldots \chi_{1,i,s,t})'$ is the $r \times 1$ vector of BVs for account i, belonging to sub-portfolio s at time t. Finally, $\mathbf{x} = (x_{1,s,t} \ldots x_{p,s,t})'$ is the $p \times 1$ vector of MVs for the sub-portfolio s at time t. The key differences with Equation (3.8) can be summarised as follows:

• **Account granularity.** Analysis is conducted at account level i, whereas Equation (3.8) relies on sub-portfolio s details.

- **Panel data frame.** For each account, a time series is considered as detailed in Section 3.2.

A link function is fitted by means of the following steps:

- **Univariate analysis.** BVs and MVs are investigated by means of univariate analysis. A selection process based on IV (or similar metrics) applies.
- **Multivariate analysis.** A short list of candidate variables is explored. The analysis focuses both on statistical significance and economic sense check.
- **Model fitting.** This process moves from the above short list, and is performed on BVs and MVs accurately discussed with business experts.

Example 3.3.3 summarises how to perform account-level model fitting.

EXAMPLE 3.3.3 PANEL GLM FITTING ANALYSIS

Let us consider the database studied in Example 3.2.1. In what follows, the model fitting process is detailed by means of:
1. Univariate analysis (focus on ageing),
2. Multivariate analysis, and
3. Model fitting.

```
# 1. Univariate analysis
# 1.1. Create train and test samples
train<- ltpd_panel %>%
dplyr::filter(sample == 'train')
test<- ltpd_panel %>%
dplyr::filter(sample == 'test')
# 1.2. Split both variables into deciles and quantiles
quantile(train$mob, prob = seq(0, 1, length = 11))
quantile(train$mob)
quantile(train$remaining_term, prob = seq(0, 1, length = 11))
quantile(train$remaining_term)
# 1.3. Remaining term analysis
train$default_event<-
dplyr::if_else(train$default_flag == 1, 0,1)
train$seasoning<- dplyr::if_else(train$remaining_term> 36,1,0)
```

The analysis of ageing shows a two-bin structure (that is, ≤ 36 or > 36 months) for remaining term (time-to-maturity). Quarterly average bad rate for accounts in the first bin is 4.1%, whereas for others, it is 0.7%. In addition to this variable, ltv_utd (loan-to-value updated) is part of the analysis. Indeed, it can easily be projected by considering property value evolution, based on house price index (HPI).

The next step is to inspect macroeconomic variables. The following set of MVs is explored: short term interest rate (IR), unemployment rate (UER), house price index (HPI), gross domestic product (GDP), consumer price index (CPI), and income. A correlation analysis is performed to point out potential overlap between pairs of candidate variables. (See Figure 3.9.)

```
# 2 Multivariate analysis
macro_vars<- train %>%
dplyr::select(ir, uer, hpi, gdp, cpi, income)
# 2.1. Correlation analysis
corr_spearman<- cor(as.matrix(macro_vars), method='spearman')
```

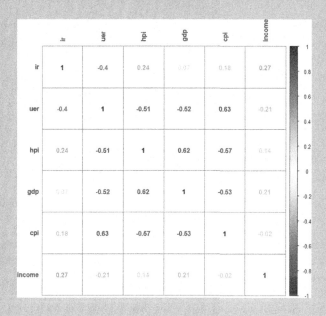

FIGURE 3.9

MV correlation analysis.

We observe that GDP and HPI together with CPI and UER have a correlation $\geq 60\%$. We then exclude variables with lower predictive power in each of these pairs.

An expert-driven process informs the choice of variables to consider for modelling purposes as shown below.

```
# 3. Model fitting
logit<- glm(default_flag~ seasoning+hpi,
family = binomial(link = 'logit'), data = train)
summary(logit)
#              Estimate Std. Error z value    Pr(>|z|)
# (Intercept) -2.984016   0.171291 -17.421 < 0.0000 ***
# seasoning   -1.934862   0.186227 -10.390 < 0.0000 ***
```

```
# hpi          -0.057738   0.007442  -7.758   0.0000 ***
# ---
# Signif. codes:  0 '***' 0.001 '**' 0.01 '*' 0.05 '.' 0.1 ' ' 1
```

A negative seasoning coefficient aligns with an expected PD reduction due to ageing. A negative HPI relationship means that an HPI decrease causes default rates to increase (and vice-versa).

It is worth noting that other variables could be included by improving both discriminatory power and correlation with DRs. Further comments will be provided in the validation section.

iii. PD shift. A distinction is made between proportional and logit shift. One may refer to Appendix B for computational details.

iv. Lifetime PDs. The last step of the process is fully aligned with Equation (3.10), described in Section 3.3.1.

The next section focuses on the validation process for both portfolio-level and account-level GLMs.

3.3.3 LIFETIME GLM VALIDATION

Checks on data, methodology and statistical testing are performed, as detailed below.

a. Data validation. The focus of data validation is on representativeness and completeness, as listed below:

- **Data representativeness.** One needs to demonstrate data consistency through time. For example, default definition should be consistent throughout the entire period under investigation. Likewise, MVs are required to adequately represent the portfolio in terms of geography, sector, and other key characteristics over each account's lifespan.
- **Data completeness.** Accounting standards do not provide specific requirements in terms of time series historical depth. Nevertheless, one should include two economic cycles or, at least, a recession period. Indeed, this is particularly important to assess model sensitivity under alternative macroeconomic situations and, in particular, under stressed conditions.

b. Methodology validation. This process relies on a review of theories and assumptions underlying a model. Methodologies need also to be tested against data availability. For example, one cannot develop an account-level GLM if panel data is unavailable.

c. Statistical testing validation. A series of analysis is required to ensure genuine statistical results, as detailed below:

- **Discriminatory power.** The ability to separate defaulted against non-defaulted accounts is crucial for a PD model. The same statistics explored in Chapter 2 may apply to lifetime PD modelling. However, one needs to pinpoint the following:
  - Portfolio-level analysis. The main focus of validation is on accuracy and sensitivity against macroeconomic fluctuations.
  - Account-level analysis. One may consider both an overall discriminatory power assessment over the entire period or investigate its evolution through time. In all cases, constraints on

BVs and MVs choice affect model's discriminatory power. Therefore one may expect to reach lower discriminatory levels compared to one-year PD models. Example 3.3.4 illustrates how to conduct the analysis, starting from Example 3.3.3.

EXAMPLE 3.3.4 ACCOUNT-LEVEL MODEL DISCRIMINATORY POWER VALIDATION

Let us consider the model developed in Example 3.3.3. The following steps are performed:

1. Score accounts (by means of the fitted model),
2. Estimate ROC curve (see Figure 3.10), and
3. Compute AUC statistics.

```
# 1. Score accounts
train$predict_logit  <- round(predict(logit,
newdata = train, type = 'response'),7)
# 2. Estimate ROC curve
library(ROCR)
pred_train<- ROCR::prediction(train$predict_logit,
train$default_flag)
perf_train<- ROCR::performance(pred_train, 'tpr', 'fpr')
```

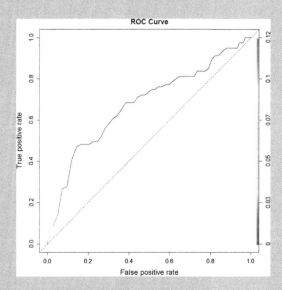

FIGURE 3.10

ROC curve.

From a visual inspection, the model shows a good discriminatory power. AUC is quantified as follows:

```
# 3. Compute AUC statistics
auc_train<- ROCR::performance(pred_train, 'auc')
# 0.6675131
```

Both train and test AUC statistics (that is, 0.67 and 0.68) pinpoint a satisfactory discriminatory power. This is particularly relevant if we consider that only one BV and one MV are taken into account. It is worthwhile noting that these statistics can be estimated over time as per Example 3.4.6 referred to survival analysis.

- **Calibration.** Few main calibration checks are required for both portfolio-level and account-level models, as detailed below:
  - **Model accuracy.** Both portfolio-level and account-level models provide a forward-looking shape to apply on top of $PD_{i,s,t}$. As a consequence, the key challenge one needs to face is to accurately capture default rate evolution through time. In this regard, one may conduct the validation exercise by focusing on actual against fitted DRs.
    Example 3.3.5 summarises the key steps one needs to perform to validate model accuracy, based on a sequence of periods $\tau_1, \ldots, \tau_J$.

EXAMPLE 3.3.5 ACCOUNT-LEVEL MODEL-PREDICTED DRS

Let us focus again on Example 3.3.3. In what follows we explore model accuracy by comparing actual against fitted DRs through time. As a synthetic measure of their relationship, one may, for example, consider correlation. The following two key steps are performed:

1. Computation of panel mean values, and
2. Correlation analysis.

```
# 1. Computation of panel mean values
train_data<- train %>%
dplyr::group_by(report_date,year) %>%
dplyr::summarise(default_rate = mean(default_flag),
pd = mean(predict_logit)) %>%
dplyr::select(report_date, year, default_rate, pd)
# 2. Correlation analysis
corr_train<- cor(train_data$default_rate, train_data$pd, method='pearson')
# 0.7380183
```

Graphical inspection of Figure 3.11 confirms a good correlation.
It is worth noting that crisis peak is not completely reached by means of the fitted model. Alternative models, including additional variables (for example, ltv_utd) would have allowed achieving such a level. In this regard, balance between parsimony and fitting is a basic aspect of the modelling *art*, and is a source of debate between modellers.

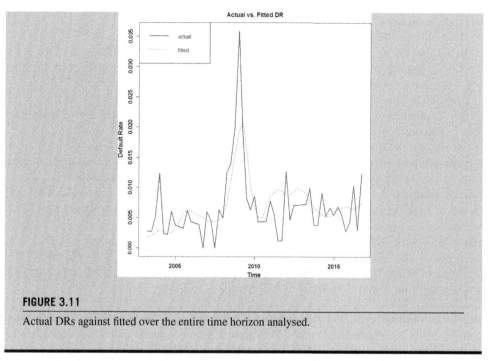

FIGURE 3.11

Actual DRs against fitted over the entire time horizon analysed.

- • **PD shift.** Checks need to be conducted both at an aggregated (portfolio) and account-level. Example 3.3.5 provides a reference for PD shift portfolio validation.
- • **Lifetime PD.** Lifetime PD validation is at the very heart of the entire process. Cohort analysis is commonly performed as detailed below:
  - – Compute historical multi-period DRs:
    - **a.** Identify a live portfolio (that is, non-defaulted accounts) at a given date.
    - **b.** Track defaults on a multi-period horizon (for example, one-year time intervals τ_j). For each period $j = 1, \ldots, J$, a default rate is computed as follows: $DR_{\tau_j} = \frac{Def_{\tau_j}}{Acc_{t_{j-1}}}.$[6]
    - **c.** Compute the cumulative default rate (for the entire portfolio) over the time horizon $h = \tau_1 + \ldots + \tau_J$. The computation is performed as follows for a given cohort:

$$DR_h^{cohort} = \prod_{j=1}^{J-1} S_{\tau_j} \cdot DR_{\tau_J}, \tag{3.12}$$

where $S_{\tau_k} = \prod_{j=1}^{k}(1 - DR_{\tau_j})$, and the superscript cohort indicates the portfolio in scope. A cohort represents a cluster of accounts live at a given starting point (that is, cohort initial point) investigated over a multi-period horizon.

---

[6]Where t_{j-1} refers to the end point of interval τ_{j-1} and beginning of interval τ, the analysis is restricted to the live portfolio at the beginning of the cohort under analysis.

- Fit multi-period PDs:
  d. Calibrate PIT (one-year) PDs at cohort's inception.
  e. Apply PD shift.
  f. Compute lifetime PDs by means of Equation (3.5). Then, summarise portfolio PDs by means of an appropriate statistic, such as portfolio mean (i.e., PD_h^{cohort}).
- Compare actual DRs against fitted:
  g. Compare DR_h^{cohort} against PD_h^{cohort}. Define acceptance thresholds by taking into account both level and volatility of default rates through time.
  h. Repeat the analysis for few different cohorts.

- **Out-of-sample and out-of-time stability.** One should verify how sensitive model parameters are on data used to develop the model and the time window chosen for the analysis.
- **Sensitivity analysis.** One needs to test how the model reacts to different economic conditions. Historical or hypothetical scenarios can be used to test it (for example, regulatory stress test scenarios).
- **BVs and MVs contribution.** Marginal analysis is widely used in finance. In our case, one may be interested to check how micro and macroeconomic variables contribute to the overall fitting. Greater MVs contribution would be expected during a crisis. Ageing is expected to play a relatively minor role in portfolios close to their maturity.
- **Reproducibility.** Model implementation is crucial to ensure an appropriate balance sheet representation. A positive replication test supports the results of the analysis. When a replication is negative, errors occurred almost surely. The question then remains whether the original study or the reproduced study in unfair. This is particularly true when large data sets are manipulated and then used to estimate lifetime PDs. A complete documentation describing the end-to-end modelling process is required. In general, incomplete documentation prevents from reproducing model development results. In all cases, inconsistency needs to be verified by means of replication exercises. The next section explores lifetime PDs from a survival modelling perspective.

3.4 SURVIVAL MODELLING

Survival modelling introduces a key innovation compared to GLM. The goal is to estimate a lifetime model at once by means of a survival function.

Few alternative approaches have been developed in the literature. Our focus is on KM (Kaplan and Meier, 1958), CPH regression (Cox, 1972), and AFT models. Figure 3.12 summarises this section's structure.

Section 3.4.1 focuses on KM approach. It allows us to familiarise with the key concepts underlying survival analysis. As a second step, Section 3.4.2 focuses on CPH regression. This model allows us to include time-varying variables, which are crucial to embed BV and MV fluctuations over time. Section 3.4.3 explores AFT models by means of few parametric functions, such as Weibull and exponential. Finally, Section 3.4.4 completes the investigation by focusing on model validation.

3.4.1 KM SURVIVAL ANALYSIS

A survival function S_τ represents the probability that an individual will not default over the interval τ. One needs to shape data structure to capture the survival curve by pointing out the role of censored data, as detailed in Figure 3.4.

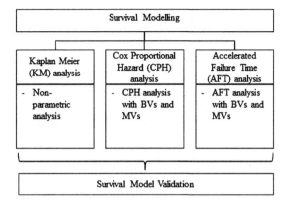

FIGURE 3.12

Workflow diagram for Section 3.4.

Example 3.4.1 introduces the KM framework.

EXAMPLE 3.4.1 INTRODUCTION TO KM SURVIVAL ANALYSIS

Let us consider the portfolio described in Table 3.9. For each ID, this table highlights last ob-servation time and default flag. Time represents either default or censoring. For example, ID 1 is censored at time 3 (without defaulting), whereas ID 2 defaults at time 3.

ID	Time	Default flag
1	3	0
2	3	1
3	6	0
4	5	0
5	1	1
6	7	0
7	3	0
8	4	1
9	2	1
10	6	1
11	8	0
12	8	0

Table 3.9 KM analysis portfolio data structure

Moving from Example 3.4.1, Table 3.9 allows us to further explore KM by focusing on each time interval. On this, let us consider two intervals τ_1 and τ_2, as detailed in Figure 3.13. Each interval τ_j has an initial and ending time, and t_0 is the starting point for both τ_1 and τ_2. On the other hand, t_{τ_1} denotes the ending point time for τ_1, and t_{τ_2} denotes the ending point for τ_2. In line with the above, if the number of accounts defaulting over a given time interval τ_j is d_j, and N_j denotes the number of

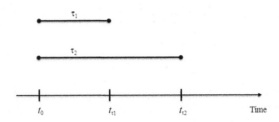

FIGURE 3.13

Survival time interval τ_j description.

accounts at risk at the beginning of τ_j (that is, accounts that will default or exit the portfolio over τ_j or later), then KM survival function is estimated as follows:

$$\hat{S}_\tau = \begin{cases} 1 & \text{if} \quad t_\tau < t_{\tau_1}, \\ \prod_{j=1}^{J} \left(1 - \frac{d_j}{N_j}\right) & \text{if} \quad t_{\tau_1} \leq t_{\tau_j} \leq t_{\tau_J}. \end{cases} \tag{3.13}$$

Example 3.4.2 provides more details on how to compute KM survival function.

EXAMPLE 3.4.2 KM SURVIVAL ANALYSIS IN DETAIL

Let us consider the portfolio described in Example 3.4.1. Firstly, one needs to re-order and aggregate accounts by time. Secondly, d_j and N_j are computed for each time j. Finally, $\left(1 - \frac{d_j}{N_j}\right)$ and $S(t_j)$ are derived, as detailed in Table 3.10. All IDs are considered separately, but the computation is performed at each t_{τ_j}.

Table 3.10 KM survival curve

ID	t_{τ_j}	Def	N_j	$\left(1 - \frac{d_j}{N_j}\right)$	S_{τ_j}
5	1	1	12	0.917	0.917
9	2	1	11	0.909	0.833
7	3	0			
1	3	0			
2	3	1	10	0.900	0.750
8	4	1	7	0.857	0.643
4	5	0	6	1.000	0.643
3	6	0			
10	6	1	5	0.800	0.514
6	7	0	3	1.000	0.514
11	8	0			
12	8	0	2	1.000	0.514

We perform the same analysis by means of the following steps:

1. Load data, and
2. Fit the survival function.

```
# 1. Load data
kmdef<-read.csv('chap3kaplanmeier.csv', header = TRUE, sep = ";", dec = ".")
attach(kmdef)
library(OIsurv)
# 2. Fit the survival function
my.surv <- Surv(Time, Status)
my.fit <- survfit(my.surv ~ 1)
detach(kmdef)
summary(my.fit)
# Call: survfit(formula = my.surv ~ 1)
# time n.risk n.event survival std.err lower 95% CI upper 95% CI
# 1     12      1     0.917   0.0798     0.773         1.000
# 2     11      1     0.833   0.1076     0.647         1.000
# 3     10      1     0.750   0.1250     0.541         1.000
# 4      7      1     0.643   0.1460     0.412         1.000
# 6      5      1     0.514   0.1639     0.275         0.961
```

The survival column in the summary table shows the same results highlighted in column S_{τ_j} of Table 3.10. Additionally, lower and upper confidence interval bands are detailed and graphically represented in Figure 3.14.

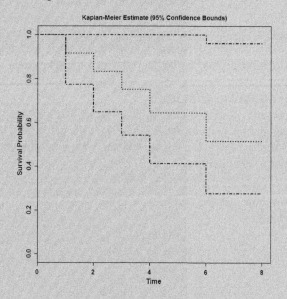

Kaplan-Meier Estimate (95% Confidence Bounds)

FIGURE 3.14

KM survival function.

Despite its simplicity, KM analysis is quite powerful and allows us to perform a series of studies to capture historical behaviour. However, one needs to link the survival function to macroeconomic variables to get forward-looking estimates. For this reason, instead of using KM, one may rely on the CPH approach, as described in the following section.

3.4.2 CPH SURVIVAL ANALYSIS

One way of analysing survival data is to rely on the following hazard function (Cox, 1972), which gives the rate of change of probability of failure at a time t

$$\lambda_t = \lim_{\tau \to 0} \frac{P(t \leq \xi < t + \tau | \xi > t)}{\tau}, \tag{3.14}$$

where ξ is a random variable associated with default time. The probability of survival at time t can be represented in terms of hazard function as follows:

$$S_\tau = \exp\left(-\int_{t_0}^{t_\tau} \lambda(u)du\right). \tag{3.15}$$

In line with ECL requirements, one needs to include a vector of covariates explaining default events. The following CHP model points out the interaction of a non-parametric proportional hazard and time-varying covariates. In terms of notation, we drop the subscript τ to avoid unnecessary complication as follows:

$$\lambda_{i,s,t|\mathbf{z}_{i,s,t}}^{CPH} = \lambda_{0,i,s,t}^{CPH} \cdot \exp(\boldsymbol{\beta}' \mathbf{z}_{i,s,t}), \tag{3.16}$$

where $\lambda_{0,i,s,t}^{CPH}$ is the hazard rate baseline function (that is, the subscript 0 denotes the concept of baseline), and $\mathbf{z}_{i,s,t}$ is an $(r + p) \times 1$ vector, including both BVs and MVs, as detailed in Equation (3.4).

Example 3.4.3 provides more details on how to deal with the CPH model.

EXAMPLE 3.4.3 CPH SURVIVAL ANALYSIS

Let us consider the portfolio described in Example 3.4.1. In this case, we distinguish between repayment (that is, RE) and interest only (that is, IO) accounts, as detailed in Table 3.11.

Armed with this enhanced data, we compare KM analysis on the new data against CPH. The following three main tasks are performed:

1. Upload data,
2. Fit KM survival function, and
3. Fit CPH survival function.

```
# 1. Upload data
coxphdef<-read.csv('chap3coxphx.csv', header = TRUE, sep = ";", dec = ".")
attach(coxphdef)
library(OIsurv)
# 2. Fit KM survival function
km.surv <- Surv(Time, Status)
```

```
km.fit <- survfit(km.surv ~ Product)
summary(km.fit)
# Product=IO
# time n.risk n.event survival std.err lower 95% CI upper 95% CI
# 2      3       1     0.667   0.272     0.2995        # 1
# 3      2       1     0.333   0.272     0.0673           1
# 4      1       1     0.000   NaN       NA              NA
# Product=RE
# time n.risk n.event survival std.err lower 95% CI upper 95% CI
# 1      9       1     0.889   0.105     0.706            1
# 6      5       1     0.711   0.180     0.433            1
# 3. Fit CPH survival function
coxph.surv <- Surv(Time, Status)
coxph.fit <- coxph(coxph.surv ~ Product , method='breslow')
summary(coxph.fit)
detach(coxphdef)
# coef exp(coef) se(coef)     z Pr(>|z|)
# ProductRE -2.43697   0.08742 1.16597 -2.09   0.0366 *
# ---
# Signif. codes:  0 '***' 0.001 '**' 0.01 '*' 0.05 '.' 0.1 ' ' 1
#            exp(coef) exp(-coef) lower .95 upper .95
# ProductRE  0.08742      11.44  0.008895    0.8592
# Concordance= 0.738  (se = 0.107 )
# Rsquare= 0.356   (max possible= 0.833 )
# Likelihood ratio test= 5.28  on 1 df,   p=0.02157
# Wald test         = 4.37  on 1 df,   p=0.03661
# Score (logrank) test = 6.82  on 1 df,   p=0.00903
```

Table 3.11 Example 3.4.1 with additional information on product type			
ID	**Time**	**Status**	**Product type**
1	3	0	RE
2	3	1	IO
3	6	0	RE
4	5	0	RE
5	1	1	RE
6	7	0	RE
7	3	0	RE
8	4	1	IO
9	2	1	IO
10	6	1	RE
11	8	0	RE
12	8	0	RE

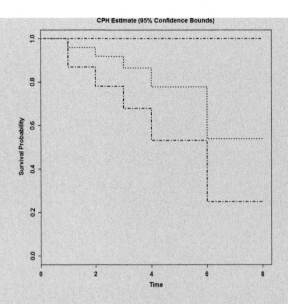

FIGURE 3.15

CPH survival function.

As a final step of the investigation, Table 3.12 compares KM and CPH estimates. (See Figure 3.15.)

Table 3.12 KM and CPH survival comparison				
Time	KM	KP RE	KM IO	CPH
1	0.917	1.000	0.889	0.958
2	0.833	0.667	0.889	0.918
3	0.750	0.333	0.889	0.865
4	0.643	0.000	0.889	0.778
5	0.643	0.000	0.889	0.778
6	0.514	0.000	0.711	0.539
7	0.514	0.000	0.711	0.539
8	0.514	0.000	0.711	0.539

Real data imply additional issues compared to what have been examined so far. One of the main challenges is to consider a database populated with accounts originating from different time periods. Based on this, the survival function described in Equation (3.15) covers an interval τ, regardless of the actual origination point. Figure 3.16 highlights how accounts are aligned to estimate the model. Left and right censoring plays an important role. The left hand-side panel is taken from Figure 3.4. The right hand-side panel shows how to align each observation in terms of time since origination. The latter is the typical view investigated in survival analysis (that is, probability of survival since origination).

Example 3.4.4 provides more details on how to deal with the CPH model with time varying variables.

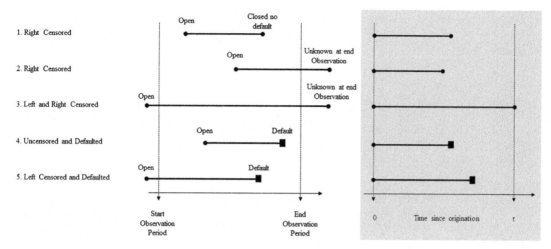

FIGURE 3.16

Re-alignment of observation along the survival horizon.

EXAMPLE 3.4.4 CPH SURVIVAL ANALYSIS

Let us start from the loan database analysed in Example 3.2.1. The following steps are performed:

1. Create train and test samples, and
2. Fit CPH model.

```
# 1. Create train and test samples
# 1.1. Create variable seasoning
ltpd_panel$seasoning<-
dplyr::if_else(ltpd_panel$remaining_term> 36,1,0)
# 1.2. Create samples
train_survcph<- ltpd_panel %>%
dplyr::filter(sample == 'train')
test_survcph<- ltpd_panel %>%
dplyr::filter(sample == 'test')
```

For each ID, a series of rows correspond to consecutive reporting dates. When default_ind is 1, a default occurred, whereas 0 indicates non-default or censoring. This variable represents the worse status throughout the entire period under analysis. The variable default_flag (not shown in Figure 3.17) aligns with loan_status to highlight a default occurrence. Additionally, TOB refers to the number of quarters since origination, whereas start_time and end_time represent the window to include into CPH function to fit the model.

```
# 2. Fit the CPH model with time-dependent variables
library(survival)
```

```
fit_coxph<- coxph(Surv(start_time,end_time,default_flag)~
ltv_utd+seasoning+hpi+ir , data=train_survcph, method = 'efron')
summary(fit_coxph)
#                coef exp(coef)  se(coef)      z Pr(>|z|)
# ltv_utd    0.394399  1.483493  0.046328   8.513  < 2e-16 ***
# seasoning -2.149792  0.116508  0.204027 -10.537  < 2e-16 ***
# hpi       -0.079905  0.923204  0.008902  -8.976  < 2e-16 ***
# ir        -0.514896  0.597563  0.096219  -5.351 8.73e-08 ***
# ---
# Signif. codes:  0 '***' 0.001 '**' 0.01 '*' 0.05 '.' 0.1 ' ' 1
```

id	report_date	year	loan_status	default_ind	tob	first_time	last_time	num_periods	start_time	end_time
1112556	2003-06-30	2003	good	1	18	17	20	4	18	19
1112556	2003-09-30	2003	good	1	19	17	20	4	19	20
1112556	2003-12-31	2003	bad	1	20	17	20	4	20	21
1112700	2003-03-31	2003	good	0	14	14	56	43	14	15
1112700	2003-06-30	2003	good	0	15	14	56	43	15	16
1112700	2003-09-30	2003	good	0	16	14	56	43	16	17
1112700	2003-12-31	2003	good	0	17	14	56	43	17	18

FIGURE 3.17

Time data structure.

All variables entering the model are highly significant. Their signs are aligned with expectations. Checks on discriminatory power and accuracy are scrutinised in the validation section. Figure 3.18 shows the evolution of the fitted survival function.

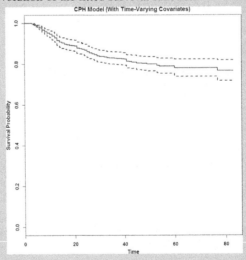

FIGURE 3.18

CPH model with time-varying covariates.

The next section describes how to approach survival modelling from the AFT perspective.

3.4.3 AFT SURVIVAL ANALYSIS

In AFT models, covariates act as acceleration factors to speed up or slow down the survival process, as compared to the baseline survival function. The hazard function is as follows:

$$\lambda_{i,s,t|\mathbf{z}_{i,s,t}}^{AFT} = \lambda_{0,i,s}^{AFT}\left[t \cdot \exp(\boldsymbol{\beta}'\mathbf{z}_{i,s,t})\right]\exp(\boldsymbol{\beta}'\mathbf{z}_{i,s,t}), \tag{3.17}$$

where, a log-linear form as $\log(t_d) = \boldsymbol{\beta}'\mathbf{z} + \sigma\epsilon$ holds. Based on this, the error term ϵ follows some distribution like, for example Weibull or exponential, and σ as an additional parameter to rescale ϵ.

The key advantage of AFT is its defining a given functional form for $\lambda_{0,i,s}^{AFT}$. The survival is then computed by means of a multiplicative relation. Indeed, $\lambda_{0,i,s}^{AFT}$ does not depend on time. On the contrary, $\lambda_{0,i,s,t}^{CPH}$ in Equation (3.16) is time-dependent and enters into the integral to compute the survival probability over a given time horizon τ.

Example 3.4.5 focuses on Weibull and exponential AFT model fitting.

EXAMPLE 3.4.5 AFT SURVIVAL ANALYSIS

Let us start from the loan database analysed in Example 3.4.4. The following steps are performed:

1. Fit Weibull survival function, and
2. Fit exponential survival function.

```
# 1. Fit Weibull survival function
library(flexsurv)
fit_weib<- flexsurvreg(Surv(start_time,end_time,default_flag,
type = 'interval') ~ ltv_utd+ seasoning + hpi+ ir,
dist = 'weibull', data = train_survcph)
# Estimates:
#                 data mean        est       L95%       U95%
# shape                 NA    1.58e+00   1.43e+00   1.76e+00
# scale                 NA    9.71e+07   3.63e+06   2.59e+09
# ltv_utd         5.17e+01   -2.41e-01  -3.05e-01  -1.77e-01
# seasoning       9.71e-01    6.36e-01   3.83e-01   8.89e-01
# hpi             3.61e+00    6.09e-02   4.83e-02   7.34e-02
# ir              3.49e+00   -1.05e-01  -1.95e-01  -1.57e-02
# 2. Fit exponential survival function
fit_exp<- flexsurvreg(Surv(start_time,end_time,default_flag,
type = 'interval') ~ ltv_utd+ seasoning + hpi+ ir,
dist = 'exp', data = train_survcph)
# Estimates:
```

```
#              data mean       est      L95%      U95%
# rate               NA   2.53e-12  2.91e-14  2.20e-10
# ltv_utd       5.17e+01   3.85e-01  2.95e-01  4.75e-01
# seasoning     9.71e-01  -1.31e+00 -1.66e+00 -9.52e-01
# hpi           3.61e+00  -9.36e-02 -1.11e-01 -7.63e-02
# ir            3.49e+00   4.27e-02 -9.81e-02  1.83e-01
```

The next section focuses on the survival modelling validation.

3.4.4 SURVIVAL MODEL VALIDATION

The validation process for survival models shares most of the activities listed for lifetime GLM. Some specific checks are summarised as follows:

a. **Data validation.** The vast majority of checks are listed in Section 3.3.3. In what follows we focus on survival specificities.

- **Data completeness.** As detailed in Section 3.4.2, one is required to align observation along the survival horizon. Consequently, lack of information usually affects highest maturities. One needs to ascertain an effective data coverage throughout the entire lifetime surface or, at least, its most important nodes.

b. **Methodology validation.** One needs to evaluate the combination of data availability and methodological framework. This is even more relevant in survival analysis, where each account is tracked through time. The choice of CPH instead of AFT modelling needs to be adequately justified and supported in terms of data availability, business, and methodological soundness.

c. **Statistical testing validation.** The focus is the following:

- **Discriminatory power.** The analysis is performed by means of the usual metrics, such as AUC and Gini index. Example 3.4.6 provides hints on how to perform it on the CPH model described in Example 3.4.4.

EXAMPLE 3.4.6 CPH DISCRIMINATORY POWER ANALYSIS

Let us consider the model developed in Example 3.4.4. Discriminatory power analysis is conducted by means of the following steps:

1. Predict based on estimated CPH model, and
2. Compute ROC curve at different time points.

```
# 1. Predict based on estimated CPH model
lp_train<- predict(fit_coxph, type = 'lp', newdata = train_survcph)
lp_test<- predict(fit_coxph, type = 'lp', newdata = test_survcph)
library(risksetROC)
# 2. Compute ROC curve at different time points
roc.test1 <- risksetROC(Stime = test_survcph$end_time,
status = test_survcph$default_flag, marker = lp_test,
predict.time = 4, method = 'Cox', main = 'Test data: ROC curve',
lty = 2, lwd = 2, col = 'red')
```

Figure 3.19 points out model's good discriminatory power for different time interval h (that is, 1y, 3y, 5y, 7y, 10y).

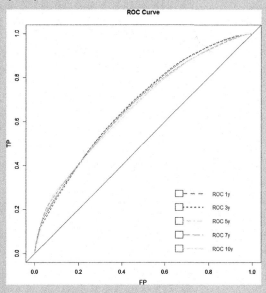

FIGURE 3.19

CPH ROC analysis over different time horizons (train set).

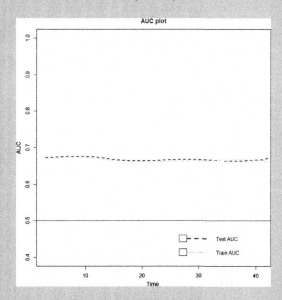

FIGURE 3.20

AUC evolution over different time horizons.

Figure 3.20 highlights a consistent high discriminatory power computed in terms of AUC over increasing time horizons for both train and test sets.

- **Calibration.** The GLM analysis, even for the survival validation model accuracy and lifetime PD, plays a crucial role as indicated below.
  - **Model accuracy.** All survival models provide an estimate over a given horizon. Nevertheless, one may be interested on sub-periods. Consequently, $\widehat{PD}_{i,s,\tau_j}$ can be derived by means of the following ratio:

$$\widehat{PD}_{i,s,\tau_j} = \widehat{PD}_{i,s,(t_{\tau_{j,init}},t_{\tau_{j,end}}]} = \frac{\hat{S}_{t_{\tau_{j,end}}} - \hat{S}_{t_{\tau_{j,init}}}}{S_{t_{\tau_{j,init}}}}, \tag{3.18}$$

where $t_{\tau_{j,init}}$ and $t_{\tau_{j,end}}$ represent the beginning and the end of the interval τ_j. As an example, one may focus on a one-year horizon as described in Example 3.4.7.

EXAMPLE 3.4.7 CPH DEFAULT RATE VALIDATION

Let us focus again on the model developed in Example 3.4.4. One-year PDs are derived by means of Equation (3.18).

Figure 3.21 compares actual DR against estimated one-year PDs over the period under analysis. Just as in the account-level modelling described in Section 3.3.2, CPH estimates allow us to capture time series key features (for example, rate jump after 2007–2009 crisis).

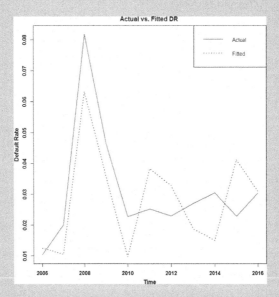

FIGURE 3.21

Actual one-year DR versus fitted PDs over time.

A 0.53 correlation between these time series provides us additional comfort on model accuracy.

Checks can be performed by means of other metrics as listed below:
- Concordance. The idea is to consider all possible pairs of observations and sort them into concordant and discordant groups, based on actual and predicted outcomes. Given the summary results of CPH regression, a very high concordance (that is, 0.754) holds for the model fitted in Example 3.4.4.
- Residuals. Residuals for survival data are somewhat different than for other types of models. This is mainly due to the censoring. Schoenfeld (1982) showed that the residuals are asymptotically uncorrelated and have expectation zero under the CPH model. Tests on residuals are usually very conservative.
- CPH proportionality. There are several options for checking the assumption of proportional hazards. Example 3.4.8 highlights how to perform the test based on the CPH model investigated so far.

EXAMPLE 3.4.8 CPH PROPORTIONALITY TEST
Let us consider Example 3.4.4. The following R code allows us to check the proportionality assumption on each of the explanatory variables included in the model.

```
# 1. Test on proportionality assumption
zph<- cox.zph(fit_coxph)
#                 rho      chisq      p
# ltv_utd     0.009475 0.049007 0.825
# seasoning  -0.061423 0.881060 0.348
# hpi         0.042260 0.770054 0.380
# ir          0.000662 0.000159 0.990
# GLOBAL            NA 2.579786 0.630
```

From the above output, the test is not statistically significant both for each covariate, and globally. We can assume proportionality to hold.

- **Lifetime PD.** For lifetime validation one may rely on what follows:
  - Cohort analysis. One may refer to the idea underlying the analysis described in Section 3.3.3. A specific cohort is chosen. Then, the evolution of this portfolio is tracked through time. For example, one may identify DR_{τ_j} as target variable. Thereafter, estimates from the model are compared against it. The process is repeated for alternative cohorts representative of the portfolio under inspection.
  - Overall portfolio dynamics. The entire portfolio is investigated over the most recent period to assess discrepancies between target and predicted. The choice of the time horizon depends upon a series of elements, such as data availability and product characteristics.
- **Out-of-sample and out-of-time stability, sensitivity analysis, and micro-macro variable contribution.** All these analyses are central throughout the validation process. The same criteria defined in Section 3.3.3 apply to survival analysis.

The next section provides the machine learning (ML) view to model lifetime PDs.

3.5 LIFETIME MACHINE LEARNING (ML) MODELLING

The key idea underlying ML is to fit data by optimising a given objective function. Two main features characterise ML. Firstly, ML is user-friendly. Secondly, it is highly data-adaptive and virtually model-assumption-free. Figure 3.22 highlights the main areas of analysis.

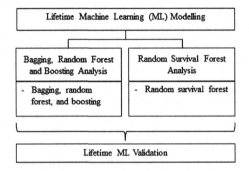

FIGURE 3.22

Workflow diagram for Section 3.5.

Section 3.5.1 focuses on bagging, random forest and boosting to fit account-level panel data. In Section 3.5.2 survival analysis is embedded within a random forest procedure. In random forests, randomisation is introduced in two forms. Firstly, a randomly drawn bootstrap sample of the data is used for growing the tree. Secondly, the tree learner is grown by splitting nodes on randomly selected predictors. Finally, Section 3.5.3 provides hints on how to validate ML lifetime modelling.

3.5.1 BAGGING, RANDOM FOREST, AND BOOSTING LIFETIME PD

As per the GLM account-level approach, the analysis is conducted by considering a restricted set of variables. Likewise, PD shift and lifetime estimates are performed, as discussed in Section 3.3.

Example 3.5.1 provides a guidance on how to estimate a link function, based on BVs and MVs.

EXAMPLE 3.5.1 LINK FUNCTION ESTIMATION VIA RANDOM FOREST

Let us consider the account-level data set first introduced in Example 3.2.1 and then studied throughout the chapter. A link function is estimated by means of the following steps:

1. Fit random forest, and
2. Predict the fitted model.

Train and test data are named train_def and test_def, as detailed below.

```
# 1. Fit random forest
# 1.1. Factor dependent variable
train_def <- ltpd_panel %>% dplyr::filter(sample=="train")
test_def <- ltpd_panel %>%  dplyr::filter(sample=="test")
train_def$def_char=as.factor(ifelse(train_def$default_flag==0,
'No','Yes'))
```

```
test_def$def_char=as.factor(ifelse(test_def$default_flag==0,
'No','Yes'))
# 1.2. Fit model
library(randomForest)
set.seed(123)
rf_def <- randomForest(def_char ~ tob+ltv_utd+
gdp+uer+cpi+hpi+ir+gdp_lag, data=train_def, mtry=3,
ntree=50, importance=TRUE, na.action=na.omit)
importance(rf_def)
#                  No       Yes MeanDecrAccuracy MeanDecrGini
# tob        2.757835  4.899592         3.374712     3.749418
# ltv_utd   53.728107 37.401487        54.123137   241.072146
# gdp       10.813693  6.458750        10.843507    17.787527
# uer       10.268828  5.461852        10.279786    31.103481
# cpi       10.547149  5.109640        10.572381    20.058706
# hpi       12.095337  6.209648        12.159406    15.495353
# ir        12.824807 11.295403        12.861711    27.378331
# gdp_lag   10.255892  7.007357        10.288429    13.546428
```

The variable ltv_utd plays an important role in explaining the phenomenon in conjunction with all MVs. On the other hand, TOB has a relatively low importance.

In terms of fitting, one may follow the same procedure described in Example 3.3.5 for comparing actual and fitted quarterly default rate time series, as pointed out in Figure 3.23. From a visual perspective, these two curves are quite close to each other. For more details on validation, one may refer to Section 3.5.3.

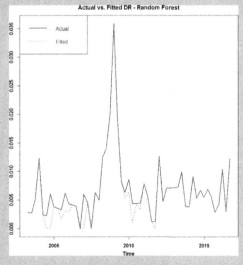

FIGURE 3.23

DR actual versus fitted analysis based on random forest model.

Example 3.5.2 performs the same analysis as above, by focusing on boosting instead of random forest.

EXAMPLE 3.5.2 LINK FUNCTION ESTIMATION VIA BOOSTING

Let us consider the same database examined in Example 3.5.1. A boosting model estimates a link function by means of the following steps:

1. Fit boosting model, and
2. Predict.

```
# 1. Fit boosting
library(gbm)
set.seed(123)
boost_shr_def <- gbm(default_flag ~ tob+ltv_utd+
gdp+uer+cpi+hpi+ir+gdp_lag, data=train_def,
distribution = 'gaussian', n.trees = 50, interaction.depth=4,
shrinkage=0.3,verbose=F)
summary(boost_shr_def)
#      var     rel.inf
# ltv_utd 55.1285498
# ir       37.7006750
# uer       2.6785451
# tob       2.2417450
# gdp_lag   0.8293945
# gdp       0.6111673
# hpi       0.4184094
# cpi       0.3915139
# 2. Predict
train_def$def_boost_shr <- predict(boost_shr_def,
newdata=train_def, n.trees=50)
test_def$def_boost_shr <- predict(boost_shr_def,
newdata=test_def, n.trees=50)
```

Figure 3.24 compares actual against fitted outcome (that is, 0, 1 default flag) distributions. It is worth noting that fitted results in some cases fall outside the [0,1] interval. Therefore one needs to impose extra constraints.

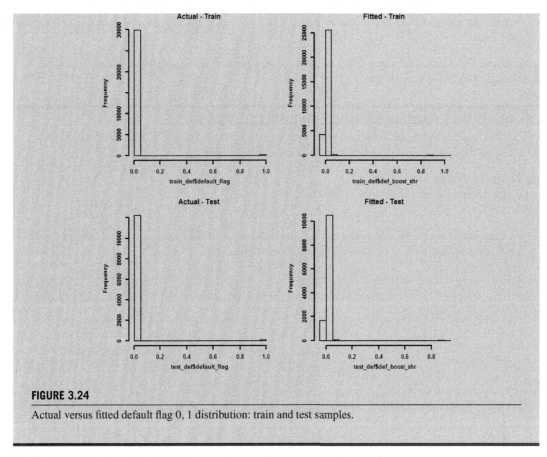

FIGURE 3.24

Actual versus fitted default flag 0, 1 distribution: train and test samples.

The next section introduces survival analysis by means of random forest.

3.5.2 RANDOM SURVIVAL FOREST LIFETIME PD

In Section 3.4 few alternative survival models were examined. Moving from KM approach, CPH was then described, and finally AFT methods was explored. It is now worth pointing out that efforts have been made to define a consistent framework sharing the goal of survival analysis and the flexibility of random forest (Ishwaran et al., 2008).

The algorithm is broadly described as follows:

- **Boostrap draws.** Draw bootstrap samples from the original data.
- **Grow tree size.** At each node of the tree, randomly select predictors for splitting, based on a given criterion. A node is split on that predictor, which maximises survival differences across daughter nodes.
- **Complete a tree.** Grow the tree to full size.
- **Hazard rate.** Calculate an ensemble cumulative hazard estimate by combining information from the trees.

- **Out-of-bag error.** Compute an out-of-bag (OOB) error rate for the ensemble derived using the fitted trees.

Example 3.5.3 provides some hints on how to perform survival analysis by means of the above-detailed random forest framework.

EXAMPLE 3.5.3 RANDOM SURVIVAL FOREST ANALYSIS

Let us consider the same database examined in Examples 3.5.1 and 3.5.2. Random survival forest modelling is performed by means of the following steps:

1. Create train and test samples,
2. Fit random survival forest model, and
3. Predict.

Data preparation relies on a process similar to that of the GLM analysis. A column for train and test identification was created on the data panel data set.

```
# 1. Create train and test samples
# 1.1. Filter the last row of each account
ltpd_surv<- ltpd_panel %>%
dplyr::filter(tob == last_time) %>%
dplyr::arrange(id, tob)
# 1.2. Train and test samples
train_surv<- ltpd_surv %>%
dplyr::filter(sample == 'train')
test_surv<- ltpd_surv %>%
dplyr::filter(sample == 'test')
# 2. Fit random survival forest model
library(randomForestSRC)
library(glmnet)
set.seed(123)
# 2.1. Fit model
rfsurv_def <- rfsrc(Surv(last_time, default_ind) ~
tob+ltv_utd+gdp+uer+cpi+hpi+ir+gdp_lag,data=train_surv,
ntree = 100, tree.err=TRUE)
print(rfsurv_def)
# Sample size: 1141
# Number of deaths: 231
# Number of trees: 100
# Forest terminal node size: 3
# Average no. of terminal nodes: 119.92
# No. of variables tried at each split: 3
# Total no. of variables: 8
# Analysis: RSF
```

```
# Family: surv
# Splitting rule: logrank
# Error rate: 5.96%
```

Figure 3.25 highlights the contribution of each variable to default phenomenon explanation. Time-on-book has a positive effect at the beginning of the mortgage life. Then, the probability of default reduces. Loan-to-value (ltv_utd), unemployment rate (UER), and consumer price index (CPI) growth have a positive relationship with default (that is, an increase in these variables is accompanied by an increase of defaults). On the other hand, gross domestic product (GDP) growth and house price index growth have a reverse relationship. A more complex relationship characterises long-term interest rates.

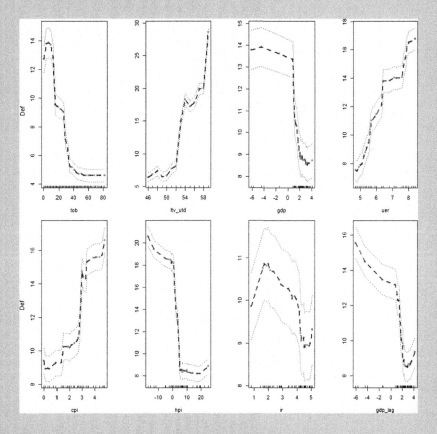

FIGURE 3.25

Variable partial contribution (random survival forest).

Figure 3.26 points out the out-of-bag survival function for the first 100 observations and their corresponding cumulative hazard rate.

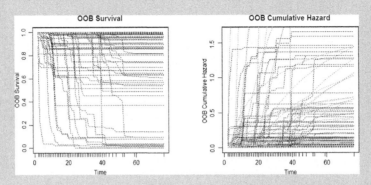

FIGURE 3.26

OOB survival and cumulative hazard.

```
# 2.2. Variable importance
vimp_srsurv <- vimp(rfsurv_def,
na.action = 'na.impute')$importance
print(data.frame(vimp_srsurv))
#          vimp_srsurv
# ltv_utd  0.12391679
# tob      0.10022866
# uer      0.07435623
# hpi      0.07178932
# cpi      0.04333724
# gdp      0.03828858
# gdp_lag  0.02907631
# ir       0.02652508
# 3. Predict model
pred_test <- predict(rfsurv_def, test_surv, n.trees=100)
print(pred_test)
# Sample size of test (predict) data: 489
# Number of deaths in test data: 79
# Number of grow trees: 100
# Average no. of grow terminal nodes: 119.92
# Total no. of grow variables: 8
# Analysis: RSF
# Family: surv
# Test set error rate: 5.01%
```

The next section focuses on ML model validation.

3.5.3 LIFETIME ML VALIDATION

ML validation is aligned with the process adopted for GLM and survival analyses. In what follows, the focus is on ML specific features.

a. **Data validation.** Checks listed in Sections 3.3.3 and 3.4.4 also apply to ML.
b. **Methodology validation.** One should compare alternative approaches by pointing out their main strengths and limitations.
c. **Statistical testing validation.** The focus is on the following:

- **Discriminatory power.** The analysis is commonly performed by means of AUC and Gini index. Example 3.5.4 serves as a guide to investigate ML discriminatory power. The focus is on random forest. Nevertheless, the procedure can easily be extended to other ML models.

EXAMPLE 3.5.4 RANDOM FOREST DISCRIMINATORY POWER ANALYSIS

Let us consider the model developed in Example 3.5.1. Discriminatory power analysis is conducted by means of the following steps:

1. Compute Gini index,
2. Calculate AUC, and
3. Investigate DR-PD correlation.

```
# 1. Compute Gini index
# 1.1. Predict RF model
train_def$def_rf <- predict(rf_def, newdata=train_def,
type='response')
train_def$def_rf_01=ifelse(train_def$def_rf=='Yes',1,0)
# 1.2. Calculate Gini index
library(optiRum)
gini_train_def<- optiRum::giniCoef(train_def$def_rf_01,
train_def$default_flag)
print(gini_train_def)
# 0.961039
# 2. Calculate AUC
library(ROCR)
pred_train<- ROCR::prediction(train_def$def_rf_01,
train_def$default_flag)
perf_train<- ROCR::performance(pred_train, 'tpr', 'fpr')
auc_train<- ROCR::performance(pred_train, 'auc')
print(auc_train@y.values[[1]])
# 0.9805195
```

Very high discriminatory power is shown by both Gini index (that is, train 0.96, test 0.86) and AUC (that is, train 0.98, test 0.93).

- **Model accuracy.** In line with Section 3.3.3, one may focus on one-year horizon to compare actual against fitted DRs. Example 3.5.5 serves as a guide to conduct the investigation.

EXAMPLE 3.5.5 RANDOM FOREST DEFAULT RATE VALIDATION

Let us focus again on the model developed in Example 3.5.1. The following steps are performed:

1. Compute average DRs (actual and fitted), and
2. Compare actual against fitted DRs.

```
# 1. Compute average DRs (actual and fitted)
train_data1<- train_def %>%
dplyr::group_by(report_date,year) %>%
dplyr::summarise(def_actual = mean(default_flag),
def_fit = mean(def_rf_01)) %>%
dplyr::select(report_date, year, def_actual, def_fit)
# 2. Compare actual against fitted DRs
corr_train<- cor(train_data1$def_actual,train_data1$def_fit)
# 0.98755
```

A very good approximation of DRs is highlighted both in train and test samples (that is, correlation 0.98 and 0.90).

- **Lifetime PD.** Lifetime validation is the crucial step of the entire process. Analysis is aligned with Sections 3.3.3 and 3.4.4.

The next section focuses on transition matrices to derive lifetime PDs.

3.6 TRANSITION MATRIX MODELLING

A common way of describing the dynamics of PDs is to use a Markov chain (Jarrow et al., 1997). Transition matrices are used to divide the PD range into a number of intervals. Each of them represents a state of the Markov chain. Figure 3.27 points out two main areas of investigation.

Section 3.6.1 focuses on PD movements (for example, one-year PDs) to reshape transition matrices, and apply the Markov property to derive lifetime PDs. Section 3.6.2 relies on Merton (1974) theory to build a sound transition matrix framework. Finally, Section 3.6.3 focuses on a non-parametric approach, where both BVs and MVs time series are used to fit rating evolutions. The goal is to fit a multi-state process rating-class time series.

3.6.1 NAÏVE MARKOV CHAIN MODELLING

A rating system uses a limited number of rating grades to rank borrowers according to their default probability. One defines a set of rating grade boundaries to translate default probability estimates into ratings. Let us assume a system with rating classes: 1, 2, 3, and a default category 4. The transition matrix for this rating system is a table listing the probabilities that an account rated 1 at the start of a period, then, has rating 1, 2, 3 or 4 at the end of the period. Rating 4 is absorbing. Therefore no migrations occur after reaching rating 4.

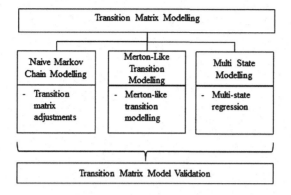

FIGURE 3.27

Workflow diagram for Section 3.6.

Table 3.13 Transition matrix scheme				
Rating	**Final**			
	1	**2**	**3**	**4**
Initial 1	$p_{\{1,1\},\tau}$	$p_{\{1,2\},\tau}$	$p_{\{1,3\},\tau}$	$p_{\{1,4\},\tau}$
2	$p_{\{2,1\},\tau}$	$p_{\{2,2\},\tau}$	$p_{\{2,3\},\tau}$	$p_{\{2,4\},\tau}$
3	$p_{\{3,1\},\tau}$	$p_{\{3,2\},\tau}$	$p_{\{3,3\},\tau}$	$p_{\{3,4\},\tau}$
4	0	0	0	1

Table 3.13 illustrates a simple transition matrix. On this basis, $p_{\{j,w\},\tau}$ represents the probability of moving from rating j (represented in row) to rating w (represented in column) over a period τ. For example, $p_{\{2,3\},\tau}$ highlights the probability to move from rating 2 to rating 3 over the interval τ (for instance, one-year).

Two major methods are usually considered to assess the probability to move from a class to another, as detailed below.

- **Cohort (frequentist) approach.** In line with cohort method, transition probabilities are estimated as follows:

$$p_{\{j,w\},\tau} = \frac{N_{\{j,w\},\tau}}{N_{\{j\},t_0}}, \tag{3.19}$$

where $N_{\{j,w\},\tau}$ is the number of accounts moving from j to w over the period τ, whereas $N_{\{j\},t_0}$ represents the number of accounts in class j at the beginning of the period (that is, t_0). If the interest is on a longer horizon $h = \tau_1 + \ldots + \tau_J$, one simply needs to define a corresponding observation interval and compute Equation (3.19) over h, instead of τ. On the other hand, if one assumes transitions to be independent across the periods under investigation, an h-period transition matrix (that is, $h = \tau_1 + \ldots + \tau_J = \tau + \ldots + \tau$) is derived by multiplying J times the τ-period matrix by itself, as detailed below:

$$\mathbf{P}_h = \underbrace{\mathbf{P}_\tau \times \ldots \times \mathbf{P}_\tau}_{J\text{-times}}, \tag{3.20}$$

where $\mathbf{P}_\tau$ is an $m \times m$ transition matrix over the time horizon τ. In line with Equation (3.19), its elements are denoted $p_{\{j,w\},\tau}$.

• **Hazard rate (duration or transition intensity) approach.** Estimates of the cohort approach are not affected by the timing and sequencing of transitions within the period. An alternative approach relies on Markov chain theory (Jarrow et al., 1997). Firstly, one needs to estimate a so-called generator matrix Λ providing a general description of the transition behaviour. The off-diagonal entries of this matrix estimated over the interval τ are as follows:

$$\lambda_{\{j,w\},\tau} = \frac{N_{\{j,w\},\tau}}{\int_{t_0}^{t_\tau} \Gamma_j(u)du}, \tag{3.21}$$

where $\Gamma_j(u)$ denotes the number of accounts rated j at time u. In both cohort and hazard approaches, we divide the number of transitions by a measure of how many accounts are at risk of experiencing the transition. In the cohort approach, the counting is performed at discrete points in time, whereas in the hazard approach accounts are enumerated at any point in time. The on-diagonal entries are constructed as follows:

$$\lambda_{\{j,j\},\tau} = -\sum_{j \neq w} \lambda_{\{j,w\},\tau}. \tag{3.22}$$

From Markov chain mechanics, a transition matrix over a horizon h is derived from the generator matrix as follows:

$$\mathbf{P}_h = \exp(\Lambda h) = \sum_{k=0}^{\infty} \frac{\Lambda^k h^k}{k!}, \tag{3.23}$$

where Λh is the generator matrix multiplied by the scalar h.

Time-homogeneous Markov chains are commonly applied. It implies that $p_{\{j,w\}}$ does not depend on t. However, lifetime estimates rely on economic fluctuations. Therefore an adjustment can be introduced by moving towards a time-inhomogeneous process. Transition probabilities are time-dependent (that is, $p_{\{j,w\},t,\tau}$).

One may then think of combining a transition matrix approach with a model summarising the impact of macroeconomic changes to build the following:

• **Naïve Markov chain.** A transition matrix is built based on the following components:

    • Link function. In line with the multi-step method, described in Section 3.3, one may think of connecting PDs to macroeconomic fluctuations by means of a link function. The easiest way to tackle this problem is to rely on a portfolio-level analysis. The fitted linked function is used for transition matrix adjustments, as detailed below.

- Transition matrix adjustments. A multi-period cumulative transition matrix can be obtained as a product of the matrix times itself. In the case of time-inhomogeneous process, the following applies:

$$P_h^{naive} = \mathbf{P}_{\tau_1} \cdot \mathbf{P}_{\tau_2} \times \ldots \times \mathbf{P}_{\tau_J}, \tag{3.24}$$

where $h = \tau_1 + \ldots + \tau_J$.

Example 3.6.1 allows us to grasp how to conduct the analysis.

EXAMPLE 3.6.1 TWO-CLASS TRANSITION MATRIX ADJUSTMENT

Let us consider the following one-year transition matrix:

$$P_{\tau_1}^{orig} = \begin{pmatrix} 96.00\% & 4.00\% \\ 0.00\% & 100.00\% \end{pmatrix},$$

where the superscript $orig$ highlights that no macroeconomic impact has been considered.

Table 3.14 reports both scenarios analysed in Example 3.3.2 and the corresponding one-year PD evolution.

Table 3.14 Multi-period macroeconomic scenario and PD evolution

	τ_1	τ_2	τ_3	τ_4	τ_5
GDP_t^{growth}	−2.94%	1.05%	1.50%	1.75%	2.00 %
UER_t	8.50%	9.00%	7.50%	7.00%	6.80%
PD	5.08%	4.98%	3.43%	2.91%	2.68%

Moving from the above, the following cumulative transition matrices are obtained by applying Equation (3.24) to what is described above:

$$\mathbf{P}_{\tau_1} = \begin{pmatrix} 94.92\% & 5.08\% \\ 0.00\% & 100.00\% \end{pmatrix},$$

$$\mathbf{P}_{[\tau_1+\tau_2]} = \begin{pmatrix} 90.20\% & 9.80\% \\ 0.00\% & 100.00\% \end{pmatrix},$$

$$\mathbf{P}_{[\tau_1+\tau_2+\tau_3]} = \begin{pmatrix} 87.10\% & 12.90\% \\ 0.00\% & 100.00\% \end{pmatrix},$$

$$\mathbf{P}_{[\tau_1+\ldots+\tau_4]} = \begin{pmatrix} 84.57\% & 15.43\% \\ 0.00\% & 100.00\% \end{pmatrix},$$

$$\mathbf{P}_{[\tau_1+...+\tau_5]} = \begin{pmatrix} 82.31\% & 17.69\% \\ 0.00\% & 100.00\% \end{pmatrix}.$$

All these matrices are in line with the cumulative analysis performed in Example 3.3.2.

One may follow few alternative schemes to make transition matrix naïve adjustments. Example 3.6.2 provides us a perspective of the mechanics one may follow in practice.

EXAMPLE 3.6.2 NAÏVE TRANSITION MATRIX ADJUSTMENTS

Let us consider the one-year transition matrix described in Table 3.15.

Table 3.15 Initial transition matrix

Rating		Final			
		1	2	3	4
Initial	1	80.00%	10.00%	8.00%	2.00%
	2	8.00%	78.00%	11.00%	3.00%
	3	6.00%	14.00%	76.00%	4.00%
	4	0.00%	0.00%	0.00%	100.00%

Based on an economic scenario, PDs increase as follows: 0.55% for rating class 1, 0.82% for rating class 2, and 1.08% for rating class 3.

Two alternative approaches are listed below:

• **Worst rating class full variation, equally distributed adjustment on other classes.** The following applies:
  ◦ The entire variation is allocated to the worst rating class. For instance, for initial rating, class 1 the entire variation is allocated to rating class 4. The following change applies class 4, 2.00% → 2.55%.
  ◦ The same variation, with opposite sign, is then equally distributed on other classes. As an example, for initial rating class 1, $\frac{-0.55\%}{3}$ is allocated to final classes 1, 2 and 3.

Table 3.16 shows post-adjustment transition matrix shape.

Table 3.16 Post adjustment matrix based on worst rating class full variation, and equally distributed adjustment on other classes

Rating		Final			
		1	2	3	4
Initial	1	79.82%	9.82%	7.82%	2.55%
	2	7.73%	77.73%	10.73%	3.82%
	3	5.64 %	13.64%	75.64%	5.08%
	4	0.00%	0.00%	0.00%	100.00%

• **Worst rating class half variation, rating-dependent distribution adjustment on other classes.** A more articulate process is followed:

- Half variation is allocated to the worst class. As an example, for initial rating class 1, $\frac{0.55\%}{2}$ is allocated to final rating class 4.
- A weighting scheme is followed to distribute the remaining variation among other rating classes. $\frac{0.55\%}{2} \cdot \frac{1}{2}$ is allocated to final rating classes 2 and 3 (above the diagonal). A 0.55% variation with sign minus is allocated to final rating class 1.

Table 3.17 summarises this framework's output.

Table 3.17 Worst rating class half variation, rating-dependent distribution adjustment on other classes

Rating		Final			
		1	**2**	**3**	**4**
Initial	1	79.45%	10.14%	8.14%	2.28%
	2	7.59%	77.59%	11.41%	3.41%
	3	5.82%	13.82%	75.82%	4.54%
	4	0.00%	0.00%	0.00%	100.00%

It is worth remarking that after naïve adjustments a transition matrix need to conserve all its fundamental characteristics (Trueck and Rachev, 2009).

In the case of time horizons of different length, one may rely on the following Taylor's expansion applied on a genericmatrix $\boldsymbol{\Gamma}$ as follows:

$$\ln(\boldsymbol{\Gamma}) = \sum_{k=1}^{\infty} \frac{(-1)^{k+1}(\boldsymbol{\Gamma}-\mathbf{I})^k}{k} = \boldsymbol{\Gamma} - \mathbf{I} - \frac{1}{2}(\boldsymbol{\Gamma}-\mathbf{I})^2 + \frac{1}{3}(\boldsymbol{\Gamma}-\mathbf{I})^3 - \ldots, \qquad (3.25)$$

and therefore:

$$\exp(\boldsymbol{\Gamma}) = \sum_{k=0}^{\infty} \frac{(\boldsymbol{\Gamma})^k}{k!} = \mathbf{I} + \boldsymbol{\Gamma} + \frac{1}{2}(\boldsymbol{\Gamma})^2 + \frac{1}{3!}(\boldsymbol{\Gamma})^3 + \ldots, \qquad (3.26)$$

where $\mathbf{I}$ is the identity matrix, and, in line with Markovian chains theory, the transition matrix for any time horizon can be calculated based on the generator matrix described in Equation (3.23).

The key drawback of naïve adjustments is a lack of a consistent economic framework. In contrast, the next section shows reliance on the Merton model to derive a multi-period transition matrix frame for lifetime PD modelling.

3.6.2 MERTON-LIKE TRANSITION MODELLING

In line with Merton (1974), a firm defaults when the value of assets falls below its liabilities. This reasoning can easily be extended to compare returns against a given threshold, as detailed in structural PD modelling in Chapter 1.[7]

---

[7]One may enrich the model by considering more than one factor, as in Example 3.3.1.

One may consider a single common factor ($\varkappa_t$),and an idiosyncratic noise component ($\epsilon_{i,s,t}$) driving normalised asset returns as follows:

$$\xi_{i,s,t} = \sqrt{\rho_{i,s}}\varkappa_t + \sqrt{1 - \rho_{i,s}}\epsilon_{i,s,t}, \qquad (3.27)$$

where $\sqrt{\rho_{i,s}}$ is the correlation between asset returns and the common factor (Duffie and Singleton, 2003), and $\varkappa_t$ and $\epsilon_{i,s,t}$ are independent and identically distributed $N(0, 1)$. Therefore $\xi_{i,s,t}$ has a standardised normal distribution.

A binary default random variable, is the starting point of the model, as detailed below:

$$y_{i,s,t} = \begin{cases} 1 & \text{for} \quad \xi_{i,s,t} \leq c_{i,s,t}, \\ 0 & \text{for} \quad \xi_{i,s,t} > c_{i,s,t}, \end{cases} \qquad (3.28)$$

where $c_{i,s,t}$ represents a default threshold. The following equation summarises the probability of default for a specific scenario x_{scen}:

$$\begin{aligned}
PD_{i,s,t|\varkappa_{scen}} &= P\left(\xi_{i,s,t} \leq c_{i,s,t} | \varkappa_{scen}\right) = \\
&= P\left(\sqrt{\rho_{i,s}}\varkappa_t + \sqrt{1 - \rho_{i,s}}\epsilon_{i,s,t} \leq c_{i,s,t} | \varkappa_{scen}\right) = \\
&= P\left(\epsilon_{i,s,t} \leq \frac{c_{i,s,t} - \sqrt{\rho_{i,s}}\varkappa_t}{\sqrt{1-\rho_{i,s}}} | \varkappa_{scen}\right) = \\
&= \Phi\left(\frac{c_{i,s,t} - \sqrt{\rho_{i,s}}\varkappa_t}{\sqrt{1-\rho_{i,s}}} | \varkappa_{scen}\right) = \\
&= \Phi\left(\frac{c_{i,s,t} - \sqrt{\rho_{i,s}}\varkappa_{scen}}{\sqrt{1-\rho_{i,s}}}\right).
\end{aligned} \qquad (3.29)$$

Instead of binary alternatives (that is, default against non-default), one may consider year-end rating classes. A series of rating bands related to cumulative probabilities of default are then used instead of a unique threshold. As an example, for a rating class CCC band, one may consider the cumulated probability of default inferred from the transition matrix as follows:[8]

$$\sum_{rating=default}^{CCC} Probability_{rating}.$$

The standard normal CDF (i.e., Φ^{-1}) is used as follows:

$$\begin{aligned}
Z_{default} &= \Phi^{-1}(P_{default}), \\
Z_{CCC} &= \Phi^{-1}(\textstyle\sum_{rating=default}^{CCC} P_{rating}), \\
Z_{B} &= \Phi^{-1}(\textstyle\sum_{rating=default}^{B} P_{rating}), \\
&\cdots
\end{aligned} \qquad (3.30)$$

where $Z_{(.)}$ represents the standard normal value, as outlined in the right-hand-side panel of Figure 3.28.

---

[8] In this example, the following rating structure applies: AAA, AA, A, BBB, BB, B, CCC, Default.

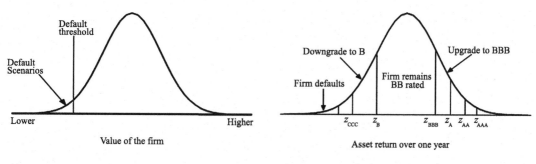

FIGURE 3.28

Structural model default threshold compared to rating bands.

The cumulative probability associated to move from rating class j to w can be represented as follows:

$$p^{cum}_{\{j,w\},s,t} = \Phi\left(\frac{c_{\{j,w\},s,t} - \sqrt{\rho_s}\,\varkappa_{scen}}{\sqrt{1 - \rho_s}}\right), \tag{3.31}$$

where $c_{\{j,w\},s,t}$ indicates a rating class threshold. Few manipulations of Equation (3.31) allow us to highlight the next relationship:

$$c_{\{j,w\},s,t} = \Phi^{-1}(p^{cum}_{\{j,w\},s,t})\sqrt{1 - \rho_s} + \rho_s\varkappa_{scen}. \tag{3.32}$$

One may consider the normalised creditworthiness index $\Psi_{s,t}$ as a representation of $\varkappa_{scen}$ by deriving the following:

$$p^{cum}_{\{j,w\},s,t} = \Phi\left(\Phi^{-1}(p^{cum}_{\{j,w\},s,t}) + \frac{\sqrt{\rho_s}}{\sqrt{1 - \rho_s}}\Psi_{s,t}\right). \tag{3.33}$$

Therefore for new projected values of $\Psi_{s,t}$, one may expect new rating bands.

Example 3.6.3 shows how to translate the above-detailed framework in practice.

EXAMPLE 3.6.3 MERTON-LIKE TRANSITION MATRIX MECHANICS

Let us consider the transition matrix described in Table 3.15. Table 3.18 shows its corresponding cumulative probabilities (that is, for each row, one needs to move from right to left by adding each column's (rating) probabilities).

Rating		Final			
		1	**2**	**3**	**4**
Initial	1	100.00%	20.00%	10.00%	2.00%
	2	100.00%	92.00%	14.00%	3.00%
	3	100.00%	94.00%	80.00%	4.00%
	4	100.00%	100.00%	100.00%	100.00%

Table 3.18 Cumulative distribution probabilities based on Table 3.15

If we then apply the standard normal inverse function to each element of Table 3.18, we obtain what is shown in Table 3.19.

Table 3.19 Inverse standard normal distribution thresholds applied to Table 3.18				
Rating	**Final**			
	1	**2**	**3**	**4**
Initial 1	N/A	−0.84	−1.28	−2.05
2	N/A	1.41	−1.08	−1.88
3	N/A	1.55	0.84	−1.75
4	N/A	N/A	N/A	N/A

We now need to make few assumptions related to Equation (3.33) implementation:

- $\rho = 0.99$.
- An overall 1.15% variation from the original setting to the new forecast condition applies.

New rating thresholds are derived, as listed in Table 3.20.

Table 3.20 Adjusted thresholds due to scenario fluctuation				
Rating	**Final**			
	1	**2**	**3**	**4**
Initial 1	N/A	−0.69	−1.13	−1.90
2	N/A	1.56	−0.93	−1.73
3	N/A	1.71	0.99	−1.60
4	N/A	N/A	N/A	N/A

As a last step, the inverse standard normal distribution is applied to the above thresholds. The new transition matrix is detailed in Table 3.21

Table 3.21 New transition matrix due to scenario fluctuation				
Rating	**Final**			
	1	**2**	**3**	**4**
Initial 1	75.51%	11.58%	10.06%	2.85%
2	5.98%	76.38%	13.45%	4.18%
3	4.40%	11.64%	78.47%	5.48%
4	0.00%	0.00%	0.00%	100.00%

Despite its appealing structure, few main drawbacks affect Merton-like transition adjustments. Firstly, difficulties arise when estimating the correlation parameter ρ. Secondly, the framework is designed for publicly traded firms. Accurate checks are required when extending this logic to privately held companies.

Another transition matrix framework is presented in the next section, where rating time series are crucial to inform the estimation process.

3.6.3 MULTI-STATE MODELLING

Moving from the idea of a cohort method, a multi-state Markov model captures movements between m states. The probability of moving away from the current state depends on the previous state. In this regard, one may consider transitions between states in continuous time, measured by an $m \times m$ intensity matrix $\mathbf{P}_t$, defined as a function of a matrix of variables $\mathbf{z}_{i,s,t}$, as follows:

$$\mathbf{P}_t = \begin{pmatrix} p_{\{1,1\},t} & p_{\{1,2\},t} & \cdots & p_{\{1,m-1\},t} & p_{\{1,m\},t} \\ p_{\{2,1\},t} & p_{\{2,2\},t} & \cdots & p_{\{2,m-1\},t} & p_{\{2,m\},t} \\ \vdots & \vdots & \ddots & \vdots & \vdots \\ p_{\{m-1,1\},t} & p_{\{m-1,2\},t} & \cdots & p_{\{m-1,m-1\},t} & p_{\{m-1,m\},t} \\ 0 & 0 & \cdots & 0 & 0 \end{pmatrix}, \tag{3.34}$$

where the transition intensity to move from state j to state w is as follows:

$$\lim_{\tau \to 0} \frac{P(Rating(t+\tau) = w | (Rating(t) = j)}{\tau}, \tag{3.35}$$

where $Rating(t)$ represents the rating at time t. The diagonal entries of $\mathbf{P}_t$ are constructed as the negative value of the sum of $p_{\{j,w\},t}$. In symbols, $p_{\{j,j\},t} = -\sum_{j \neq w}^{m} p_{\{j,w\},t}$.

We rely on the following equation to capture the role of both microeconomic and macroeconomic variables on the transition from rating j to w for a given account:

$$p_{\{j,w\},t} = p_{\{j,w\}}^{0} \exp\left(\boldsymbol{\beta}_{\{j,w\}}' \mathbf{z}_t \right), \tag{3.36}$$

where $\mathbf{z}_t$ denotes the set of both BVs and MVs affecting the probability of moving from state j to w. The intercept (that is, $p_{\{j,w\}}^{0}$) is specific to the transition intensity in t_0.

One may refer to *msm* package for R implementation. One of the major issues has to do with the need for large data sets to allow optimisation algorithms to converge. The next section focuses on PD transition matrix validation.

3.6.4 TRANSITION MATRIX MODEL VALIDATION

The validation process for transition matrix modelling does not substantially differ from what has been examined in previous validation sections. With regard to statistical testing, one needs to bear in mind that transition matrices need to conserve their features (for example, Markovian processes). Furthermore, specific attention needs to be devoted on off-diagonal distributions. Smooth decays usually applied to avoid unexpected jumps between contiguous classes need to be carefully inspected and tested.

3.7 SAS LABORATORY

Three main approaches are explored in what follows. Firstly, the focus is on GLM lifetime modelling. Secondly, attention moves towards survival analysis. Finally machine learning methods are investigated. An overview of SAS implementation is provided by considering all major examples already studied by means of R throughout the chapter.

SAS laboratory 3.7.1 focuses on GLM.

SAS LABORATORY 3.7.1 LIFETIME GLM ANALYSIS

Let us consider Example 3.3.3. As a starting point, one needs to upload the same data file, then the analysis is replicated by means of the following steps:

1. Create table mean DR,
2. Train and test samples,
3. Create new variables,
4. Perform correlation analysis, and
5. Fit logit regression.

```
/* 1. Create table mean DR */
data lifetimepd;
set work.chap3datasetpanel;
run;
proc sql;
create table mean_DR as select distinct
report_Date,
mean(default_flag) as DR

from lifetimepd
group by report_date;
quit;

proc sgplot data=mean_dr;
series x=report_date y=DR;
run;

/* 2. Train and test samples */
proc sort data=lifetimepd;by id default_ind;run;
proc surveyselect data=lifetimepd out=stratified_lifetimepd
method=srs rate=0.7 outall seed=2122;
strata id default_ind;run;

proc freq data=work.stratified_lifetimepd;
table Selected*default_ind /sparse norow nocol ;
```

```
run;

/* 3. Create new variables */
proc sql;
create table mean_DR as select distinct *,
mean(default_flag) as DR

from stratified_lifetimepd
group by report_date;
quit;
proc rank data=work.mean_DR (where=(selected=1))
groups=10 out=quantiles;
var remaining_term;
ranks R_remaining_Term;
run;
proc sql;
create table remaining_terms_bins as select distinct

R_remaining_term,
max(remaining_term) as max_bin,
mean(DR) as mean_DR
from quantiles

group by r_remaining_term;
quit;

data seasoning;
set quantiles;
if remaining_term < 36 then seasoning=1;
else seasoning=0;
run;

/* 4. Perform correlation analysis */
proc corr data=seasoning spearman;
var ir uer hpi gdp cpi income;
run;
ods graphics on;

/* 5. Fit logit regression */
proc genmod data=seasoning plots=all descending;
model default_flag=seasoning hpi/link=logit dist=binomial;
run;
```

SAS laboratory 3.7.2 provides some hints on survival analysis implementation.

SAS LABORATORY 3.7.2 SURVIVAL ANALYSIS

Let us consider the small dataset investigated in Example 3.4.1 and what has already been investigated in SAS laboratory 3.7.1. The following steps are performed to fit survival analysis, based on Kaplan Meier (KM) and Cox proportional hazard (CPH) approaches:

1. Fit KM survival function (on the small dataset of Example 3.4.1).
2. Fit CPH survival function.

```
/* 1. Fit KM survival function*/
data KM;
set work.'chap3coxphx (1)'n;
rename Status=Default;
run;
proc sort data=km; by time Default;run;

proc lifetest data=km plots=survival;
time time*default(0);
run;

/* 2. Fit CPH survival function*/
/* data seasoning */
proc phreg data=seasoning plots=survival;
model tob*default_flag(0)=ltv_utd seasoning hpi ir/
rl=both ties=efron;
run;
```

SAS laboratory 3.7.3 provides some hints on machine learning PD lifetime analysis.

SAS LABORATORY 3.7.3 ML LIFETIME ANALYSIS

Let us consider what has already been investigated in previous SAS laboratories. The following steps are performed to fit random forest and boosting:

1. Fit random forest, and
2. Fit boosting.

```
/* 1. Fit random forest */
proc hpforest data=seasoning criterion=Variance
maxtrees=100 vars_to_try=4 splitsize=200 leafsize=100
maxdepth=8 alpha=0.05;
target default_flag / level=interval;
input tob ltv_utd gdp uer cpi hpi ir gdp_lag / level=interval;
ods output fitstatistics=fitstats;
save file = 'C:\random_forest_pd_rules.bin';
run;
```

```
quit;

/* 2. Fit boosting */
proc treeboost data=seasoning exhaustive=5000 iterations=100
leafsize=50 maxdepth=2 shrinkage=0.3;
target default_flag / level=interval;
input tob ltv_utd gdp uer cpi hpi ir gdp_lag / level=interval;
score out=scored_GradientBoost;
importance out=imp;
quit;
```

3.8 SUMMARY

As a starting point, an overview on data to use for lifetime PD modelling was provided. Our main focus was on account-level panel time series necessary to study both behavioural variables (BVs) and macroeconomic variables (BVs). Alternative modelling approaches were then considered.

Firstly, generalised linear models (GLMs) were explored by focusing on two alternatives. On the one hand, a portfolio-level approach was introduced as a viable solution in the case of limited data availability. On the other hand, a data-intensive driven methodology inspired the account-level analysis. Based on this, a panel GLM model was developed to capture both BVs and MVs.

As a second step, survival analysis was investigated to estimate the entire lifetime PD curve all at once. Three approaches were studied: Kaplan–Meier (KP), Cox proportional hazard (CPH), and accelerated failure time (AFT). In this regard, KM was the first survival approach proposed in literature. It served the purpose of describing the key concepts underlying survival analysis. Then, CPH and AFT were considered as alternatives to build models based on both time-varying BVs and MVs.

Thirdly, machine learning (ML) methods were studied by focusing on bagging, random forest and boosting. These methodologies, introduced in Chapter 2, were tested against a time-dependent framework. A lifetime framework was then investigated, based on quarterly (or yearly) projected time series. Furthermore, random survival forest was used to link survival analysis and ML.

Finally, moving from Markov chain modelling, the last section focused on lifetime PDs, based on transition matrices. The main difference of transition matrix approaches, compared to other lifetime PDs, was reliance on rating classes instead of binary (that is, default, non-default) classes. Three main perspectives were inspected. Firstly a naive Markov chain model was presented. A Merton-like transition model was then considered to avoid the lack of economic justification challenging the previous approach. Eventually, multi-state modelling was briefly studied. Validation was examined as a crucial area to assess how genuine was the proposed methodology in combination with data availability.

Data and complementary examples' software code are available at www.tizianobellini.com.

SUGGESTIONS FOR FURTHER READING

Bellotti and Crook (2009) provide an overview of forward-looking lifetime PD analysis. Breeden and Thomas (2016) explore the relationship between PDs and macroeconomic variables through the lenses of a stress-testing framework. A reader-friendly and non-complex introduction to survival analysis is provided by Thomas et al. (2017). Dirick et al. (2017) provide benchmarks for time to default analysis via survival modelling. Additional details on how to fit Cox proportional hazard and accelerated failure time models by means of SAS can be found in Baesens et al. (2016). Reduced form models and Markov chains are extensively studied in credit risk. One may refer to Jarrow et al. (1997) for a formal dissertation and extensive description of Markov chains on transition matrices. For the conditional transition matrix approach, one may also refer to Belkin et al. (1998) and Malik and Thomas (2012).

APPENDIX A. PORTFOLIO-LEVEL PD SHIFT

A distinction operates between proportional and logit shift as listed below:

a. **Proportional shift.** One applies a PD variation to all accounts within the sub-portfolio s in line with the relative shift of $\Psi_{t,s}$, as detailed below[9]:

$$\dot{PD}^{pl,ps}_{i,s,t,\Delta} = PD_{i,s,t_0} \cdot \frac{\hat{\Psi}_{s,\Delta}}{\Psi_{s,t_0}}, \tag{3.37}$$

where the superscripts pl and ps indicate portfolio-level and proportional shift, and $\dot{PD}$ refers to a shifted PD.[10] The subscript Δ indicates a macroeconomic scenario. PD_{i,s,t_0} is the PIT account PD, and $\hat{\Psi}_{s,\Delta}$ is the estimated creditworthiness index, based on a given macroeconomic scenario (i.e., $\mathbf{x}_\Delta$).

Example 3.8.1 shows how to implement the proportional shift.

EXAMPLE 3.8.1 PROPORTIONAL SHIFT

Let us consider a portfolio made by 5 accounts described in Example 3.3.2. Table 3.22 reports it again to ease example's reading.

Table 3.22 Corporate and SME portfolio

ID	Segment	$PD_{i,s,t}$
1	Corporate	0.50%
2	Corporate	2.00%
3	Corporate	3.00%
4	SME	3.50%
5	SME	4.00%

---

[9]The subscript τ is omitted to ease the notation.
[10]The superscript · refers to the final outcome of a process, not to its variation.

Let us consider the linear model described in Example 3.3.1 together with the following macroeconomic scenario:

- UK GDP reduces by -2.94% $(GDP_{t,lag}^{growth})$.
- UK UER moves to 8.50% (UER_t).

Table 3.23 summarises the linear model coefficients, macroeconomic scenario values x_Δ, and the corresponding impact on the creditworthiness index.

Table 3.23 Scenario analysis on $\Psi_{s,t}$. † Level of UER (i.e., 8.50%)				
Variable	**Coefficient**	x_Δ		
intercept	-0.05204			
$GDP_{t,lag}^{growth}$	-0.21198	-0.02940		
UER_t	1.40331	0.08500 †		
Ψ_{s,t_0}			5.83%	
$\hat{\Psi}_{s,\Delta}$			7.35%	
$\frac{\hat{\Psi}_{s,\Delta}}{\Psi_{s,t_0}}$				1.26

Starting from Table 3.23, we apply the proportional variation $\frac{\hat{\Psi}_{s,\Delta}}{\Psi_{s,t_0}} = 1.26$ to each account. Table 3.24 summarises the impact of the above-described scenario on the corporate portfolio PDs under analysis.

Table 3.24 Proportional shift PDs				
ID	**Segment**	PD_{t_0}	$\frac{\hat{\Psi}_{s,\Delta}}{\Psi_{s,t_0}}$	$PD_{i,s,t,\Delta}^{pl,ps}$
1	Corporate	0.50%	1.26	0.63%
2	Corporate	2.00%	1.26	2.52%
3	Corporate	3.00%	1.26	3.78%
4	SME	3.50%	1.26	4.41%
5	SME	4.00%	1.26	5.04%

b. Logit Shift. Despite the intuitiveness of the proportional shift method, risk managers usually prefer a more sophisticated approach based on the logit modelling. In this regard, one can write the conditional PD, based on a given realisation of the creditworthiness index $\Psi_{s,t}^* \in [0, 1]$, as follows:

$$PD_{i,s,t} = P\left(y_{i,s,t} = 1 | \Psi_{s,t}^*\right) = \frac{1}{1 + e^{-(\varsigma_{i,s,t} | \Psi_{s,t}^*)}}, \tag{3.38}$$

where $\varsigma_{i,s,t}$ depends on both BVs and the creditworthiness index, as follows:

$$\varsigma_{i,s,t | \Psi_{s,t}^*} = \beta_{i,s,0} + \beta_{i,s,1}\chi_{1,t}^* + \ldots + \beta_{i,s,k-1}\chi_{k-1,t}^* + \epsilon_{i,s,t}, \tag{3.39}$$

where the vector $\chi = (\chi^*_{1,t}, \ldots, +\chi^*_{k-1,t})'$ contains BVs for the realisation $\Psi^*_{s,t}$. Additionally, $\beta = (\beta_{i,s,0}, \ldots, \beta_{i,s,k-1})'$ is the vector of coefficients, and $\epsilon_{i,s,t}$ is an error component. One may assume a linear relationship between $\varsigma_{i,s,t}$ and the variation of $\Psi_{s,t}$. Therefore we can project the creditworthiness index estimated through Equation (3.8) by means of a suitable macroeconomic scenario, as follows:

$$\hat{\Psi}_{s,\Delta} = \hat{\eta}_{s,0} + \hat{\eta}_{s,1}x_{1,\Delta} + \ldots + \hat{\eta}_{s,p}x_{p,\Delta}, \tag{3.40}$$

where $\mathbf{x}_\Delta = (x_{1,\Delta}, \ldots, x_{p,\Delta})'$ is the vector of macroeconomic forecast. The difference between $(\hat{\Psi}_{s,\Delta})$ and (Ψ_{s,t_0}) log-odds is a key ingredient of the overall framework, as shown below:

$$\Delta\varsigma_{s,\Delta} = \ln\left(\frac{\hat{\Psi}_{s,\Delta}}{1 - \hat{\Psi}_{s,\Delta}}\right) - \ln\left(\frac{\Psi_{s,t_0}}{1 - \Psi_{s,t_0}}\right), \tag{3.41}$$

where $\Delta\varsigma_{s,\Delta}$ is common for all accounts belonging to the s sub-portfolio.[11] This variation is added on top of the initial log-odds to obtain the following shifted PD:

$$\dot{P}D^{pl,ls}_{i,s,t,\Delta} = \frac{1}{1 + e^{-(\varsigma_{i,s,t} + \Delta\varsigma_{s,\Delta})}}, \tag{3.42}$$

where $\dot{P}D^{pl,ls}_{i,s,t,\Delta}$ indicates portfolio-level pl, logit shift ls account i PD computed on $\mathbf{x}_\Delta$ scenario forecast.

Example 3.8.2 summarises each step of the above-detailed process.

EXAMPLE 3.8.2 LOGIT SHIFT

Let us consider the same portfolio investigated in Example 3.8.1. We rely on the same $\Psi_{s,t}$ creditworthiness index, the same linear function, and macroeconomic projections. Table 3.25 summarises the impact on the creditworthiness index, based on the logit shift approach.

Table 3.25 Logit shift scenario analysis

Variable		
Ψ_{s,t_0}	5.83%	
$\ln\left(\frac{\hat{\Psi}_{s,t_0}}{1-\Psi_{s,t_0}}\right)$	-2.78	
$\hat{\Psi}_{s,\Delta}$	7.35%	
$\ln\left(\frac{\hat{\Psi}_{s,\Delta}}{1-\hat{\Psi}_{s,\Delta}}\right)$	-2.53	
$\Delta\varsigma_{s,\Delta}$		0.25

---

[11] For the sake of clarity, Δ in front of ς. indicates a variation.

Starting from Table 3.25, we apply a logit variation $\varsigma_{s,\Delta} = -2.53 + 2.78 = 0.25$ to each account. Table 3.26 summarises the impact of the above-described scenario on the corporate portfolio PDs under analysis.

Table 3.26 Shifted PDs

ID	Segment	PD_{t_0}	ς_{i,s,t_0}	$\Delta\varsigma_{s,\Delta}$	$\varsigma_{i,s,t_0} + \Delta\varsigma_{s,\Delta}$	$\dot{PD}^{pl,ls}_{i,s,t,\Delta}$
1	Corporate	0.50%	−5.29	0.25	−5.04	0.64%
2	Corporate	2.00%	−3.89	0.25	−3.64	2.55%
3	Corporate	3.00%	−3.48	0.25	−3.23	3.82%
4	SME	3.50%	−3.32	0.25	−3.07	4.45%
5	SME	4.00%	−3.18	0.25	−2.93	5.08%

It is worth noting that the differences between proportional and logit shift are relatively small. On this basis, the projected values summarised in Tables 3.24 and 3.26 show that these differences are more relevant for higher PDs. They are also affected by the magnitude of macroeconomic scenario changes.

APPENDIX B. ACCOUNT-LEVEL PD SHIFT

Computational details for both proportional and logit shift for account-level estimates are listed below:

a. Proportional Shift. The framework is aligned with the portfolio-level proportional shift described in Section 3.3.1. The main changes are detailed as follows:

$$\dot{PD}^{al,ps}_{i,s,t,\Delta} = PD_{i,s,t_0} \cdot \frac{\widehat{PD}^{al}_{i,s,\Delta}}{\widehat{PD}^{al}_{i,s,t_0}}, \tag{3.43}$$

where $\widehat{PD}^{al}_{i,s,\Delta}$ is the account-level PD derived from Equation (3.11) by considering a given macroeconomic scenario $\mathbf{x}_{s,\Delta} = (x_{1,s,\Delta}, \ldots x_{p,s,\Delta})'$, and BVs evolution $\chi_{i,s,\Delta} = (\chi_{1,i,s,\Delta}, \ldots, \chi_{r,i,s,\Delta})'$. On the other hand, $\widehat{PD}^{al}_{i,s,t_0}$ is the account-level PD, based on BVs and MVs in t_0. A question arises: why not directly use $\widehat{PD}^{al}_{i,s,\Delta}$? One could use the results of the panel GLM model. However, these estimates may not be completely aligned with PD_{i,s,t_0}. Therefore Equation (3.43) provides an effective answer for account-level panel GLM calibration.

b. Logit Shift. The following equation holds:

$$PD_{i,s,t} = P\left(y_{i,s,t} = 1 | \chi_{i,s,t}, \mathbf{x}_{s,t}\right) = \frac{1}{1 + e^{-(\varsigma_{i,s,t} | \chi_{i,s,t}, \mathbf{x}_{s,t})}}, \tag{3.44}$$

where $PD_{i,s,t}$ has the same meaning of Equation (3.38). Based on the functional relationship highlighted in Equation (3.11), one may compute the log-odds variation, based on a given macroeconomic scenario $\mathbf{x}_\Delta = (x_{1,s,\Delta}, \ldots, x_{p,s,\delta})'$ in conjunction with a set of BVs $\chi_{i,\Delta} = (\chi_{1,i,s,\Delta}, \ldots, \chi_{r,i,s,\delta})'$, as detailed below:

$$\Delta\Theta_{i,s,\Delta} = \ln\left(\frac{\hat{\theta}_{i,s,\Delta}}{1 - \hat{\theta}_{i,s,\Delta}}\right) - \ln\left(\frac{\theta_{i,s,t_0}}{1 - \theta_{i,s,t_0}}\right). \tag{3.45}$$

As in Section 3.3.1, this variation is added on top of the initial log-odds to obtain the following shifted PD:

$$\dot{P}D^{al,ls}_{i,s,t,\Delta} = \frac{1}{1 + e^{-(\varsigma_{i,s,t} + \Delta\Theta_{i,s,\Delta})}}, \tag{3.46}$$

where $\dot{P}D^{al,ls}_{i,s,t,\Delta}$ stands for account-level logit-shifted PD, based on macroeconomic scenario $\mathbf{x}_\Delta = (x_{1,s,\Delta}, \ldots, x_{p,s,\Delta})'$, and updated BVs $\chi_{i,\Delta} = (\chi_{1,i,s,\Delta}, \ldots, \chi_{r,i,s,\delta})'$.

Despite the differences in terms of estimates, the shifting computational procedure is aligned with portfolio-level mechanics.

EXERCISES

Exercise 3.1. Based on Example 3.3.3, derive the lifetime PD term structure as defined in Equation (3.15).

Exercise 3.2. Let us consider the model estimated in Example 3.3.3. Perform a cohort validation by means of the steps indicated in Section 3.3.3.

Exercise 3.3. Let us consider Example 3.4.5. Perform the following analyses:

- Fit survival AFT model by relying on exponential function and considering additional variables apart from those already included in Example 3.4.5.
- Validate the model both in terms of discriminatory power and accuracy.

REFERENCES

Baesens, B., Rosh, D., Scheule, H., 2016. Credit Risk Analytics: Measurement Techniques, Applications, and Examples in SAS. Wiley, Hoboken.

Belkin, B., Suchower, S., Forest, L., 1998. A One-Parameter Representation of Credit Risk and Transition Matrices. JP Morgan Credit-Metrics Monitor. Third Quarter.

Bellini, T., 2017. Stress Testing and Risk Integration in Banks: A Statistical Framework and Practical Software Guide (in Matlab and R). Academic Press, San Diego.

Bellotti, T., Crook, J., 2009. Support vector machines for credit scoring and discovery of significant features. Expert Systems with Applications 36, 3302–3308.

Breeden, J.L., Thomas, L.C., 2016. Solution to specification errors in stress testing models. Journal of the Operations Research Society 67, 830–840.

Cox, D.R., 1972. Regression models and life-tables. Journal of the Royal Statistical Society, Series B 34 (2), 187–220.

Dirick, L., Claeskens, G., Baesens, B., 2017. Time to default in credit scoring using survival analysis: a benchmark study. Journal of the Operational Research Society 68, 652–665.

Duffie, D., Singleton, K.J., 2003. Credit Risk Pricing, Measurement and Management. Princeton University Press, Princeton.

Hamilton, J., 1994. Time Series Analysis. Princeton University Press, Princeton.

Ishwaran, H., Kogalur, U., Blackstone, E., Lauer, M., 2008. Random survival forests. The Annals of Applied Statistics 2, 841–860.

Jarrow, R., Lando, D., Turnbull, S., 1997. Markov model for the term structure of credit risk spreads. Review of Financial Studies 10, 481–523.

Kaplan, E., Meier, P., 1958. Nonparametric estimation from incomplete observations. Journal of the American Statistical Association 53, 457–481.

Malik, M., Thomas, L.C., 2012. Transition matrix models of consumer credit ratings. International Journal of Forecasting 28, 261–272.

Merton, R., 1974. On the pricing of corporate debt: the risk structure of interest rates. Journal of Finance 29 (2), 449–470.

Schoenfeld, D., 1982. Partial residuals for the proportional hazards regression model. Biometrika 69, 239–241.

Thomas, L., Crook, J., Edelman, D., 2017. Credit Scoring and Its Applications (Mathematics in Industry).

Trueck, S., Rachev, S., 2009. Rating Based Modeling of Credit Risk: Theory and Application of Migration Matrices. Academic Press, San Diego.

LGD MODELLING

Loss given default (LGD) represents the portion of a non-recovered credit in case of default. Two extremes can easily be identified. On the one hand, a full recovery is associated with 0% LGD. On the other hand, a zero recovery scenario leads to a 100% LGD. A series of partial recoveries may also occur in practice resulting in LGD usually being bounded between 0% and 100%. Contrary to PD that enters expected credit loss (ECL) computation only for non-defaulted accounts, LGD is needed both for non-defaulted and defaulted instruments.

As a starting point to develop an LGD model, one needs to rely on a suitable database. Its goal is to collect all information needed to assess recoveries throughout the so-called "workout process" until an account is fully cured or written-off.

From a modelling standpoint, firstly a micro-structure LGD modelling is introduced to provide a comprehensive view of the post-default recovery process. A fundamental distinction is drawn between cured and written-off accounts. The focus is on probability of cure and severity. The investigation is conducted by considering both historical and forward-looking perspectives.

The next step of our journey focuses on regression techniques. Tobit, beta and other regression methods are firstly studied as silos approaches, and then combined in mixture models to improve both goodness-of-fit and model predictive power.

Thirdly, machine learning (ML) modelling is explored. Classification and regression trees are natural candidates to fit LGDs. Bagging, random forest and boosting are also studied as a valid enhancement of the most traditional ML methods.

In recent years, few attempts to model LGDs by means of survival analysis have been performed. Some hints are provided on how to apply Cox proportional hazard (CPH), and accelerated failure time (AFT) models to LGDs.

Finally, scarce data issues, together with low default portfolios, are investigated by pointing out the need for simpler approaches. Qualitative assessments play a key role.

As per the previous chapters, examples are examined by means of R software. The final section focuses on SAS.

KEY ABBREVIATIONS AND SYMBOLS

$CO_{l,t}$	Operational costs for product l at time t
$CO_{i_{wo},l,t}$	Operational costs for written-off account i, belonging to product l at time t
$EAD_{l,t=def}$	Exposure at default for product l at time $t = default$
$EAD_{i_{cu},l,t=def}$	Exposure at default for cured account i, belonging product l at time $t = default$
$EAD_{i_{wo},l,t=def}$	Exposure at default for written-off account i, belonging to product l at time $t = default$
LGD_l	LGD for a given product l
$P_{cu,l}$	Probability of cure for product l

IFRS 9 and CECL Credit Risk Modelling and Validation. https://doi.org/10.1016/B978-0-12-814940-9.00012-8

$SEV_{cu,l}$	Severity for cured accounts belonging to product l
$SEV_{non\text{-}cu,l}$	Severity for non-cured accounts belonging to product l
$RE_{l,t}$	Recoveries for product l at time t
$RE_{i_{cu},l,t}$	Recoveries for cured account i, belonging to product l at time t
$RE_{i_{wo},l,t}$	Recoveries for written-off account i, belonging to product l at time t

4.1 INTRODUCTION

Loss given default (LGD) is usually defined as a ratio of losses to an exposure at default. In the literature, three main classes of LGDs are commonly studied: internal data-based workout analysis, market-based estimate, and implied market LGDs (Schuermann, 2003). Our main focus is on workout LGDs. Indeed, banks are required to assess their expected credit losses, based on their experience and forward-looking projections. In this regard, workout LGD is derived from a set of estimated cash flows resulting from the recovery collection process discounted back to default date.

LGD is commonly estimated at product level (that is, l) as a synthetic metric. On the one hand, this approach facilitates the estimation process. On the other, it makes implementation easier. Therefore one may think of LGD as the average loss for account sharing similar characteristics and computed as follows:

$$LGD_l = 1 - \frac{\sum_{t_{re}=1}^{T_{re}} PV(RE_{l,t_{re}}) - \sum_{t_{co}=1}^{T_{co}} PV(CO_{l,t_{co}})}{EAD_{l,t=def}}, \quad (4.1)$$

where PV stands for present value, $RE_{l,t_{re}}$ are the recovery flows for product l at time $t_{re} = 1, \ldots, T_{re}$, whereas $CO_{l,t_{co}}$ are operational costs. $EAD_{l,t=def}$ stands for product l exposure at default (that is, $t = def$).

Figure 4.1 summarizes the chapter's path.

- **LGD data preparation.** Historical data are at the very heart of LGD modelling. Model sophistication and robustness are strictly linked to the quality of workout process data. Section 4.2 highlights the key elements a LGD database relies on.
- **LGD micro-structure approach.** Section 4.3 introduces micro-structure LGD modelling by focusing on two main elements: probability of cure and severity. Few methods are explored for fitting purposes. Then, a distinction is made between non-defaulted and defaulted accounts LGDs. A forward-looking perspective is investigated to align with accounting requirements. As a final step, a specific model is studied for real estate portfolios.
- **LGD regression methods.** Contrary to the micro-structure LGD modelling, Section 4.4 shows how regression methods capture all workout outcomes in one go. One needs to rely on bounded outcomes between the interval [0,1]. Flexibility is also required in terms of functional distribution (for example, beta regression). Furthermore, a combination of many approaches can be used to adequately capture product (portfolio) specific features, and project LGDs according to forward-looking scenarios.
- **LGD machine learning (ML) modelling.** If one thinks of LGD_l as an average loss for accounts sharing similar (product l) characteristics, ML methods are natural candidates for LGD estimates, as detailed in Section 4.5.

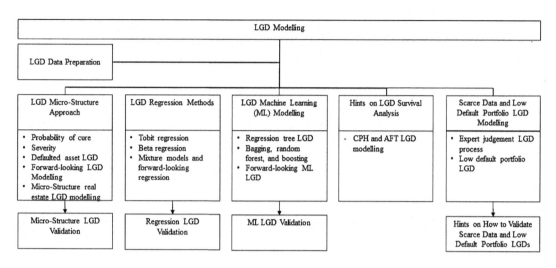

FIGURE 4.1

Chapter's workflow diagram.

- **Hints on LGD survival analysis.** Despite the appealing statistical structure, survival analysis has not been widely used for LGD modelling. Section 4.6 describes the key elements one needs to focus on when developing a survival LGD model.
- **Scarce data and low default portfolio LGD modelling.** One of the major issues one needs to face to develop an LGD model is data gathering. Poor data quality usually characterizes the workout process. Section 4.7 focuses on procedures to follow in the case of scarce data, and methods to embrace for low default portfolios LGD modelling.

For each of the above modelling schemes, a specific section is devoted to model validation. A systematic process to ensure integrity on data, methodology, and statistical appropriateness is crucial to ensure a consistent ECL estimation.

Examples and case studies are examined by means of R software throughout the chapter. Finally, Section 4.8 provides SAS details on the chapter's key exemplifications.

4.2 LGD DATA PREPARATION

ECL computation relies on homogeneous default definition across PD, LGD, and EAD modelling. For this reason, we refer to Chapter 2 for a detailed description of default triggers. On the other hand, the attention is now on the workout process. Section 4.2.1 (following) focuses on the theoretical concepts informing LGD estimates and corresponding information needs, whereas Section 4.2.2 focuses on LGD database characteristics.

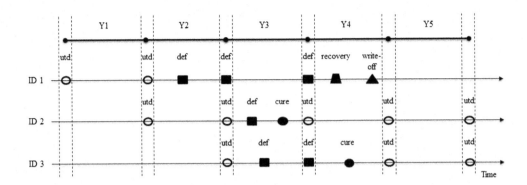

FIGURE 4.2

Default and workout time-line: instant cure default definition.

4.2.1 LGD DATA CONCEPTUAL CHARACTERISTICS

Figure 4.2 investigates three accounts (that is, ID 1, ID 2, ID 3) to point out the key elements needed to estimate LGDs. Let us start by focusing on ID 1. This account[1] is up-to-date at the beginning of the first year, and it does not default in year 1. In contrast, it defaults in year 2 and does not cure. Some recoveries are recorded in year 4. Finally, it is then written-off during the same year 4. ID 2 appears in the portfolio in year 2, and a its default takes place in year 3. It is cured within the same year 3 and remains up-to-date moving forward.[2] Finally, moving to ID 3, the main difference between ID 3 and ID 2 is the length of the permanence in default status.

In line with Figure 4.2, the key elements one needs to focus on are listed below:

- **Default event.** LGD analysis is conducted on defaulted accounts only.
- **Cure.** The likelihood of returning to the up-to-date status after a default occurrence plays a key role in LGD estimation. Specific model components can be estimated to capture this phenomenon (that is, probability of cure).
- **Recoveries.** One may distinguish between lump-sum and recovery streams. Collaterals are usually a key recovery source. For this reason, collateral information plays a key role throughout the entire LGD modelling journey.
- **Costs.** One needs to distinguish between direct and indirect costs. The former refer to expenses specifically encountered for the account under investigation. On the other hand, indirect costs refer to general expenditure pro-quota allocated to defaulted accounts.
- **Time value of money.** Workout process length has an important impact on the overall credit loss. One needs to identify the interest rate for discounting recovery and cost flows. Bank's funding structure needs to be considered to assess the corresponding cost.

---

[1]Without loss of generality, and to ease the description, the assumption, one customer one account, holds.
[2]One needs to bear in mind that the adoption of a probationary period (for example, six-month, one-year) would postpone the return to the up-to-date status.

Example 4.2.1 lists some of the key features of a LGD database. The focus is on a retail mortgage portfolio. However, it can easily be tweaked to meet corporate portfolio needs. Recoveries refer to a lump-sum amount derived from property sale. In contrast, costs are spread along the workout process. A discount factor is applied, based on portfolio's risk profile.

EXAMPLE 4.2.1 RETAIL MORTGAGE LGD DATABASE

Let us consider an account (that is, ID 1) belonging to a retail portfolio. Table 4.1 summarizes the key information required to develop an LGD model.

Table 4.1 LGD database structure ($ Thousands)

ID	Rep. date	Def. flag	Bal- ance	Coll. type	Cost	Poss. flag	Prop. value	HPI var %	Sale flag	Sale price
1	Q1/Y1	0	100.00	Resid.		0	150.00	1.00%	0	
1	Q2/Y1	1	101.00	Resid.		0	150.00	1.10%	0	
1	Q3/Y1	1	102.00	Resid.		0	150.00	1.20%	0	
1	Q4/Y1	0	98.00	Resid.		0	150.00	2.00%	0	
1	Q1/Y2	0	96.00	Resid.		0	160.00	1.50%	0	
1	Q2/Y2	1	97.00	Resid.		0	160.00	1.00%	0	
1	Q3/Y2	1	98.00	Resid.		0	160.00	1.00%	0	
1	Q4/Y2	1	102.00	Resid.	3.00	0	160.00	1.50%	0	
1	Q1/Y3	1	103.00	Resid.		0	160.00	1.50%	0	
1	Q2/Y3	1	104.00	Resid.		1	160.00	1.50%	0	
1	Q3/Y3	1	108.00	Resid.	3.00	1	160.00	1.50%	0	
1	Q4/Y3	1	111.00	Resid.	2.00	1	160.00	2.00%	1	80.00

Each field is detailed as follows:

- **ID.** Information is usually available at account, product and customer level. Data granularity is crucial for the entire analysis. Therefore one needs to identify a suitable level of data availability to start developing an LGD model.
- **Default flag.** Starting from an up-to-date status, a first default occurs in the second quarter of year 1 (that is, Q2/Y1). An instant cure default definition is adopted. In Q4/Y1 this account returns to the up-to-date status. A new default event takes place in Q2/Y2, and the account does not recover.
- **Balance.** This column highlights the outstanding balance through time. It is worth noting that accrual interest (for example, $1 thousand per quarter) is added on top of the principal when no payments are made. In contrast, quarterly payments reduce the balance. Recovery costs are added on top of the principal when occurring.
- **Collateral type.** Firstly, one needs to verify whether a collateral exists. Secondly, the assessment of its value is crucial, as described in column Property Value.
- **Cost.** This column refers to direct cost sustained to carry on with property possession and sale. Additional indirect cost may arise and different rules inform accounting standards for their inclusion in LGD modelling.

- **Possession flag.** One may split the process in pre-possession and post-possession. After possession a property is usually sold, and a haircut on property value usually applies.
- **Property value.** An updated collateral valuation allows us to assess exposure coverage. Missing or outdated information undermines LGD model accuracy.
- **HPI variation %.** This macroeconomic variable (MV) allows us to infer potential real estate market fluctuations, and their connections with sale prices.
- **Sale flag.** It indicates the occurrence of a sale event.
- **Sale price.** This information is needed to assess actual losses.

One should also consider other information, such as written-off amount, to have a full reconciliation of economic and accounting representation in the recovery process.

In line with the above, one needs to gather as much information as possible and organize it accordingly. The next section provides a guide on how to build a consistent LGD database.

4.2.2 LGD DATABASE ELEMENTS

The following scheme is a key reference to structure an LGD database. Information is organized across few main areas, such as exposure, customer, external information and recovery procedure, as listed below:

a. **Exposure.** A series of key drivers can be identified, starting from product types. The following distinction between collateral and no-collateral is usually beneficial:

- **Collateral.** The presence of a collateral provides a warranty in the event of default. One may distinguish among different collateral types. A wide range of financial guarantees can be put in place (for example, publicly traded bonds are the most liquid assets). Personal warranties may also be considered, but they are often difficult to liquidate. As an additional example, real estate collaterals play a major role. Given their physical nature, in the case of a default, one needs to trigger executive procedures. A relatively long period of time may be necessary for their translation into recovery cash flows.
- **No-collateral.** Products without a collateral are usually exposed to higher losses compared to those with a collateral. The recovery process varies dramatically among different portfolio, such as retail and corporate. It also depends upon product types (for example, credit card, overdraft).
- **Type of exposure.** A key distinction arises between on and off-balance exposures. In the latter case, the likelihood of actual balance disposal is an additional component one needs to model.

b. **Customer.** Attributes related to the customer are usually important drivers to assess LGDs. Few examples of the potential areas of interest are listed below:

- **Segment.** One may distinguish among business, regulatory and legal entity segments. Retail portfolios, for example, are usually treated separately from small medium enterprises (SMEs), and corporates.
- **Sector.** This attribute mainly applies to SMEs and corporate portfolios.
- **Size.** This characteristic mainly applies to SMEs and corporates. A typical portfolio segmentation refers to turnover.

Table 4.2 LGD risk drivers

Category	Type	Risk driver
a. Exposure	i. Collateral	Collateral type
		Loan to value
		Number of pledged securities
	ii. Non-collateral	Facility type
		Limit (e.g., 1 year prior to default)
		Time to maturity
		Utilisation intensity
	iii. Type of exposure	On balance, off-balance sheet
b. Customer	i. Segment	Business segment
		Internal segment
		Legal entity
	ii. Sector	Industry, sector
	iii. Size	Turnover
	iv. Credit quality	Rating (e.g., 1 year prior to default)
		Rating deterioration
		Seniority
	v. Relationship	Length of business relationship
		Intensity of business relationship
c. External info	i. Macroeconomic variables	Variables from different sources
	ii. Other exogenous factors	Default rates
d. Recovery procedure	i. Resolution period	Resolution period

- **Credit quality.** PD bands or rating classes, in some cases, are considered as a driver for LGD as long as a potential correlation with losses can be detected.
- **Relationship.** A long term relationship may encompass the possibility to activate recovery channels that are not necessarily available for the short term ones.

c. **External information.** Information referring to the overall economic evolution and creditworthiness indices are crucial to develop forward-looking LGDs.

d. **Recovery procedure.** The legal environment where an entity operates is crucial to estimate the resolution period and assess recovery flows.

Table 4.2 provides a summary of LGD risk drivers, starting from the above-detailed characteristics. The next section describes how to combine this information for LGD estimation.

4.3 LGD MICRO-STRUCTURE APPROACH

In line with the previous section, LGD modelling relies on defaulted accounts. Figure 4.3 proposes to split this population into two subsets. On the one hand, cured accounts (that is, the number of these

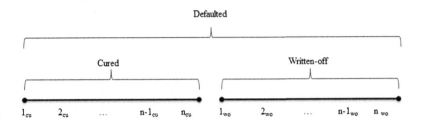

FIGURE 4.3

Defaulted population: cured vs. written-off accounts.

accounts in our database n_{cu}). On the other hand, written-off accounts (that is, the number of these accounts in our database n_{wo}).

The idea underlying LGD micro-structure approach is to develop two separate models and combine them. The tree structure depicted in Figure 4.4 pinpoints the relevance of these two outcomes. One may consider other potential workout outcomes like, for example, restructuring. Nevertheless, the framework does not substantially change.

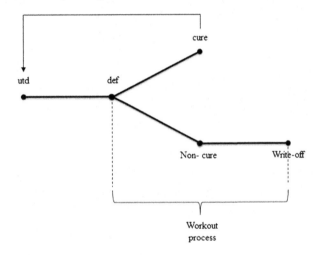

FIGURE 4.4

Workout process: defaulted against non-defaulted accounts.

In light of the above, one can then rewrite Equation (4.1) as follows:

$$
LGD_l = \left[1 - \frac{\sum_{i_{wo}=1}^{n_{wo}} \left[\sum_{t_{re}=1}^{T_{i_{wo},re}} PV(RE_{i_{wo},l,t_{re}}) - \sum_{t_{co}=1}^{T_{i_{wo},co}} PV(CO_{i_{wo},l,t_{co}}) \right]}{\sum_{i_{wo}=1}^{n_{wo}} EAD_{i_{wo},l,t=def}} \right] \cdot (1 - P_{cu,l}) \quad (4.2)
$$

$$
+ \frac{\sum_{i_{cu}=1}^{n_{cu}} \sum_{t_{cu}=1}^{T_{i_{cu},co}} PV(CO_{i_{cu},l,t_{cu}})}{\sum_{i_{cu}=1}^{n_{cu}} EAD_{i_{cu},l,t=def}} \cdot P_{cu,l} =
$$

$$
SEV_{wo,l} \cdot (1 - P_{cu,l}) + SEV_{cu,l} \cdot P_{cu,l},
$$

where the subscript i_{wo} stands for written-off, whereas i_{cu} indicates a cured account. In both cases, accounts belong to the product (or facility) type l. One may also develop LGD models to include forward-looking information. A time dimension needs to be added (that is, $LGD_{l,t}$). All other notation being the same as in Equation (4.1); the focus is on the following components:

- **Probability of cure** $P_{cu,l}$. This is the likelihood of returning to the up-to-date status after being defaulted.
- **Severity** SEV_l. One may distinguish between severity in case of cure $SEV_{cu,l}$, and severity in case on write-off $SEV_{wo,l}$.
- **Discount rate.** Present value computation relies on interest rates derived by considering the following ingredients:
  - Risk-free rate. A risk-free rate can be seen as a risk-neutral measure of a time value of money, and is typically represented by a yield of government security, such as a Treasury bill or Treasury bond.
  - Default premium. A default premium included in the contract rate embeds a compensation for expected default.
  - Risk premium. A risk-averse entity demands compensation for the volatility of actual cash-flows from expected ones. Hence a risk-premium is added to the discount rate.

Figure 4.5 describes how the micro-structure modelling journey is organized throughout Section 4.3.

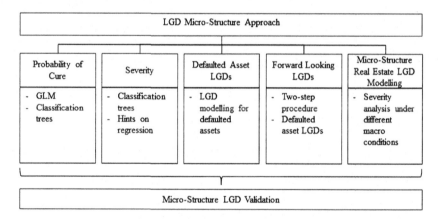

FIGURE 4.5

Workflow diagram for Section 4.3.

Section 4.3.1 investigates probability of cure modelling by means of logistic regression and classification trees. Severity is studied in Section 4.3.2 by focusing on regression trees, and few hints are provided on regression methods. Defaulted asset LGD is the subject covered in Section 4.3.3. These analyses do not consider any forward-looking perspective. They cannot be directly used for ECL purposes. Then, Section 4.3.4 builds a bridge between LGD and macroeconomic variables (MVs). Indeed, a need for embedding forward-looking information is at the root of expected credit losses. Specific attention is then addressed to real estate LGD modelling. In this regard, Section 4.3.5 focuses on the link between severity, and house price index (HPI) fluctuations. Finally, Section 4.3.6 provides some hints on how to validate LGD micro-structure models.

4.3.1 PROBABILITY OF CURE

In line with Figure 4.4, one may consider a binary outcome representing cure against non-cure. As a first approach, one may rely on logit regression. This approach is widely used due to its simplicity. As an alternative, practical and intuitive interpretation is the key advantage of techniques based on decision trees. Basic classifier trees are commonly used to model the probability of cure. Nevertheless, for more complex portfolios, bagging, random forest, and boosting may also apply. For less sophisticated portfolios, which usually collapse on a few drivers identified by an expert panel (see Section 4.7.1), one may rely on expert-driven methods.

Example 4.3.1 provides some hints on how to tackle the probability of cure estimation task by means of logit regression. As stated above, this model does not embed any forward looking perspective. (See Section 4.3.4.)

EXAMPLE 4.3.1 PROBABILITY OF CURE ESTIMATION

Let us consider a retail mortgage portfolio. Its structure is aligned with Table 4.1. Its major explanatory variables can be summarized as follows: balance_at_default (balance at default), ltv_utd (loan to value updated), time_since_default (time since default), repayment_type_segment (repayment type), TOB (time-on-book), months_to_maturity (months-to-maturity), region.

Probability of cure analysis is performed by means of the following steps:

1. Updload data,
2. Explorative analysis,
3. Create train and test samples,
4. Binning analysis,
5. Fit regression, and
6. Predict and compute Gini index.

It is worth noting that sold accounts—in our database—correspond to non-cured accounts. Therefore flag_sold is used as dependent variable. Model output needs to be interpreted as an estimate of $(1 - P_{cu})$. It corresponds to the probability of selling a property after experiencing default.

```
# 1. Updload data
data_lgd<- read.csv('data_lgd.csv',
header = TRUE, sep=';')
# 2. Explorative analysis
# 2.1 Box-plot months to maturity vs. flag_sold (see Figure 4.6)
boxplot(data_lgd$months_to_maturity~data_lgd$flag_sold,
horizontal=T, frame=F, col='light blue',
main='Months to Maturity (Sold=1 vs. Non-Sold=0)')
```

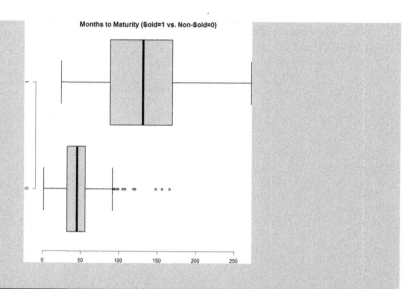

FIGURE 4.6

Box-plot: months-to-maturity vs. flag sold.

```
# 3. Create train and test samples
data_lgd$flag_sold_1<- dplyr::if_else(data_lgd$flag_sold == 1,0,1)
library(caret)
set.seed(2122)
train_index <- caret::createDataPartition(data_lgd$flag_sold_1, p = .7,
list = FALSE)
train <- data_lgd[ train_index,]
test  <- data_lgd[-train_index,]
# 4. Binning analysis
# 4.1 IV analysis
library(smbinning)
iv_analysis<- smbinning.sumiv(df=train,y='flag_sold_1')
```

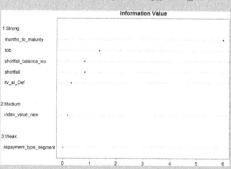

FIGURE 4.7

Information value (IV) analysis.

The following variables are considered for the analysis: months_to_maturity (months-to-maturity), ltv_utd (loan to value updated), and TOB (time-on-book). (See Figure 4.7.)

A binning analysis is also performed. Figure 4.8 refers to the variable months_to_maturity.

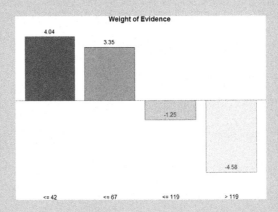

FIGURE 4.8

Weight of evidence (WOE) analysis for the variable months_to_maturity.

Correlation between pairs of variables is investigated. In our case, the maximum correlation reaches 0.29. Therefore the following stepwise regression is performed on the above-described three variables: months_to_maturity (months-to-maturity), ltv_utd (loan-to-value updated), and TOB (time-on-book).

```
# 5. Fit regression
# See complementary examples' software code for binning analysis
library(MASS)
attach(train)
logit_full<- glm(flag_sold~ woe_months_to_maturity+woe_ltv_utd+
woe_tob, family = binomial(link = 'logit'), data = train)
logit_stepwise<- stepAIC(logit_full,
k= qchisq(0.05, 1, lower.tail=F), direction = 'both')
detach(train)
#Inspect results:
summary(logit_stepwise)
#                 Estimate Std. Error z value    Pr(>|z|)
# (Intercept)      -1.0634     0.3381  -3.146    0.001657 **
# woe_months_to_m -5.1115     1.0198  -5.012 0.000000539 ***
# woe_ltv_utd  1.0867     0.2460   4.417 0.000009989 ***
# woe_tob          -1.3932     0.3805  -3.661    0.000251 ***
# ---
# Signif. codes:  0 '***' 0.001 '**' 0.01 '*' 0.05 '.' 0.1 ' ' 1
```

```
# 6. Predict and compute Gini index
# 6.1 Predict
predict_logit_train<- predict(logit_stepwise,
newdata = train, type = 'response')
train$predict_logit  <- predict(logit_stepwise,
newdata = train, type = 'response')
# 6.2 Gini index calculation
library(optiRum)
gini_train<- optiRum::giniCoef(train$predict_logit,
train$flag_sold)
# 0.8862348
```

High Gini index for both train and test samples (that is, 0.88 and 0.90, respectively) high-lights a good model discriminatory power.

The next section focuses on severity analysis.

4.3.2 SEVERITY

An important distinction arises when computing severity. Indeed, one may compute SEV as an average, based on exposures or number of defaulted accounts, as listed below:

$$SEV_l^{EAD} = \left[1 - \sum_{i_{wo}=1}^{n_{wo}} \left[\frac{\sum_{t_{re}=1}^{T_{iwo,re}} PV(RE_{i_{wo},l,t_{re}}) - \sum_{t_{co}=1}^{T_{iwo,co}} PV(CO_{i_{wo},l,t_{co}})}{EAD_{i_{wo},l,t=def}} \right. \right.$$
$$\left. \left. \cdot \frac{EAD_{i_{wo},l,t=def}}{\sum_{i_{wo}=1}^{n_{wo}} EAD_{i_{wo},l,t=def}} \right] \right], \tag{4.3}$$

where the superscript EAD indicates averaging by exposure, and i_{wo} stands for written-off account. One may also consider the following alternative weighting scheme:

$$SEV_l^{\#} = \left[1 - \sum_{i_{wo}=1}^{n_{wo}} \left[\frac{\sum_{t_{re}=1}^{T_{iwo,re}} PV(RE_{i_{wo},l,t_{re}}) - \sum_{t_{co}=1}^{T_{iwo,co}} PV(CO_{i_{wo},l,t_{co}})}{EAD_{i_{wo},l,t=def}} \cdot \frac{1}{n_{wo}} \right] \right], \tag{4.4}$$

where the superscript # indicates the number of accounts. For portfolios, where exposures are highly volatile, one may prefer Equation (4.3) instead of (4.4). The opposite applies for homogeneous portfolios.

A wide range of regression approaches have been considered in the literature (Bellotti and Crook, 2012). Tobit and beta regression are natural candidates. These techniques will be studied in Section 4.4. Hereafter we rely on the simplicity of decision trees to summarize a phenomenon requiring deep business expertise. Example 4.3.2 provides hints on how to use regression trees for the purpose of estimating severity on a retail mortgage portfolio. Section 4.3.4 provides some hints on how to embed a forward looking perspective.

EXAMPLE 4.3.2 SEVERITY ESTIMATION

Let us consider the same retail mortgage portfolio investigated in Example 4.3.1. Severity is estimated by means of the following steps:

1. Upload data,
2. Fit regression tree,
3. Prune, and
4. Predict pruned tree.

```
# 1. Upload data
# 1.1. Data import
lgd_data_tree_sel <- data_lgd %>%
dplyr::select('flag_sold', 'balance_at_default','ltv_utd',
'time_since_default', 'repayment_type_segment',
'tob', 'months_to_maturity', 'region' , 'shortfall_balance_wo')
lgd_data_sev <- lgd_data_tree_sel %>%
dplyr::filter(flag_sold==1)
# 1.2. Create variable based on loan to value < or > 70%
lgd_data_sev<-lgd_data_sev %>%
dplyr::mutate(ltv_lower_70=ifelse(test=(ltv_utd <=0.7),
yes = 1, no=0))
# 1.3. Sampling
library(caret)
set.seed(123)
train_index_sev <- caret::createDataPartition(
lgd_data_sev$ltv_lower_70, p = .7, list = FALSE)
train_sev <- lgd_data_sev[ train_index_sev,]
test_sev  <- lgd_data_sev[-train_index_sev,]
# 2. Fit regression tree
library(tree)
lgd_reg_tree_sev <- tree(shortfall_balance_wo~.
-flag_sold-ltv_lower_70, data=train_sev)
summary(lgd_reg_tree_sev)
# Variables actually used in tree construction:
# 'ltv_utd' 'region'
# Number of terminal nodes:  8
# Residual mean deviance:  0.008469 = 0.9654 / 114
# 2.1. Prediction on test sample
#sold_char_test<- ifelse(test$flag_sold==0,'No','Yes')
lgd_reg_tree_predict_sev <- predict(lgd_reg_tree_sev,
test_sev)
mse_lgd_reg_sev <- mean((lgd_reg_tree_predict_sev-
test_sev$shortfall_balance_wo)^2)
```

```
# 0.02350271
# 3. Pruning
lgd_reg_tree_prune_sev <- prune.tree(lgd_reg_tree_sev,
best=3)
summary(lgd_reg_tree_prune_sev)
# Variables actually used in tree construction:
# 'ltv_utd' 'region'
# Number of terminal nodes:  3
# Residual mean deviance:  0.01631 = 1.94 / 119
```

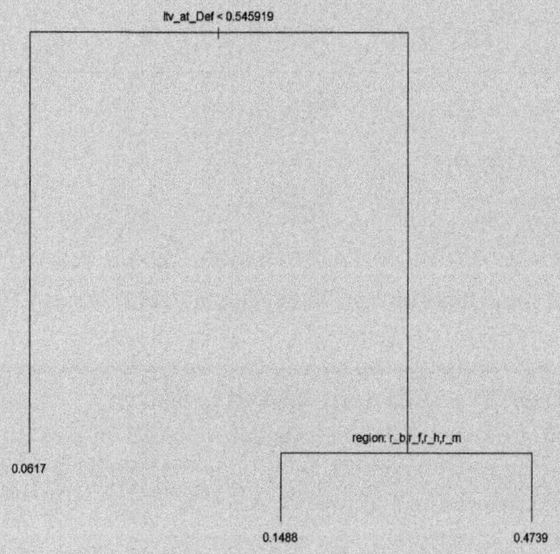

FIGURE 4.9

Pruned tree for severity analysis.

```
# 4. Predict pruned tree
lgd_reg_tree_predict_prune_sev <- predict(lgd_reg_tree_prune_sev,
test_sev)
mse_lgd_reg_sev <- mean((lgd_reg_tree_predict_prune_sev-
test_sev$shortfall_balance_wo)^2)
# 0.02350271
```

Loan-to-value plays the key role in assessing severity. As a second variable, geographical area is the additional factor emerging from regression tree analysis. In both non-pruned and pruned trees, the residual mean deviance is less than 2%. The mean squared error of the predicted model on the test sample is less than 2.5% for both non-pruned and pruned trees. (See Figure 4.9.)

Defaulted accounts deserve a bespoke treatment, as detailed in the next section.

4.3.3 DEFAULTED ASSET LGD

One needs to compute ECLs for both non-defaulted and defaulted assets. For assets in default, both the probability of cure and the severity need to be assessed conditionally on the workout process status. In this regard, the probability of cure for an account at the very beginning of the workout process is usually higher than at its end. Likewise, severity depends upon the status reached on the workout process. Time bands are usually created to facilitate the analysis. For example, one may think of the following time since default intervals: [0,1Y], (1Y,2Y], (>2Y). In what follows, we adapt Equation (4.2) to account for interval j evolution, as listed below:

$$LGD_{l,j} = \tag{4.5}$$

$$\left[1 - \frac{\sum_{i_{wo_j}=1}^{n_{wo_j}} \left[\sum_{t_{re}=1}^{T_{i_{wo_j},re}} PV(RE_{i_{wo_j},l,t_{re}}) - \sum_{t_{co}=1}^{T_{i_{wo_j},co}} PV(CO_{i_{wo_j},l,t_{co}}) \right]}{\sum_{i_{wo_j}=1}^{n_{wo_j}} EAD_{i_{wo_j},l,t=def}} \right] \cdot (1 - P_{cu_j})$$

$$+ \frac{\sum_{i_{cu_j}=1}^{n_{cu_j}} \sum_{t_{co}=1}^{T_{i_{cu},co}} PV(CO_{i_{cu_j},l,t_{co}})}{\sum_{i_{cu_j}=1}^{n_{cu_j}} EAD_{i_{cu_j},l,t=def}} \cdot P_{cu_j}.$$

Example 4.3.3 provides some hints on how to develop defaulted asset LGD, based on a retail mortgage portfolio.

EXAMPLE 4.3.3 DEFAULTED ASSET LGD MODELLING

Let us consider the portfolio investigated in Example 4.3.1. The focus is now on defaulted asset LGD. We follow a regression tree approach by relying on nested trees. A conditional structure on time since default is organized as follows:

1. Upload data, and
2. Fit regression tree.

```
# 1. Upload data
lgd_data_tree_yy <- read.csv('data_lgd_year.csv',
header = TRUE, sep=';')
# 1.1. Select a subset of variable
lgd_data_tree_sel_year <- lgd_data_tree_yy %>%
dplyr::select('flag_sold', 'balance_at_default','ltv_utd',
'time_since_default', 'repayment_type_segment',
'tob', 'months_to_maturity', 'region',
'shortfall_balance_wo', 'year')
# 1.2. Filter out NAs
lgd_data_tree_year <- lgd_data_tree_sel_year %>%
na.omit(lgd_data_tree_sel_year)
# 1.3. Stratified sampling
library(caret)
set.seed(123)
```

```
train_index <- caret::createDataPartition(
lgd_data_tree_year$flag_sold, p = .7, list = FALSE)
train_year <- lgd_data_tree_year[ train_index,]
test_year  <- lgd_data_tree_year[-train_index,]
# 2. Fit regression tree
library('partykit')
lgd_da_1 <- ctree(shortfall_balance_wo~year,data=train_year,
maxdepth = 1)
plot(lgd_da_1)
```

In line with Figure 4.10 a split is made between $[0 - 1Y]$ and $(> 1Y)$. The box-plot shows that when we are in the first interval (that is, $[0 - 1Y]$) LGD is very low (close to zero). In contrast, for time since default greater than one-year, the median severity is around 20%.

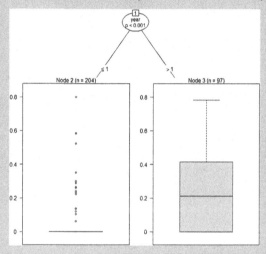

FIGURE 4.10

Defaulted asset LGD node 1.

```
# 2.1. Node 2
lgd_da_2 <- ctree(shortfall_balance_wo ~ year + .
-flag_sold, data=train_year,
subset = predict(lgd_da_1, type = 'node') == 2)
plot(lgd_da_2)
```

Figure 4.11 focuses on node 2 of Figure 4.10. The tree highlights that the variable months-to-maturity effectively discriminates between severity close to zero and greater than zero.

```
# 2.2. Node 3
lgd_da_3 <- ctree(shortfall_balance_wo ~ year + .
-flag_sold, data=train_year,
```

```
subset = predict(lgd_da_1, type = 'node') == 3)
plot(lgd_da_3)
```

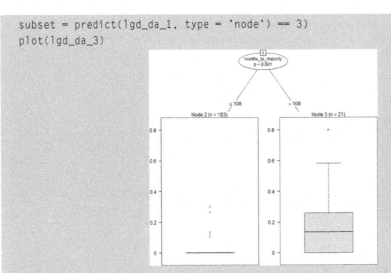

FIGURE 4.11

Defaulted asset LGD node 2.

Finally, Figure 4.12 focuses on node 3 of Figure 4.10. In this case, both loan-to-value and months-to-maturity are considered. On this basis, it is worth noting that the relative small number of units of sub-node 4 may cause some inconsistencies. Indeed, from a business perspective, one would expect an increase in severity for higher loan-to-values. This inconsistency can potentially be addressed via expert judgement.

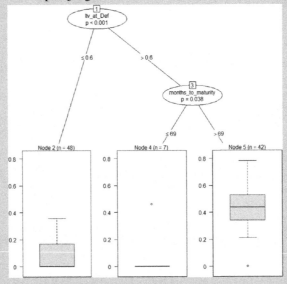

FIGURE 4.12

Defaulted asset LGD node 3.

The next section describes how the micro-structure modelling can be used to derive forward-looking LGD estimates.

4.3.4 FORWARD-LOOKING MICRO-STRUCTURE LGD MODELLING

In line with IASB (2014) and FASB (2016) requirements, ECL relies on point-in-time, unbiased, forward-looking credit risk measures. A multi-step procedure is inspected hereafter to embed a forward-looking perspective. Section 4.3.5 introduces a separate framework for real estate LGD modelling.

The overall micro-structure modelling described so far relies on two main components: probability of cure and severity. In this regard, one may develop a multi-step procedure to capture the relationship between $P_{cu,l,t}$ and $SEV_{l,t}$ against MVs, as listed below:

- **Probability of cure and severity starting point.** P_{cu,l,t_0} and SEV_{l,t_0} constitute the starting point for the multi-step estimation procedure.
- **Link function.** The second step is to fit product or portfolio-level probability of cure and severity against MVs (that is, $\mathbf{x}_t$). In practice, product-level time series are difficult to build because of data sparseness. For this reason, one may rely on portfolio information. Furthermore, one may think of developing a model directly on LGD (instead of its sub-components).
- **Model shift.** The third step of the procedure is to compute relative variations to apply on top of current estimates, as follows:
  - **Probability of cure:**

$$\dot{P}_{cu,l,t,\Delta} = P_{cu,l,t_0} \cdot \frac{P_{cu,\Delta}^{ptf}}{P_{cu,t_0}^{ptf}}, \tag{4.6}$$

where $\dot{P}_{cu,l,t,\Delta}$ denotes the updated probability of cure due to scenario $\mathbf{x}_\Delta$, related to product l at time t. The superscript $\cdot$ refers to the final outcome of a process. A proportional shift computed at portfolio is represented by means of $\frac{P_{cu,\Delta}^{ptf}}{P_{cu,t_0}^{ptf}}$.
  - **Severity:**

$$S\dot{E}V_{l,t,\Delta} = SEV_{l,t_0} \cdot \frac{SEV_{\Delta}^{ptf}}{SEV_{t_0}^{ptf}}, \tag{4.7}$$

where $S\dot{E}V_{l,t,\Delta}$ indicates the updated severity. A proportional shift is represented by means of $\frac{SEV_{\Delta}^{ptf}}{SEV_{t_0}^{ptf}}$.
  - **Overall LGD:**

$$L\dot{G}D_{l,t,\Delta} = LGD_{l,t_0} \cdot \frac{LGD_{\Delta}^{ptf}}{LGD_{t_0}^{ptf}}, \tag{4.8}$$

where $L\dot{G}D_{l,t,\Delta}$ indicates the updated LGD.

Example 4.3.4 details how to estimate the relationship between LGD and macroeconomic variables.

EXAMPLE 4.3.4 FORWARD-LOOKING REGRESSION ANALYSIS

Moving from the LGD database used throughout the chapter, a portfolio time series is created (that is, LGD_t^{ptf}). MVs are stuck in an $n \times p$ matrix $\mathbf{x}_t$ (t refers to a semester). Scarce data prevented conducting the analysis on a more granular basis.

One needs to bear in mind that economic conditions after t may affect recoveries and, therefore, LGD_t. Let us consider, for example, $LGD_{t2007-01}$ (see Figure 4.13), and let us assume a workout period length of 3 years. Recoveries take place over: 2007, 2008 and 2009. This implies a link between LGD_t and MVs over the following 3 years. As a consequence, one may require MVs with a time lead.

A regression is performed by means of the following steps:

1. Upload data,
2. Fit regression, and
3. Fit regression with lead variables.

```
# 1. Upload data
lgd.ts <- read.csv('lgd_timeseries.csv', header = TRUE,
sep=';')
lgd.ts$date <- as.Date(lgd.ts$date,format = '%d/%m/%Y')
# 2. Fit regression
# 2.1. Inclusion of all variables
ee<-18
lgd.lm.full <- lm(lgd~.-date, data = lgd.ts[1:ee,])
#summary(lgd.lm)
# 2.2. Stepwise regression
library(MASS)
lgd.stepwise<- stepAIC(lgd.lm.full, direction = 'both')
summary(lgd.stepwise)
#             Estimate Std. Error t value Pr(>|t|)
# (Intercept) -0.8974    3.2751   -0.274  0.78760
# ir           2.9689    0.9004    3.297  0.00455 **
# ---
# Signif. codes:  0 '***' 0.001 '**' 0.01 '*' 0.05 '.' 0.1 ' ' 1
# Residual standard error: 4.021 on 16 degrees of freedom
# Multiple R-squared:  0.4046,  Adjusted R-squared:  0.3674
# F-statistic: 10.87 on 1 and 16 DF,  p-value: 0.004546
```

Stepwise regression points out the similarity between LGD and interest rate time series. Nevertheless, this link may be, at least to some extent, spurious.

Figure 4.13 pinpoints a peak in LGD approximately in 2007–2008, whereas the drop in GDP, and increase in unemployment rate, occurred later in 2009.

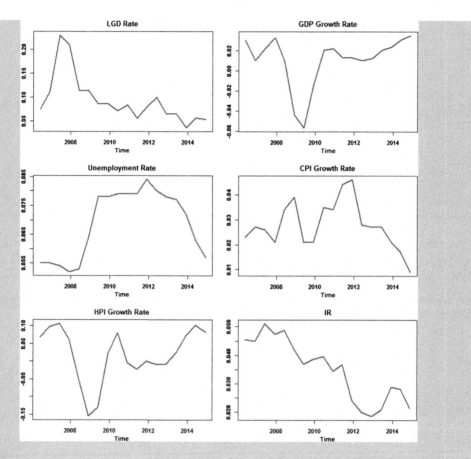

FIGURE 4.13

LGD and MVs time series (semi-annual data).

Due to time misalignment, a lead relationship is additionally investigated, as detailed in the following:

```
# 3. Fit regression with lead variables
# 3.1. Create 3 semesters ahead moving average gdp growth
gdp_ma3 <- matrix(0,ee,1)
for(i in 1:ee)
{
gdp_ma3[i] <-0.33*(lgd.ts$gdp[i+1]+lgd.ts$gdp[i+2]+lgd.ts$gdp[i+3])
}
lgd.lm.lead.ma <- lm(lgd[1:ee]~gdp_ma3[1:ee], data = lgd.ts)
summary(lgd.lm.lead.ma)
```

```
#   Estimate Std. Error t value Pr(>|t|)
# (Intercept)    11.2576      1.0631  10.589 1.23e-08 ***
# gdp_ma3[1:ee]  -1.6767      0.4812  -3.484  0.00306 **
# ---
# Signif. codes:  0 '***' 0.001 '**' 0.01 '*' 0.05 '.' 0.1 ' ' 1
# Residual standard error: 3.93 on 16 degrees of freedom
# Multiple R-squared:  0.4314,  Adjusted R-squared:  0.3959
# F-statistic: 12.14 on 1 and 16 DF,  p-value: 0.003064
```

A linear model with 3 semesters moving average lead GDP growth captures relatively well LGD time series shape. Attempts to include additional variables should be performed. However, simplicity, in this case, is considered a priority.

Example 4.3.5 completes the multi-step framework by focusing on a very simple portfolio. The output of Example 4.3.4, together with a given macroeconomic scenario, are the key inputs to project LGDs over a multi-period horizon.

EXAMPLE 4.3.5 LGD PROPORTIONAL SHIFT

Let us consider a simple portfolio made by three accounts, as listed in Table 4.3.

Table 4.3 LGD for Corporate and SME accounts

ID	Segment	LGD_{i,t_0}
1	Corporate	7.50%
2	Corporate	6.00%
4	SME	10.50%

Table 4.4 highlights the GDP growth moving average macroeconomic scenario needed to feed the (second) model developed in Example 4.3.4 (t refers to a semester).

It is worth noting that, in line with the regression model estimated in Example 4.3.4, $GDP_t^{growth,ma}$ represents the moving average over the next three semesters.

Table 4.4 LGD projection over a multi-period macroeconomic scenario

		t_1	t_2	t_3	t_4	t_5
$GDP_t^{growth,ma}$		−1.51%	−0.70%	0.46%	0.61%	0.70%
$\hat{\beta}_0$	11.2576					
$\hat{\beta}_1$	−1.6767					
$\widehat{LGD}_{t,\Delta}^{ptf}$		13.79%	12.43%	10.49%	10.23%	10.08%
$\widehat{LGD}_{t_0}^{ptf}$	8.16%					
$ID1$	7.50%	12.67%	11.43%	9.64%	9.41%	9.27%
$ID2$	6.00%	10.14%	9.14%	7.71%	7.53%	7.41%
$ID3$	10.50%	17.74%	16.00%	13.49%	13.17%	12.98%

It is worth remarking that the above-described framework can easily be extended to defaulted as-set LGDs. Indeed, assets that are already in default as per the reporting date are affected by future macroeconomic conditions.

The next section focuses on a forward-looking framework for real estate exposures.

4.3.5 MICRO-STRUCTURE REAL ESTATE LGD MODELLING

The key idea underlying micro-structure real estate lending LGD is to rely on haircut estimates. They are computed as a ratio between indexed property value and net sale price. Indeed, once this haircut is estimated, property value indices (for example, HPI) can be used to project future values of a property, and assess a loss corresponding to the mismatch between EAD, and estimated sale price. Example 4.3.6 provides all details to grasp how this method works.

EXAMPLE 4.3.6 MICRO-STRUCTURE REAL ESTATE LGD MODELLING

Let us consider, as an illustrative exemplification, the three defaulted accounts listed in Table 4.5. The EAD of account ID 1 is $105.00 thousand. The value of the property at default is $100.00 thousand. This property is sold after 1 year from default and the corresponding HPI index (from default time to sale) is 120%. As a consequence, the estimated price value of the property is $120.00 thousand. On the other hand, the actual net sale price is $95.00 thousand. The absolute haircut is $25.00 thousand. It corresponds to a 20.83% percentage haircut. Similar reasoning applies to account IDs 2 and 3. However, for them, sale events occur after 2 and 3 years, respectively.

Table 4.5 Micro-structure real estate LGD modelling key ingredients ($ Thousands)

ID	EAD	Property value at default	HPI	Indexed property value	Net sale price	Haircut	Haircut %
1	105.00	100.00	120%	120.00	95.00	25.00	20.83%
2	200.00	150.00	125%	187.50	140.00	47.50	25.33%
3	300.00	180.00	130%	234.00	160.00	74.00	31.62%

Table 4.6 summarizes severity estimation process. Indeed, one needs to compute the present value of recoveries. Then, the absolute estimated loss is derived as a difference between EAD and the present value of net recoveries. The ratio between estimated loss and EAD provides the loss severity percentage.

Table 4.6 Loss estimate ($ Thousands)

ID	Discount factor	Discounted haircut	Estimated recovery	Estimated loss	Loss severity %
1	0.98	24.50	93.10	11.90	11.33 %
2	0.96	45.60	134.40	65.60	32.80 %
3	0.94	69.56	150.40	149.60	49.87 %

One can decide to use a synthetic measure of severity (for example, average) or consider a more structured way of dealing with projections. From Table 4.6, one may compute a weighted average haircut of 27.67%. In contrast, weighted average loss severity is 37.54%.

Table 4.7 shows how to use the framework in practice. An up-to-date account is considered. Two alternative scenarios are then investigated to compare estimated losses based on HPI dynamics.

- **First scenario: haircut approach.** Focusing on the first row, we start from a $200.00 thousand EAD, and a property value of $400.00 thousand. The following columns show the projected value of the property, according to HPI forecast. Therefore based on the estimated average 27.67% haircut, the estimated (present value) recovery is $155.94 thousand. The corresponding loss is $244.06 thousand (that is, $400.00–$155.94 thousand) which accounts for 61.02% of the EAD.
- **Second scenario: haircut approach.** On the other hand, in the case where HPI grows to 190%, the corresponding loss is $130.65 thousand, which accounts for 32.66% of the EAD.
- **First and second scenario: loss severity approach.** If one relies on the historical estimated severity (that is, 37.54%), external economic conditions do not affect LGD assessment. In both cases we would estimate $ 150.15 thousand loss, corresponding to 37.54% of the EAD.

Table 4.7 Application of the haircut-based modelling ($ Thousands)

Scenario	EAD	Property value at default	HPI	Indexed property value	Haircut %	Estimated recovery	Estimated loss	Loss %
Low HPI	400.00	200.00	110%	220.00	27.67%	155.94	244.06	61.02%
High HPI	400.00	200.00	190%	380.00	27.67%	269.35	130.65	32.66%

The focus os the next section is on micro-structure LGD model validation.

4.3.6 MICRO-STRUCTURE LGD VALIDATION

Checks focus on data, methodology, and statistical testing are performed as listed below:

a. **Data validation.** One of the main issues one needs to face is data integration among different systems used when accounts are up-to-date and then default. Attention should be addressed to:

- **Data representativeness.** Firstly, one needs to specify data granularity (e.g., account-level). Secondly, in line with Section 4.2, one needs to use a consistent definition of default. Furthermore, updated collateral evaluation is vital to ensure LGD representativeness. Then, accrued interest, expenses and other recovery related elements need to be integrated into the LGD database with the same granularity as other key information.
- **Variable appropriateness.** One may face LGD data quality issues. Limitations need to be accurately pointed out. Additionally, both BVs and MVs need to be appropriately sourced in terms of product type, collateral, geography, sector, and other key characteristics of the portfolio under analysis.

- **Data completeness.** Short historical depth may be a critical issue. One should aim to include two economic cycles, or—at least—a recession period. This is particularly relevant to assess model sensitivity on alternative macroeconomic conditions.

b. **Methodology validation.** Theoretical validation is conducted by comparing alternative approaches. The micro-structure approach described in this section can be challenged by considering other methods, such as regression, machine learning and survival analysis, as detailed in the next sections. In all cases methodologies need to be tested against data availability.

c. **Statistical testing validation.** Statistical validation ensures genuine modelling results, as detailed below:

- **Discriminatory power.** As detailed in Section 4.3.1, probability of cure is a crucial component of micro-structure modelling. One may check model discriminatory power by means of alternative metrics, as discussed in previous chapters while focusing on PDs.
- **Model accuracy.** The micro-structure framework relies on the two main components: probability of cure and severity. If discriminatory analysis is used to validate the first component, other metrics are needed for the second one. One should embrace the entire LGD assessment by jointly considering probability of cure and severity, as detailed in Example 4.3.7.

EXAMPLE 4.3.7 MODEL PREDICTION AGAINST ACTUAL LOSSES

Let us focus on the LGD database used throughout the chapter. The validation process relies on the comparison between fitted and actual losses. Based on this, a simplification is made by assuming zero loss in the case of cure. The following steps are followed:

- Compute actual LGDs.
- Use Equation (4.2) to estimate LGDs by means of fitted probability of cure and severity.
- Compute the difference between fitted and actual LGDs.
- Investigate the distribution of fitting errors, and summarize them through a suitable metric, such as mean or median.

We use the logit model developed in Example 4.3.1 for the probability of cure (or the complementary probability of write-off). The decision tree explored in Example 4.3.2 is considered to assess severity.

The analysis is conducted by means of the following steps:

1. Create a validation database,
2. Compare fitted and actual LGD, and
3. Compute a synthetic metric of accuracy.

```
# 1. Create a validation database
reg_list1 <- c('r_b','r_f','r_h','r_m')
reg_list2 <- c('other','r_a','r_c','r_d','r_e','r_g','r_l')
# 1.1. Apply severity to each account based on rules
train_val<-train %>%
dplyr::mutate(sev_band=ifelse(test=(ltv_utd <=0.545919),
yes = 0.0617,
```

```
no=ifelse(test=(region %in% reg_list1 & ltv_utd >0.545919),
yes = 0.1488,
no=ifelse(test=(region %in% reg_list2 & ltv_utd >0.545919),
yes = 0.4739,
no='na'))))
# 2. Compare fitted and actual LGD
# 2.1. Compute fitted LGD
train_val$sev_band <- as.numeric(train_val$sev_band)
train_val$lgd_tree <- train_val$predict_logit*train_val$sev_band
# 2.2. Compute squared differences
train_val$lgd_diff <- (train_val$lgd_tree -
train_val$shortfall_balance_wo)^2
# 2.3. Derive square root differences
train_val$lgd_diff_sqrt <- (train_val$lgd_diff)^0.5
```

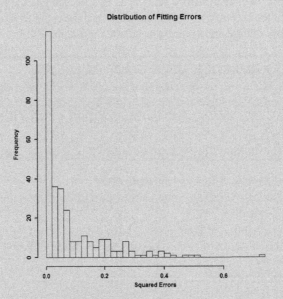

FIGURE 4.14

Error distribution: actual vs. fitted LGDs.

Graphical inspection shows a good model fitting. (See Figure 4.14.) Additionally, one may be interested in summarizing accuracy by means of the following metrics:

```
# 3. Compute a synthetic metric of accuracy
# 3.1. Root mean squared error
lgd_rmse <- sqrt(mean(train_val$lgd_diff))
# 0.1383988
```

```
# 3.2. Weighted average LGD preparation
train_val$lgd_shortfall_def <-
train_val$shortfall_balance_wo*train_val$balance_at_default
train_val$lgd_tree_def <-
train_val$lgd_tree*train_val$balance_at_default
train_val2<- train_val %>%
dplyr::summarise(lgd_shortfall_def1=sum(lgd_shortfall_def),
balance_at_default1=sum(balance_at_default),
lgd_tree_def1= sum(lgd_tree_def))
# 3.3. Weighted average LGD: actual
lgd_actual <-train_val2$lgd_shortfall_def1 /
train_val2$balance_at_default1
# 0.0797918
# 3.4 Weighted average LGD: fitted
lgd_fit<-train_val2$lgd_tree_def1 /
train_val2$balance_at_default1
# 0.08569076
```

This analysis confirms how close actual and fitted average LGDs are (that is, RMSE 7.97% for actual and 8.56% for fitted).

With regard to the forward-looking modelling, Example 4.3.4 highlights a commonly used metric to assess model accuracy (that is, R^2). Other measure of closeness can be considered (for example, mean square root error).

- **Calibration.** Despite its intuitiveness, LGD estimation is affected by a series of issues. One of the most important has to do with the length of the workout process. Consequently, a PIT LGD estimate relies on a time horizon sufficient to embrace the entire recovery process. Data scarcity may also cause some troubles when assessing a calibration target. Therefore one needs to accurately identify the period on which to base LGD calibration. Then apply techniques already explored in previous chapters with regards to probability of cure, and opportunely rescale severity based on the target.
- **Out-of-sample and out-of-time stability.** Parameter stability and overall portfolio fitting are two of the major checks one should perform as part of the out-of-sample and out-of-time validation process. The process is similar to what have been described in previous chapters.
- **Sensitivity analysis.** The goal is to test how the model reacts to different BVs and MVs. The joint investigation of model accuracy and sensitivity to economic fluctuations is crucial throughout the validation process.
- **Reproducibility.** Model implementation needs to align with the framework resulting from development. A positive replication test supports the results of the analysis. Detailed documentation is crucial to ensure a comprehensive understanding of all details underlying the modelling process.

The next section focuses on regression methods.

4.4 LGD REGRESSION METHODS

The micro-structure approach studied in the previous sections relies on the key distinction between cured accounts, incurring very low losses, against non-cured, with non-zero losses. The idea underlying regression modelling is to consider the entire process in one go. Therefore a full spectrum of potential outcomes ranging from 0% fo 100% LGD needs to be considered.

Figure 4.15 summarizes this section's structure.

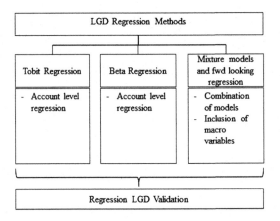

FIGURE 4.15

Workflow diagram for Section 4.4.

Section 4.4.1 focuses on Tobit regression. In contrast, Section 4.4.2 performs the LGD analysis, based on beta regression (Gupton and Stein, 2005). Finally, Section 4.4.3 relies on a mixture of model approaches to embed forward-looking information for LGD projection.

4.4.1 TOBIT REGRESSION

Tobit model (Tobin, 1958) has been widely used in the recent years for LGD modelling (Bellotti and Crook, 2012). In its standard form, the dependent variable is left-censored at zero. Since LGD is both left- and right-censored, one needs to rely on a generalization of the standard model as detailed below:

$$LGD^*_{i,l} = \mathbf{x}'_{i,l}\boldsymbol{\beta}_l + \epsilon_{i,l}, \tag{4.9}$$

and

$$LGD_{i,l} = \begin{cases} 0 & \text{if } LGD^*_{i,l} \leq 0, \\ LGD^*_{i,l} & \text{for } 0 < LGD^*_{i,l} < 1, \\ 1 & \text{for } LGD^*_{i,l} \geq 1, \end{cases} \tag{4.10}$$

where i refers to an account, whereas l indicates a product.

Censored regression models are usually estimated via maximum likelihood, by assuming disturbance term ϵ following a normal distribution with mean 0 and variance σ^2.

Example 4.4.1 explores Tobit regression in the retail mortgage portfolio investigated throughout this chapter.

EXAMPLE 4.4.1 TOBIT LGD MODELLING

Let us consider the portfolio studied in Example 4.3.1. We aim to use Equations (4.9) and (4.10) to estimate the corresponding LGD by means of the following steps:

1. Upload data,
2. Create train and test samples, and
3. Fit Tobit regression.

```
library(AER)
# 1. Upload data
data_lgd<- read.csv('data_lgd.csv', header = TRUE, sep=';')
# 1.1. Overview of the database structure
library(dplyr)
dplyr::glimpse(data_lgd)
# 1.2. Histogram of the variable: ltv_utd
data_lgd$lossrate<-data_lgd$shortfall/
data_lgd$balance_at_default
hist(data_lgd$lossrate)
# 2. Create train and test samples
data_lgd$flag_sold_1<-
dplyr::if_else(data_lgd$flag_sold == 1,0,1)
library(caret)
set.seed(2122)
train_index <- caret::createDataPartition(data_lgd$flag_sold_1,
p = .7, list = FALSE)
train <- data_lgd[ train_index,]
test  <- data_lgd[-train_index,]
# 3. Fit tobit regression
fit_tobit <- tobit(lossrate ~ ltv_utd, data = train)
summary(fit_tobit)
# Coefficients:
#             Estimate Std. Error z value Pr(>|z|)
# (Intercept) -0.43016    0.09211   -4.670 3.01e-06 ***
# ltv_utd      0.31687    0.12297    2.577 0.00997 **
# Log(scale)  -0.75157    0.08790   -8.550 < 2e-16 ***
# ---
# Signif. codes:  0 '***' 0.001 '**' 0.01 '*' 0.05 '.' 0.1 ' ' 1
# Scale: 0.4716
# Gaussian distribution
# Number of Newton-Raphson Iterations: 3
```

```
# Log-likelihood: -164.8 on 3 Df
# Wald-statistic:  6.64 on 1 Df, p-value: 0.0099708
```

Figure 4.16 summarizes portfolio loss rate.

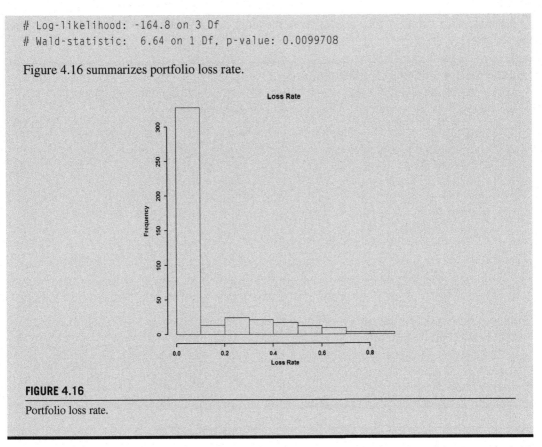

FIGURE 4.16

Portfolio loss rate.

As a next step, one needs to predict the estimated model. Tobit function used in Example 4.4.1 does not directly rescale outcomes. Therefore an extra step is performed by assuming that the probability of a non-zero observation is $\Phi(\frac{\mu}{\sigma})$, where Φ is the normal cumulative distribution function. The conditional expectation is then $\mu + \sigma \cdot \lambda(\frac{\mu}{\sigma})$, where $\lambda(\cdot)$ is the inverse of Mills ratio (Tobin, 1958). The unconditional expectation is obtained as the product of these two components: $\Phi(\frac{\mu}{\sigma}) \cdot \left[\mu + \sigma \cdot \lambda(\frac{\mu}{\sigma})\right]$.

Example 4.4.2 predicts LGDs, based on parameter estimates detailed in Example 4.4.1.

EXAMPLE 4.4.2 PREDITC TOBIT LGDS

Moving from Example 4.4.1, predictions are computed as follows:

```
my_range = range(train$lossrate, predict(fit_tobit))
```

Figure 4.17 shows actual and fitted loss rates. The left panel reports actuals as circles, whereas fitted values are linked by means of a solid line. It is worth noting that all non-cured accounts are stuck in the initial rows of the dataset (that is, low index on the horizontal axis).

In contrast, cured accounts (with a 0% loss rate) have higher index values. Consequently, one would expect to have higher loss rates for non-cured accounts on the left hand-side, and a series of 0% losses on the right hand-side of the graph.

Fitted values are constantly below 0%. This is further highlighted on the right panel showing fitted values distribution.

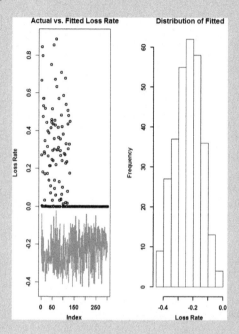

FIGURE 4.17

Loss rate before applying Tobit-specific rescaling adjustment. Left panel: actual (circles) and fitted (solid line). Right panel: fitted loss distribution.

A rescaling adjustment is performed as follows:

```
mu <- fitted(fit_tobit)
sigma <- fit_tobit$scale
p0 <- pnorm(mu/sigma)
lambda <- function(x) dnorm(x)/pnorm(x)
ey0 <- mu + sigma * lambda(mu/sigma)
ey <- p0 * ey0
```

Figure 4.18 shows the predicted values, based on re-scaled outcomes. All fitted loss rates are positive. Nevertheless, the regression is not able to effectively capture portfolio characteristics. Indeed, fitted values do not exceed 16.00%, whereas actual loss rates in some cases exceed 80.00%.

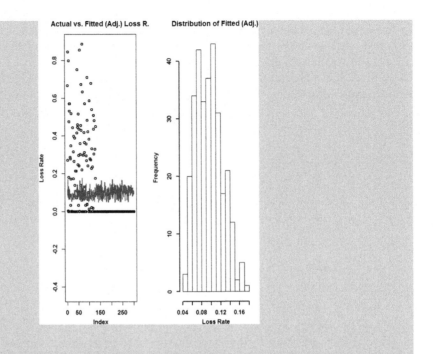

FIGURE 4.18

Loss rate after applying Tobit-specific rescaling adjustment. Left panel: actual (circles) and fitted (solid line). Right panel: fitted loss distribution.

Due to both dataset size and high percentage of cured accounts, the model does not seem to accurately capture loss rate dynamics. Graphical inspection highlights that written-off accounts are approximately characterized by the same loss rate as fully cured accounts.

The next section focuses on beta regression.

4.4.2 BETA REGRESSION

Beta distribution has widely been used to model LGD. As an example, it is the reference function for Moody's $LossCalc^{TM}$ (Gupton and Stein, 2005). From a formal perspective, if we consider LGD as a random variable y following a beta distribution defined within the interval $[0,1]$, then

$$Beta(y|\alpha, \beta) = \frac{1}{\mathbf{B}(\alpha, \beta)} y^{\alpha-1}(1-y)^{\beta-1}, \tag{4.11}$$

where $\alpha > 0$, $\beta > 0$, and $\mathbf{B}(\alpha, \beta) = \int_0^1 u^{\alpha-1}(1-u)^{\beta-1}du$ is the so-called beta function. It is worth noting that $\mathbb{E}(y) = \frac{\alpha}{\alpha+\beta}$ and $Var(y) = \frac{\alpha\beta}{(\alpha+\beta+1)(\alpha+\beta)^2}$.

Example 4.4.3 provides some hints on how Beta regression works in practice.

EXAMPLE 4.4.3 BETA REGRESSION MODELLING

Let us consider, the portfolio investigated in Example 4.4.1. We fit a beta regression, as detailed below:

```
#1. Fit beta regression
library(betareg)
train <- train %>%
dplyr::mutate(lossrate_new= ifelse(lossrate==1,0.9999,
no=ifelse(lossrate==0,0.0001,lossrate)))
fit_beta <- betareg( lossrate_new ~ ltv_utd+tob+region,
data = train)
summary(fit_beta)
# Coefficients (mean model with logit link):
#    Estimate Std. Error z value Pr(>|z|)
# (Intercept) -1.099031   0.340944  -3.223  0.00127 **
# ltv_utd      -0.039932   0.242363  -0.165  0.86913
# tob          -0.003612   0.001247  -2.896  0.00378 **
# regionr_a    -0.202287   0.393928  -0.514  0.60759
# regionr_b    -0.726486   0.290892  -2.497  0.01251 *
# regionr_c    -0.499296   0.258363  -1.933  0.05329 .
# regionr_d    -0.730752   0.231716  -3.154  0.00161 **
# regionr_e    -0.270251   0.292677  -0.923  0.35581
# regionr_f    -0.852346   0.232715  -3.663  0.00025 ***
# regionr_g    -0.328371   0.339179  -0.968  0.33298
# regionr_h    -0.532569   0.310901  -1.713  0.08672 .
# regionr_i    -0.647459   1.077997  -0.601  0.54810
# regionr_l    -0.512263   0.387691  -1.321  0.18640
# regionr_m    -0.837124   0.476516  -1.757  0.07896 .
#    ---
# Signif. codes:  0 '***' 0.001 '**' 0.01 '*' 0.05 '.' 0.1 ' ' 1
# Type of estimator: ML (maximum likelihood)
# Log-likelihood:  1217 on 15 Df
# Pseudo R-squared: 0.2486
# Number of iterations: 69 (BFGS) + 2 (Fisher scoring)
```

Despite the statistical non-significance of the variable ltv_utd, its economic relevance suggests the inclusion in the model. Furthermore, one would potentially need to further group the variable region in order to obtain significant bins. Nevertheless, the analysis (as it is) provides interesting elements to reflect on.

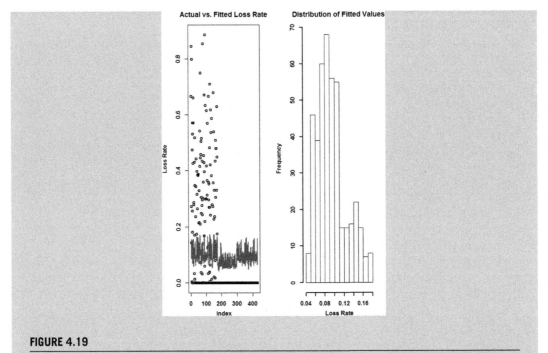

FIGURE 4.19

Beta regression loss rate. Left panel: actual (circles) and fitted (solid line). Right panel: fitted loss distribution.

A 0.25 pseudo-R-squared shows a relatively low fitting. This is graphically confirmed by the comparison of actual and fitted loss rates in the left hand-side panel of Figure 4.19. Indeed, fitted values lie in the interval 5.00%–20.00% range, whereas actuals are scattered over a much wider interval.

For portfolios with observations polarized on extremes (that is, zero loss or 100% loss), inflated beta may help the fitting process by means of the following distribution:

$$
BetaInf(y|\alpha, \beta, \omega_0, \omega_1) = \begin{cases} \omega_0 & \text{for} \quad y = 0, \\ (1 - \omega_0 - \omega_1)\frac{1}{\mathbf{B}(\alpha,\beta)} y^{\alpha-1}(1-y)^{\beta-1} & \text{for} \quad 0 < y < 1, \\ \omega_1 & \text{for} \quad y = 1, \end{cases} \quad (4.12)
$$

where $0 < \omega_0 < 1$ and $0 < \omega_1 < 1 - \omega_0$. The parameters of a beta-inflated function can be estimated by means of a link function (for example, logit) by relying on a $k \times 1$ vector $\boldsymbol{\chi} = (\chi_1, \dots, \chi_k)'$ of explanatory variables.

In case of defaulted asset LGD, one needs to devote specific focus on time since default. Indeed, as detailed in Section 4.3.3, the account's LGD is deeply affected by the point reached on the workout process.

In the next section a combination of models is proposed to improve accuracy and model flexibility. Additionally, MVs embed a forward-looking perspective.

4.4.3 MIXTURE MODELS AND FORWARD-LOOKING REGRESSION

A combination of regression models can also be used instead of a single one. Indeed, following Bellotti and Crook (2012), one may rely on a mixture model by means of decision tree and sub-models for each branch of the tree. Figure 4.20 summarizes the key steps one may follow in this process.

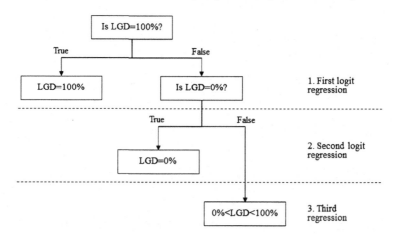

FIGURE 4.20

Mixture model summary.

In more detail, one may rely on logit regressions for the first two levels of the tree:

1. **First logit regression.** Consider a binary problem for 100% against 0% LGD. A probability of 100% LGD is computed by means of logit regression. The outcome of this first regression is $P_{1,i,l}$ (that is, probability of 100% loss).
2. **Second logit regression.** Consider another binary problem once 100% LGD cases are isolated. The outcome of this regression is $P_{0,i,l}$, representing the probability of 0% loss. Therefore $(1 - P_{0,i,l})$ indicates the probability of either 100% LGD or $0\% < LGD < 100\%$.
3. **Third regression.** Run another regression for cases, where $0\% < LGD < 100\%$.

LGD forecast for a given account i is computed as the expected value of the above three sub-models:

$$LGD_{i,l} = (1 - P_{0,i,l}) \cdot [P_{1,i,l} + (1 - P_{1,i,l}) \cdot L_{i,l}], \qquad (4.13)$$

where:

- $P_{1,i,l}$ is the probability of LGD 100% for account computed from the first logit regression model;
- $P_{0,i,l}$ is the probability of LGD 0% for account computed from the second logit regression model;
- $L_{i,l}$ is the loss estimated through the third regression model.

It is worth noting that the model under analysis may rely on both BVs and MVs. This allows us to use the framework to obtain forward-looking estimates. In this regard, one should think of using panel regression to perform an analysis similar to what was shown in Chapter 3. In all cases, if the process becomes too complex, or when LGD database does not support panel analysis, one may also consider a two-step procedure, as described in Section 4.3 for micro-structure modelling. A similar reasoning applies to defaulted assets, where one needs to track account evolution throughout the workout process.

The next section focuses on the validation process throughout all regression models examined so far.

4.4.4 REGRESSION LGD VALIDATION

The validation process for regression methods is aligned with what was described in Section 4.3.6. Few peculiarities applicable to regression are listed below:

a. **Data validation.** With regard to data, one may refer to Section 4.3.6. Indeed, no additional specific checks apply to regression methods.
b. **Methodology validation.** As detailed in 4.3.6, one should evaluate advantages and disadvantages of alternative methods, including micro-modelling, regression, machine learning, and others.
c. **Statistical testing validation.** In what follows, the attention is mainly focused on model accuracy. Few hints are also provided in terms of sensitivity analysis and reproducibility. For mixture models, discriminatory power can be assessed by means of techniques already examined in Section 4.3.6.

- **Model accuracy.** Goodness of fit tests are required to point out model fitting. One should perform both a component-specific validation and an overall model validation. In line with Section 4.3.6, a comparison of actual and fitted losses needs to inform the analysis. A specific focus is required on loss distribution and not simply on summary metrics, such as mean or median loss rate. A cohort perspective also helps understanding the model's behaviour under different economic circumstances.
- **Sensitivity analysis.** One needs to point out how BVs and MVs fluctuations impact projections by considering both historical and hypothetical scenarios.
- **Reproducibility.** As per all other models, both data and model outputs are subject to replication exercises. In this regard, one needs to ascertain an adequate documentation of all steps of the end-to-end process.

In the next section LGD is explored through the lenses of machine learning (ML) techniques.

4.5 LGD MACHINE LEARNING (ML) MODELLING

A wide spectrum of machine learning (ML) techniques can be used for LGD modelling. Classification and regression trees have already been used for micro-structure LGD modelling in Section 4.3. Here, the focus is on methods to estimate LGD all in one go. In this regard, when the dependent variable is numeric, as we have seen in Section 4.4, regression trees play a key role. Additional techniques, such as bagging, random forest, and boosting have recently gained consensus both in the literature and among practitioners. They can be used as a main LGD reference, utilised to improve some elements of the LGD framework, or be considered as a challenger model.

Figure 4.21 summarizes this section's structure.

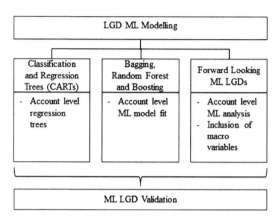

FIGURE 4.21

Workflow diagram for Section 4.5.

Section 4.5.1 focuses on the standard regression tree structure. It paves the way to Section 4.5.2, where bagging, random forest and boosting are applied. Section 4.5.3 describes how to use ML procedures to obtain forward-looking LGD estimates. Finally, Section 4.5.4 focuses on validation.

4.5.1 REGRESSION TREE LGD

A regression tree operates through a series of logical if-then conditions. The algorithm begins with a root node containing all observations. Then, it searches over all possible binary splits to minimize intra-subset volatility.

The approach followed in Section 4.3.2 (that is, Example 4.3.2) to estimate severity can be easily extended to the entire population without making a distinction between probability of cure and severity. In other words, Section 4.3 relies on a clear distinction between cured and non-cured accounts. Separate models are used to capture these features. One may also develop a regression tree on the entire population by leaving the algorithm to detect the most effective way to capture portfolio LGD features.

Example 4.5.1 describes how to implement this approach on the LGD database used throughout the chapter.

EXAMPLE 4.5.1 REGRESSION TREE MODELLING

Let us consider the portfolio studied throughout the chapter. All observations are taken into account. No distinction is made between cured and non-cured (written-off) accounts. The following steps are implemented to estimate LGD:

1. Upload data,

2. Fit regression tree (dependent variable shortfall_balance_wo),
3. Predict, and
4. Prune.

```
# 1. Upload data
lgd_data_tree <- read.csv('data_lgd.csv', header = TRUE, sep=';')
# 1.1. Select a subset of relevant variables
lgd_data_tree_sel_orig <- lgd_data_tree %>%
dplyr::select('flag_sold', 'balance_at_default','ltv_utd',
'time_since_default', 'repayment_type_segment', 'tob',
'months_to_maturity', 'region' , 'shortfall_balance_wo')
# 1.2. Filter out NAs
lgd_data_tree_sel <- lgd_data_tree_sel_orig %>%
na.omit(lgd_data_tree_sel_orig)
# 1.3. Create train and test samples
library(caret)
set.seed(123)
train_index <- caret::createDataPartition(
lgd_data_tree_sel$flag_sold, p = .7, list = FALSE)
train <- lgd_data_tree_sel[ train_index,]
test  <- lgd_data_tree_sel[-train_index,]
# 2. Fit regression tree
library(tree)
lgd_reg_tree <- tree(shortfall_balance_wo~.-flag_sold, data=train)
summary(lgd_reg_tree)
# Variables actually used in tree construction:
# 'months_to_maturity' 'region' 'ltv_utd'
# 'balance_at_default'
# Number of terminal nodes:  13
# Residual mean deviance:  0.005391 = 1.553 / 288
# 3. Predict
tree_predict_train <- predict(lgd_reg_tree, train)
rmse_lgd_reg_train <- sqrt(mean((tree_predict_train
-train$shortfall_balance_wo)^2))
# 0.07182237
```

The regression tree includes the key variables already inspected in previous sections. With regard to the predicted values, root mean square error (RMSE) is 7.18% for train and 12.82% for test sample, respectively.

```
# 4. Prune
lgd_reg_tree_prune <- prune.tree(lgd_reg_tree, best=4)
summary(lgd_reg_tree_prune)
```

```
# Variables actually used in tree construction:
# 'months_to_maturity' 'ltv_utd' 'region'
# Number of terminal nodes:  4
# Residual mean deviance:  0.01189 = 3.532 / 297
# 4.1. Apply the pruned tree on test sample
tree_predict_prune_train <- predict(lgd_reg_tree_prune, train)
rmse_prune_train <- sqrt(mean((tree_predict_prune_train
-train$shortfall_balance_wo)^2))
# 0.1083208
```

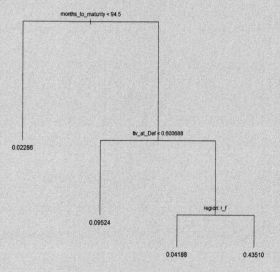

FIGURE 4.22

Pruned tree LGD modelling.

Figure 4.22 summarizes the pruned tree structure. Three key variables are considered: months_to_maturity, ltv_utd (that is, loan-to-value updated), and region. With regard to the predicted values, for both train and test samples, RMSE is greater than in the non-pruned case. For the train sample RMSE for pruned tree, it is 10.83% against 7.18%. For the test sample, it is 15.22% against 12.82%.

Figure 4.23 summarizes the fitting for non-pruned and pruned trees by distinguishing between train and test samples. An optimal model would align fitted values on a 45-degree diagonal. The tree structure is such that, for a given tree leaf, all accounts have the same LGD. This phenomenon is much more clear in the bottom panel, where the pruning process reduces the number of final nodes.

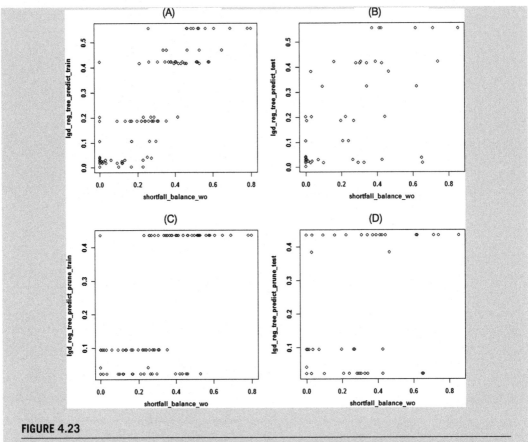

FIGURE 4.23

Decision tree predicted vs. actual LGDs. Train and test sample outcomes for non-pruned and pruned trees. (A) Train no-pruning; (B) Test no-pruning; (C) Train pruning; (D) Test no-pruning.

The next section explores how to use random forest and boosting to estimate LGDs.

4.5.2 BAGGING, RANDOM FOREST, AND BOOSTING LGD

The regression tree procedure described in Section 4.5.1 is very intuitive. However, some space is left for fitting improvement. Based on this, one may consider ML techniques already explored in previous chapters. Example 4.5.2 relies on random forest.

EXAMPLE 4.5.2 RANDOM FOREST LGD

Moving from the train and test sample already created for Example 4.5.1, the following steps are implemented to apply a random forest algorithm:

1. Fit random forest, and
2. Predict.

```
# 1. Fit random forest
library(randomForest)
set.seed(123)
rf_lgd <- randomForest(shortfall_balance_wo~.-flag_sold,
data=lgd_data_tree_sel[train_index,],mtry=4, ntree=100,
importance=TRUE, na.action=na.omit)
# Type of random forest: regression
# Number of trees: 100
# No. of variables tried at each split: 4
# Mean of squared residuals: 0.01128358
# % Var explained: 63.31
```

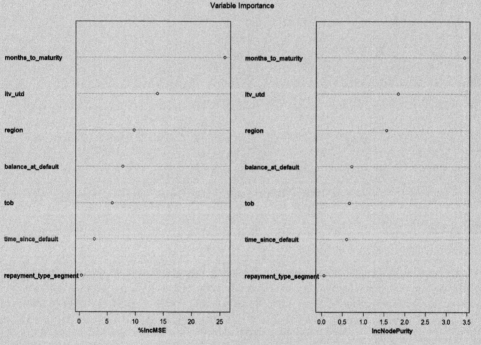

FIGURE 4.24

Random forest importance variable plot.

In line with all previous examples, the most relevant variables are: months_to_maturity, ltv_utd and region. (See Figure 4.24.)

Remark. It is worth noting that time_since_default is considered as part of the explanatory variables despite its relatively low contribution. This variable should always be included for defaulted asset LGDs.

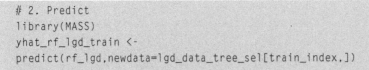

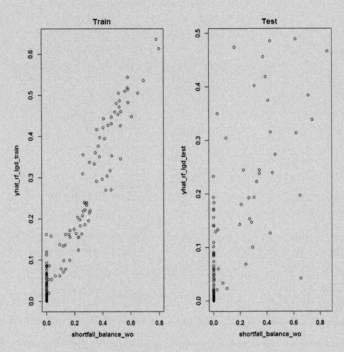

FIGURE 4.25

Random forest predicted vs. actual LGDs: train and test samples.

In Figure 4.25, perfect modelling is represented by means of a 45-degree diagonal. The left hand-side plot highlights a very good sample fitting (that is, train data). It confirms what was previously highlighted in terms of mean of squared residuals (that is, 0.01128358 as per the output of random forest). Moving to the right hand-side plot of Figure 4.25, test sample prediction is characterized by higher dispersion.

Example 4.5.2 highlights random forest fitting improvements compared to regression tree, introduced in Section 4.5.1. The next step is to investigate how boosting may further improve model fitting. Example 4.5.3 provides some hints on how to apply the algorithm.

EXAMPLE 4.5.3 BOOSTING LGD

Let us proceed from Example 4.5.2 by means of the same train and test samples. Likewise, shortfall_balance_wo is the variable to fit. The following steps serve the purpose of implementing the boosting:

1. Fit boosting,
2. Predict, and
3. Apply a shrinkage.

```
# 1. Fit boosting
library(gbm)
set.seed(123)
boost_lgd=gbm(shortfall_balance_wo~.-flag_sold,
data=lgd_data_tree_sel[train_index,],
distribution='gaussian',n.trees=100,interaction.depth=4)
summary(boost_lgd)
# var      rel.inf
# months_to_maturity       months_to_maturity 54.7337061
# ltv_utd                             ltv_utd 25.4350546
# region                               region 13.9906140
# balance_at_default       balance_at_default  4.1704502
# tob                                     tob  1.1696537
# time_since_default       time_since_default  0.5005214
# repayment_type_segment repayment_type_segment  0.0000000
```

The output of the model ranks explanatory variables in terms of relative importance. Once again, the two most relevant are: months_to_maturity and ltv_utd. As per random forest analysis, time_since_default would need to be used for defaulted asset LGD.

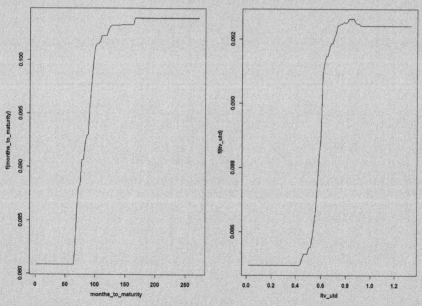

FIGURE 4.26

Incremental analysis for months_to_maturity and ltv_utd.

Figure 4.26 highlights an approximate S shape for both months_to_maturity and ltv_utd.

```
# 2. Predict
yhat_boost_lgd_train=predict(boost_lgd,
newdata=lgd_data_tree_sel[train_index,],n.trees=100)
```

One may additionally apply a shrinkage to the above-detailed model, as listed in the following:

```
# 3. Apply a shrinkage
boost_lgd_shr=gbm(shortfall_balance_wo~.-flag_sold,
data=lgd_data_tree_sel[train_index,],
distribution='gaussian',n.trees=100,interaction.depth=4,
shrinkage=0.2,verbose=F)
yhat_boost_lgd_train_shr=predict(boost_lgd_shr,
newdata=lgd_data_tree_sel[train_index,],n.trees=100)
```

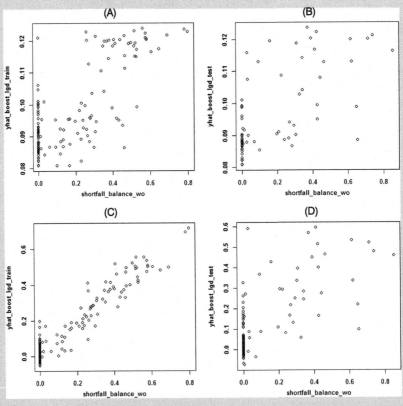

FIGURE 4.27

Boosting predicted vs. actual LGDs. Train and test sample outcomes for non-pruned and pruned trees. (A) Train no-shrinkage; (B) Test no-shrinkage; (C) Train shrinkage; (D) Test shrinkage.

Figure 4.27 points out the role of applying a 0.20 shrinkage to the initial boosting. Visual inspection pinpoints an improvement in terms of alignment between actual and fitted values. This is particularly evident from the comparison of panels A and C. Indeed, the latter shows a greater alignment with the diagonal (where fitted values are perfectly aligned with actuals) than in panel A. A more comprehensive goodness-of-fit analysis is provided in Section 4.5.4, where the full validation process is described.

The next section focuses on forward-looking ML methods.

4.5.3 FORWARD-LOOKING MACHINE LEARNING LGD

One needs to capture an LGD link with MVs to make the projections required by IASB (2014) and FASB (2016). The most intuitive way to tackle this issue via ML algorithms is to include MVs in our dataset. On the other hand, when ML procedures fail to capture this relationship because of scarce data or other specific features, the two-step procedure, described in Section 4.3.4, may be used on top of the LGD estimated via ML techniques.

Example 4.5.4 provides some hints on how to perform the analysis by means of random forest.

EXAMPLE 4.5.4 FORWARD-LOOKING RANDOM FOREST

Let us include some MVs aligned with Example 4.3.4 to enrich the database explored throughout the chapter. The analysis is performed by means of the following steps:

1. Upload data,
2. Fit random forest, and
3. Perform sensitivity analysis.

```
# 1. Upload data
lgd_fwd_macro <- read.csv('lgd_fwd_timeseries.csv',
header = TRUE, sep=";")
lgd_fwd_macro$sem_def <- as.Date(lgd_fwd_macro$sem_def,
format = "%m/%d/%Y")
# 1.1. Select a subset of variable
library(dplyr)
lgd_fwd_macro_sel_all <- lgd_fwd_macro %>%
dplyr::select('flag_sold', 'balance','ltv_utd',
'repayment_type_segment', 'tob', 'months_to_maturity',
'region' , 'shortfall_balance_wo',
'gdp', 'uer', 'cpi', 'hpi', 'ir')
# 1.2. Filter historical data set
lgd_fwd_macro_sel <- lgd_fwd_macro_sel_all[1:430,]
# 1.3. Create train and test samples
library(caret)
set.seed(123)
train_index_macro <- caret::createDataPartition(
```

```
      lgd_fwd_macro_sel$flag_sold, p = .7, list = FALSE)
      train_macro <- lgd_fwd_macro_sel[ train_index_macro,]
      test_macro  <- lgd_fwd_macro_sel[-train_index_macro,]
      # 2. Fit random forest
      library(randomForest)
      set.seed(123)
      rf_lgd_macro <- randomForest(shortfall_balance_wo~.-flag_sold,
      data=train_macro, mtry=4, ntree=100, importance=TRUE,
      na.action=na.omit)
      importance(rf_lgd_macro)
      #                            %IncMSE  IncNodePurity
      # balance                  4.86474453    0.76112841
      # ltv_utd                  9.36220657    1.42821186
      # repayment_type_segment   0.62289506    0.04335664
      # tob                      4.14651824    0.79965450
      # months_to_maturity      23.65134307    3.38916587
      # region                   8.42960916    1.46487030
      # gdp                      1.92656656    0.20465696
      # uer                     -0.88452101    0.13651496
      # cpi                     -0.04802177    0.15972731
      # hpi                      2.72183410    0.27207836
      # ir                       1.66505158    0.22570846
```

Sensitivity analysis is performed on a small sub-sample of the portfolio. The purpose is not to replicate the investigation performed in Example 4.3.4, but to show how to forecast LGD values by relying on alternative economic conditions. For this purpose, the following baseline and adverse scenarios are considered see Table 4.8.

Table 4.8 Macroeconomic scenarios: baseline vs. adverse

	gdp	uer	cpi	hpi	ir
Baseline	3.50%	5.25%	0.85%	8.50%	2.50%
Adverse	−5.50%	7.50%	2.00%	−12.50%	2.00%

```
      # 3. Perform sensitivity analysis
      lgd_data_macro_base <- lgd_fwd_macro_sel_all[431:499,]
      lgd_data_macro_stress <- lgd_fwd_macro_sel_all[500:568,]
      yhat_rf_lgd_macro_base <- predict(rf_lgd_macro,
      newdata=lgd_data_macro_base)
      yhat_rf_lgd_macro_stress <- predict(rf_lgd_macro,
      newdata=lgd_data_macro_stress)
```

The comparison of the baseline LGDs and adverse LGD shown in Figure 4.28 points out the role of MVs in projecting LGDs. The majority of accounts is on the upper side of the diagonal.

This is particularly relevant for higher LGD values when adverse economic conditions cause LGDs to increase, especially for accounts that are not likely to cure.

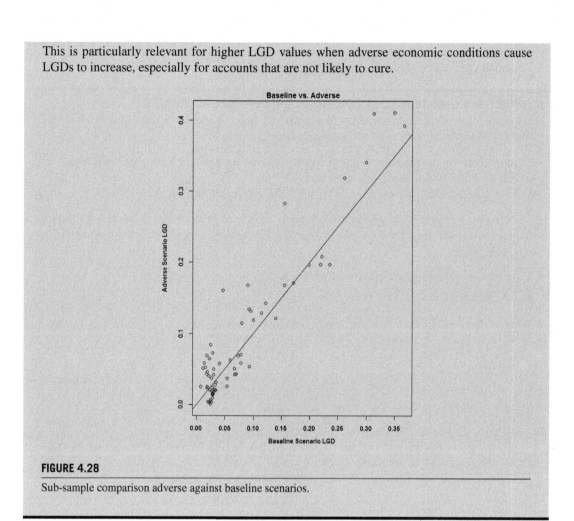

FIGURE 4.28

Sub-sample comparison adverse against baseline scenarios.

The next section focuses on the ML validation process.

4.5.4 MACHINE LEARNING LGD VALIDATION

The process to validate machine learning LGD models aligns with Section 4.3.6. In what follows, the focus is on ML peculiarities.

a. **Data validation.** Section 4.3.6 applies to ML LGDs.
b. **Methodology validation.** Comparison of alternative methods is vital, as made known in the previous validation sections. When focusing on ML methods, one needs to pay particular attention to balance easy interpretation and model sophistication. This applies in particular when other more traditional techniques have already been used and embraced within a firm.
c. **Statistical testing validation.** The focus is on model accuracy as listed below:

- **Model accuracy.** One should be able to show how close actual and fitted losses are, both in sample and out of sample. Example 4.5.5 provides some hints on how to set-up this process.

EXAMPLE 4.5.5 ML MODEL PREDICTION AGAINST ACTUAL LOSSES

Let us focus on models examined in Examples 4.5.1, 4.5.2 and 4.5.3. One may refer to the following steps as an indication of model accuracy assessment:

- Investigate the distribution of fitting errors, and summarize them through a suitable metric (for example, root mean square error RMSE).
- Compare portfolio average fitted and actual LGDs to check for bias.

As a starting point, we consider the regression tree model described in Example 4.5.1. Similar steps can be followed for Examples 4.5.2 and 4.5.3. Validation is performed by means of the following steps:

1. Compute root mean squared error (RMSE), and
2. Estimate regression tree average LGD

```
# 1. Compute RMSE
rmse_lgd_reg_train <-sqrt(mean((tree_predict_train-
train$shortfall_balance_wo)^2))
# 0.07182237
rmse_prune_train <- sqrt(mean((tree_predict_prune_train-
train$shortfall_balance_wo)^2))
# 0.1083208
```

Train sample RMSE is 7.18% and 10.83% for the tree without and with pruning, respectively. With regard to the test sample, RMSE is 12.82% and 15.22%, respectively. The increase in volatility is due both to the size of the test sample and its characteristics.

```
# 2. Estimate regression tree average LGD
# 2.1. Train sample elementary values
train$lgd_shortfall_def <-
train$shortfall_balance_wo*train$balance_at_default
train$lgd_tree_train <-
tree_predict_train*train$balance_at_default
train$lgd_tree_prune_train <-
tree_predict_prune_train*train$balance_at_default
# 2.2. Train sample sum of values
train_sum<- train %>%
dplyr::summarise(lgd_shortfall_def1=sum(lgd_shortfall_def),
balance_at_default1=sum(balance_at_default),
lgd_tree_train= sum(lgd_tree_train), lgd_tree_prune_train=
sum(lgd_tree_prune_train))
```

```
# 2.3. Train sample weighted average computation
lgd_actual_train <-
train_sum$lgd_shortfall_def1/train_sum$balance_at_default1
# 0.07651254
lgd_fit_tree_train<-
train_sum$lgd_tree_train/train_sum$balance_at_default1
# 0.07616479
lgd_fit_tree_prune_train<-
train_sum$lgd_tree_prune_train/train_sum$balance_at_default1
# 0.0804189
```

The actual weighed average LGD value for the train sample is 7.65%. The corresponding average estimate, based on the non-pruned tree, is 7.61%; whereas for the pruned tree, it is 8.04%. Moving to the test sample, the actual weighed average LGD is 8.40%. The corresponding average estimate, based on the non-pruned tree, is 7.64%; whereas for the pruned tree, it is 9.28%. These fluctuations are due both to the characteristics of the tree structure, and the differences between development sample and test.

Table 4.9 summarizes train and test results for each ML model investigated so far. Random forest and boosting with shrinkage provide the best in sample fitting. However, the out-of-sample analysis highlights some bias, probably due to the small subset size used for the analysis.

Table 4.9   RMSE and mean values for alternative ML approaches: train and test samples

	Train		Test	
Actual	**RMSE %**	**Mean %**	**RMSE %**	**Mean %**
Actual		7.65		8.41
Regression tree	7.18	7.61	12.82	7.64
Regression tree pruned	10.83	8.04	15.22	9.28
Random forest	4.71	7.69	12.82	8.89
Boosting	16.51	8.82	18.25	8.92
Boosting shrinkage	4.44	7.61	12.71	9.55

The next section provides some hints on survival analysis.

4.6 HINTS ON LGD SURVIVAL ANALYSIS

There are two main reasons why survival analysis could be used for LGD estimation. Firstly, some accounts in the dataset are still being paid. They can easily be treated as censored, and include them in model building. Secondly, recovery rate distribution is far from being normal. Survival analysis models can handle these problems by means of alternative distribution, as the non-parametric Cox proportional hazard (CPH) or accelerated failure time (AFT) models.

Both CPH and AFT are built for modelling recovery rates. Here, the event of interest is debt write-off. Therefore written-off debts are treated as uncensored. On the other hand, paid-off debts and those in the process of being paid are treated as censored.

AFT models do not handle 0 in target variable. Therefore cured account would require ad hoc treatment.

Survival analysis has only recently been considered for LGD modelling. Its application is still in early phases. On the one hand, this is due to its relatively higher complexity. On the other hand, its structure is particularly appealing when recoveries occur at once.

The next section provides some guidance on how to tackle issues related to lack of data and low default portfolios.

4.7 SCARCE DATA AND LOW DEFAULT PORTFOLIO LGD MODELLING

All methods described in previous sections rely on a reasonable set of historical information. Nevertheless, one may face two extra challenges. Firstly, recovery process information is not appropriately collected. Therefore one cannot heavily rely on statistical techniques. Secondly, for low default portfolios other solutions need to be considered, for example, information enrichment and benchmarking.

Section 4.7.1 (following) explores the key steps of an expert judgement assessment, whereas Section 4.7.2 provides some hints on low default portfolio LGD treatment. Section 4.7.3 completes the journey by defining principles informing a validation process, when statistical models are not the primary estimation resource.

4.7.1 EXPERT JUDGEMENT LGD PROCESS

When a complete statistical modelling framework is not a viable solution, due to data availability, an expert judgement framework may provide reassurance in terms of resilience and accuracy. Top-down and bottom-up interactions are deemed to ensure robustness to LGD estimates. Indeed, an overarching view of the phenomenon needs to be supported by factual evidence on historical, current, and foreseeable future. The following key areas are usually scrutinized:

- **Expert panel identification.** As a first step, one needs to identify experts to involve throughout the LGD process. Risk management usually plays a key role in terms of coordination. However, competences are commonly required among different teams, such as recovery, finance and accounting. An adequate governance around the expert assessment process is vital to ensure clear ownership and consistent assessment.
- **Default definition.** When people with different backgrounds are involved in a complex process, basic agreements are crucial. A common understanding of both quantitative and qualitative events triggering default needs to inform all steps of the journey.
- **Portfolio segmentation.** Corporate and retail portfolios are usually treated separately. Collateralized products commonly embed lower LGDs than those not assisted by collaterals. Product characteristics, geography, and other additional features may also play a relevant role as segmentation drivers.

- **Data.** Structured or unstructured data are used to support business experts assessments. Indeed, historical track records of written-off positions are crucial both to reach an agreement and justify it outside the expert panel consensus.
- **Method.** One needs to clarify metrics underlying LGD estimates. In line with the micro-structure approach described in Section 4.3, one may rely on:
  - Probability of cure. Expert panel is required to express its own view on historical and prospective cure dynamics.
  - Severity. Recovery assessment needs to represent current and foreseeable internal and external conditions.
- **LGD risk drivers.** In line with Table 4.2, a set of elements driving LGD needs to be defined.
- **Forward-looking view.** Given the dynamic nature of the banking business, one needs to check whether historical recoveries align with current and expected future recovery practice. Indeed, portfolio changes or external condition movements may lead to profound modifications (for example, selling part of defaulted assets or creating a more dynamic recovery business). These elements need to be considered as part of the projection process, together with the inclusion of macroeconomic factor fluctuations.
- **Defaulted assets.** A detailed assessment informs defaulted assets estimation. Specific focus needs to be addressed regarding potential changes on recovery strategies.
- **Governance.** Rules informing expert judgements need to be adequately structured and documented. Roles and responsibilities need to be clearly defined. Additionally, metrics, data sources and other elements informing the assessment process need to be structured, and continuously revised to ensure continuous alignment with business procedures.

Example 4.7.1 details how an expert judgement process can be organized for a corporate portfolio.

EXAMPLE 4.7.1 EXPERT JUDGEMENT CORPORATE LGD MODELLING

Let us consider a portfolio with scarce information available over a limited time horizon. The following process is followed:

- **Expert panel identification.** Corporate recovery team together with finance, risk management, and business are involved in the assessment. Risk management team takes the lead of the work stream. Other ad hoc representatives intervene on demand on specific topics according to their competences.
- **Default definition.** An instant cure definition is adopted to facilitate the analysis. Both quantitative and qualitative elements are taken into account. Bankruptcy and 90 days past due are the primary events triggering a default.
- **Portfolio segmentation.** Three main sectors are identified, as listed below:
  - Income-producing real estate (IPRE). Funding is provided to real estate firms (for example, office buildings to let, retail space, multifamily residential buildings), where the prospects for repayment and recovery primarily depends upon cash flows generated by the financial assets.
  - Construction. This industry includes the construction of infrastructure and buildings, their maintenance, and disposal.

- Manufacturing. This sector is part of the goods-producing industries group. It comprises entities operating in the mechanical, physical, or chemical transformation of materials, substances, or components into new products.
- **Data.** The following information is available for major defaults occurred in the last three years:
  - Sector indicator,
  - Bankruptcy and 90 days past due information,
  - Balance at write-off,
  - Accrued interests and expenses,
  - Total recovery amount,
  - Indication of written-of or cured position with corresponding date, and
  - Proxy value of collateral at origination is available only for few big operations.
- **Method.** LGD is assessed based on Equation (4.2), summarized as follows:

$$LGD_l = SEV_{wo,l} \cdot (1 - P_{cu,l}) + SEV_{cu,l} \cdot P_{cu,l},$$

where l can be considered as portfolio segment (that is, IPRE, construction, manufacturing).
  - Probability of cure. A set of accounts is chosen on the pool of historical defaults. Their key characteristics are jointly discussed by experts. An agreement is reached on cure, in line with the above default definition. Average cure rates per year are computed, based on historical information. A comparison is then performed over the most recent period to account for point-in-time. As a final decision, an average probability of cure is defined for each segment.
  - Severity. A more complex process characterizes severity assessment. Indeed, a key distinction arises between accounts with collateral against uncollateralized positions. Furthermore, a clear separation is posed between residential real estate, commercial real estate, and other collaterals (for example, machineries and instrumental tools). As a consequence, the risk driver analysis listed below becomes crucial.
  - LGD risk drivers. Table 4.10 summarizes the key elements on the basis of which experts provide their views.

Table 4.10	Risk drivers	
Category	**Type**	**Risk driver**
a. Exposure	i. Collateral	Collateral type and seniority
	ii. Non-collateral	Facility type
b. Customer	i. Segment	IPRE, construction, manufacturing

A tree structure is the output of the expert judgement process. Indeed, probability of cure and severity are provided for each of the following nodes:
  - IPRE:
    - Collateral type and seniority.
    - Facility type.
  - Construction:

- · Collateral type and seniority.
  - · Facility type.
  - Manufacturing:
    - · Collateral type and seniority.
    - · Facility type.
  Collateral types are adequately clustered together with seniority to effectively represent the current portfolio in scope.
- **Forward-looking view.** Scarce data availability over time suggests the use of external available data to capture LGD fluctuations over the last economic cycle. A regression exercise, similar to Section 4.3.4, is conducted. Then, a scalar is applied to capture LGD movements due to macroeconomic variations.
- **Defaulted assets.** For defaulted assets, a simplified approach is adopted. Indeed, no sufficient historical information corroborates a detailed investigation. Nevertheless, an expert assessment, based on historical experience, suggests applying an upward scalar for more than two years since default assets.
- **Governance.** All above-detailed elements are described in a document summarizing the expert judgement process. Monitoring and validation principles are also detailed.

The next section focuses on low default portfolios.

4.7.2 LOW DEFAULT PORTFOLIO LGD

Though the low default portfolio (LDP) problem affects all components of the expected loss (PD, LGD and EAD), most focus has, so far, been on the estimation of PD (Tasche, 2013). Apart from pooling of data, suggested remedies are unfortunately not applicable on LGD estimation.

Two main approaches can be followed to estimate LDP LGD. On the one hand, workout LGD is estimated, based on cash flow recoveries, as examined throughout the entire chapter. On the other hand, market LGD is derived from the prices of defaulted bonds. The decision to go for workout, or market LGD, is essentially the choice of when to observe the recovery rate. Workout LGD relies on ultimate recoveries from the workout process, whereas market LGD estimations use the trading prices at some time after default. The advantage of the workout is that it uses the true values of recoveries, whereas market LGD, affected by the supply and demand, risk aversion and liquidity of the post-default market, has been found to systematically underestimate the true recovery rates.

Expedients, such as the inclusion of near-defaults or the use of transition matrices, sometimes adopted to estimate LDP PDs, can hardly apply to LGD. The one remedy, which has a substantial effect is to pool data, and base the estimation not only on banks' own LGD observations. Since the number of historical LGD observations is low, also after pooling, it could be tempting to use an approach based on market prices. Workout LGD, based on pooled data, would be a viable solution, only if enough data are available. Also a Market LGD estimation approach could be justified to use on a LDP from a theoretical viewpoint, since it increases the possible sample with defaults that historically occurred. However, not all securities that might be in an LDP are traded on a market. Furthermore, the market prices are based on the market's estimation of the future recovery, and the prices are affected by liquidity aspects and risk aversion.

A qualitative approach, similar to what is described in Section 4.7.1, is usually crucial. Indeed, when both workout LGD on pooled data and market LGD are not able to fully represent the phenomenon under analysis, a further step is needed. A comprehensive understanding of contractual features (for example, seniority and collateral type), together with a broader economic landscape representation (for example, downturn and sector specificities), is at the very root of a reliable LGD estimation.

In the case of sovereigns, and public sector entities, one also needs to figure out intervention mechanics triggered by a default. Indeed, details on international and national regulations may help quantifying recoveries. As a consequence, a combination of assessments relying on workout data, market experience, and expert assessment is the preferred way to overcome the intrinsic data scarcity issue related to LDPs. The next section provides some hints on the validation process.

4.7.3 HINTS ON HOW TO VALIDATE SCARCE DATA AND LOW DEFAULT PORTFOLIO LGDS

The usual interdependence of data, methodology, and statistical validation, reflected in previous sections, assumes much deeper importance in case of scarce data and LDPs. Far from a mechanical and servile mindset, one needs to fully grasp the key elements characterizing recovery process. A deep dive into product characteristics, contractual specificities, and collateral peculiarities is a must. Additionally, data analysis, based on both workout process and market, constitute the key ingredient of a comprehensive validation. In all cases, one needs to bear in mind the role of economic conditions, which are crucial for forward-looking estimates, as required both by IFRS 9 and CECL. The next section focuses on SAS LGD modelling.

4.8 SAS LABORATORY

Micro-structure, regression, and machine learning LGD modelling are explored by means of SAS in what follows. An overview is provided by relying on all major examples already studied by means of R throughout the chapter.

SAS laboratory 4.8.1 focuses on micro-structure LGD.

SAS LABORATORY 4.8.1 MICRO-STRUCTURE LGD MODELLING

Let us consider Examples 4.3.1 and 4.3.2. As a starting point, one needs to upload the same data files used for such examples, then the analysis is replicated in SAS by means of the following steps:

1. Create cure table,
2. Train and test samples (cure),
3. Calculate WoE and IV,
4. Fit logit regression,
5. Create severity table,
6. Train and test samples (severity), and
7. Fit regression tree.

```
/* 1. Create cure table */
```

```
proc sort data=uk_data_lgd;by flag_sold;run;
proc boxplot data=uk_data_lgd;
plot months_to_maturity*flag_sold;
run;
data flag_sold_1;
set uk_data_lgd;
if flag_sold=1 then flag_sold_1=0;
else flag_sold_1=1;
run;

/* 2. Train and test samples (cure) */
proc surveyselect data=flag_sold_1 out=stratified_Data method=srs
rate=0.7 outall;
run;
data train test;
set stratified_data;
if selected=1 then output train;
else output test;
run;

/* 3. Calculate WoE and IV  */
proc hpbin data=train numbin=5;
id _all_;
input months_to_maturity tob shortfall_balance_wo
shortfall ltv_utd index_Value_new ;
ods output mapping=mapping;
run;
ods trace on;
ods output woe=WOE infovalue=IV;
proc hpbin data=train WOE bins_meta=mapping output=binned_dataset;
id _all_;
target flag_sold_1/level=nominal;
run;
proc contents data=binned_dataset;
run;
proc sql;
create table woe_append as select distinct

a.*,
b1.woe as months_to_maturity_woe,
b2.woe as tob_woe,
b3.woe as shortfall_balance_wo_woe,
b4.woe as shortfall_woe,
```

```
b5.woe as ltv_utd_woe,
b6.woe as index_value_new_woe

from binned_dataset as a

left join woe as b1 on a.bin_months_to_maturity=b1.bin and
lowcase(b1.binnedvariable)='bin_months_to_maturity'
left join woe as b2 on a.bin_tob=b2.bin and
lowcase(b2.binnedvariable)='bin_tob'
left join woe as b3 on a.bin_shortfall_balance_wo=b3.bin and
lowcase(b3.binnedvariable)='bin_shortfall_balance_wo'
left join woe as b4 on a.bin_shortfall=b4.bin and
lowcase(b4.binnedvariable)='bin_shortfall'
left join woe as b5 on a.bin_ltv_utd=b5.bin and
lowcase(b5.binnedvariable)='bin_ltv_utd'
left join woe as b6 on a.bin_index_value_new=b6.bin and
lowcase(b6.binnedvariable)='bin_index_value_new'

;quit;

/* 4. Fit logit regression */
proc genmod data=woe_append desc;
model flag_sold_1=months_to_maturity_woe ltv_utd_woe tob_woe/
link=logit dist=binomial;
quit;

/* 5. Create severity table */
data severity;
set work.uk_data_lgd;
where flag_sold=1;
severity=shortfall/balance_at_Default;
if ltv_utd <= 0.7 then ltv_le_70=1;
else ltv_le_70=0;
run;

/* 6. Train and test samples (severity) */
proc surveyselect data=severity out=stratified_Data method=srs
rate=0.7 outall;
run;
data train test;
set stratified_data;
if selected=1 then output train;
else output test;
```

```
run;
ods graphics on;

/* 7. Fit regression tree */
proc hpsplit data=train leafsize=10 maxdepth=8 plots=zoomedtree;
target severity / level=interval;
input shortfall_balance_wo index_value_new tob
ltv_utd /level=interval;
input ltv_le_70 region repayment_type_segment /level=ordinal;
prune costcomplexity;
output growthsubtree=growth importance=factor_imp
nodestats=node_stats;
run;
quit;
```

SAS Laboratory 4.8.2 focuses on regression methods.

SAS LABORATORY 4.8.2 LGD REGRESSION METHODS

Let us consider Examples 4.4.1 and 4.4.3. After uploading the corresponding data file, the analysis is replicated in SAS by means of the following steps:

1. Fit Tobit regression, and
2. Fit beta regression.

```
/* 1. Fit tobit regression */
data severity_calc;
set work.uk_data_lgd;
severity=shortfall/balance_at_Default;
run;
proc qlim data= severity_calc outest=parms;
class region repayment_type_segment;
model severity= ltv_utd region repayment_type_segment ;
endogenous severity ~ censored (LB=0 UB=1);
OUTPUT OUT=OUT XBETA EXPECTED;RUN;
proc corr data=out spearman;
var severity Expct_severity;run;
proc sgplot data=out;
scatter x=severity y=Expct_severity;run;

/* 2. Fit beta regresssion */
proc glimmix data=severity_calc;
model severity=ltv_utd/dist=beta link=logit solution;
output out=betaout predicted;run;
```

SAS laboratory 4.8.3 focuses on machine learning methods.

SAS LABORATORY 4.8.3 RANDOM FOREST LGD

Let us consider Example 4.5.2. After uploading the corresponding data file, the analysis is replicated in SAS as follows:

```
/* 1. Fit random forest */
proc hpforest data=train criterion=Variance
maxtrees=100 vars_to_try=4 splitsize=200 leafsize=100
maxdepth=8 alpha=0.05;
target severity / level=interval;
input shortfall_balance_wo index_value_new tob
ltv_utd /level=interval;
input ltv_le_70 region repayment_type_segment /level=ordinal;
ods output fitstatistics=fitstats;
save file = 'C:\random_forest_lgd_rules.bin';
run;
quit;
```

4.9 SUMMARY

An overview of LGD modelling was provided by considering alternative approaches. The main focus was on workout LGD, whereas minor attention was devoted to market-based estimate, and implied market methods.

Our scrutiny started from data. Indeed, a suitable modelling process relies on adequate information regarding recoveries collected over a reasonable historical period. Neither IASB (2014), nor FASB (2016), pose specific requirements around a minimum period to be covered. Nevertheless, the need to adequately represent a suitable time horizon, by including a recession, was pointed out.

From a modelling standpoint, the study began from a micro-structure approach, where a key distinction arose between cured and written-off accounts. In this regard, generalized linear models (GLMs) and classification trees were adopted to estimate probability of cure and severity. A forward-looking perspective was also investigated by pointing out the relationship between LGD components and macroeconomic variables (MVs). A real estate micro-structure model was also scrutinized by highlighting the link with house price index (HPI), and similar variables.

As an alternative to micro-structure modelling, the focus moved towards regression methods including Tobit and beta regression. The key advantage of these regressions was performing the estimation all at once. Nevertheless, mixture modelling was also considered to capture a forward-looking perspective.

Few hints on survival modelling were provided before moving onto the machine learning space. Bagging, random forest, and boosting were proven as powerful instruments to capture LGD key features.

Finally, attention was devoted to LGD estimation, when scarce data are available, and in the case of low default portfolios. In both cases, a mix of quantitative and qualitative elements constituted the foundation for the assessment.

Validation was examined as a crucial area to assess each modelling approach.

Examples were examined by means of R software, whereas in the final section SAS was utilised. **Data and complementary examples' software code are available at www.tizianobellini.com.**

SUGGESTIONS FOR FURTHER READING

As an initial step, one may find it useful referring to Schuermann (2003) for a reader-friendly and non-complex introduction to LGD modelling. Loeffler and Posch (2011) also provide an easy-to-grasp overview of LGD modelling. Engelmann and Rauhmeier (2011) provide a comprehensive view of credit risk parameter estimation, with a Basel II perspective. A reference point in financial industry is the work of Gupton and Stein (2005), where LossCalc method is described. Bellotti and Crook (2012) provide an up-to-date view on how to estimate LGD by incorporating macroeconomic variables. With regard to machine learning, Hastie et al. (2009) provide a useful theoretical introduction, whereas James et al. (2013) follow a hands-on perspective by means of examples in R.

EXERCISES

Exercise 4.1. Based on Example 4.3.1, estimate probability of cure by relying on CART.

Exercise 4.2. Let us consider the model estimated in Example 4.4.3. Perform an overall validation by comparing actual against fitted losses, as detailed in Example 4.3.7.

Exercise 4.3. Let us consider the model estimated in Example 4.5.3. Perform sensitivity analysis by considering a severely adverse scenario over a three-year horizon.

REFERENCES

Bellotti, T., Crook, J., 2012. Loss given default models incorporating macroeconomic variables for credit cards. International Journal of Forecasting 28 (1), 171–182.

Engelmann, B., Rauhmeier, R., 2011. The Basel II Risk Parameters. Springer-Verlag, Berlin, Heidelberg.

FASB, 2016. Accounting Standards Updata No. 2016-13, Financial Instruments-Credit Losses (Topic 326). June 16, 2016. Financial Accounting Series. Financial Accounting Standards Board.

Gupton, G., Stein, R., 2005. Losscalc V2: Dynamic Prediction of LGD, Modelling Methodology. Moody's KMV Company.

Hastie, T., Tibshirani, R., Friedman, J., 2009. Elements of Statistical Learning: Data Mining, Inference and Prediction. Springer, New York.

IASB, 2014. IFRS 9 Financial Instruments. Technical report, July 2014. International Accounting Standards Board.

James, G., Witten, D., Hastie, T., Tibshirani, R., 2013. An Introduction to Statistical Learning with Applications in R. Springer, New York.

Loeffler, G., Posch, P., 2011. Credit Risk Modeling Using Excel and VBA. Wiley, Chichester.

Schuermann, T., 2003. What do We Know About Loss Given Default? Federal Reserve Bank of New York.

Tasche, D., 2013. The art of probability-of-default curve calibration. Journal of Credit Risk 9, 63–103.

Tobin, J., 1958. Estimation of relationship for limited dependent variables. Econometrica 26, 24–36.

PREPAYMENTS, COMPETING RISKS AND EAD MODELLING

Exposure at default (EAD) represents the balance on which expected credit loss (ECL) is computed. A key distinction operates between committed products (for example, loans) and uncommitted facilities (for instance, overdrafts).

Loan-type products usually cover a multi-year horizon. Consequently, economic conditions may cause a deviation from the originally agreed repayment scheme. As a first step of our journey, the focus is on full prepayments and overpayments (partial prepayments). The investigation is conducted by means of generalized linear models (GLMs) and machine learning (ML). Hints on survival analysis are also provided to estimate and project prepayment outcomes.

A silos analysis characterized all ECL risk component investigated throughout the book. In contrast, growing attention is devoted both by researchers and practitioners on competing risks. As a second step of our investigation, the focus will be on a framework to jointly model full prepayments, defaults and overpayments. On the one hand, we tackle the issue by means of a multinomial regression. In this case, when the outcome is not binary (for example, overpayment) beta and Tobit regression are also used to capture overpayment specific features. On the other hand, full prepayments and overpayments are jointly investigated by means of ML models.

Finally, as a third focus area, uncommitted facilities are inspected by means of a specific framework. One needs to deal with additional challenges comprising accounts with zero or negative utilization at reporting date, and positive exposure at default. All states of the world that practice ECL computation are scrutinized from different angles.

As per the previous chapters, examples and cases are examined by means of R software. In the final section SAS is utilized as analytical means.

KEY ABBREVIATIONS AND SYMBOLS

DB_{i,t_0}	Drawn balance for account i at time t_0
$\mathbb{E}(U_{i,t_D} \mid D_{(t_0,t_h]})$	Expected utilization for account i given default occurring over the interval $(t_0, t_h]$
h	Time horizon: $h = \tau_1 + \tau_2 + \ldots + \tau_J$
L_{i,t_0}	Limit for account i at time t_0
$PP_{i,s,t}$	Probability of prepayment for account i, sub-portfolio s at time t
$SP_{i,s,\tau}$	Survival probability for account i, sub-portfolio s over the period τ
U_{i,t_0}	Utilization for account i at time t_0
τ_j	Time interval j
$\Xi_{i,s,t,\tau}$	Full prepayment indicator function for account i, sub-portfolio s at time t over the period τ

IFRS 9 and CECL Credit Risk Modelling and Validation. https://doi.org/10.1016/B978-0-12-814940-9.00013-X

5.1 INTRODUCTION

Banks play a key role in addressing customer financial needs over different time horizons. Firstly, loan-type products (for example, corporate loans and retail mortgages) usually follow a well-defined repayment schedule. Nevertheless, contracts allow borrowers to deviate from the original schedule as in the case of full prepayments and overpayments (that is, excess payments compared to the amount due).[1] Secondly, interactions between risks play a central role. For example, one may be interested to investigate the relationship between defaults and prepayments. For this reason, special focus is dedicated to competing risks modelling. As a third area of interest, in the short-run, uncommitted and revolving facilities help customers to manage temporary liquidity mismatches. Our goal is to estimate their exposure at default (EAD) by considering a variety of situations, including cases where, at reporting date, utilization is zero or negative.

Figure 5.1 summarizes how these topics are tackled throughout this chapter.

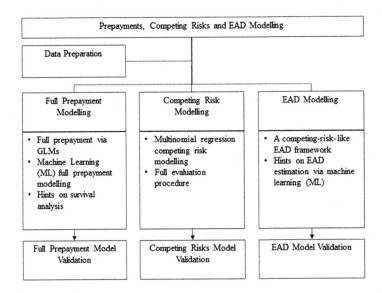

FIGURE 5.1

Chapter's workflow diagram.

- **Data preparation.** Historical prepayments, overpayments and balance data before default are required to model long-run deviations from loan schedules, and adequately represent short-term evolution of uncommitted and revolving facilities. Section 5.2 describes how to build datasets for these purposes.

---

[1]Overpayments and partial prepayments are used as synonyms throughout the chapter.

- **Full prepayment modelling.**[2] A full prepayment is the most extreme deviation from the repayment schedule. Indeed, the loan is repaid in full at some point before maturity. Few alternative approaches are explored in Section 5.3. Firstly, the problem is tackled by focusing on GLMs. This method has already been investigated for both PD and LGD modelling. Here, the binary outcome is represented by prepayment events. In line with previous chapters, machine learning (ML) tools are explored. Finally, few hints on how to use survival analysis are provided.
- **Competing risk modelling.** Contrary to PDs and LGDs, full prepayment modelling relies on accounts outside the default perimeter. Indeed, the goal is to investigate loan balance evolution, based on live accounts to assess their exposure at date. Focus is first fixed on defaults as competing risk against prepayments. Then, overpayments are included as part of the study. Multinomial regression is utilized for analysing full prepayments and defaults, whereas extra effort is needed when considering overpayments. In this case, Tobit and beta regression are useful tools to estimate overpayments as a portion of the outstanding balance at a given reporting date.
- **EAD modelling.** Section 5.5 focuses on EAD modelling by considering a broader spectrum of products, and potential behaviours. It moves from the uncommitted product archetype to investigate the evolution of credit line utilization until the event of default. Firstly, a competing risk perspective is followed. Then, the problem is tackled following an ML perspective.

Examples and case studies are examined by means of R software. Finally, Section 5.6 provides SAS details on the key examples investigated in the chapter.

5.2 DATA PREPARATION

If in previous chapters the focus was on accounts experiencing default events, here we consider both: non-defaulted and defaulted accounts. Indeed, the study of prepayments and overpayments does not rely on defaults, whereas EAD reflects the dynamics of defaulted instruments.

The main focus of Section 5.2.1 is on prepayments and overpayments. Hints are also provided on defaulted accounts to consider both in a competing risk framework and for EAD estimation.

5.2.1 HOW TO ORGANIZE DATA

Data structure required to run account-level analysis is similar to what is used for lifetime PD modelling. As in Chapter 3, one may consider a time frame, as described in Figure 5.2. Indeed, one needs to fit a model on historical data. Then, starting from t_0, a projection takes place.

In what follows, a distinction is made among the three main areas of analysis informing the chapter:

- **Full prepayment.** Unlike PD model development, prepayment analysis relies on non-defaulted accounts. One needs to collect historical information by focusing on the distinction between accounts that fully prepay against others. A deep investigation is a prerequisite to define a prepayment event. As a second step, one may create a flag indicating prepayment occurrence, as

---

[2]In what follows, full prepayment and prepayment are used interchangeably. In both cases, a complete payment of the remaining balance applies.

FIGURE 5.2

Time series structure and notation.

Table 5.1 Quarterly prepayment flag. † Prepayment event. ‡ Maturity date

ID	Reporting date	Prepayment flag
1	$Q1/Y1$	0
1	$Q2/Y1$	0
1	$Q3/Y1$	0
1	$Q4/Y1$	0
1	$Q1/Y2$	1†
2	$Q1/Y3$	0
2	$Q2/Y3$	0
2	$Q3/Y3$	0
2	$Q4/Y3$	0
2	$Q1/Y4$	0‡

listed below. Table 5.1 summarizes the quarterly prepayment flag evolution by means of two account IDs. Indeed, ID 1 (fully) prepays in $Q1/Y2$. In contrast, ID 2 reaches maturity without making any (full) prepayment. It is worth highlighting that a (full) prepayment is an absorbing status.

It is worth remarking a distinction between a physical prepayment and contract modification entitling de-recognition. In the second case, one needs to define criteria to qualify prepayment events.

One needs to stack BVs and MVs information for each row to build a comprehensive database structure, including both dependent and explanatory (independent) variables.

• **Competing risks.** In the next sections prepayments, defaults, and overpayments are considered as competing risks. Table 5.2 summarizes how to build the flag to use as a dependent variable throughout the investigation. Contrary to Table 5.1, where full prepayment was indicated with 1, in Section 5.4 when a full prepayment occurs flag $= 2$ is used. As a consequence, ID 1 experiencing a full prepayment is flagged 2 in $Q1/Y2$. ID 2 does not experience any prepayment, default, or overpayment. The account matures in $Q1/Y4$ (that is, flag 0). ID 3 defaults in $Q4/Y3$ (flag 1). Finally, ID 4 overpays in $Q2/Y2$, $Q3/Y2$, $Q4/Y2$ (that is, flag 3). With regard to this account, extra information is required. Indeed, one needs to estimate the amount of overpayments compared with the original schedule. Consequently, column $Overpayment\%$ reports the percentage amount of overpayment compared to its corresponding outstanding balance. In line with the full prepayment data structure, one needs to stack BVs and MVs information for each row by creating a comprehensive database, including all variables needed to model the phenomena under analysis.

Table 5.2 Competing risk flags. † Prepayment event; ‡ Maturity date; †† Default; ‡‡ Overpayment

ID	Reporting date	Event flag	Overpayment %
1	$Q2/Y1$	0	
1	$Q3/Y1$	0	
1	$Q4/Y1$	0	
1	$Q1/Y2$	2†	
2	$Q1/Y3$	0	
2	$Q2/Y3$	0	
2	$Q3/Y3$	0	
2	$Q4/Y3$	0	
2	$Q1/Y4$	0‡	
3	$Q1/Y3$	0	
3	$Q2/Y3$	0	
3	$Q3/Y3$	0	
3	$Q4/Y3$	1 ††	
4	$Q1/Y2$	0	
4	$Q2/Y2$	3 ‡‡	1.50%
4	$Q3/Y2$	3 ‡‡	1.20%
4	$Q4/Y2$	3 ‡‡	1.10%

- **EAD.** For uncommitted and revolving facilities, one needs to assess the portion of credit limit utilized at default. In other words, if an account has a $100.00 thousand limit, one needs to assess how much of this credit is drawn at default. Two main challenges arise. On the one hand, one needs to specify the time horizon to consider (for example, 12-month interval). On the other hand, drawn amount at default needs to be estimated. As a result, first, one needs to focus on defaulted accounts. A flag needs to align with default definition adopted for other credit models (that is, PD, LGD). Then, information about balance evolution is required as a dependent variable, whereas BVs and MVs are required as explanatory variables.

The next section kicks-off modelling analysis by focusing on full prepayments.

5.3 FULL PREPAYMENT MODELLING

Prepayments may have different determinants. A distinction usually arises between loans (corporate) and mortgages. In all cases, one may consider the following two main drivers causing full prepayment:

- **Excess cash.** Cash availability, exceeding ordinary needs, may induce to fully prepay a loan or a mortgage. In this case, the bank receives an amount corresponding to the outstanding (principal) balance, and the loan is cancelled.

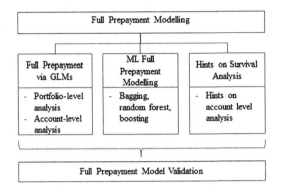

FIGURE 5.3

Workflow diagram for Section 5.3.

- **Refinancing and contract modification.** A new agreement may cause a complete renovation of the original contract. This event needs to be adequately inspected and validated against IASB (2014) and FASB (2016) rules. Indeed, the original contract needs to be de-recognized due to significant modification. In this case, no cash transfer takes place. Nevertheless, the original contract expires, and a new one is made.

Once full prepayments have been identified, in adherence with accounting rules, modelling relies on a binary outcome: non-occurrence or occurrence of prepayment. In line with PD and LGD modelling, already examined in the previous chapters, a natural way of tackling the problem is to use GLMs, machine learning (ML), or consider survival analysis. Figure 5.3 describes how the journey is organized throughout Section 5.3.

In Section 5.3.1, full prepayments are investigated by means of two alternative approaches: portfolio-level and account-level analysis. The focus is then on panel regression. Section 5.3.2 performs the investigation by means of ML procedures. Section 5.3.3 provides some hints on survival analysis. Finally, Section 5.3.4 describes how to conduct a full prepayment model validation.

5.3.1 FULL PREPAYMENT VIA GLM

In line with accounting requirements, an unbiased, point-in-time, and forward-looking estimate informs ECL computation. As a result, one needs to consider both behavioural variables (BVs) and macroeconomic variables (MVs) to avoid any delay in loss recognition. Two main alternatives can be followed to estimate the probability of a full prepayment as listed below:

i. **Portfolio-level analysis.** An index is built at a portfolio- (or sub-portfolio-) level, representing the average prepayment rate experienced over an interval τ (for example, a quarter or a year). This index is built on internal data, or is derived from external sources. Just as portfolio-level lifetime PD analysis, it is linked to macroeconomic variables via regression.

ii. Account-level GLM analysis. Account-level information can be used to infer the relationship between prepayments ($PP_{i,s,t}$) against both BVs and MVs via panel regression. A full prepayment indicator function related to account i can be represented as follows:

$$\Xi_{i,s,t,\tau} = \begin{cases} 1, & \text{full prepayment,} \\ 0, & \text{no-full-prepayment,} \end{cases} \tag{5.1}$$

where the subscript s indicates a sub-portfolio, t refers to the time of the assessment, and τ stands for the corresponding prepayment time horizon (for example, a quarter or a year).

In line with the methodology described in Chapter 3, a sequence of forward-looking probabilities of prepayment feeds the following lifetime prepayment equation:

$$PP_{i,s,h} = SP_{i,s,\tau} \cdot PP_{i,s,(t_\tau,t_h]}, \tag{5.2}$$

where $SP_{i,s,\tau}$ represents the survival probability referred to account i, sub-portfolio s, over the time horizon τ (i.e., $\tau \leq h$). The first element of the equation refers to the probability of no-prepayment over the interval $(t_0, t_\tau]$. On the other hand, $PP_{i,s,(t_\tau,t_h]}$ encompasses the probability of prepaying between t_τ and the end of time interval h (that is, t_h).[3]

Example 5.3.1 provides some hints on how to implement the above-described GLM full prepayment model by considering both BVs and MVs.

EXAMPLE 5.3.1 MORTGAGE GLM FULL PREPAYMENT MODELLING

Let us consider a panel data mortgage portfolio spanning over a multi-year horizon. On the one hand, for each account a prepayment flag is available, as detailed in Section 5.2.1. On the other, explanatory variables include both BVs (for example, time-on-book (TOB), loan-to-value updated (ltv_utd)) and MVs (for example, gross domestic product (GDP) variation, and unemployment rate (UER)). These variables are aligned with those used in Chapter 3 for PDs and Chapter 4 for LGDs. The analysis is performed by means of the following steps:

1. Upload data,
2. Perform GLM analysis, and
3. Inspect time series fitting.

```
# 1. Upload data
bal_prep<- read.csv('bal_prep.csv', header=TRUE,
sep = ',', dec = '.')
# 1.1. Format date
library(dplyr)
library(vars)
bal_prep <- dplyr::mutate_at(bal_prep,
```

---

[3]Square brackets include extremes, whereas parentheses do not include extremes. Additionally, t indicates a point in time, whereas τ and h are time intervals. In more detail, $h = \tau_1 + \tau_2 + \ldots + \tau_J$.

```
vars(contains('date')), funs(as.Date))
# 1.2. Train and test samples
set.seed(1234)
train_sample_prep <- caret::createDataPartition(bal_prep$year,
p=0.7, list=FALSE)
train_prep <- bal_prep[train_sample_prep, ]
test_prep <- bal_prep[-train_sample_prep, ]
# 2. Perform GLM analysis
library(MASS)
logit_prep_full <- glm(prep_flag ~ tob+ltv_utd + uer+gdp+
cpi+hpi+ir, data=train_prep, family = binomial(link = 'logit'))
logit_prep<- stepAIC(logit_prep_full,
k = qchisq(0.05, 1, lower.tail=F), direction = 'both')
summary(logit_prep)
#              Estimate Std. Error z value  Pr(>|z|)
# (Intercept) 93.502785  2.018254  46.329  < 2e-16 ***
# tob          0.002870  0.000761   3.772 0.000162 ***
# ltv_utd     -1.308816  0.026771 -48.889  < 2e-16 ***
# uer         -3.338496  0.087984 -37.944  < 2e-16 ***
# gdp          0.241397  0.026492   9.112  < 2e-16 ***
# cpi         -0.629288  0.068070  -9.245  < 2e-16 ***
# hpi          0.093384  0.008095  11.536  < 2e-16 ***
# ir          -2.018241  0.080944 -24.934  < 2e-16 ***
# ---
# Signif. codes:  0 '***' 0.001 '**' 0.01 '*' 0.05 '.' 0.1 ' ' 1
# (Dispersion parameter for binomial family taken to be 1)
# Null deviance: 14894  on 26143  degrees of freedom
# Residual deviance: 10486  on 26136  degrees of freedom
# AIC: 10502
# Number of Fisher Scoring iterations: 7
```

Stepwise regression proposes a model with the following BVs: TOB (time-on-book), ltv_utd (loan to value updated). A list of MVs is also part of the output: UER (unemployment rate), GDP_growth, CPI, HPI, and IR (interest rate). Signs are aligned with expectations. For, one would expect a reduction in prepayments when unemployment rate increases. On the other hand, one expects an increase of prepayments when a positive GDP growth occurs.

The top-left plot of Figure 5.4 compares fitted against actual prepayments. Dotted line shows that the model, over and under, shoots actual prepayments for some quarters. All other plots point out an MV-dynamic along the period under investigation.

Section 5.3.4 provides a series of goodness of fit metrics including discriminatory power analysis and correlation inspection.

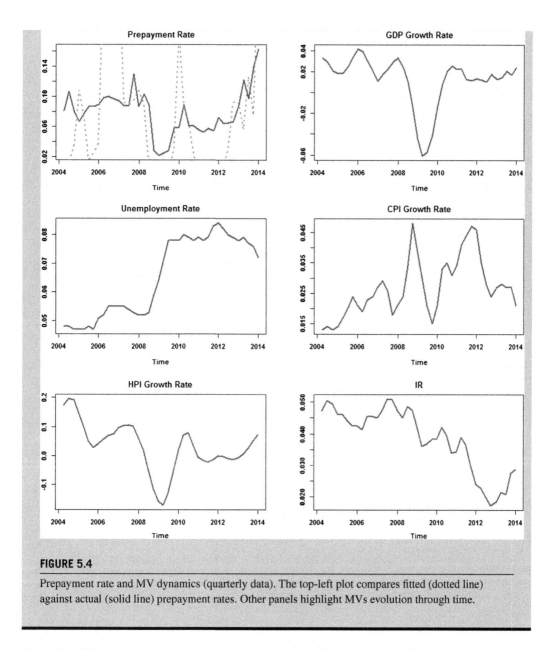

FIGURE 5.4

Prepayment rate and MV dynamics (quarterly data). The top-left plot compares fitted (dotted line) against actual (solid line) prepayment rates. Other panels highlight MVs evolution through time.

Remark. Lifetime prepayment curve $PP_{i,s,h}$, described in Equation (5.2), is estimated by relying on prepayment probabilities PP_{i,s,τ_j}, estimated by means of GLMs, and projected over subsequent interval τ_j to cover the entire horizon h under investigation.

The next section focuses on machine learning procedures to model (full) prepayments.

5.3.2 MACHINE LEARNING (ML) FULL PREPAYMENT MODELLING

Just as account-level modelling, explored in the previous section, machine learning can be used to estimate full prepayments by considering both BVs and MVs. Example 5.3.2 provides some hints on how to utilize random forest for this purpose.

EXAMPLE 5.3.2 FULL PREPAYMENT MODELLING VIA RANDOM FOREST

Let us consider the portfolio studied in Example 5.3.1. The following steps are performed to estimate full prepayments via random forest:

1. Upload data,
2. Perform random forest analysis, and
3. Predict (train and test samples).

```
# 1. Upload data
bal_prep<- read.csv('bal_prep.csv', header=TRUE,
sep = ',', dec = '.')
library(dplyr)
library(vars)
bal_prep <- dplyr::mutate_at(bal_prep,
vars(contains('date')), funs(as.Date))
# 1.1. Train and test samples
set.seed(1234)
train_sample_prep <- caret::createDataPartition(bal_prep$year,
p=0.7, list=FALSE)
train_prep <- bal_prep[train_sample_prep, ]
test_prep <- bal_prep[-train_sample_prep, ]
# 1.2. Convert prep_flag
prep_char=ifelse(train_prep$prep_flag==0,'No','Yes')
train_prep=data.frame(train_prep,prep_char)
prep_char=ifelse(test_prep$prep_flag==0,'No','Yes')
test_prep=data.frame(test_prep,prep_char)
# 2. Perform random forest analysis
library(randomForest)
set.seed(123)
rf_prep <- randomForest(prep_char ~ tob+ltv_utd+uer+gdp+
cpi+hpi+ir,data=train_prep,mtry=2, ntree=50,
importance=TRUE, na.action=na.omit)
importance(rf_prep)
#                No       Yes MeanD.Accuracy MeanD.Gini
# tob       6.358853  4.796162     7.20182     43.76593
# ltv_utd  61.123296 53.958619    65.31530   2028.15728
# uer      11.241792 10.218423    11.60880    408.39120
# gdp      14.221225 10.949830    14.61431    190.22267
```

```
# cpi          9.380757  9.217934   10.00395    204.82349
# hpi          9.888206 12.123049   10.99514    167.33674
# ir          11.885669 11.197375   12.60618    252.46956
# 3. Predict train and test samples
# 2.1. Predict train
train_prep$prep_rf <- predict(rf_prep, newdata=train_prep)
table(train_prep$prep_rf, train_prep$prep_char)
#          No    Yes
# No   23987    127
# Yes      0   2030
# 2.2. Predict test
test_prep$prep_rf <- predict(rf_prep, newdata=test_prep)
table(test_prep$prep_rf, test_prep$prep_char)
#          No    Yes
# No   10318     52
# Yes      0    832
```

A very good fitting is highlighted both in train and test samples. Figure 5.5, additionally, points out random forest model capability to capture prepayment events throughout the entire period under analysis.

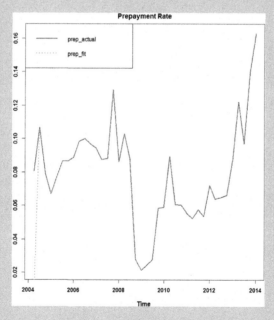

FIGURE 5.5

Random forest fitted (dotted line) against actual (solid line) prepayment rates.

Example 5.3.3 provides an alternative to random forest to estimate prepayments on the same portfolio studied in Example 5.3.1.

EXAMPLE 5.3.3 FULL PREPAYMENT MODELLING VIA BOOSTING

Let us consider the portfolio studied in Example 5.3.1. Boosting analysis is conducted by means of the following steps:

1. Perform boosting (with shrinking) analysis, and
2. Predict train and test samples.

```
# 1. Perform boosting analysis
library(gbm)
set.seed(123)
boost_shr_prep <- gbm(prep_flag ~ tob+ltv_utd+uer+gdp+
cpi+hpi+ir, data=train_prep, distribution = 'gaussian',
n.trees = 50, interaction.depth=4, shrinkage=0.2, verbose=F)
summary(boost_shr_prep)
# var     rel.inf
# uer             uer 42.460637
# ltv_utd     ltv_utd 24.909894
# ir               ir 17.293710
# hpi             hpi  8.493897
# cpi             cpi  4.246965
# gdp             gdp  2.594896
# tob             tob  0.000000
```

The same variables selected through GLM stepwise regression and random forest also play a key role in boosting. It is useful to take note of the relative importance of UER (unemployment rate), ltv_utd (loan-to-value updated), and IR (interest rate) to explain prepayment events by means of boosting.

Figure 5.6 compares fitted against actual prepayment events for both train and test samples. They are very close to each other. Nevertheless, one needs to point out that boosting outcomes are not bounded in the [0,1] interval. Additional constraints are required in addition to the fitting procedure.

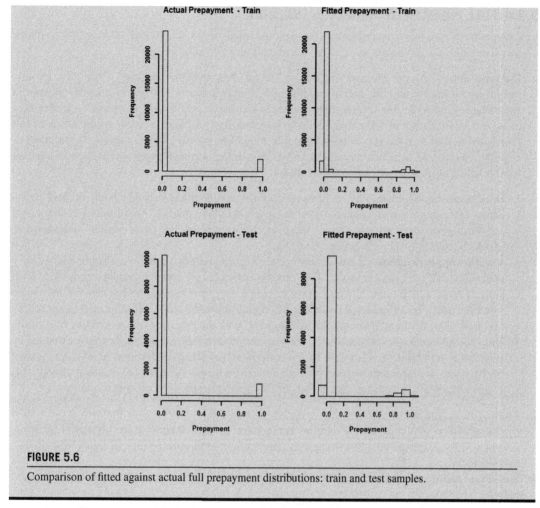

FIGURE 5.6

Comparison of fitted against actual full prepayment distributions: train and test samples.

Both random forest and boosting outperform logistic regression in capturing full prepayment events. Further analyses, listed in Section 5.3.4, point out how ML procedures are probably able to embed features difficult to be captured by means of the most traditional methods (for example, GLM).

The lifetime prepayment curve is derived as detailed in Equation (5.2). All above ML models provided prepayment probabilities over an interval τ_j (that is, PP_{i,s,τ_j}).

5.3.3 HINTS ON SURVIVAL ANALYSIS

Survival analysis appears like a natural way to model full prepayments. Indeed, one may consider time-varying covariates to capture survival linkages with both BVs and MVs. Based on this, Cox Proportional Hazard (CPH) and accelerated failure time (AFT) models, introduced in Chapter 3, can be easily applied for full prepayment modelling purposes. One may refer to Chapter 3 for a comprehensive view.

The next section enters into the details of full prepayment validation.

5.3.4 FULL PREPAYMENT MODEL VALIDATION

Full prepayment validation is organized through the same steps considered in previous chapters. Checks focus on data, methodology, and statistical testing, as detailed below:

a. **Data validation.** As per PD and LGD, even for full prepayment, data play a key role. Despite the easy intuition beyond full prepayment, actual IT infrastructures are not necessarily aligned to spontaneously provide this information. Indeed, changes in facility IDs or product number may cause the identification of full prepayments to be particularly difficult. A clear specification of full prepayment event is at the very root of the entire modelling process. In this regard, a joint effort of risk management, IT data, finance, and technical accounting is crucial to provide a suitable database for modelling purposes and ensure what follows:

   • **Data representativeness.** Full prepayments are usually identified based on bank internal logics. Scarce information on this phenomenon are available in the market. Additionally, external data are not necessarily representative of bank-specific processes. For these reasons, internal data should be used for full prepayment modelling.
   • **Variable appropriateness.** Lack of appropriate historical depth, together with poor quality, may undermine full prepayment model development. Products are often aggregated at facility level both in retail and wholesale loans. As a consequence, information inconsistencies may arise when the analysis is conducted based on different granularity detail. Missing amortizing schedules may also prevent performing the investigation with the precision one would like to achieve.
   • **Data completeness.** As pointed out in previous chapters, no specific requirements are defined by accounting standards on the length of the underlying historical observation period. As detailed for PDs, one should aim to include two economic cycles, and—at least—a recession period. This is particularly important to assess model sensitivity on alternative economic conditions.

b. **Methodology validation.** Alternative approaches should be considered to perform a theoretical model validation. A comparison of their advantages and disadvantages is at the very heart of the assessment. This, in particular, needs to be evaluated in light of the competing risk analysis described in Section 5.4.

c. **Statistical testing validation.** Statistical validation ensures genuine modelling results, as detailed below:

   • **Discriminatory power.** In line with previous chapters, this analysis can be performed by means of alternative metrics, as detailed in Example 5.3.4.

EXAMPLE 5.3.4 FULL PREPAYMENT DISCRIMINATORY POWER ANALYSIS

Let us start by focusing on the model developed in Example 5.3.1. A crucial part of the full prepayment model validation is to assess the capability to discriminate between prepaying and non-prepaying accounts. The analysis is conducted by means of the following steps:

1. Calculate Gini index, and
2. Compute AUC statistics.

The following R code refers to Example 5.3.1. It can easily be extended to other models examined so far.

```
# 1. Calculate Gini index
# 1.1. Train sample
library(optiRum)
train_prep$predict_prep_logit  <- predict(logit_prep,
newdata = train_prep, type = 'response')
gini_train_prep<- optiRum::giniCoef(train_prep$predict_prep_logit,
train_prep$prep_flag)
print(gini_train_prep)
# 0.7034126
# 2. Calculate AUC statistics
# 2.1. Train sample
pred_train<- ROCR::prediction(train_prep$predict_prep_logit,
train_prep$prep_flag)
auc_train<- ROCR::performance(pred_train, 'auc')
print(auc_train@y.values[[1]])
# 0.8520629
```

Table 5.3 provides a summary of AUC for the alternative models examined in previous sections (that is, Examples 5.3.1, 5.3.2 and 5.3.3).

Table 5.3 AUC values for alternative prepayment models. Train and test samples		
	AUC train	**AUC test**
Logistic regression	0.85	0.85
Random forest	0.97	0.97
Boosting (shrinking)	1.00	1.00

- **Model accuracy.** The accuracy of the developed framework can be captured by comparing actual balance against projected. The full prepayment model is applied over a given time horizon, and compared against actual occurrences. One may rely on correlation (or squared correlation) and other measures of closeness. Example 5.3.5 provides some hints on how to perform the analysis.

EXAMPLE 5.3.5 GOODNESS-OF-FIT OVER TIME

Let us focus on Example 5.3.1. We aim to point out the model's capability to capture economic fluctuations over time by means of the following steps:

1. Compute quarterly prepayment rates (for train and test samples),
2. Compute annual prepayment rates, and
3. Estimate correlation between actual and fitted values.

```
# 1. Compute quarterly mean prepayment rates (train set)
train_data<- train_prep %>%
```

```
dplyr::group_by(report_date,year) %>%
dplyr::summarise(prep_actual = mean(prep_flag),
prep_fit = mean(predict_prep_logit)) %>%
dplyr::select(report_date, year, prep_actual, prep_fit)
# 2. Compute annual mean prepayment rates
train_data<- train_data %>%
dplyr::group_by(year) %>%
dplyr::summarise(prep_actual_year = sum(prep_actual),
prep_fit_year = sum(prep_fit)) %>%
dplyr::select(year, prep_actual_year, prep_fit_year)
# 3. Estimate correlation between actual and fitted values
corr_train<- cor(train_data$prep_actual_year,
train_data$prep_fit_year, method = 'pearson')
#  0.5669538
```

Table 5.4 provides a summary of correlation for models examined in previous sections (that is, Examples 5.3.1, 5.3.2 and 5.3.3).

Table 5.4 Correlation values for alternative prepayment models. Train and test samples

	Correlation train	Correlation test
Logistic regression	0.57	0.60
Random forest	0.97	0.97
Boosting (shrinking)	0.98	0.97

One should also check how the model works when applied to actual balance. In cohort analysis the estimated model is applied to a given portfolio at a given reporting date. It is then tracked through time and compared against actual balance evolution. Errors are investigated trough time, and eventually compared against tolerance thresholds.

- **Calibration.** ECL computation relies on point-in-time estimates. One should ascertain model's ability to represent the most recent full prepayment events. For example, a comparison between actual against fitted prepayment rates should be considered. Misalignments should be adequately treated to avoid biased projections.
- **Out-of-sample and out-of-time stability.** As illustrated above, the distinction between train and test data is crucial for model validation. Moreover, one would need to consider some extra data points to check how the model behaves after the development period. One should perform the following analysis:
  - Parameter stability. As a first validation test, one should check whether model parameters are severely affected by the choice of the data on which the model is developed. One should verify how sensitive model parameters are to these choices.
  - Overall portfolio fitting. The overall fitting can be checked against historical average prepayment rates. Cohort analysis is extremely useful in this case.

- **Sensitivity analysis.** As per other credit risk parameters, the goal of this exercise is to test how the model reacts to different economic conditions. One may consider historical or hypothetical scenarios to test it.
- **Reproducibility.** Checks are required to ensure an appropriate balance projection in production environment. A positive replication test supports the results of the analysis. A complete documentation describing the end-to-end modelling process is also required. In general, incomplete documentation does not allow model replication.

5.4 COMPETING RISK MODELLING

In the most recent years, growing attention has been devoted both by practitioners and researchers (Dirick et al., 2017) to develop frameworks to jointly model different risks. For example, in a slowdown scenario, one would expect an increase in default rates and decrease in retail mortgage prepayments.[4] On the other hand, a growth scenario would be probably accompanied by default rate reduction and increase of retail mortgage prepayments.

In what follows, few alternative approaches are explored to model competing risks. Figure 5.7 describes how the journey is organized throughout Section 5.4.

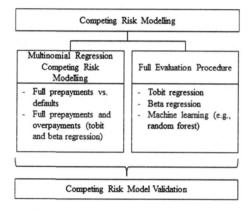

FIGURE 5.7

Workflow diagram for Section 5.4.

Section 5.4.1 focuses on multinomial regression to assess competing event likelihood. Firstly, focus is on full prepayment and defaults. Then, a two-step procedure is used to jointly model: full prepayments, defaults and overpayments. In the latter case, a multinomial regression is used to identify event occurrence. Then, overpayment magnitude is estimated by means of Tobit and beta regressions. In Section 5.4.2 full prepayments and overpayments are jointly estimated. The idea is to consider as target a variable with domain in the interval [0, 1]. As a further method, the reader may refer to Dirick et al. (2017) for details on survival analysis applied to competing risks.

---

[4]For corporate loans, more variables should be considered by including, among others, product type and sector.

5.4.1 MULTINOMIAL REGRESSION COMPETING RISKS MODELLING

When a target variable assumes more than two categories, multinomial logistic regression seems a natural candidate for their modelling. In this regard, let us start by focusing on two competing risks: (loan) full prepayment and default. Overpayments will be included as a simple extension of this initial framework.

Let $\pi_{i,j,t,\tau}$ represent loan i probability of being active, prepay, or default over the period τ as listed below:

* $\pi_{i,0,t,\tau}$. Probability of loan i staying active over the period τ.
* $\pi_{i,1,t,\tau}$. Probability of loan i prepaying sometime during the interval τ.
* $\pi_{i,2,t,\tau}$. Probability of loan i defaulting during the period τ.

Multinomial regression model can be represented as follows[5]:

$$\ln\left(\frac{\pi_{i,j,t}}{\pi_{i,J,t}}\right) = \beta_{0,j} + \mathbf{z}'_{i,t}\boldsymbol{\beta}_j, \tag{5.3}$$

where $\beta_{0,j}$ is a constant, and $\boldsymbol{\beta}_j$ is a vector of coefficients for $j = 1, \ldots, J-1$. The vector $\mathbf{z}_{i,t}$ includes both BVs and MVs.

This model is analogous to a logistic regression, except that the probability distribution of the response is multinomial instead of binomial, and there are $J-1$ equations instead of one. The $J-1$ multinomial logit equations contrast each of categories $1, 2, \ldots, J-1$ with category J. On the other hand, the single logistic regression equation is a contrast between successes and failures. If $J = 2$, the multinomial logit model reduces to the usual logistic regression model.

The multinomial logit model may also be written in terms of the original probabilities $\pi_{i,j,t}$ rather than the log-odds. Starting from Equation (5.3), assuming $\eta_{i,j,t} = \beta_{0,j} + \mathbf{z}'_{i,t}\boldsymbol{\beta}_j$, and adopting the convention that $\eta_{i,J,t} = 0$, the following applies:

$$\pi_{i,j,t} = \frac{\exp(\eta_{i,j,t})}{\sum_{k=1}^{J} \exp(\eta_{i,k,t})}. \tag{5.4}$$

Example 5.4.1 provides some hints on how to apply multinomial regression to jointly model full prepayment and default events.

EXAMPLE 5.4.1 FULL PREPAYMENT AND DEFAULT MODELLING VIA MULTINOMIAL REGRESSION

Let us consider an account-level database, where full prepayment and default are recorded. A competing risk model is estimated by means of the following steps:

1. Upload data,
2. Perform multinomial analysis, and
3. Predict.

---

[5] τ is omitted to ease the notation.

```
# 1. Upload data
bal_def_prep <- read.csv('bal_def_prep.csv')
library(dplyr)
library(vars)
bal_def_prep <- dplyr::mutate_at(bal_def_prep,
vars(contains('date')), funs(as.Date))
# 1.2. Create train and test database
set.seed(1234)
train_def_prep_sample <- caret::createDataPartition(
bal_def_prep$year, p=0.7, list=FALSE)
train_def_prep <- bal_def_prep[train_def_prep_sample, ]
test_def_prep <- bal_def_prep[-train_def_prep_sample, ]
# 2. Perform multinomial analysis
library(nnet)
library(foreign)
library(stargazer)
mod_multi <- multinom(multi_flag ~ tob+ltv_utd+uer+gdp+
cpi+hpi+ir, data=train_def_prep)
stargazer(mod_multi, type='text')
# ===============================================
#                          Dependent variable:
#                       -----------------------------
#                            1              2
#                           (1)            (2)
# ---------------------------------------------------
# tob                      -0.007*        0.003***
#                          (0.004)        (0.001)
#
# ltv_utd                  5.188***      -1.303***
#                          (0.067)        (0.027)
#
# uer                     10.775***      -3.216***
#                          (0.378)        (0.087)
#
# gdp                     -1.839***       0.273***
#                          (0.185)        (0.028)
#
# cpi                     -1.908***      -0.650***
#                          (0.437)        (0.070)
#
# hpi                     -0.021          0.120***
#                          (0.066)        (0.009)
#
```

```
# ir                      3.563***      -2.229***
#                        (0.555)        (0.084)
#
# Constant              -364.083***     93.162***
#                        (0.024)        (2.023)
#
#
# ------------------------------------------------
#   Akaike Inf. Crit.   10,924.590    10,924.590
# ================================================
#   Note:              *p<0.1; **p<0.05; ***p<0.01
```

Default is indicated with 1, whereas 2 refers to full prepayment. All signs are aligned with expectations. They are opposite for these two phenomena. As an example, when ltv_utd increases, one would expect default rate to increase. In contrast, full prepayment is expected to decrease. Such a reasoning can be extended to all variables included in the analysis. (See Figure 5.8.)

```
# 3. Predict
pred_sc_def_prep_train <- predict (mod_multi,
train_def_prep, 'probs')
pred_class_def_prep_train <- predict (mod_multi,
train_def_prep)
```

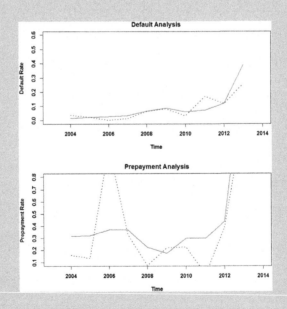

FIGURE 5.8

Default and prepayment rate time series: comparison of actual (solid line) vs. fitted (dotted line).

What is stated above can easily be extended to other risks. In particular, one may be interested in capturing overpayments. In this regard, a full prepayment implies principal to be fully paid. Therefore a binary outcome applies. Likewise, the consequence of default is the account being expelled from the (performing) portfolio. On the other hand, overpayments do not cause an account to exit the portfolio. Indeed, an overpayment causes the outstanding balance to be lower than expected, based on the original amortizing schedule. Consequently, in addition to identifying overpayment events, one needs to estimate their magnitude.

Two main approaches can be followed to capture both full prepayments and overpayments. In this section a two-step procedure is followed. On the one hand, one needs to identify the event. On the other hand, a conditional overpayment estimation is performed. Section 5.4.2 focuses on a full evaluation framework, which allows us to estimate full prepayments and overpayments in one go.

The two-step estimation process is performed as follows:

- **Overpayment and other events occurrence.** The competing risk framework above investigated (based on multinomial regression) is a natural candidate to jointly estimate probability of overpayment, full prepayment, and potentially other events.
- **Overpayment magnitude estimation.** Conditional on overpayment occurrence, one needs to estimate its entity as a fraction of the outstanding principal balance. On this Tobit and beta regression, and similar techniques are useful reference tools.

Example 5.4.2 provides some hints on how to implement the above-described two-step process.

EXAMPLE 5.4.2 TWO-STEP PROCEDURE: OVERPAYMENT AND FULL PREPAYMENT

Let us consider an account-level database, where overpayments and full prepayments are recorded. A competing risk modelling framework is organized through the following steps:

1. Upload data,
2. Run multinomial regression,
3. Predict multinomial regression,
4. Filter overpayments, and
5. Run beta regression.

```
# 1. Upload data
bal_prep <- read.csv('bal_prep_part.csv')
library(dplyr)
library(vars)
bal_prep <- dplyr::mutate_at(bal_prep,
vars(contains('date')), funs(as.Date))
# 1.1. Training and Test Data
set.seed(1234) #set seed in order to reproduce sampling results
train_prep_sample <- caret::createDataPartition(bal_prep$year,
p=0.7, list=FALSE)
train_prep <- bal_prep[train_prep_sample, ]
test_prep <- bal_prep[-train_prep_sample, ]
```

```
# 2. Run multinomial regression
library(nnet)
library(foreign)
library(stargazer)
mod_multi <- multinom(multi_flag ~ tob+ltv_utd+uer+gdp+
cpi+hpi+ir, data=train_prep)
# ===============================================
#                        Dependent variable:
#                    -----------------------------
#                         2              3
#                        (1)            (2)
# -----------------------------------------------
# tob                   0.001          -0.001*
#                      (0.001)         (0.001)
#
# ltv_utd             -1.086***       -1.203***
#                      (0.022)         (0.022)
#
# uer                 -2.764***       -2.700***
#                      (0.079)         (0.068)
#
# gdp                  0.183***        0.222***
#                      (0.024)         (0.021)
#
# cpi                 -0.317***        0.775***
#                      (0.062)         (0.039)
#
# hpi                  0.069***       -0.097***
#                      (0.007)         (0.007)
#
# ir                  -1.698***       -1.849***
#                      (0.074)         (0.059)
#
# Constant            77.155***       81.868***
#                      (1.661)         (1.559)
#
# -----------------------------------------------
# Akaike Inf. Crit.   23,449.210     23,449.210
# ===============================================
# Note:                 *p<0.1; **p<0.05; ***p<0.01
```

Full prepayment is indicated with 2, whereas overpayment is flagged with 3. BV and MV signs are substantially aligned with expectations. Indeed, a negative sign for ltv_utd shows that an increase of loan-to-value causes a reduction of both the probability of full prepayment and overpayment. The same applies to UER, CPI, and IR. Positive relationship with GDP is aligned with expectations, including HPI, and linked to full prepayments.

```
# 3. Predict multinomial regression
pred_sc_prep_test <- predict (mod_multi, test_prep, 'probs')
pred_class_prep_test <- predict (mod_multi, test_prep)
# 3.1. Confusion matrix
table(pred_class_prep_test, test_prep$multi_flag)
# pred_class_prep_test    0     2     3
#                    0 9021   534   516
#                    2    0   134   117
#                    3    0   216   664
```

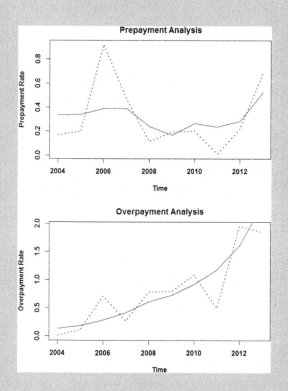

FIGURE 5.9

Prepayment rate and overpayment rate time series: comparison of actual (solid line) vs. fitted (dotted line).

Figure 5.9 summarizes the evolution of prepayments and overpayments through time. The next step is to estimate overpayments by means of Tobit and beta regression.

```
# 4. Filter overpayments
bal_prep <- bal_prep %>%
dplyr::filter(multi_flag==3)
# 4.1. Cast 1 as 0.9999 and 0 as 0.0001
bal_prep <- bal_prep %>%
dplyr::mutate(fppp_perc_new= ifelse(fppp_perc==1,0.9999,
no=ifelse(fppp_perc==0,0.0001,fppp_perc)))
# 4.2. Train and test samples
set.seed(1234)
train_prep_sample <- caret::createDataPartition(bal_prep$year,
p=0.7, list=FALSE)
train_prep <- bal_prep[train_prep_sample, ]
test_prep <- bal_prep[-train_prep_sample, ]
# 5. Run beta regression
library(betareg)
beta_prep <- betareg(fppp_perc_new ~ tob+ltv_utd+
uer+gdp+cpi+hpi+ir, data=train_prep)
summary(beta_prep)
# Coefficients (mean model with logit link):
#   Estimate Std. Error z value Pr(>|z|)
# (Intercept)  5.2497401  0.2578144  20.362  < 2e-16 ***
# tob          0.0006149  0.0001537   3.999 6.35e-05 ***
# ltv_utd     -0.1404878  0.0034395 -40.845  < 2e-16 ***
# uer         -0.3226291  0.0128227 -25.161  < 2e-16 ***
# gdp          0.1071198  0.0048244  22.204  < 2e-16 ***
# cpi         -0.0344076  0.0112439  -3.060  0.00221 **
# hpi          0.1348660  0.0012862 104.857  < 2e-16 ***
# ir           0.0793228  0.0124439   6.374 1.84e-10 ***
#
# Phi coefficients (precision model with identity link):
# Estimate Std. Error z value Pr(>|z|)
# (phi)  210.025      5.432    38.66   <2e-16 ***
# ---
# Signif. codes:0 '***' 0.001 '**' 0.01 '*' 0.05 '.' 0.1 ' ' 1
#
# Type of estimator: maximum likelihood
# Log-likelihood:  9004 on 9 Df
# Pseudo R-squared: 0.7984
# Number of iterations: 34 (BFGS) + 5 (Fisher scoring)
```

Figure 5.10 summarizes the key features of the fitted model by comparing time series and distribution against actual overpayments.

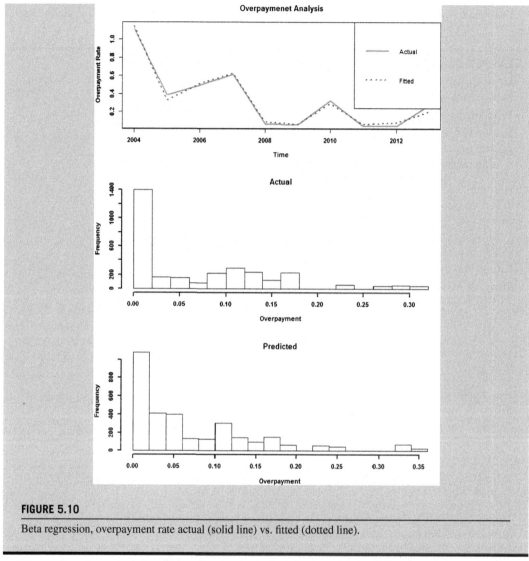

FIGURE 5.10

Beta regression, overpayment rate actual (solid line) vs. fitted (dotted line).

The next section presents a full evaluation procedure by focusing on full prepayments and overpayments.

5.4.2 FULL EVALUATION PROCEDURE

Full prepayment and overpayments are jointly considered. They are represented as a fraction of the outstanding principal balance. This fraction is 0 when neither prepayment, nor overpayment occur. It is 1 when a full prepayment takes place. It assumes values in the interval (0, 1) when overpayments take place. Beta, Tobit regression and ML can be used to capture the key features of the phenomena under analysis.

Example 5.4.3 provides some hints on how to implement the above-described full evaluation process.

EXAMPLE 5.4.3 FULL EVALUATION PROCEDURE

Let us consider the same database used in Example 5.4.2. Alternative approaches are considered, as listed below:

1. Upload data,
2. Run beta regression,
3. Run tobit regression, and
4. Run random forest.

```
# 1. Upload data
bal_prep <- read.csv('bal_prep_part.csv')
library(dplyr)
library(vars)
# 1.1. Create a new variable in the interval (0,1)
bal_prep <- bal_prep %>%
dplyr::mutate(fppp_perc_new= ifelse(fppp_perc==1,0.9999,
no=ifelse(fppp_perc==0,0.0001,fppp_perc)))
# 1.2. Train and test samples
set.seed(1234)
train_prep_sample <- caret::createDataPartition(bal_prep$year,
p=0.7, list=FALSE)
train_prep <- bal_prep[train_prep_sample, ]
test_prep <- bal_prep[-train_prep_sample, ]
# 2. Run beta regression
library(betareg)
beta_prep <- betareg(fppp_perc_new ~ ltv_utd+uer+cpi+hpi+ir,
data=train_prep)
# Coefficients (mean model with logit link):
#              Estimate Std. Error z value Pr(>|z|)
# (Intercept) 11.255662   0.325088  34.623  < 2e-16 ***
# ltv_utd     -0.170652   0.004241 -40.242  < 2e-16 ***
# uer         -0.434251   0.015844 -27.409  < 2e-16 ***
# cpi          0.060818   0.013019   4.671 2.99e-06 ***
# hpi          0.013813   0.001264  10.931  < 2e-16 ***
# ir          -0.280410   0.018066 -15.522  < 2e-16 ***
#
# Phi coefficients (precision model with identity link):
# Estimate Std. Error z value Pr(>|z|)
# (phi) 0.479051   0.004035   118.7    <2e-16 ***
# ---
# Signif.codes:0 '***' 0.001 '**' 0.01 '*' 0.05 '.' 0.1 ' ' 1
```

```
# Type of estimator: maximum likelihood
# Log-likelihood: 1.302e+05 on 7 Df
# Pseudo R-squared: 0.1751
# Number of iterations: 46 (BFGS) + 1 (Fisher scoring)
```

Beta regression provides very poor fitting (that is, pseudo R^2=0.1751). A graphical inspection reveals the difficulty to capture extremes, in particular, full prepayment events.

As an alternative, let us consider a Tobit regression, as detailed below.

```
# 3. Run tobit regression
library(VGAM)
tobit_prep <- vglm(fppp_perc_new ~ ltv_utd+uer+gdp+cpi+hpi+ir,
tobit(Lower=0, Upper=1, type.f = 'cens'), data=train_prep)
# Coefficients:
# Estimate Std. Error  z value Pr(>|z|)
# (Intercept):1  3.6648472  0.0799123   45.861  < 2e-16 ***
# (Intercept):2 -1.3514251  0.0059439 -227.363  < 2e-16 ***
# ltv_utd       -0.0502564  0.0009892  -50.805  < 2e-16 ***
# uer           -0.1271445  0.0042498  -29.917  < 2e-16 ***
# gdp      0.0044213  0.0013269    3.332 0.000862 ***
# cpi           0.0110864  0.0033785    3.281 0.001033 **
# hpi           0.0036145  0.0003988    9.062  < 2e-16 ***
# ir           -0.0580580  0.0046814  -12.402  < 2e-16 ***
# ---
# Signif. codes:  0 '***' 0.001 '**' 0.01 '*' 0.05 '.' 0.1 ' ' 1
# Number of linear predictors:  2
# Names of linear predictors: mu, loge(sd)
# Log-likelihood: -1765.14 on 52280 degrees of freedom
# Number of iterations: 11
```

Even in this case a poor fitting characterizes the analysis (for example, correlation is 0.3645, whereas squared correlation is 0.1329).

As an alternative, a random forest approach is used as follows.

```
# 4. Run random forest
library(randomForest)
set.seed(123)
rf_prep <- randomForest(fppp_perc_new ~ tob+ltv_utd+uer+
cpi+hpi+ir, data=train_prep, mtry=2, ntree=100,
importance=TRUE, na.action=na.omit)
importance(rf_prep)
# %IncMSE IncNodePurity
# tob      19.98485      87.84917
# ltv_utd 73.47817     556.56908
# uer      21.66024     227.01771
```

```
# cpi    14.71911    69.66765
# hpi    14.98561    85.64826
# ir     18.38738    93.40319
```

Train sample correlation is 0.8000, and squared correlation is 0.6410. Test sample correlation is 0.7685, whereas the squared correlation is 0.5906. Figure 5.11 highlights a good fitting of the model both in terms of time series evolution (that is, in the top plots, the solid line represents actuals, whereas the dotted line shows fitted values) and distribution within the [0,1] interval.

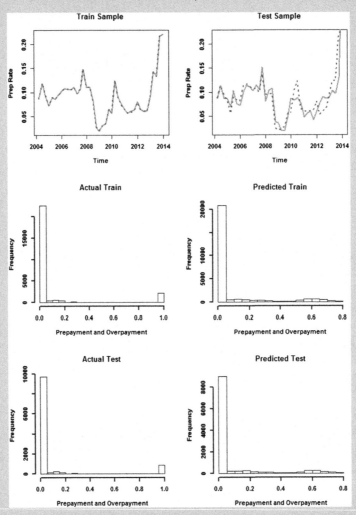

FIGURE 5.11

Full prepayment and overpayment analysis via random forest. Train and test sample, actual (solid line) vs. fitted (dotted line) comparison.

The next section focuses on competing risk model validation.

5.4.3 COMPETING RISK MODEL VALIDATION

This section highlights substantial differences in the validation activities compared to what emerged in Section 5.3.4, as detailed below:

a. Data validation. Checks and controls on data are substantially aligned with those described in Section 5.3.4. In the case of multinomial regression, one should additionally verify empty or small cells. Indeed, if a cell has very few cases, the model may become unstable, or it might not even run at all. Multinomial regression uses a maximum likelihood estimation method; it requires a large sample size. It also uses multiple equations. This implies an even larger sample size than ordinal or binary logistic regression.

b. Methodology validation. The adoption of a model encompassing prepayments (that is, full prepayments and overpayments), in conjunction with default, constitutes a step forward, compared to the traditional split between probability of default and behavioural modelling. A comprehensive investigation of advantages and disadvantages needs to inform the choice of the most appropriate competing risk modelling framework.

c. Statistical testing validation. From a statistical perspective, separate tests are required on silos risks, together with an integrated check, to capture their interdependencies. In what follows, the focus is on an integrated framework, as listed below:

- **Discriminatory power.** As detailed in Section 5.4.1, one needs to check model discriminatory power. In line with previous chapters, this analysis can be performed by means of alternative metrics, as detailed in Example 5.4.4.

EXAMPLE 5.4.4 FULL PREPAYMENT AND DEFAULT DISCRIMINATORY POWER ANALYSIS

Let us consider the model developed in Example 5.4.1. The analysis is conducted by means of the following steps:

1. Calculate confusion matrix, and
2. Compute multi-class AUC.

In what follows we skip data import and model estimation because they have already been discussed.

```
# 1. Calculate confusion matrix
# 1.1. Predict test
pred_sc_def_prep_test <- predict (mod_multi, test_def_prep, 'probs')
pred_class_def_prep_test <- predict (mod_multi, test_def_prep)
# 1.2. Confusion matrix
table(pred_class_def_prep_test, test_def_prep$multi_flag)
# pred_class_def_prep_test    0     1     2
#                       0 10124    37   675
#                       1     0    84     0
#                       2     0     0   266
```

```
mean(as.character(pred_class_def_prep_test)
!= as.character(test_def_prep$multi_flag))
# 0.06365099
# 2. Compute multi-class AUC
library(pROC)
pred_class_test_dp <- as.numeric(pred_class_def_prep_test)
roc_multi_test <- multiclass.roc(test_def_prep$multi_flag,
pred_class_test_dp)
auc(roc_multi_test)
# Multi-class area under the curve: 0.6987
```

The classification error for the train sample is 0.0636, whereas the multi-class AUC is 0.6987.

- **Model accuracy.** The accuracy of the developed framework can be captured by comparing actual balance against projected. Based on this, the full prepayment model is applied over a given time horizon and compared against actual occurrences. Example 5.4.5 focuses on time series correlation analysis.

EXAMPLE 5.4.5 DEFAULT AND PREPAYMENT RATE GOODNESS-OF-FIT OVER TIME

Let us focus on Example 5.4.1. The following analysis allows us to summarize model capability to capture macroeconomic fluctuations through time:

1. Compute quarterly prepayment rates,
2. Estimate correlation for default rates, and
3. Estimate correlation for prepayment rates.

```
# 1. Compute quarterly mean default and prepayment rates
train_def_prep$pred_def  <- pred_sc_def_prep_train[,2]
train_def_prep$pred_prep  <- pred_sc_def_prep_train[,3]
train_quarter_def_prep <- train_def_prep %>%
dplyr::group_by(report_date,year) %>%
dplyr::summarise(def_actual = mean(default_flag),
def_fit = mean(pred_def), prep_actual = mean(prep_flag),
prep_fit = mean(pred_prep)) %>%
dplyr::select(report_date, year,def_actual, def_fit,
prep_actual, prep_fit)
# 1.1. Estimate correlation for default rates
corr_def_train<- cor(train_quarter_def_prep$def_actual,
train_quarter_def_prep$def_fit, method = 'pearson')
# 0.8154796
# 1.1. Estimate correlation for prepayment rates
corr_prep_train<- cor(train_quarter_def_prep$prep_actual,
train_quarter_def_prep$prep_fit, method = 'pearson')
# 0.7102749
```

> With regard to the test sample, default correlation is 0.8155, whereas for prepayment, it
> is 0.7103.

The next section focuses on exposure at default modelling by mainly focusing on uncommitted and
revolving facilities.

5.5 **EAD MODELLING**

The focus of previous sections was on loan-type products. Our primary goal was to model balance
projections by considering amortization schedule, in conjunction with full prepayments and overpayments. Attention is now devoted to uncommitted and revolving facilities. Two main issues arise in this
case:

- **Exposure estimate.** As per balance projection, the aim is to assess an account exposure in the event
  of default. In this regard, a useful distinction arises between the following two main categories:
  - **Revolving facilities with no commitment to a given maturity.** This is the typical case of over-
    draft (and similar products), where a bank commits to provide lending up to a given amount
    (that is, limit) over a given time horizon. Despite the uncommitted nature of these facilities, in
    practice, banks allow using a credit line until a review is performed. In other words, theoretically,
    a bank may instantaneously withdraw its credit line. In practice, it does not usually occur. There-
    fore one needs to estimate the period a credit line can be used. Indeed, accounting principles do
    not allow considering limit variations, but require estimating utilization (given a credit line limit
    at reporting date) over a lifetime horizon.
  - **Facilities with commitment until a given maturity.** For products, such as committed credit
    lines or bond-guaranteed-indemnities (BGIs), the bank has a commitment until a given maturity.
    A credit line operates up to a given limit, and drawings are defined both in terms of amount
    and maturity. As a consequence, the utilization may change over time until maturity within the
    agreed limit.
- **Time horizon to consider.** With regard to revolving facilities with no commitment to a given maturity, a common practice is to perform a credit review on an annual basis. Consequently, one should
  refer the lifetime horizon to a 12-month period. Similar reasoning applies to credit cards, but in this
  case the horizon is usually longer. A practical shortcut is to consider an average time to closure.
  One may refer to Appendix for a simplistic framework, based on a constant closure rate. A more
  sophisticated mechanics may rely on variable closure rates, depending upon economic fluctuations.

In what follows, the main focus is on revolving facilities. For products with a commitment until a
given maturity a combination of competing risks and revolving models applies. Figure 5.12 describes
how Section 5.5 is organized.

Section 5.5.1 describes how to extend the competing-risk framework, inspected in Section 5.4, to
uncommitted facilities modelling. Section 5.5.2 provides some hints on how to conduct the analysis by
means of machine learning procedures. Indeed, these methods have already been investigated for other
purposes. Section 5.5.3 focuses on EAD validation.

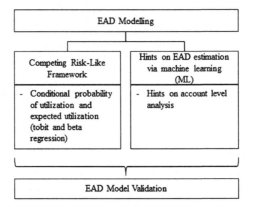

FIGURE 5.12

Workflow diagram for Section 5.5.

5.5.1 A COMPETING-RISK-LIKE EAD FRAMEWORK

Let us start our journey by focusing on an overdraft-type product. Similar reasoning applies to credit cards and other similar products. A given limit $L_{i,h}$ holds for account i over a given horizon h. A point in time utilization rate is defined as follows:

$$U_{i,t_0} = \frac{DB_{i,t_0}}{L_{i,h,t_0}}, \qquad (5.5)$$

where U_{i,t_0} stands for account i utilization rate in t_0, whereas DB_{i,t_0} is the drawn balance, and L_{i,h,t_0} is the limit over the period h.

Aiming to estimate the expected utilization at default, few alternatives may be explored, by relying on Equation (5.5), as listed below:

- **Zero or negative utilization at reporting date:** $DB_{i,t_0} \leq 0$. This case is particularly challenging. Firstly, one needs to assess the probability to trigger a positive $U_{i,t}$. Secondly, one needs to estimate the utilization rate.
- **Positive utilization within the limit at reporting date:** $DB_{i,t_0} \leq L_{i,h,t_0}$. This is the typical case, where the utilization is greater than zero, and lower than the agreed limit. We can distinguish between drawn and undrawn balance (that is, headroom) as follows: $DB_{i,t} + UB_{i,t} = L_{i,h,t_0}$. In other words, for any $t_0 < t \leq t_h$, the sum of drawn and undrawn balance equals the limit holding in t_0. In line with accounting standards, no change in limit applies over the entire lifetime horizon on which expected credit losses are computed.
- **Extra limit utilization at reporting date:** $DB_{i,t_0} \geq L_{i,h,t_0}$. This case may occur in practice. However, for simplicity, in what follows the assumption $DB_{i,t_0} \leq L_{i,h,t_0}$ is made. Additionally, $DB_{i,t} \leq L_{i,h,t_0}$.

The following equation summarizes our EAD modelling framework:

$$\mathbb{E}(U_{i,t_D}|D_{(t_0,t_h]}) = \qquad (5.6)$$

$$P(U_{i,t_D} > 0 | DB_{i,t_0} \leq 0, D_{(t_0,t_h]}) \cdot \mathbb{E}(U_{i,t_D} | DB_{i,t_0} \leq 0, D_{(t_0,t_h]}) +$$
$$P(U_{i,t_D} > 0 | 0 < DB_{i,t_0} \leq L_{i,h,t_0}, D_{(t_0,t_h]}) \cdot \mathbb{E}(U_{i,t_D} | 0 < DB_{i,t_0} \leq L_{i,h,t_0}, D_{(t_0,t_h]}),$$

where U_{i,t_D} represents the utilization rate at default (that is, the subscript t_D indicates the time when a default occurs), and $D_{(t_0,t_h]}$ stands for default occurrence within the interval $(t_0, t_h]$. Hereafter, without loss of generality, the interval h is assumed to be 12 months. Leow and Crook (2016) proposed a two-step procedure to perform the estimation, as listed below[6]:

- **Conditional probability.** If we consider $P(U_{i,t_D} > 0 | DB_{i,t_0} \leq 0, D_{(t_0,t_h]})$ and $P(U_{i,t_D} > 0 | 0 < DB_{i,t_0} \leq L_{i,h,t_0}, D_{(t_0,t_h]})$, we obtain the probability of $U_{i,t_D} > 0$ conditional on a default event. The bipartition (that is, $DB_{i,t_0} \leq 0$ and $0 < DB_{i,t_0} \leq L_{i,h,t_0}$) allows us to capture two relevant initial conditions: non-utilization and utilization of the credit limit. This binary outcome can easily be modelled through a logistic regression by considering both BVs and MVs as explanatory variables.
- **Expected utilization.** As a second step, one may estimate the expected utilization by means of Tobit or beta regression. Indeed, given a certain limit defined at reporting date, one can effectively define U_{i,t_D} within the [0,1] interval and use tools already studied in Section 5.4.

From a practical perspective, one may collapse the above-described two-phase process into a one-step full expected utilization estimate. The focus is on the following alternative target variables[7]:

i. **Exposure at default factor (EADF).** In this case, the target variable is defined by means of the following ratio:

$$EADF_{i,D} = \frac{DB_{i,t_D}}{L_{i,h,t_0}}, \tag{5.7}$$

where the subscript D stands for default, $L_{i,h,t_0} > 0$, and, given the assumption $DB_{i,t_D} \leq L_{i,h,t_0}$, $EADF_{i,D} \in [0, 1]$. As a consequence, one may, for example, estimate the expected exposure by means of beta regression. In terms of projection, the following applies:

$$\mathbb{E}(U_{i,t_D}^{EADF}) = \frac{DB_{i,t_D}}{L_{i,t_0}} \cdot L_{i,t_0}. \tag{5.8}$$

ii. **Credit conversion factor (CCF).** In this case, the focus is on the relationship between drawn balance at default and in t_0 as detailed below:

$$CCF_{i,D} = \frac{DB_{i,t_D}}{DB_{i,t_0}}, \tag{5.9}$$

where the assumption $DB_{i,t_0} > 0$ holds. In this case, $EADF_{i,D} \in (0, \infty)$. Tobit regression with lower truncation at 0 is a potential candidate model. In terms of projection, the following applies:

$$\mathbb{E}(U_{i,t_D}^{CCF}) = \left[DB_{i,t_0} \cdot \frac{DB_{i,t_D}}{DB_{i,t_0}} \right] \cdot L_{i,t_0}. \tag{5.10}$$

---

[6]For accounting purposes, we need to stick to the initial credit limit L_{i,t_0}.
[7]One needs to bear in mind that cases where $DB_{i,t_0}|D_{(t_0,t_h]} \leq 0$ are usually negligible for a reasonably extended h horizon.

iii. **Loan equivalent exposure (LEQ).** Leow and Crook (2016) refer to the ratio $\frac{DB_{i,t_D}-DB_{i,t_0}}{L_{i,t_0}-DB_{i,t_0}}$ to represent LEQ target variable. The following slightly different formulation may also apply:

$$LEQ_{i,D} = \frac{DB_{i,t_D} - DB_{i,t_0}}{L_{i,t_0}}, \tag{5.11}$$

where the assumption $L_{i,t_0} > 0$ holds, and $LEQ_{i,D} \in [-1,1]$. Tobit regression with lower an upper truncation is a potential candidate model. In terms of projection, the following holds:

$$\mathbb{E}(U_{i,t_D}^{LEQ}) = \left[\frac{DB_{i,t_0}}{L_{i,t_0}} + \frac{DB_{i,t_D} - DB_{i,t_0}}{L_{i,t_0}}\right] \cdot L_{i,t_0}. \tag{5.12}$$

Example 5.5.1 suggests how to estimate Equation (5.7).

EXAMPLE 5.5.1 EADF MODELLING

Let us consider an overdraft database. The analysis focuses on defaulted accounts. The target variable, defined in Equation (5.7), is available in the database. The fitting process is performed by means of the following steps:

1. Upload data.
2. Run beta regression.

```
# 1. Upload data
ead <- read.csv('ead.csv')
library(dplyr)
# 1.1. Train and test samples
set.seed(1234) #set seed in order to reproduce sampling results
train_sample <- caret::createDataPartition(ead$year,
p=0.7, list=FALSE)
train_ead <- ead[train_sample, ]
test_ead <- ead[-train_sample, ]
# 2. Run beta regression
library(betareg)
beta_ead <- betareg(uti_def ~ uti_ini+gdp, data=train_ead)
# Coefficients (mean model with logit link):
#             Estimate Std. Error z value Pr(>|z|)
# (Intercept)   0.2584    0.1771   1.459   0.145
# uti_ini       1.1446    0.8431   1.358   0.175
# gdp          -0.2948    0.0232 -12.707   <2e-16 ***
#
# Phi coefficients (precision model with identity link):
# Estimate Std. Error z value Pr(>|z|)
# (phi)   2.5301    0.2029   12.47   <2e-16 ***
# ---
# Signif. codes:  0 '***' 0.001 '**' 0.01 '*' 0.05 '.' 0.1 ' ' 1
```

```
# Type of estimator: maximum likelihood
# Log-likelihood: 107.4 on 4 Df
# Pseudo R-squared: 0.3388
# Number of iterations: 16 (BFGS) + 1 (Fisher scoring)
```

In terms of economic interpretation, coefficient signs are aligned with expectations. From a fitting point of view, Figure 5.13 top panel shows a good fitting through time. Bottom panels highlight a close relationship between actual against fitted distributions.

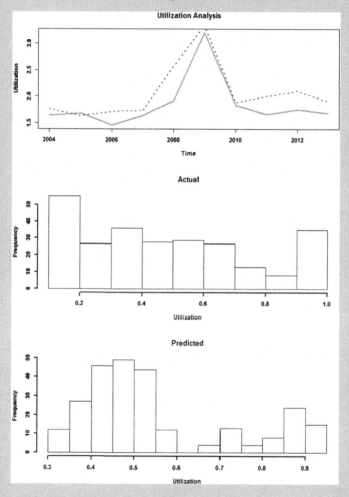

FIGURE 5.13

EADF actual vs. fitted. Top panel: actual (solid line) vs. fitted (dotted line) EADF through time. Bottom panels: EADF actual and fitted distributions.

Example 5.5.2 suggests how to estimate Equation (5.9) by means of Tobit regression.

EXAMPLE 5.5.2 CCF MODELLING

Let us consider the database explored in Example 5.5.1. CCF, defined in Equation (5.9), is estimated by means of the following Tobit regression:

```
# 1. Run tobit regression
library(VGAM)
tobit_ead <- vglm(ccf_ratio ~ uti_ini+gdp,
tobit(Lower=0, Upper=25, type.f = 'cens'), data=train_ead)
# Coefficients:
#                 Estimate Std. Error z value Pr(>|z|)
# (Intercept):1   6.62006    0.32377   20.45   <2e-16 ***
# (Intercept):2   0.60913    0.04740   12.85   <2e-16 ***
# uti_ini        -17.07323   1.57294  -10.85   <2e-16 ***
# gdp             -0.40412   0.03823  -10.57   <2e-16 ***
# ---
# Signif. codes:  0 '***' 0.001 '**' 0.01 '*' 0.05 '.' 0.1 ' ' 1
# Number of linear predictors:  2
# Names of linear predictors: mu, loge(sd)
# Log-likelihood: -523.2433 on 512 degrees of freedom
# Number of iterations: 6
# No Hauck-Donner effect found in any of the estimates
```

An inverse relationship with GDP growth is in line with economic theory. In terms of fitting, Figure 5.14 top panel shows a good fitting through time. Bottom panels show a close relationship between actual against fitted distributions.

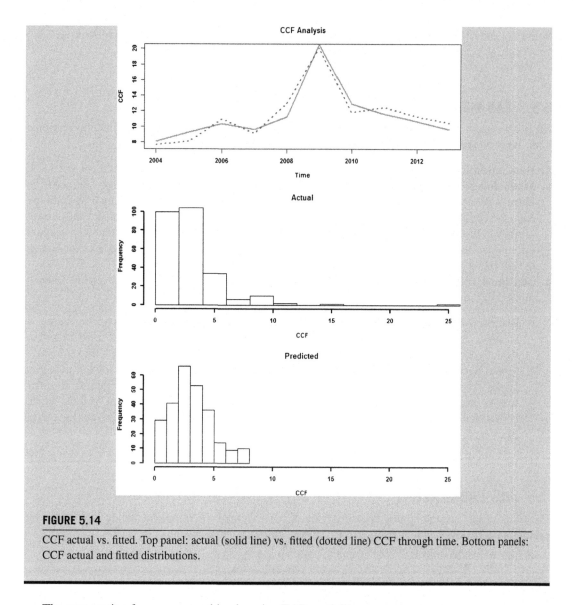

FIGURE 5.14

CCF actual vs. fitted. Top panel: actual (solid line) vs. fitted (dotted line) CCF through time. Bottom panels: CCF actual and fitted distributions.

The next section focuses on machine learning EAD modelling.

5.5.2 HINTS ON EAD ESTIMATION VIA MACHINE LEARNING (ML)

The regression procedure described in the previous section is quite intuitive and easy to grasp. The machine learning (ML) frame, already studied throughout this book, seems a natural way to estimate EAD, as detailed in Equation (5.6), and following. In more detail, bagging, random forest and boosting may be used to directly estimate the expected EAD, based on historical (account-level) information.

Both BVs and MVs need to be considered as explanatory variables to obtain a forward-looking EAD projection, as detailed in Examples 5.5.1 and 5.5.2.

The next section focuses on EAD validation.

5.5.3 EAD MODEL VALIDATION

All main checks applicable to EAD have already been investigated in previous validation sections. Some hints on specific inspections one may conduct follow:

a. **Data validation.** Checks and controls on data align with those described in Sections 5.3.4 and 5.4.3.
b. **Methodology validation.** Few important choices inform EAD modelling. Firstly, one needs to identify product categories to model. As a second step, the time horizon on which to compute expected credit losses is crucial. In this regard, one should consider both business model and current practice. Thirdly, the alternative between two-step (Leow and Crook, 2016) or one-step method informs the validation process. Finally, one needs to support the choice of using an exposure at default factor instead of credit conversion factor, or loan equivalent exposure.
c. **Statistical testing validation.** Few statistical tests need to be performed, based on the chosen method to estimate EAD, as detailed below:

   - **Discriminatory power.** This check is required only in cases where a two-step procedure is adopted, as detailed in Equation (5.6). Metrics like Gini index, AUC can be used to assess model's discriminatory power over the entire period under scrutiny, or by considering cohorts.
   - **Model accuracy.** One may conduct the same analysis performed in previous section to assess model accuracy. Once again, cohort inspection should be part of the investigation. In other words, one needs to apply the estimated model on exposures at a given point in time. Then, both actual and fitted values are tracked. Error rates are scrutinized and summarized (for example, via correlation or similar metrics).

5.6 SAS LABORATORY

The focus of this section is on competing risks. An overview of SAS implementation is provided by exploring examples already investigated in the previous sections by means of R.

SAS Laboratory 5.6.1 focuses on GLM.

SAS LABORATORY 5.6.1 COMPETING RISK ANALYSIS

Let us consider Example 5.4.1. Firstly, one needs to upload the corresponding data file, then the analysis is replicated by means of the following steps:

1. Train and test samples,
2. Fit multinomial regression,
3. Calculate default and prepayment rates,
4. Calculate average prediction, based on multi-flag, and
5. Plot actual vs. fitted.

```
/* 1. Train and test samples */
proc sort data=work.uk_bal_def_prep;by year;run;
proc surveyselect data=work.uk_bal_def_prep out=stratified_data
method=srs rate=0.7 outall seed=2122;
strata year;
run;

/* 2. Fit multinomial regression*/
proc genmod data=stratified_data (where=(selected=1))
order=data desc;
model multi_flag=mob ltv_utd uer gdp_Growth cpi hpi
ir10/dist=multinomial aggregate=multi_flag;
output out=out predicted=predict;
quit;

/* 3. Calculate default and prepayment rates */
proc sql;
create table mean_Rate as select distinct
*,
mean(default_flag) as DR,
mean(prep_flag) as PR
from out
group by report_date;
quit;

/* 4. Calculate average prediction based on multi-flag */
proc sql;
create table mean_prediction as select distinct
_order_,
report_date,
DR,
PR,
mean(predict) as predicted

from mean_rate
group by _order_,report_Date;
quit;

/* 5. Plot actual vs. fitted */
proc sgplot data=mean_prediction;
series x=report_date y=DR;
series x=report_date y=predicted;
where _order_=2;
```

```
run;
```

5.7 SUMMARY

An introduction to data preparation for prepayments, overpayments and competing risk was provided, paving the way to behavioural modelling.

As a starting point, loan-type products were investigated by focusing on full prepayments. Generalized linear models (GLMs) and machine learning (ML) were extensively scrutinized, and hints on survival analysis were provided.

A competing risk framework was introduced to deal with complementary events, such as default, full prepayment and overpayment. Multinomial regression was used as a reference to model event occurrence. With regard to overpayments, an additional step was considered to estimate the magnitude of the partial prepayment by means of Tobit and beta regressions. Few machine learning techniques, including bagging, random forest, and boosting were also adopted by showing their profound capability to capture complex phenomena.

Finally, uncommitted facilities were investigated by means of a competing-risk-like framework. Few alternative target variables were adopted, such as exposure at default factor (EADF), credit conversion factor (CCF), and loan equivalent exposure (LEQ). Empirical analyses were conducted by means of Tobit and beta regressions. Hints on machine learning were also provided.

Validation was studied as an integral step to ensure model reliability. As per the previous chapters, practical cases were examined by means of R, whereas a SAS laboratory provided details on the most relevant examples.

Data and complementary examples' software code are available at www.tizianobellini.com.

SUGGESTIONS FOR FURTHER READING

Therneau et al. (2018) provide an overview of competing risk modelling from a statistical angle. Dirick et al. (2017) describe how to use survival analysis in the context of credit scoring and competing risks. One may also find useful referring to Therneau (2018) on this topic. Qi (2009) elaborates a comprehensive EAD modelling framework for credit cards. Likewise, Leow and Crook (2016) provide an exhaustive overview on EAD modelling by focusing on card's peculiarities. The reader interested in machine learning may find it useful referring to Hastie et al. (2009) for a theoretical introduction, whereas James et al. (2013) provide a more hands-on perspective by means of examples in R.

APPENDIX. AVERAGE CLOSURE RATE SHORTCUT

Our goal is to describe a simplified method to represent average closure rate for uncommitted and revolving products, such as overdrafts. Few strong assumptions are made. Results are deeply affected by these overarching constraints.

Let us assume estimating lifetime expected credit loss (ECL) in a continuous time setting, as listed below:

$$ECL_{lifetime} = \int_0^\infty PD(t)LGD(t)EAD(t)dt. \tag{5.13}$$

If lifetime horizon is relatively short and variables $PD(t)$, and $LGD(t)$ do not experience extreme volatility under scenarios adopted for the analysis, one may isolate $PD(t)$ and $LGD(t)$ by focusing on $EAD(t)$ over a lifetime horizon. The average closure time is derived by imposing the following constraint:

$$\int_0^\infty EAD(t)dt = \int_0^{\bar{T}} EAD^*(t)dt, \tag{5.14}$$

where $\bar{T}$ represents the average closure time and EAD^* is our objective function. If we assume an exponentially distributed closure rate probability with constant intensity λ, the following applies:

$$P_{cl,t} = \lambda e^{-\lambda t}, \tag{5.15}$$

where $P_{cl,t}$ indicates the instantaneous probability of closure at time t. Based on this assumption, the average closure time corresponds to $\frac{1}{\lambda}$, where λ is estimated based on historical data.

The cumulative distribution function (CDF) for an exponentially distributed density is as follows:

$$CDF_{cl,t} = 1 - \int_0^t e^{-\lambda u}du. \tag{5.16}$$

Finally, one may derive the survival probability (that is, probability not to close) up to the average closure time as follows:

$$\int_0^\infty e^{-\lambda u}du = \int_0^{\frac{1}{\lambda}} du. \tag{5.17}$$

This equation implies that, on the basis of all above assumptions, one may consider a constant balance, instead of a decaying balance, over a period $\frac{1}{\lambda}$ corresponding to the average closure rate horizon.

EXERCISES

Exercise 5.1. Analyse the competing risks explored in Example 5.4.1 by means of the framework detailed by Therneau et al. (2018) and Therneau (2018).

Exercise 5.2. Perform the analysis conduced through Examples 5.5.1 and 5.5.2 by means of random forest and boosting.

Exercise 5.3. Let us consider the models applied in the previous exercise. Perform statistical validation by pointing out model accuracy.

REFERENCES

Dirick, L., Claeskens, G., Baesens, B., 2017. Time to default in credit scoring using survival analysis: a benchmark study. Journal of the Operational Research Society 68, 652–665.

FASB, 2016. Accounting Standards Updata No. 2016–13, Financial Instruments-Credit Losses (Topic 326). June 16, 2016. Financial Accounting Series. Financial Accounting Standards Board.

Hastie, T., Tibshirani, R., Friedman, J., 2009. Elements of Statistical Learning: Data Mining, Inference and Prediction. Springer, New York.

IASB, 2014. IFRS 9 Financial Instruments. Technical report, July 2014. International Accounting Standards Board.

James, G., Witten, D., Hastie, T., Tibshirani, R., 2013. An Introduction to Statistical Learning with Applications in R. Springer, New York.

Leow, M., Crook, J., 2016. A new mixture model for the estimation of credit card exposure. European Journal of Operational Research 249, 487–497.

Qi, M., 2009. Exposure at Default of Unsecured Credit Cards. Office of the Comptroller of the Currency. Working paper.

Therneau, T., 2018. Multi-State Models as a Data Exploration Tool. Cran R-Project.

Therneau, T., Crowson, C., Atkinson, E., 2018. Multi-State Models and Competing Risks. Financial services authority. Cran R-Project.

SCENARIO ANALYSIS AND EXPECTED CREDIT LOSSES

Expected credit losses (ECLs) are usually computed by relying on the product of three main risk parameters: probability of default (PD), loss given default (LGD) and exposure at default (EAD).

As discussed in previous chapters, a forward-looking view is central for the overall estimate. In this regard, the first goal of this chapter is to study multivariate time series to analyse and forecast macroeconomic scenarios. The focus is on vector auto-regression (VAR) and vector error-correction (VEC) models. Hints are also provided regarding global vector auto-regression (GVAR) modelling.

As a second step of the journey, a practical case study allows us to grasp how to compute ECL by relying on parameters investigated throughout the book. Emphasis is given to IFRS 9 and CECL comparison.

Finally, full ECL validation is scrutinized. Indeed, the presumed independence between risk parameters and lack of concentration effects is challenged by means of a portfolio analysis. Historical validation is also inspected as part of a full ECL validation process.

Examples and case studies are examined by means of R software and SAS.

KEY ABBREVIATIONS AND SYMBOLS

$CLoss_g$	Credit loss for simulation g
$EAD_{i,t}$	Exposure at default for account i at time t
ECL_{pt}^{life}	Lifetime expected credit loss for portfolio pt
$L^{(\cdot)}$	Lag operator
$LGD_{i,t}$	Loss given default for account i at time t
$PD_{i,t}$	Probability of default for account i at time t
PV_t	Present value operator at time t
$\mathbf{x}_t$	Vector of macroeconomic variables (MVs) at time t
$\mathbf{x}_{t+h|t}$	h-step ahead macroeconomic variables (MVs) forecast
Δx_t	First difference operator: $x_t - x_{t-1}$
ϵ_t	White noise process or error term with specific distribution

---

6.1 INTRODUCTION

IFRS 9 specifically requires projections under alternative scenarios and the adoption of a weighting scheme to compute ECL. FASB (2016) is not prescriptive in this regard. Nevertheless, no restrictions

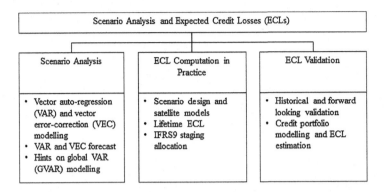

FIGURE 6.1

Chapter's workflow diagram.

are imposed on this topic. Consequently, one may consider a multi-scenario setting both for IFRS 9 and CECL. Nonetheless, a reversion towards long-term mean loss rate is central under FASB (2016). Therefore two key issues need to be addressed in such a setting. On the one hand, one needs to specify a suitable time horizon for the reversion. On the other hand, a long-term loss rate needs to be estimated. Time series analysis plays a key role to address these issues. Based on this, structural models are often challenged by econometric methods to explain macroeconomic fluctuations. Flexibility and statistical reliability are the major advantages of vector auto-regression (VAR) and vector error-correction (VEC) models.

Three main goals inspire this chapter. Firstly, one needs to become familiar with the most common econometric tools to fit macroeconomic time series and make scenario projections. Secondly, we aim to bring together all credit risk components studied throughout the entire book to estimate ECL. The third goal is to create a framework to validate the overall ECL estimate. Indeed, risk component silos validation does not necessarily ensure a consistent ECL outcome.

Figure 6.1 summarizes how these three areas are investigated throughout the chapter.

- **Scenario analysis.** Section 6.2 introduces multivariate time series analysis. Details on how to perform VAR and VEC are provided. Since scenario analysis is at the very heart of the entire ECL computation, MVs analysis and impulse response analysis are studied. Some hints on global vector auto-regression (GVAR) modelling are also provided.
- **ECL computation in practice.** Credit risk models investigated throughout the book, together with scenarios above-detailed, are the key ingredients for computing ECL, as summarized in Section 6.3. In more detail, a practical guide on how to perform ECL computation is scrutinized by considering both IFRS 9 and CECL. Finally, the focus is on the staging allocation process prescribed by IASB (2014).
- **ECL validation.** In Section 6.4 the focus is on an overall ECL validation. Indeed, a silos risk parameter validation does not necessarily ensure a consistent ECL output. Two main perspectives are considered. On the one hand, historical credit losses are studied as a paradigm for ECL validation. On the other hand, a credit portfolio modelling perspective is followed to validate ECL results.

Examples and case studies are examined by means of R software throughout the chapter.

6.2 SCENARIO ANALYSIS

Starting from the traditional VAR and VEC models, the essential tool-kit to deal with macroeconomic time series is presented. Estimation, simulation and forecast are components of a comprehensive process to use for ECL scenario analysis and forecast.

Figure 6.2 describes how the journey is organized throughout Section 6.2.

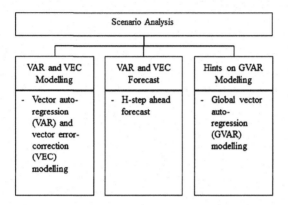

FIGURE 6.2

Workflow diagram for Section 6.2.

Section 6.2.1 presents VAR model as a flexible tool to capture statistical patterns. It is also possible to use this approach to represent theory-based relationships. The VEC model is then introduced to deal with integrated time series. Moving from the need to utilize macroeconomic scenario for estimating ECLs, Section 6.2.2 provides details on VAR and VEC forecasts. Impulse response analysis is also part of the tool-kit for projecting consistent scenarios. Finally, Section 6.2.3 provides some hints on global VAR (GVAR) modelling to extend VAR and VEC archetype over a multi-country setting.

6.2.1 VECTOR AUTO-REGRESSION AND VECTOR ERROR-CORRECTION MODELLING

Let $\mathbf{x}_t = (x_{1,t}, \ldots, x_{k,t})'$ denote a $p \times 1$ vector of time series variables. The basic $k\text{-}lag$ VAR(k) model has the following form:

$$\mathbf{x}_t = \mathbf{c} + \boldsymbol{\Phi}_1 \mathbf{x}_{t-1} + \ldots + \boldsymbol{\Phi}_k \mathbf{x}_{t-k} + \boldsymbol{\epsilon}_t, \tag{6.1}$$

$$\underbrace{\begin{bmatrix} x_{1,t} \\ \vdots \\ x_{p,t} \end{bmatrix}}_{\mathbf{x}_t} = \underbrace{\begin{bmatrix} c_1 \\ \vdots \\ c_p \end{bmatrix}}_{\mathbf{c}} + \underbrace{\begin{bmatrix} \phi 1_{1,1} & \cdots & \phi 1_{1,p} \\ \vdots & \ddots & \vdots \\ \phi 1_{p,1} & \cdots & \phi 1_{p,p} \end{bmatrix}}_{\boldsymbol{\Phi}_1} \underbrace{\begin{bmatrix} x_{1,t-1} \\ \vdots \\ x_{p,t-1} \end{bmatrix}}_{\mathbf{x}_{t-1}} + \ldots +$$

$$
+ \underbrace{\begin{bmatrix} \phi_{k_{1,1}} & \cdots & \phi_{k_{1,p}} \\ \vdots & \ddots & \vdots \\ \phi_{k_{p,1}} & \cdots & \phi_{k_{p,p}} \end{bmatrix}}_{\boldsymbol{\Phi}_k} \underbrace{\begin{bmatrix} x_{1,t-k} \\ \vdots \\ x_{p,t-k} \end{bmatrix}}_{x_{t-k}} + \underbrace{\begin{bmatrix} \epsilon_{1,t} \\ \vdots \\ \epsilon_{p,t} \end{bmatrix}}_{\epsilon_t},
$$

where $\boldsymbol{\Phi}_{1,\dots,k}$ are $p \times p$ matrices of coefficients, and ϵ_t is a $p \times 1$ zero mean white noise vector process (serially uncorrelated or independent), with time invariant covariance matrix $\boldsymbol{\Sigma}$. The VAR(k) model has the following form in lag operator notation:

$$
\boldsymbol{\Phi}(L)\mathbf{x}_t = \mathbf{c} + \epsilon_t, \tag{6.2}
$$

where $\boldsymbol{\Phi}(L) = \boldsymbol{I}_p - \boldsymbol{\Phi}_1 L - \dots - \boldsymbol{\Phi}_k L^k$. The VAR($k$) is stable if the eigenvalues of the companion matrix

$$
\mathbf{C} = \begin{bmatrix} \boldsymbol{\Phi}_1 & \boldsymbol{\Phi}_2 & \cdots & \boldsymbol{\Phi}_p \\ \mathbf{I}_p & \mathbf{0} & \cdots & \mathbf{0} \\ \mathbf{0} & \ddots & \mathbf{0} & \vdots \\ \mathbf{0} & \mathbf{0} & \mathbf{I}_p & \mathbf{0} \end{bmatrix}, \tag{6.3}
$$

have modulus less than one.

Example 6.2.1 introduces multivariate time series modelling. It highlights how to generate a VAR(1) process.

EXAMPLE 6.2.1 SIMULATING A VAR(1) MODEL

Let us consider the next VAR(1) model:

$$
\begin{bmatrix} x_{1,t} \\ x_{2,t} \end{bmatrix} = \begin{bmatrix} 0.2 \\ 0.2 \end{bmatrix} + \begin{bmatrix} 0.3 & 0.2 \\ 0.2 & 0.3 \end{bmatrix} \begin{bmatrix} x_{1,t-1} \\ x_{2,t-1} \end{bmatrix} + \begin{bmatrix} \epsilon_{1,t} \\ \epsilon_{2,t} \end{bmatrix},
$$

where the covariance matrix $\boldsymbol{\Sigma}$ is as follows:

$$
\begin{bmatrix} 1.0 & 0.8 \\ 0.8 & 1.0 \end{bmatrix}.
$$

The following R code simulates the above VAR(1) model by means of the next steps:

1. Define simulation parameters, and
2. Simulate 50 realizations of the above-detailed VAR(1). (See Figure 6.3.)

```
# 1. Define simulation parameters
# 1.1. Vector of constants
ka <- matrix(c(0.2,0.2),2,1)
# 1.2. Covariance matrix
Omega <- matrix(c(1.0, 0.8, 0.8, 1.0),2,2)
```

```
Om <- chol(Omega)
# 1.3. VAR matrix
A1 <- matrix(c(0.3,0.2,0.2,0.3),2,2)
# 1.4. Simulation matrix
mX <- matrix(0.0, 2, 50)
# 1.5. Initial values
mX[,1] <- c(1.0420, 1.0720)
# 2. VAR(1) simulation
set.seed(123)
mZeta <- matrix(rnorm(2*50),2,50)
for (t in 2:ncol(mX))
{ mX[,t] <- ka + A1 %*% mX[,t-1] +t(Om) %*% mZeta[,t] }
```

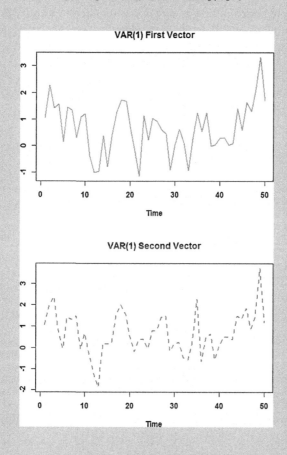

FIGURE 6.3

VAR(1) model simulation.

For both IFRS 9 and CECL, scenarios play a key role. No specific requirement is pointed out in terms of Monte Carlo simulations. Nevertheless, mechanics described in Example 6.2.1 allows us to simulate paths from which to derive densities, and support scenario projections under alternative conditions.

Stationarity assumption plays a key role when dealing with time series. Nonetheless, it does not necessarily hold in practice. In this regard, a cointegrated framework may help the analysis. A $p \times 1$ vector of variables $\mathbf{x}_t = (x_{1,t}, \ldots x_{p,t})'$, $t = 1, \ldots, T$, is said to be cointegrated if at least one non-zero $p \times 1$ vector $\boldsymbol{\beta}_l$ exists, such that $\boldsymbol{\beta}_l' x_t$ is trend stationary (Johansen, 1988). In this case, $\boldsymbol{\beta}_l$ is called cointegrating vector. If r such linearly independent vectors exist, $\mathbf{x}_t$ is cointegrated with cointegrating rank r. Starting from the $p \times r$ matrix of cointegrating vectors $\boldsymbol{\beta} = (\boldsymbol{\beta}_1, \ldots, \boldsymbol{\beta}_r)$, the r elements of the vector $\boldsymbol{\beta}' \mathbf{x}_t$ are trend-stationary, and $\boldsymbol{\beta}$ is called the cointegrating matrix.

The cointegration matrix $\boldsymbol{\beta}$ is not unique, since for any scalar c the linear combination $c\boldsymbol{\beta}' \mathbf{x}_t = \boldsymbol{\beta}^{*'} \mathbf{x}_t \sim I(0)$. Hence, some normalisation assumption is required to identify $\boldsymbol{\beta}$. The reader may refer to Juselius (2006) for an interesting dissertation on identification. According to Johansen (1996), the cointegrated VAR can be represented in the form of VEC, as follows:

$$\Delta \mathbf{x}_t = \boldsymbol{\Pi} \mathbf{x}_{t-1} + \boldsymbol{\Gamma}_1 \Delta \mathbf{x}_{t-1} + \ldots + \boldsymbol{\Gamma}_{k-1} \Delta \mathbf{x}_{t-k+1} + \boldsymbol{\epsilon}_t, \tag{6.4}$$

$$
\underbrace{\begin{bmatrix} \Delta x_{1,t} \\ \vdots \\ \Delta x_{p,t} \end{bmatrix}}_{\Delta \mathbf{x}_t} = \underbrace{\begin{bmatrix} \pi_{1,1} & \cdots & \pi_{1,p} \\ \vdots & \ddots & \vdots \\ \pi_{p,1} & \cdots & \pi_{p,p} \end{bmatrix}}_{\boldsymbol{\Pi}} \underbrace{\begin{bmatrix} x_{1,t-1} \\ \vdots \\ x_{p,t-1} \end{bmatrix}}_{\mathbf{x}_{t-1}} + \underbrace{\begin{bmatrix} \gamma 1_{1,1} & \cdots & \gamma 1_{1,p} \\ \vdots & \ddots & \vdots \\ \gamma 1_{p,1} & \cdots & \gamma 1_{p,p} \end{bmatrix}}_{\boldsymbol{\Gamma}_1} \underbrace{\begin{bmatrix} \Delta x_{1,t-1} \\ \vdots \\ \Delta x_{p,t-1} \end{bmatrix}}_{\Delta \mathbf{x}_{t-1}} + \ldots +
$$

$$
+ \underbrace{\begin{bmatrix} \gamma_{k-1 1,1} & \cdots & \gamma_{k-1 1,p} \\ \vdots & \ddots & \vdots \\ \gamma_{k-1 p,1} & \cdots & \gamma_{k-1 p,p} \end{bmatrix}}_{\boldsymbol{\Gamma}_{k-1}} \underbrace{\begin{bmatrix} \Delta x_{1,t-k+1} \\ \vdots \\ \Delta x_{p,t-k+1} \end{bmatrix}}_{\Delta \mathbf{x}_{t-k+1}} + \underbrace{\begin{bmatrix} \epsilon_{1,t} \\ \vdots \\ \epsilon_{p,t} \end{bmatrix}}_{\boldsymbol{\epsilon}_t},
$$

where $\mathbf{x}_t = (x_{1,t} \ldots x_{p,t})'$ is the $p \times 1$ vector of variables, and Δ is the first difference operator, $\Delta \mathbf{x}_t = \mathbf{x}_t - \mathbf{x}_{t-1}$.[1]

---

[1] In the case where $\boldsymbol{\Pi}$ has a reduced rank, the following equation holds: $\boldsymbol{\Pi} = \boldsymbol{\alpha}\boldsymbol{\beta}'$, where $\boldsymbol{\alpha}$ and $\boldsymbol{\beta}$ are $p \times r$ matrices, $r \leq p$. $\boldsymbol{\beta}$ is the above-described cointegrating matrix, and $\boldsymbol{\Gamma}_1, \ldots, \boldsymbol{\Gamma}_{k-1}$ are $p \times p$ parameter matrices. Errors are assumed to be normally distributed $\boldsymbol{\epsilon}_t \sim N(\mathbf{0}, \boldsymbol{\Sigma})$, where $\boldsymbol{\Sigma}$ represents the $p \times p$ covariance matrix. In addition, one could consider a vector $\mathbf{D}_t = (D_{1,t}, \ldots, D_{g,t}, \mu_0)'$ containing g (binary) dummies and a constant. The following three cases need to be considered when assessing the rank of $\boldsymbol{\Pi}$.

$$rank(\boldsymbol{\Pi}) = p,$$
$$rank(\boldsymbol{\Pi}) = 0,$$
$$0 < rank(\boldsymbol{\Pi}) \leq p.$$

Example 6.2.2 (following) outlines how to deal with cointegration modelling. UK time series covering the period 2000–2013 are investigated.

EXAMPLE 6.2.2 VEC ANALYSIS

Let us consider the following UK time series: nominal gross domestic (GDP), consumer price index (CPI), nominal equity price index (EQ), exchange rate in US dollars (ER), nominal short-term interest rate per annum in percent (R^{ST}), nominal long-term interest rate per annum in percent (R^{LT}). The analysis covers the period 2000–2013. A suitable variable transformation is summarised in Table 6.1.

Table 6.1 UK variable transformation used for VEC analysis

Descriptions	Symbols and analytical formulas
Real output (GDP)	$z_t = \ln(GDP_t/CPI_t)$
ln CPI	$\pi_t = \ln(CPI_t)$
Real equity price	$eq_t = \ln(EQ_t/CPI_t)$
Real exchange rate	$er_t = \ln(ER_t/CPI_t)$
Short term interest rate	$r_t^{ST} = 0.25\ln(1 + R_t^{ST}/100)$
Long term interest rate	$r_t^{LT} = 0.25\ln(1 + R_t^{LT}/100)$

The analysis is performed by means of the following steps:

1. Upload data,
2. Check for stationarity: ADF test,
3. Model estimation, and
4. Conduct diagnostic checks.

```
# 1. Upload data
macv_init<-(read.csv('uk_macv.csv', header = TRUE,
sep = ';', dec='.'))
macv<- macv_init[2:54,]
```

Figure 6.4 shows UK time series over the period 2000–2013.

In the first case, all p linearly independent combinations must be stationary. In the second case, no linear combination exists to make Πx_t stationary, except for the trivial solution. The most important case is the third one, where the rank of Π is greater than zero, but lower than p. As stated above, when the matrix has no full rank, it can be decomposed into the product of two $p \times r$ matrices α and β such that $\alpha\beta'$. Hence $\alpha\beta'x_t$ is stationary. The r linear independent columns of β are the cointegrating vectors. Each vector represents one long-run relationship between the individual series of x_t.

In line with the above identification issue, the parameters of the matrices α and β are undefined, because any non-singular matrix Θ would yield $\alpha\Theta\left(\beta\Theta^{-1}\right)' = \Pi$. It implies that only the cointegration space spanned by β can be determined. The obvious solution is to normalise one element of β to one. The elements of α determine the speed of adjustment to the long-run equilibrium.

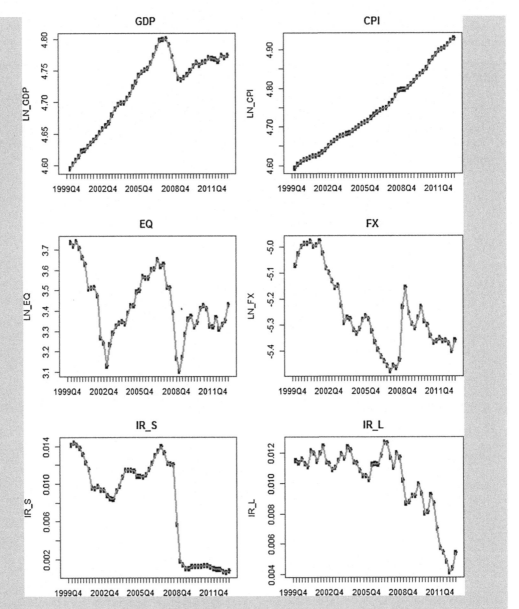

FIGURE 6.4

UK macroeconomic time series analysis from 2000 to 2013.

Augmented Dickey–Fuller (ADF) test verifies time series stationarity (Lutkepohl, 2007). According to this test, the following table shows that the unit root null hypothesis cannot be rejected for the original time series. On the other hand, the unit root hypothesis is rejected for all first differenced time series. (See Table 6.2.)

```
# 2. Check for stationarity: ADF test
```

Table 6.2 ADF test for original variables and their first differences		
	Original variable	**Δ Variable**
	p-value	**p-value**
z_t	0.9491	0.0872
π_t	0.9597	< 0.01
eq	0.6166	< 0.01
er	0.7820	< 0.01
r^{ST}	0.8710	< 0.01
r^{ST}	0.7082	< 0.01

Model estimation and selection take place in conjunction with diagnostic checking. The focus is on the VEC model with one lag (and constant).

```
# 3. Model estimation
library(tseries)
library(urca)
library(vars)
macv$LN_GDP_D <- diff(macv_init[,"LN_GDP"], lag = 1)
macv$LN_CPI_D <- diff(macv_init[,"LN_CPI"], lag = 1)
macv$LN_EQ_D <- diff(macv_init[,"LN_EQ"], lag = 1)
macv$LN_FX_D <- diff(macv_init[,"LN_FX"], lag = 1)
macv$IR_S_D <- diff(macv_init[,"IR_S"], lag = 1)
macv$IR_L_D <- diff(macv_init[,"IR_L"], lag = 1)
VECM2<- ca.jo(macv[, c('LN_GDP_D','LN_CPI_D', 'LN_EQ_D',
'LN_FX_D', 'IR_S_D', 'IR_L_D')],
type = 'trace',ecdet='none', K =2, spec ='transitory')
# Values of teststatistic and critical values of test:
#            test 10pct  5pct   1pct
# r <= 5 |   7.16  6.50  8.18   11.65
# r <= 4 |  17.51 15.66 17.95   23.52
# r <= 3 |  38.55 28.71 31.52   37.22
# r <= 2 |  60.66 45.23 48.28   55.43
# r <= 1 | 107.84 66.49 70.60   78.87
# r = 0  | 162.91 85.18 90.39  104.20
```

The following diagnostic checks highlight that the model cannot be rejected based on common assumptions. The reader interested in performing additional analysis aimed to detect atypical observation may refer to Bellini (2016).

```
# 4. Diagnostic checks
# 4.1. VEC to VAR transformation
```

```
vec2var<-vec2var(VECM2,r=2)
# 4.2. Tests
vec2var.norm<- normality.test(vec2var)
vec2var.norm$jb.mul
# JB-Test (multivariate)
# data:  Residuals of VAR object vec2var
# Chi-squared = 8.7552, df = 12, p-value = 0.7237
# Skewness only (multivariate)
# data:  Residuals of VAR object vec2var
# Chi-squared = 4.2288, df = 6, p-value = 0.6458
# Kurtosis only (multivariate)
# data:  Residuals of VAR object vec2var
# Chi-squared = 4.5265, df = 6, p-value = 0.6058
```

The next section focuses on the main theoretical assumptions to project VAR and VEC models.

6.2.2 VAR AND VEC FORECAST

Let us start the forecast analysis from the following one-step ahead predictor for a VAR model:

$$\mathbf{x}_{t+1|t} = \mathbf{c} + \boldsymbol{\Phi}_1 \mathbf{x}_t + \ldots + \boldsymbol{\Phi}_k \mathbf{x}_{t-k+1}. \tag{6.5}$$

A forecast for a longer horizon h relies on the following chain-rule:

$$\mathbf{x}_{t+h|t} = \mathbf{c} + \boldsymbol{\Phi}_1 \mathbf{x}_{t-1+h|t} + \ldots + \boldsymbol{\Phi}_k \mathbf{x}_{t-k+h|t}, \tag{6.6}$$

and the h-step forecast errors is

$$\mathbf{x}_{t+h} - \mathbf{x}_{t+h|t} = \sum_{r=0}^{h-1} \boldsymbol{\psi}_r \boldsymbol{\epsilon}_{t-r+h}, \tag{6.7}$$

where the matrices $\boldsymbol{\psi}_r$ are determined by recursive substitution:

$$\boldsymbol{\psi}_r = \sum_{l=1}^{k-1} \boldsymbol{\psi}_{r-l} \boldsymbol{\Phi}_l, \tag{6.8}$$

with $\boldsymbol{\psi}_0 = \boldsymbol{I}_p$ and $\boldsymbol{\Phi}_l = \mathbf{0}$ for $l > k$. Hence, let us consider forecasting $\mathbf{x}_{t+h}$, when the parameters of the VAR process are estimated by using multivariate least squares. The best linear predictor is as follows:

$$\hat{\mathbf{x}}_{t+h|t} = \hat{\boldsymbol{\Phi}}_1 \hat{\mathbf{x}}_{t-1+h|t} + \ldots + \hat{\boldsymbol{\Phi}}_k \hat{\mathbf{x}}_{t-k+h|t}, \tag{6.9}$$

where $\hat{\boldsymbol{\Phi}}_{(\cdot)}$ is the estimated parameter matrix.

Since multivariate forecast errors are asymptotically normally distributed, $\mathbf{x}_{t+h}$ can be simulated by generating multivariate normal random variables with zero mean and covariance matrix $\hat{\boldsymbol{\Sigma}}(h) = \sum_{r=0}^{h-1} \hat{\boldsymbol{\xi}}_r \hat{\boldsymbol{\Sigma}} \hat{\boldsymbol{\xi}}_r'$, with $\hat{\boldsymbol{\xi}}_r = \sum_{l=1}^r \hat{\boldsymbol{\xi}}_{r-l} \hat{\boldsymbol{\Sigma}}_l$. Lutkepohl (2007) gives an approximation of $MSE(\mathbf{x}_{t+h} - \hat{\mathbf{x}}_{t+h|t})$, which may be interpreted as finite sample correction to the above-detailed covariance matrix.

Asymptotic confidence intervals for h-step ahead forecast may be obtained by relying on the normal distribution assumption.

When dealing with large sets of variables, extensive samples are required. However, they are not necessarily available. Additionally, lagged values tend to produce high correlation, and parameter estimates lose their robustness. Doan et al. (1984) proposed the use of Bayesian prior information (that is, Minnesota prior). This approach has been widely used in practice. The reader may refer to LeSage (1999) for a useful dissertation and detailed software implementation.

With regard to CECL, one needs to identify a suitable period for mean reversion and the corresponding level of long-term average losses. One may rely on a long term historical sub-portfolio loss rate, or consider the output of credit risk models, fed through a suitable mean-reverting scenario. Impulse response analysis may help in this respect. Indeed, an auto-regression process can be represented as an infinite sum of past errors with decaying weights. In a similar way, a covariance stationary VAR process has a so-called *Wold* representation of the form

$$\mathbf{x}_t = \mu + \epsilon_t + \boldsymbol{\psi}_1 \epsilon_{t-1} + \boldsymbol{\psi}_2 \epsilon_{t-2} + \dots, \tag{6.10}$$

where the $p \times p$ moving average $\boldsymbol{\psi}_r$ is determined recursively using Equation (6.8). One should be tempted to interpret the elements of $\boldsymbol{\psi}_r$ as the dynamic multiplier, or impulse response. However, this is only possible if $var(\boldsymbol{\epsilon}) = \boldsymbol{\Sigma}$ is a diagonal matrix, so that errors are uncorrelated. One way to obtain an uncorrelated error matrix is to estimate a triangular structural VAR, represented as follows:

$$\mathbf{B}\mathbf{x}_t = \mathbf{c} + \boldsymbol{\Phi}_1 \mathbf{x}_{t-1} + \dots + \boldsymbol{\Phi}_k \mathbf{x}_{t-k} + \boldsymbol{\eta}_t, \tag{6.11}$$

where $\mathbf{B}$ is a lower triangular matrix with ones along the diagonal. The uncorrelated orthogonal errors $\boldsymbol{\eta}_t$ are regarded as structural errors; the triangular structure imposes a recursive casual ordering. The ordering, for example, $\mathbf{x}_1 \rightarrow \mathbf{x}_2 \rightarrow \mathbf{x}_3$ imposes the restriction that $\mathbf{x}_1$ affects $\mathbf{x}_2$ and $\mathbf{x}_3$, but the latter variable may not affect $\mathbf{x}_1$. Hence, the ordering depends on the context and its economic justification.

Given a recursive ordering, the *Wold* representation of $\mathbf{x}_t$, based on the orthogonal errors $\boldsymbol{\eta}_t$, is as follows:

$$\mathbf{x}_t = \mu + \boldsymbol{\Theta}_0 \boldsymbol{\eta}_t + \boldsymbol{\Theta}_1 \boldsymbol{\eta}_{t-1} + \boldsymbol{\Theta}_2 \boldsymbol{\eta}_{t-2} + \dots, \tag{6.12}$$

where $\boldsymbol{\Theta}_0 = \mathbf{B}^{-1}$ is a lower triangular matrix.

Exercise 6.2.3 shows how to implement the impulse response analysis in practice.

EXAMPLE 6.2.3 VEC, VAR AND IMPUSE RESPONSE ANALYSIS

Let us consider the time series scrutinized in Example 6.2.2. An impulse response analysis is performed by relying on the estimated model transformed into VAR form (that is, *vec2var*), as follows.

```
# 1. Impulse response analysis
irf_eq<- irf(vec2var, impulse="LN_EQ_D", response="LN_GDP_D",
n.ahead=10, boot=TRUE, ci = 0.99)
irf_fx<- irf(vec2var, impulse="LN_FX_D", response="LN_GDP_D",
n.ahead=10, boot=TRUE, ci = 0.99)
irf_irs<- irf(vec2var, impulse="IR_S_D", response="LN_GDP_D",
```

```
n.ahead=10, boot=TRUE, ci = 0.99)
irf_irl<- irf(vec2var, impulse="IR_L_D", response="LN_GDP_D",
n.ahead=10, boot=TRUE, ci = 0.99)
```

Figure 6.5 shows a 10-step ahead GDP variation due to independent shocks on equity, exchange rate, short-term and long-term interest rates.

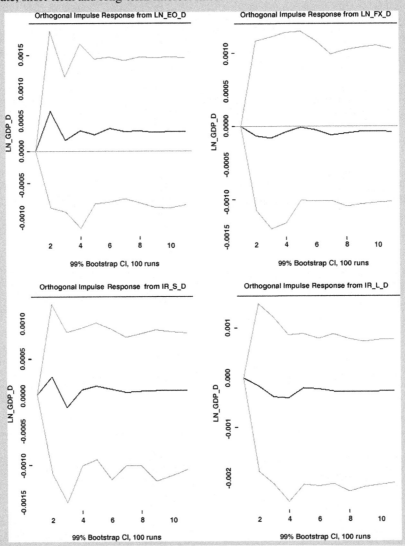

FIGURE 6.5

Impulse response analysis: 10-step ahead GDP variation due to independent shocks on: equity, exchange rate, short-term and long-term interest rates.

From a CECL perspective, this analysis helps understanding the extent of a macroeconomic shock on variables included in a scenario. A mean reversion process can be structured accordingly.

The global nature of economic interdependencies induces both researcher and practitioners to use global VAR models (GVAR). Based on this, Pesaran et al. (2004) provide a fundamental reference. A useful Matlab implementation is provided by Bellini (2017). The next section provides some hints on how to perform a GVAR analysis.

6.2.3 HINTS ON GVAR MODELLING

Let us consider an economy with S countries indexed $s = 0, \ldots, S$. Country 0 is the reference one. A GVAR model is outlined starting from a typical VARX$(2, 2)$,[2] as follows:

$$
\begin{aligned}
\mathbf{x}_{s,t} = \mathbf{c}_{s,0} + \mathbf{c}_{s,1} t + \boldsymbol{\Phi}_{s,1} \mathbf{x}_{s,t-1} + \boldsymbol{\Phi}_{s,2} \mathbf{x}_{s,t-2} + \\
+ \boldsymbol{\Lambda}_{s,0} \mathbf{x}_{s,t}^* + \boldsymbol{\Lambda}_{s,1} \mathbf{x}_{s,t-1}^* + \boldsymbol{\Lambda}_{s,2} \mathbf{x}_{s,t-2}^* + \mathbf{u}_{s,t},
\end{aligned}
\tag{6.13}
$$

where $\mathbf{x}_{s,t}$ is the $p_s \times 1$ vector of country specific variables, and $\mathbf{x}_{s,t}^*$ is the $p_s^* \times 1$ vector of foreign variables. $\mathbf{c}_{s,0}$ is the constant term, whereas $\mathbf{c}_{s,1}$ is the trend coefficient. $\boldsymbol{\Phi}_{s,(\cdot)}$ and $\boldsymbol{\Lambda}_{s,(\cdot)}$ are the matrix coefficients for the domestic and foreign variables. $\mathbf{u}_{s,t}$ represents the error component, which is assumed to be a serially uncorrelated and cross-sectionally weakly dependent process.

The foreign variable vectors have the following weighting structure:

$$
\mathbf{x}_{s,t}^* = \sum_{r=0}^{S} \mathbf{w}_{s,r} \mathbf{x}_{r,t}, \quad \mathbf{w}_{ss} = 0,
\tag{6.14}
$$

where $w_{s,r}$ are weights such that $\sum_{r=0}^{S} w_{s,r} = 1$. Weights can change over time. However, a fixed weight scheme facilitates the dissertation. Foreign-specific variables are weighted averages of the corresponding domestic variable. Weights are usually set according to international trade flows.

The error correction form of the VARX$(2, 2)$ outlined in Equation (6.13) is represented as follows:

$$
\begin{aligned}
\Delta \mathbf{x}_{s,t} = \mathbf{c}_{s,0} - \boldsymbol{\alpha}_s \boldsymbol{\beta}_s' \left[\boldsymbol{\zeta}_{s,t-1} - \boldsymbol{\gamma}_s (t - 1) \right] + \\
\boldsymbol{\Lambda}_{s,0} \mathbf{x}_{s,t}^* + \boldsymbol{\Gamma}_s \Delta \boldsymbol{\zeta}_{s,t-1} + \mathbf{u}_{s,t},
\end{aligned}
\tag{6.15}
$$

where $\boldsymbol{\zeta}_{s,t} = \left(\mathbf{x}_{s,t}', \mathbf{x}_{s,t}^{*'} \right)'$, $\boldsymbol{\alpha}_s$ is a $p_s \times r_s$ matrix of rank r_s, and $\boldsymbol{\beta}_s$ is a $(p_s + p_s^*) \times r_s$ matrix, or rank r_s.

For each country, models are estimated separately, conditional on $\mathbf{x}_{s,t}^*$. The latter is treated as long run or $I(1)$, weakly exogenous with regards to Equation (6.15) parameters. Though the estimation is done on a country basis, the GVAR model is solved for the international economy as a whole. Conditional on a given estimate of $\boldsymbol{\beta}_s$, the remaining parameters are estimated via ordinary least square

---

[2]VARX$(2, 2)$ stands for VAR with 2 lags on the domestic country, and 2 lags on the foreign countries.

regressions as follows:

$$\Delta \mathbf{x}_{s,t} = \mathbf{c}_{s,0} + \delta_s ECM_{s,t-1} + \Lambda_{s,0}\mathbf{x}_{s,t}^* + \Gamma_s \Delta \mathbf{x}_{s,t-1} + \mathbf{u}_{s,t}, \qquad (6.16)$$

where $ECM_{s,t-1}$ are the error correction terms of the sth country model.

When a set of macroeconomic variable projection is available, one should rely on conditional forecast. Robertson and Tallman (1999) provide an interesting framework. Bellini (2017) provides some hints on how to implement it for stress testing purposes.

The next section shows the interaction between macroeconomic scenarios and ECLs.

6.3 ECL COMPUTATION IN PRACTICE

In line with IASB (2014), and considering FASB (2016) probability of default method, ECLs are computed by relying on the following product[3]:

$$ECL = \mathbb{E}(PD \cdot LGD \cdot EAD), \qquad (6.17)$$

whereby, in case of independence, the following applies:

$$ECL = \mathbb{E}(PD) \cdot \mathbb{E}(LGD) \cdot \mathbb{E}(EAD). \qquad (6.18)$$

This assumption plays a key role. Indeed, it subsumes absence of contagion and does not account for the role of concentration (that is, name and sector) threatening banks' resilience under adverse scenarios (Duffie and Singleton, 2003). A more extensive discussion on these assumptions is provided in Section 6.4. In what follows, the focus is on how to implement Equation (6.18), considering a given scenario generation process. In this regard, one needs to point out that IASB (2014) explicitly requires multiple scenarios, whereas FASB (2016) does not prescribe multiple scenarios adoption.

Figure 6.6 describes how Section 6.3 is organized.

Section 6.3.1 provides some hints on how to design scenarios and link credit risk satellite models. Section 6.3.2 brings together all models examined throughout the book to describe how to compute ECL by following a lifetime perspective. Finally, Section 6.3.3 focuses on IFRS 9 staging allocation. Indeed, IASB (2014) requires credits to be allocated in buckets (that is, stages 1, 2, 3), based on a significant increase in credit risk criterion. One-year ECL applies to stage 1, whereas lifetime ECLs hold for stages 2 and 3.

6.3.1 SCENARIO DESIGN AND SATELLITE MODELS

Mindful of ECL complexity, the narrative accompanying its computation plays an important role. Banks are required to describe their key assumptions and detail the most relevant variable projections.

As an example, Business Case 6.3.1 summarizes an IFRS 9 scenario narrative.

---

[3] A present value estimation is assumed to be embedded in credit risk parameter estimates.

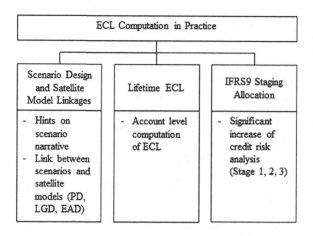

FIGURE 6.6

Workflow diagram for Section 6.3.

BUSINESS CASE 6.3.1 SCENARIO NARRATIVE FOR IFRS 9 ECL ESTIMATION

The bank uses three economic scenarios to estimate ECL under IFRS 9 rules. These scenarios represent a *most likely outcome* (that is, central scenario) and two less likely scenarios on either side of the central (that is, upside and a downside, respectively).

For the central scenario, key assumptions are defined for variables, such as GDP growth, inflation, unemployment and policy rates, using either the average of external forecasts for most economies, or market prices and internal estimates.

Upside and downside scenarios are designed to be cyclical, in that GDP growth, inflation and unemployment usually revert back to the central scenario after the first three years for major economies. We determine the maximum divergence of GDP growth from the central scenario using the 10th and the 90th percentile of the entire distribution of forecast outcomes for major economies. Using externally available forecast distributions ensures independence in scenario construction. Whereas key economic variables are set with reference to external distributional forecasts, we also align the overall narrative of the scenarios to the macroeconomic risks described in bank's top and emerging risks. This ensures that scenarios remain consistent with the more qualitative assessment of risks captured in top, and emerging risks.

Under the central scenario for the next three years, global GDP growth is expected to be around 2.5%. This rate is marginally higher than the average growth experienced over the last few years. Core inflation is assumed to remain stable, and inflation in the US and euro area is expected to slowly converge back towards central bank targets over the next two years. As a consequence, US and euro area central banks are expected to raise rates very gradually. In the UK, the Bank of England is expected to look through near-term, above-target inflation, and raise interest rates slowly. Unemployment rates displayed considerable positive cyclical momentum, which is expected to continue to underpin labour market performance in the forecast period.

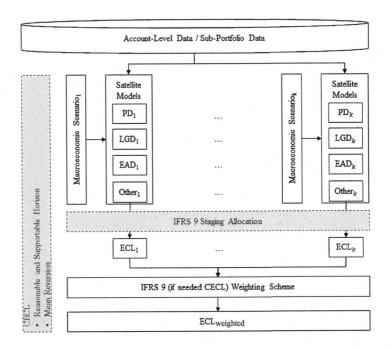

FIGURE 6.7

Data, scenario, satellite model links, and ECL.

> Central scenario forecasts of the unemployment rate are stable and, for some markets, at historical lows. Stabilisation of oil prices in 2017, helped by the Organization of Petroleum Exporting Countries' output cuts, and a fall in inventory, enable a stronger price outlook to develop.

IASB (2014) requires a scenario weighting scheme (that is, probability-weighted). Item B5.5.42 may be interpreted in the sense that in some cases, relatively simple modelling may be sufficient. In other situations, the identification of scenarios that specify the amount and timing of the cash flows for particular outcomes, and their estimated probability, is required. In those situations, the expected credit losses shall reflect at least two outcomes (see paragraph 5.5.18).

One may infer an upper limit to the number of scenarios from Section BC5.265. *The calculation of an expected value need not be a rigorous mathematical exercise, whereby an entity identifies every possible outcome and its probability.* Consequently, the requirement of a simulation-based approach over thousands of scenarios can be disregarded.

Figure 6.7 summarizes the framework needed to link account information, macroeconomic scenarios and credit risk satellite model (for example, PD, LGD, EAD) to estimate ECLs. If staging allocation is a typical step required as part of the IFRS 9 procedure, all other components may also apply to CECL. Based on this, one may exclude multiple scenarios, if not considered as part of the estimation frame. Furthermore, one needs to include both a step to identify a reasonable (supportable) horizon for long-term ECL computation, and a mean reversion target.

One may summarize the process as follows:

- **Data.** At reporting date, a set of information is needed as a starting point to assess ECL. Both performing and defaulted portfolios information is needed.
- **Macroeconomic scenarios.** Given ECL forward-looking nature, scenarios are required both for IFRS 9 and CECL. In more detail, IFRS 9 explicitly required a multi-scenario framework. In contrast, CECL is not prescriptive. Nevertheless, one may organize CECL by relying on a multiple-scenario scheme, as per IFRS 9.
- **Satellite models.** Credit risk models, such as PD, LGD, EAD, in conjunction with a set of other frames (for example, effective interest rate) rely on account-level, portfolio-level data, and scenarios. Projections are drawn over a lifetime horizon both for IFRS 9 and CECL. As part of the lifetime curve, IFRS 9 requires one-year parameters to estimate stage 1 ECL.
- **IFRS 9 staging allocation.** Staging rules apply to each financial instrument, based on criteria aligned with IASB (2014) requirements.
- **ECL computation for each scenario.** The output of credit-risk satellite models feed ECL engine. If FASB (2016) relies on lifetime estimates, IASB (2014) requires a distinction between one-year and lifetime ECLs, based on the staging allocation process described in Section 6.3.3.
- **Weighting scheme and final ECL estimation.** As a final step of the process, ECL is obtained as a weighted average of $ECL_1, \ldots, ECL_k$, estimated by relying on alternative scenarios. For CECL, if only one scenario is used, ECL is estimated as part of the previous step: *ECL computation for each scenario*.

All these components are further investigated in the next two sections. Firstly, lifetime ECL is scrutinized from a hands-on perspective. Then, IFRS 9 staging allocation is studied by considering alternative approaches and practical expedients.

6.3.2 LIFETIME ECL

In line with Equation (6.18), expected credit loss can be represented as the product of three main parameters: PD, LGD and EAD. An unbiased, forward-looking, lifetime perspective informs both IFRS 9 and CECL. The aim is to anticipate loss provisioning by avoiding a late recognition of credit depreciation in financial statements.

A lifetime perspective is followed (that is, IFRS 9 staging allocation, treated in Section 6.3.3). The granular (that is, account-level) perspective informing the entire book also applies to the following:

$$ECL_{pt}^{life}(\mathbf{x}_t^*) = \sum_{i=1}^{n_{pt}} \left[\sum_{t=1}^{T_i} PV_t \left(PD_{i,t} \cdot LGD_{i,t} EAD_{i,t} | \mathbf{x}_t^* \right) \right], \tag{6.19}$$

where the superscript $life$ stands for lifetime, whereas the subscript pt indicates the portfolio on which the analysis is conducted (that is, a portfolio is made-up by n_{pt} accounts). $PV_t(\cdot)$ represents the present value operator. Computations are conducted at account level i, over a lifetime horizon T_i. Finally, the forward-looking perspective is captured by conditioning both credit risk parameters and present value estimate on macroeconomic scenario $\mathbf{x}_t^*$.

In this regard, as detailed in previous sections, IFRS 9 explicitly requires multiple scenarios, whereas CECL is not prescriptive. Nevertheless, we can assume the use of a plurality of scenarios to estimate ECL. Business Case 6.3.2 provides some hints on how this process may be inspected from an IFRS 9 standpoint.

BUSINESS CASE 6.3.2 MULTIPLE SCENARIOS AND WEIGHTING SCHEME FROM IFRS 9 STANDPOINT

The ECL recognised in the financial statements, reflects the effect on expected credit losses of a range of possible outcomes, calculated on a probability-weighted basis, based on the economic scenarios described above, including management overlays where required. The probability-weighted amount is typically a higher number than would result from using only the central (most likely) economic scenario. Expected losses typically have a non-linear relationship to the many factors, which influence credit losses, such that more favourable macroeconomic factors do not reduce defaults as much as less favourable macroeconomic factors increase defaults.

Each outer scenario is consistent with a probability of 15%, whereas the central scenario is assigned the remaining 70%. This weighting scheme is deemed appropriate for the computation of unbiased ECL. Key scenario assumptions are set using the average of forecasts from external economists. This helps to ensure that the IFRS 9 scenarios are unbiased, and maximise the use of independent information.

Moving from the framework described in Figure 6.7, Example 6.3.1 points out how to apply Equation (6.19) to a small illustrative portfolio.

EXAMPLE 6.3.1 ECL LIFETIME MECHANICS

Let us consider a loan portfolio made up by five accounts. Table 6.3 summarizes starting-point (that is, t_0) one-year credit risk parameters for each of them. These parameters do not include a forward-looking perspective; that will be included later on in the example.

Table 6.3 Starting-point (that is, t_0) one-year credit risk parameters, before including a forward-looking perspective

	PD_{t_0}	LGD_{t_0}	EAD_{t_0}
ID1	2.00%	20.00%	80.00
ID2	5.00%	20.00%	500.00
ID3	8.00%	20.00%	60.00
ID4	1.00%	20.00%	40.00
ID5	0.50%	20.00%	20.00

Three scenarios are considered to compute ECLs, as listed below:

- Baseline: 50% probability;
- Upside: 20% probability;
- Adverse: 30% probability.

Credit risk parameters are projected according to one of the methods described throughout the book. Details on how this process is performed are omitted to ease our dissertation.

Few additional assumptions inform ECL computation, as listed below:

- Computations are performed on a yearly basis. Banks usually run their models based on a higher frequency (for example, monthly or quarterly). Nevertheless, this simplifying assumption helps summarizing the process to its essence.
- Portfolio maturity is three years. All accounts are assumed to expire at the end of t_3.
- No prepayments or overpayments are assumed to take place.
- Parameters already embed a present value assessment. Therefore no additional $PV_t(\cdot)$ estimate is needed.

In line with the above, Table 6.4 summarizes marginal PDs over the period under investigation. A distinction is made among baseline, upside and adverse scenarios.

Table 6.4 PD evolution under alternative scenarios (that is, baseline, upside and adverse)

	PD_{t_0}	PD_{t_1}	PD_{t_2}	PD_{t_3}
Baseline				
ID1	2.25%	2.18%	2.11%	2.05%
ID2	5.60%	5.24%	4.91%	4.60%
ID3	8.93%	8.06%	7.29%	6.60%
ID4	1.13%	1.10%	1.08%	1.06%
ID5	0.56%	0.55%	0.55%	0.54%
Upside				
ID1	1.96%	1.88%	1.80%	1.75%
ID2	4.90%	4.56%	4.24%	4.01%
ID3	7.84%	7.08%	6.39%	5.86%
ID4	0.98%	0.95%	0.92%	0.90%
ID5	0.49%	0.48%	0.46%	0.46%
Adverse				
ID1	2.56%	2.59%	2.77%	2.22%
ID2	6.34%	6.17%	6.31%	4.86%
ID3	10.06%	9.38%	9.16%	6.80%
ID4	1.28%	1.32%	1.43%	1.16%
ID5	0.64%	0.66%	0.73%	0.59%

Table 6.5 shows LGD evolution over the three-year horizon under analysis.

Table 6.5 LGD evolution under alternative scenarios (that is, baseline, upside and adverse)

	LGD_{t_0}	LGD_{t_1}	LGD_{t_2}	LGD_{t_3}
Baseline	20.00%	19.35%	18.77%	18.21%
Upside	18.50%	17.29%	16.20%	15.20%
Adverse	22.73%	21.99%	21.33%	20.69%

An amortizing scheme applies on each portfolio account, as detailed in Table 6.6.

Table 6.6 EAD under the hypothesis of no prepayments ($ Thousands)

	EAD_{t_0}	EAD_{t_1}	EAD_{t_2}	EAD_{t_3}
ID1	80.00	60.00	40.00	20.00
ID2	500.00	375.00	250.00	125.00
ID3	60.00	45.00	30.00	15.00
ID4	40.00	30.00	20.00	10.00
ID5	20.00	15.00	10.00	5.00

Based on the above, Table 6.7 summarizes ECL estimates for all three scenarios above detailed.

Table 6.7 ECL under alternative scenarios ($ Thousands)

	ECL_{t_0}	ECL_{t_1}	ECL_{t_2}	ECL_{t_3}	Total
Baseline					
ID1	0.36	0.25	0.16	0.07	0.85
ID2	5.60	3.80	2.30	1.05	12.75
ID3	1.07	0.70	0.41	0.18	2.36
ID4	0.09	0.06	0.04	0.02	0.21
ID5	0.02	0.02	0.01	0.00	0.05
Total	7.15	4.83	2.92	1.33	16.23
Upside					
ID1	0.29	0.19	0.12	0.05	0.65
ID2	4.53	2.95	1.72	0.76	9.97
ID3	0.87	0.55	0.31	0.13	1.87
ID4	0.07	0.05	0.03	0.01	0.16
ID5	0.02	0.01	0.01	0.00	0.04
Total	5.78	3.76	2.18	0.96	12.69
Adverse					
ID1	0.47	0.34	0.24	0.09	1.14
ID2	7.20	5.08	3.36	1.26	16.91
ID3	1.37	0.93	0.59	0.21	3.10
ID4	0.12	0.09	0.06	0.02	0.29
ID5	0.03	0.02	0.02	0.01	0.07
Total	9.19	6.46	4.26	1.59	21.50

According to the above weighting scheme (that is, baseline 50%, upside 20% and adverse 30%), portfolio ECL is $ 16.23 \cdot 0.5 + 12.69 \cdot 0.2 + 21.50 \cdot 0.3 = \$17.10$ thousands.

Moving from the framework described in Figure 6.7, one needs to identify for CECL a reasonable and supportable horizon to revert toward a long-term average. The reversion period has widely been interpreted in practice as the nine-quarters CCAR stress testing scenario (FRB, 2014), followed by an approximately four-quarters mean reversion process. When a PD, LGD, and EAD framework is adopted for CECL, one may rely on the relationship with scenarios to revert towards the average loss rate. In other words, one may leave MV dynamics to drive the long-range ECL by means of satellite

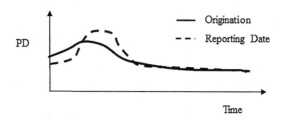

PD

Time

Origination
--- Reporting Date

FIGURE 6.8

Marginal lifetime PD comparison: origination vs. reporting date.

linkages. On the other hand, when a pool approach is adopted (for example, loss rate or vintage), a historical credit loss needs to be estimated, linked with a corresponding scenario adjustment.

Aside from the lifetime ECL above illustrated, IASB (2014) requires a credit classification in three buckets (stages). Based on this allocation, a distinction applies between one-year and lifetime ECL, as described in the next section.

6.3.3 IFRS 9 STAGING ALLOCATION

The main purpose of a staging allocation process is to determine whether an account has experienced significant increase in credit risk since origination. In line with IASB (2014), credits are allocated among three different buckets, as listed below:

- **Stage 1.** No significant deterioration in credit risk, since origination is experienced at reporting date. In this case a one-year ECL applies.
- **Stage 2.** At reporting date, a significant increase in credit risk since origination is recorded. ECL is computed over a lifetime horizon.
- **Stage 3.** This bucket includes defaulted accounts. Lifetime ECL applies.

Three main elements characterize the staging assessment:

i. **Quantitative element.** One needs to compare PD term structure at origination and at reporting date. In line with common practice, this comparison is not performed based on account's original lifetime, but on its residual lifetime. For example, a 10-year loan originated 4 years ago has a 6-year residual maturity. In line with the above, a 6-year lifetime PD comparison applies.

ii. **Qualitative element.** Those elements not included in the PD models that may reflect a significant increase in credit risk (for example, types of forbearance or watch list).

iii. **Backstop indicator.** A rebuttable presumption prescribes allocating to stage 2 accounts more than 30 days past due (equivalently one month in arrears). One may rebut this presumption by showing that this criterion does not affect bank's credit process.

Figure 6.8 provides some hints on how to perform the comparison, based on a quantitative approach (that is, quantitative element above described).

Few questions need to be addressed, as detailed below:

- **How to weight curves based on scenarios?** It is worth noting that scenarios need to be projected both at origination and reporting date. In terms of marginal PD computation, two main alternatives can be followed. On the one hand, one may compute PDs for alternative scenarios and average them for each time t. On the other hand, one may average scenarios, and derive marginal curves based on lifetime modelling.

- **How to perform the comparison?** A first intuitive approach is to compare cumulative PDs (that is, curve defined at origination and at reporting date) at maturity date. As an alternative, one may average PDs over the entire period under analysis.
- **Relative or absolute metric?** A relative comparison relies on the ratio between origination and reporting date PDs. As an example, if the average PD over the residual maturity life computed at origination is 2.00%, and at reporting date is 3.50%, a relative comparison highlights a 175.00% increase. On the other hand, an absolute comparison points out a 1.50% increase (that is, absolute difference between origination and reporting date PDs).
- **How to set a tolerance threshold?** In our previous example, if a threshold is set in terms of ratio at 150.00%, then a significant increase in credit risk occurred. The account is allocated in stage 2. In contrast, if such a threshold is set at 200.00%, no significant increase in credit risk took place. Therefore the account is allocated in stage 1. Let us now consider an absolute threshold set at 3.00%. In our case 3.50% > 3.00%. Therefore the account is allocated to stage 2. Contrastingly, if the threshold is set at 4.00%, the account is allocated to stage 1. Additionally, one may use a combination of relative and absolute barriers according to bank's appetite. Portfolio can be split into clusters, where relative or absolute comparisons are performed. In this regard, when comparing origination against reporting date PDs, one needs to bear in mind that: for small PDs (for example, $<= 1\%$), a relative comparison (that is, ratio between reporting date vs. origination) may end-up with aberrant values. As a consequence, an absolute threshold may be preferable. For greater PDs, a relative comparison may be considered in conjunction with an absolute threshold.

Example 6.3.2 provides some additional hints on how to structure a staging framework.

EXAMPLE 6.3.2 STAGING THRESHOLD DEFINITION

Let us assume a staging mechanism based on clusters. A set of criteria is defined based on average PD over the residual time to maturity. The following cluster is identified:

- Lower risk: average PD at reporting date $\leq 1.50\%$.
- Medium risk: average PD at reporting date $1.50\% < PD \leq 3.50\%$
- Higher risk: average PD at reporting date > 3.50%.

Thresholds based on these three clusters are defined as follows:

- For the first cluster (i.e., lower risk) an absolute threshold is defined in terms of 30 basis points. In this case, if the difference between average PD at reporting date and origination is higher than 30 basis points, the account is allocated to stage 2.
- For the second PD band (i.e., medium risk) a 75 basis point absolute threshold holds.
- For the third PD band (i.e., higher risk) a relative threshold is set as ratio between reporting date and origination PD. When this ratio exceeds 200.00% (i.e., PD doubles), an account is allocated to stage 2.

Once thresholds are defined, few more options may be considered to finalize ECL computation as listed below:

- **Option a.** A weighted average lifetime PD is used to allocate accounts to stage 1 or stage 2, based on what follows:
  - Staging allocation is based on the weighted average lifetime PD.
  - Weighted average lifetime PD is compared against staging threshold.
  - The account is allocated to one stage.

  Example 6.3.3 provides some hints on how to implement this framework.

EXAMPLE 6.3.3 STAGING ALLOCATION OPTION A

Let us consider a 6.00% staging threshold for a given account under analysis. Three scenarios, denoted as A, B and C in Table 6.8, are considered. One-year and lifetime PDs are shown as a function of scenarios. The simplifying assumption of constant LGD applies. From a financial standpoint, we rely on a bullet instrument repaying both principal and interest at maturity.

An account is allocated to stage 1, based on the weighted average lifetime PD. In our case, the average lifetime PD is 5.55% (that is, $2.00\% \cdot 30.00\% + 5.50\% \cdot 50.00\% + 11.00\% \cdot 20.00\%$). Since 5.55% < 6.00%, the account is allocated to stage 1. Therefore ECL is $22.20 thousand (that is, one-year estimate).

Table 6.8 Staging allocation framework. Option a ($ Thousands)

Scenario	Weight	One-year PD	Lifetime PD	LGD	EAD	One-year ECL	Lifetime ECL	One-year ECL weighted	Lifetime ECL weighted
A	30.00%	1.00%	2.00%	60.00%	1,000.00	6.00	12.00	1.80	3.60
B	50.00%	4.00%	5.50%	60.00%	1,000.00	24.00	33.00	12.00	16.50
C	20.00%	7.00%	11.00%	60.00%	1,000.00	42.00	66.00	8.40	13.20
Average PD			5.55%						
ECL								22.20	33.30

- **Option b.** Lifetime PD associated to the most likely scenario informs account allocation to stage 1 or stage 2. The process works as follows:
  - Staging allocation is based on the most likely scenario.
  - Lifetime PD corresponding to the most likely scenario is compared against staging threshold.
  - The account is allocated to one stage.

  Based on Example 6.3.3, scenario B is the most likely. In this case, lifetime PD is 5.50%, which is lower than the 6.00% threshold. Therefore the account is allocated to stage 1. On the other hand, ECL is computed as a weighted average, based on scenarios A, B, and C. As a consequence, ECL is $ 22.20 thousand (corresponding to one-year estimate), as in Example 6.3.3.

- **Option c.** For each scenario the allocation process is performed. ECL is computed as a weighted average of ECLs related to each scenario, as follows:
  - For each individual scenario, lifetime PD is compared against the transfer criteria threshold.
  - Based on the above, one-year of lifetime ECL is computed for each scenario.

• ECL is then calculated as an average of scenario ECLs already computed.

Example 6.3.4 helps us to grasp how option c works.

EXAMPLE 6.3.4 STAGING ALLOCATION OPTION C

Let us consider Example 6.3.3 setting in terms of staging threshold, scenarios, and credit risk parameters. For each scenario the account is allocated to one stage. The final ECL is the weighted average of each scenario ECL.

Table 6.9 Staging allocation framework. Option c ($ Thousands)

Scenario	Weight	One-year PD	Life-time PD	LGD	EAD	One-year ECL	Life-time ECL	Stage	ECL
A	30.00%	1.00%	2.00%	60.00%	1,000.00	6.00	12.00	1	1.80
B	50.00%	4.00%	5.50%	60.00%	1,000.00	24.00	33.00	1	12.00
C	20.00%	7.00%	11.00%	60.00%	1,000.00	42.00	66.00	2	13.20
Total									27.00

The last column of Table 6.9 shows that ECL is $27.00 thousand.

The next section focuses on ECL validation process.

6.4 ECL VALIDATION

The final step of our journey is to verify ECL reliability from a holistic perspective. Few limitations affect ECL framework, based on Equation (6.18). Firstly, one may challenge credit risk parameter independence (Bellotti, 2017). Secondly, the implicit absence of concentration assumption is not aligned with practical experience. Indeed, both name and sector concentration play a key role, in particular, during a crisis (Bellini, 2017). Some additional challenges are also detailed in Business Case 6.4.1.

BUSINESS CASE 6.4.1 IFRS 9 VS. IAS 39: EVIDENCE FROM THE MARKET

As per January 2018, major institutions across the globe started adopting IFRS 9 rules. A simple comparison of provisions under IAS 39 and IFRS 9 may help focusing on the key elements informing the next generation of financial statements.

Figure 6.9 compares the overall coverage (that is, ratio between provisions and gross exposure) for a set of UK operating banks (that is, Barclays, HSBC, Lloyds and Royal Bank of Scotland) under IAS 39 and IFRS 9 (that is, bubble size represents IFRS 9 provisions). Data refer to 1 January 2018 transition note. For all banks, an increase in provisions is experienced. Nevertheless, the magnitude of this increase varies. Indeed, Royal Bank of Scotland (RBS) provisions increase sits in the range of 15–20%, HSBC and Lloyds growth is in the range of 30–35%, whereas Barclays provisions rose more than 50%.

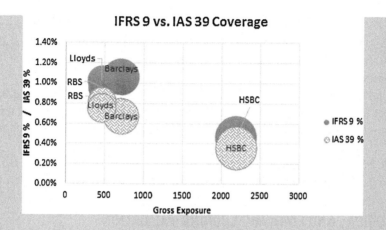

FIGURE 6.9

IAS 39 vs. IFRS 9 provisions for a set of UK operating banks as per 1 January 2018 transition note ($ Millions).

As an additional step, one may investigate how these increases may be affected by staging. Figure 6.10 compares all banks under investigation by summarizing portfolio composition by stage. Barclays experienced the major contribution of stage 2, followed by Lloyds. For both of them, the contribution of stage 2 is in the range of 10–15%. On the other hand, stage 2 accounts for approximately 6% of gross exposure for both HSBC and RBS.

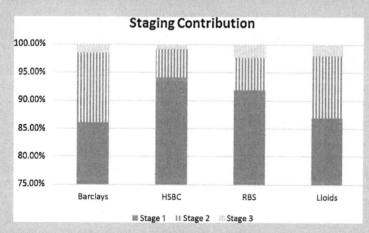

FIGURE 6.10

Staging contribution for a set of UK operating banks.

In line with Business Case 6.4.1, one of the first questions one needs to address is whether ECL figures, both for IFRS 9 and CECL, are representative of portfolio potential losses. Indeed, a silos validation of PD, LGD and EAD does not allow us to capture more sophisticated linkages underlying credit loss mechanics. As an additional element characterizing IFRS 9, one should also validate a staging process. Indeed, Business Case 6.4.1 clearly highlights how staging may drive ECL estimates by requiring one-year of lifetime estimates.

Two main perspectives can be followed to validate ECL as a whole. On the one hand, one may follow a historical perspective to back-test estimated ECLs. On the other hand, a forward-looking perspective informed by credit portfolio modelling may provide a relevant guidance to assess ECL consistency.

Section 6.4.1 follows a historical perspective, whereas Section 6.4.2 provides some hints on how credit portfolio modelling may help validating ECL moving from a scenario simulation viewpoint.

6.4.1 HISTORICAL AND FORWARD-LOOKING VALIDATION

One of the most intuitive ways to validate ECL is to perform a historical comparison. Based on this, one may apply models back in time and follow a sound foresight perspective. Model estimates are compared against actual losses. A cohort study can be performed as follows:

- **Portfolio in scope.** Firstly, one needs to identify a consistent portfolio to compare. Particular attention needs to be devoted to its changes through time in terms of factors, such as size, geography and business type.
- **Clusters.** Due to financial instrument intrinsic differences, one should structure the analysis by focusing on homogeneous sub-portfolios. This process facilitates the comparison through time, and allows us to better understand credit peculiarities (for example, geography and product type).
- **Vintages.** Life-cycle characteristics usually play an important role in driving credit losses. This particularly applies to long-run products, for example, retail mortgages. Additionally, for long-run products, one may encounter some difficulties in collecting historical data over decades.
- **Macroeconomic conditions.** In line with Section 6.3, ECL is computed by considering alternative scenarios. In reality, only one scenario at a time affects the business. Consequently, a cohort analysis, including a crisis (for example, 2007–2009), may help understanding loss dynamics under stressed conditions.

Comparison can be performed both in terms of synthetic metrics, such as average losses, or by focusing on distributions. What if analyses help understanding discrepancies between actual and expected losses and provide a justification.

In line with Business Case 6.4.1, one needs to pay particular attention to the staging allocation process adopted for IFRS 9. Indeed, the mechanics involved heavily affects ECL outcomes. Discrepancies between historical and expected losses may be explored by challenging staging criteria. Sensitivity analysis is particularly useful even in this context.

In all cases, one needs to adopt a flexible mindset to point out key strengths and limitations of the complex framework informing ECL estimates, both under IASB (2014) and FASB (2016).

The next section explores an alternative approach to validate ECL by focusing on credit portfolio models.

6.4.2 CREDIT PORTFOLIO MODELLING AND ECL ESTIMATION

If historical analysis provides an important anchor point, a comprehensive validation also needs to explore inexperienced conditions. In this regard, credit portfolio modelling provides a suitable framework to assess ECL estimates under alternative settings.

The aim of a portfolio model is to derive a credit loss distribution, starting from an overarching framework, fed through risk parameters, such as PDs, LGDs and EADs. Such a distribution is built on the principle that account i may be insolvent and, in the case of default, its exposure may not be fully recovered. In this regard, the probability of default (PD_i) represents the likelihood of the insolvency. Loss given default (LGD_i) summarizes the non-recovered portion of an asset exposure (EAD_i).

Alternative portfolio approaches have been developed in the recent past (Koyluoglu and Hickman, 1998). Some models rely on a closed formula Gordy (2003), but more commonly, a Monte Carlo simulation is used to derive such a distribution. In the latter case, for each simulation $g = 1, \ldots, G$, a credit loss is derived from the product of a given default indicator ($\mathbb{1}^{def}_{i,s,\Delta,g}$) times $LGD_{i,s,\Delta,g}$ and $EAD_{i,s,\Delta,g}$. Portfolio credit loss ($CLoss_g$) is computed as listed below:

$$CLoss_g = \sum_{i=1}^{n} \mathbb{1}^{def}_{i,s,\Delta,g} LGD_{i,s,\Delta,g} EAD_{i,s,\Delta,g}, \qquad (6.20)$$

where s stands for portfolio, Δ indicates a scenario specifically denoted g. One may repeat the random process and obtain a distribution aligned with Figure 6.11. This curve highlights a typical asymmetric profile, where small losses have higher chance than greater losses. At the same time, Figure 6.11, points out the distinction between expected loss (EL) and unexpected loss (UL). The latter is computed as a difference between a given quantile of the distribution (that is, credit value at risk $VaR_{credit,(1-\alpha)}$) and EL.

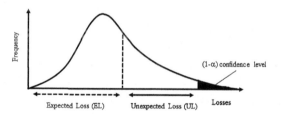

FIGURE 6.11

Loss distribution. Expected loss (EL) versus unexpected loss (UL).

From an ECL standpoint, the focus is on portfolio average loss (that is, expected loss). In contrast, BIS (2006) focuses on unexpected loss. In this regard, Basel II does not rely on accounting ECL, but on expected losses computed by relying on internal rating-based (IRB) models. A misalignment may arise between accounting ECL and EL computed under Basel II. Therefore the potential increase in provisions, due to IASB (2014) and FASB (2016), may impact capital absorption and, consequently, capital ratios, as described in Chapter 1.

Credit portfolio models usually focus on a one-year horizon. They consider PD as stochastic, whereas LGD and EAD are deterministic. Nevertheless, one may easily remove these restrictions by considering a multi-period setting, where all parameters are allowed to fluctuate based on economic movements. This becomes a natural framework to validate ECL estimates.

Figure 6.12 summarizes our portfolio credit loss framework to validate ECL.

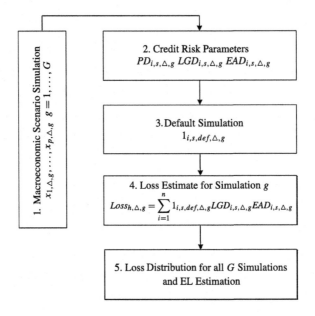

FIGURE 6.12

Portfolio credit loss framework to validate ECLs.

One needs to perform the following steps:

1. **Macroeconomic scenario simulation.** Scenarios are generated over a lifetime horizon. In line with Section 6.2, time series analysis is useful not only to fit historical data and project one scenario, but also to randomly generate macroeconomic paths $\mathbf{x}_{\Delta,g} = (x_{1,\Delta,g}, \ldots, x_{p,\Delta,g})'$, $g = 1, \ldots, G$.[4]

---

[4] As an alternative, one may simulate macroeconomic variables by relying on their historical distribution. A multivariate copula or mixture model allows us to capture macroeconomic joint patterns in line with historical occurrences. Following a mixture approach, the density of the macroeconomic variables $\mathbf{x}_t = (x_{1,t}, \ldots, x_{p,t})'$ may be written as follows:

$$g(\mathbf{x}_t) = \sum_{r=1}^{p} \lambda_r \phi_r(x_{r,t}),\qquad(6.21)$$

where $(\lambda, \phi) = (\lambda_1, \ldots, \lambda_p, \phi_1, \ldots, \phi_p)$ denotes the vector of parameters, whereas λ_r are weights and sum to unity. The normal function parametric family, among others, may be a useful starting point to simulate macroeconomic scenarios by relying on Equation (6.21).

2. **Credit risk parameters**. Credit risk parameters are projected at an account level. The probability of default $PD_{i,s,\Delta}$ feeds both default simulation process and loss estimation. On the other hand, $LGD_{i,s,\Delta}$ and $EAD_{i,s,\Delta}$ enter into loss estimation only.
3. **Default simulation**. As a starting point, each account belongs to a specific sub-portfolio $s = 1, \ldots, S$. For each macroeconomic scenario, a copula is used to generate a random vector $\mathbf{u}_g = (u_{1,g}, \ldots, u_{S,g})'$, where $0 \leq u_{s,g} \leq 1$. Default occurs when $PD_{i,s,\Delta,g} \geq u_{s,g}$. In this case, $\mathbb{1}_{i,s,\Delta,g}^{def}$ of Equation (6.20) assumes value 1. It is worth noting that copula parameters are required to reflect interdependencies among sub-portfolios. Example 6.4.1 analyses how to fit a Student T copula on real time series.

EXAMPLE 6.4.1 HOW TO FIT COPULA PARAMETERS

Quarterly default rate time series from 1990 to 2010 may be used as creditworthiness index Ψ_s. A Student T copula is fitted on these time series by means of the following steps:

1. Upload data,
2. Set parameters, and
3. Fit data with Student-T copula.

```
# 1. Upload data
library(copula)
t_orig <- as.data.frame(read.csv("sector5.csv", header = TRUE,
sep = ";", dec="."))
sector_5 <- as.matrix(read.csv("sector5head.csv", header = TRUE,
sep = ";", dec="."))
SIMcustomer_5 <- as.data.frame(read.csv("sector5val.csv",
header = TRUE, sep = ";", dec="."))
# 2. Set parameters
set.seed(1234567)
t_d<-t_orig[,2:6]
mat_cor_td<- cor(t_d, method="kendall")
cor_td<- mat_cor_td[upper.tri(mat_cor_td,diag=FALSE)]
n_row_td<- nrow(t_d)
n_col_td<- ncol(t_d)
nSimI <- 1000
# 3. Fit data with Student-T copula
t_cop1 <- tCopula(cor_td,dim=n_col_td, dispstr="un",df=5,df.fixed=TRUE)
aa<- rep(0, n_col_td*(n_col_td-1)/2)
u <- apply(t_d, 2, rank) / (n_row_td + 1) ## pseudo-observations
fit_tau <- fitCopula(t_cop1, u, method="itau")
param_estimate<-attributes(fit_tau)$estimate
fitted_t_copula<- tCopula(param_estimate, dim=n_col_td, dispstr="un",
df=5, df.fixed=TRUE)
```

4. **Loss estimate for simulation g.** For each simulation g a loss is computed as per Equation (6.20).

5. **Loss distribution for all G simulations.** Losses computed for each simulation g are ranked to derive a loss distribution. Then, the expected loss is computed as an average of the distribution. For a lifetime estimation, the process needs to be repeated throughout the lifetime horizon by conditioning each path on previous time occurrences. In other words, if an account defaults at the first time step, it will be discarded from the portfolio, as detailed in Figure 6.13.

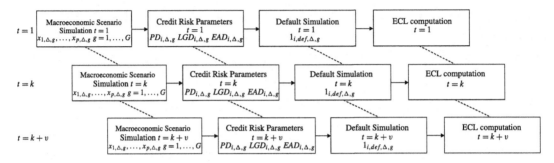

FIGURE 6.13

Lifetime ECL simulation framework.

Example 6.4.2 provides some hints on how to conduct the analysis over a lifetime (three-year) horizon.

EXAMPLE 6.4.2 HOW TO SIMULATE CREDIT PORTFOLIO LOSSES

Moving from the estimated Student T copula from Example 6.4.1, the following steps are performed to simulate portfolio credit loss distribution:

1. Simulate random generations,
2. Merge simulations with sector data,
3. Merge database simulation and accounts (by row),
4. Simulate defaults (a simplistic coding is used to help understanding each step of the process), and
5. Compute loss metrics.

```
# 1. Simulate random generations
r_t_copula1 <- rCopula(nSimI,fitted_t_copula)
r_t_copula2 <- rCopula(nSimI,fitted_t_copula)
r_t_copula3 <- rCopula(nSimI,fitted_t_copula)
# 2. Merge simulations with sector data
rand_copula1<-cbind(sector_5,t(as.matrix(r_t_copula1)))
```

```
rand_copula2<-cbind(sector_5,t(as.matrix(r_t_copula2)))
rand_copula3<-cbind(sector_5,t(as.matrix(r_t_copula3)))
# 3. Merge database simulation and accounts (by row)
mm1 <- as.matrix(SIMcustomer_5$SECTOR)
colnames(mm1)<- c("SECTOR")
rand_copula_1 <- merge(mm1, rand_copula1, by.x = "SECTOR",
by.y = "SECTOR")
rand_copula_pd1<-as.matrix(rand_copula_1[1:200,2: ncol(rand_copula_1)] )
rand_copula_2 <- merge(mm1, rand_copula2, by.x = "SECTOR",
by.y = "SECTOR")
rand_copula_pd2<-as.matrix(rand_copula_2[201:400,2: ncol(rand_copula_2)] )
rand_copula_3 <- merge(mm1, rand_copula3, by.x = "SECTOR",
by.y = "SECTOR")
rand_copula_pd3<-as.matrix(rand_copula_3[401:600,2: ncol(rand_copula_3)] )
# 4. Simulate defaults
cr_customer  <- 200
intrate<- 0.02
# 4.1. Year 1
sim_default1cr <- matrix(NaN, nrow=cr_customer,ncol=nSimI)
sim_def_flag1 <- matrix(NaN, nrow=cr_customer,ncol=nSimI)
for (i in 1:cr_customer)
 for (j in 1:nSimI)
 {
  {
   verif <- SIMcustomer_5[i,4]- rand_copula_pd1[i,j]
   if(verif>=0)
   {
    sim_default1cr[i,j]<- (1-SIMcustomer_5[i,5])
    sim_def_flag1[i,j]<- 0
   }
   else
   {
    sim_default1cr[i,j]<- 1
    sim_def_flag1[i,j]<- 1
   }
  }
 }
pv1 <- 1/(1+intrate)
loss1y <- pv1*(sum(SIMcustomer_5[1:cr_customer,3])-
 t(SIMcustomer_5[1:cr_customer,3])%*%sim_default1cr)
# 4.2. Year 2
sim_default2cr <- matrix(NaN, nrow=cr_customer,ncol=nSimI)
sim_def_flag2 <- matrix(NaN, nrow=cr_customer,ncol=nSimI)
```

```
for (i in 1:cr_customer)
 for (j in 1:nSimI)
 {
  {
   verif <- SIMcustomer_5[i+cr_customer,4]-
   rand_copula_pd2[i,j]
   if(verif>=0)
    {
    sim_default2cr[i,j]<-(1-SIMcustomer_5[i+cr_customer,5])*
    sim_def_flag1[i,j]
    sim_def_flag2[i,j]<- 0
    }
   else
    {
    sim_default2cr[i,j] <- 1 *sim_def_flag1[i,j]
    sim_def_flag2[i,j]<- 1
    }
  }
 }
pv2 <- 1/(1+intrate)^2
loss2y <- pv2*(t(SIMcustomer_5[201:400,3])%*%sim_def_flag1-
        t(SIMcustomer_5[201:400,3])%*%sim_default2cr)
# 4.3. Year 3
sim_default3cr <- matrix(NaN, nrow=cr_customer,ncol=nSimI)
sim_def_flag3 <- matrix(NaN, nrow=cr_customer,ncol=nSimI)
for (i in 1:cr_customer)
 for (j in 1:nSimI)
 {
  {
   verif <-   SIMcustomer_5[i+(2*cr_customer),4]-
   rand_copula_pd3[i,j]
   if(verif>=0)
    {
    sim_default3cr[i,j]<- (1-SIMcustomer_5[i+(2*cr_customer),5])*
    sim_def_flag2[i,j]
    sim_def_flag3[i,j]<- 0
    }
   else
    {
    sim_default3cr[i,j] <- 1 *sim_def_flag2[i,j]
    sim_def_flag3[i,j]<- 1
    }
  }
```

```
}
pv3 <- 1/(1+intrate)^3
loss3y <- pv3*(t(SIMcustomer_5[401:600,3])%*%sim_def_flag2-
    t(SIMcustomer_5[401:600,3])%*%sim_default3cr)
# 5. Compute loss metrics
lossyy<-rbind(loss1y,loss2y,loss3y)
cumloss <- colSums(lossyy)
mean(cumloss)
# 300214.8
```

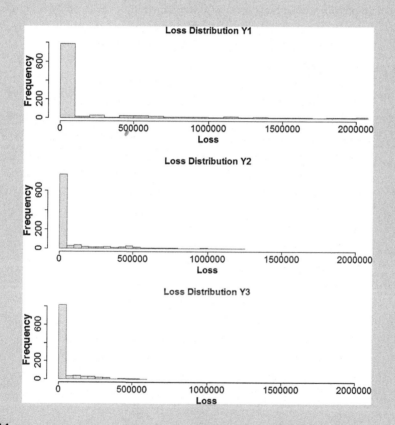

FIGURE 6.14

Credit loss distribution based on a Student T simulation for year 1, year 2 and year 3 ($).

When relying on a Student T copula estimated on empirical data, the cumulative present value mean loss is $300,214. In case of zero correlation, this loss reduces to $289,413, which is very close to $281,321 lifetime ECL, computed as a present value of the product $PD \times LGD \times EAD$. (See Figure 6.14.)

In line with the above, average loss is compared against IFRS 9 or CECL estimate. At least two settings may be considered to appreciate the role of correlation:

- **No correlation.** A first run should rely on the presumed independence assumption underlying Equation (6.18).
- **Correlation.** The introduction of this ingredient may cause potential misalignment of accounting ECL and credit portfolio modelling ECL. This is where senior management needs to be involved for an overall assessment of ECL estimates. Likewise, auditors and external validator should also inspect potential reasons for misalignment with financial reporting figures.

The next section provides some hints on how to implement time series analysis by means of SAS.

6.5 SAS LABORATORY

SAS Laboratory 6.5.1 focuses on time series analysis, as discussed in Examples 6.2.2 and 6.2.3.

SAS LABORATORY 6.5.1 MULTIVARIATE TIME SERIES ANALYSIS

Let us consider Examples 6.2.2 and 6.2.3. Firstly, one needs to upload the corresponding data file, then the analysis is replicated by means of the following steps:

1. ADF-test original variables,
2. ADF-test first difference, and
3. Fit model.

```
/* 1. ADF test original variables */
proc varmax data=data_;
model LN_GDP LN_CPI LN_EQ LN_FX IR_S IR_L / p=1
dftest print=(estimates roots);
run;

/* 2. ADF test first difference */
proc varmax data=data_;
model LN_GDP LN_CPI LN_EQ LN_FX IR_S IR_L / p=1
dftest dify=(1) print=(estimates roots) ;
run;

/* 3. Fit model */
/* ods option enables impulse response graphics */
/* lead option provides forecasts */
ods graphics on;
proc varmax data= data_ plots=all;
model LN_GDP    LN_CPI    LN_EQ LN_FX IR_S IR_L / p=1
lagmax=3 print=(impulse covpe(5) decompose(10));
```

```
output lead=10;
run;
```

6.6 SUMMARY

The chapter introduced some of the key concepts to analyse multivariate time series by means of vector auto-regression (VAR) and vector error-correction (VEC) models. Hints were also provided on global vector auto-regression (GVAR) modelling. All these models were studied as a basis to develop macroeconomic scenarios feeding our expected credit loss (ECL) framework.

Data, scenarios, credit risk satellite models were funnelled into a mechanism to compute ECL. Few distinctive elements characterized IFRS 9 compared to CECL. Indeed, a staging process was inspected for IFRS 9 purposes, to separate credits according to a significant increase of credit risk criterion. Based on that, one-year or lifetime ECL applied. In addition, the need to converge over a long-run loss rate was addressed by focusing on scenario design to meet CECL requirements.

As a final step of our journey, the overall ECL validation challenge was tackled by considering two perspectives. On the one hand, a historical view was followed. On the other hand, credit portfolio modelling was adopted to embed a forward-looking perspective to perform the analysis. Criticisms were pointed out with regard to the independence assumption underlying ECL computed as a product of probability of default, loss given default, and exposure at default. As a final remark, warnings were pointed out about a potential for procyclicality, due to the forward-looking perspective informing the renewed credit loss frame informing both IFRS 9 and CECL.

Data and complementary examples' software code are available at www.tizianobellini.com.

SUGGESTIONS FOR FURTHER READING

Time series analysis is described in classical books, such as, Hamilton (1994). Johansen (1996) and Juselius (2006) focus on cointegration by highlighting both theory and practical exemplifications. Additionally, Lutkepohl (2007) proposes a very interesting analysis of VAR and VEC models by means of the software JMulti (that is, a software application explicitly devoted to VAR, VEC and other time series analysis). Following a more marked software perspective, Pfaff (2008) shows how to analyse integrated and cointegrated time series with R. Following Pesaran et al. (2004), the high number of recent papers on GVAR show the growing interest in this subject. Among these researches, it is worth mentioning Dees et al. (2007) and Castren et al. (2010). Apart from the easy-to-implement framework proposed by Robertson and Tallman (1999), a useful reference for conditional forecasting is Pesaran et al. (2007). Starting from the seminal documents produced at the eve of the credit portfolio management, CreditMetrics (1997), CSFB (1997) and Wilson (1997) show the key ideas behind the methodologies still in use in the current risk practice. Bellini (2013, 2017) enriches the investigation by proposing an integrated perspective, where credit, market, interest rate, and liquidity risks are jointly modelled.

EXERCISES

Exercise 6.1. The file chap6ex1.xlsx contains time series spanning from 1993 to 2010. The focus is on the following quarterly variables: default rate (DR), gross domestic product (GDP), unemployment rate (UER), real estate price index (RE), exchange rate Euro against $ (ER), 3-month euribor (EUR3M), and 10-year interest rate swap (IRS10). Perform the following analyses:

- Perform Johansen trace test.
- Check residual properties.

Exercise 6.2. Based on the model applied in Exercise 6.1, perform the following analyses:

- Run the impulse response analysis after having converted the VEC into VAR model.
- Forecast 50 paths of the estimated model over a 10 quarters.

Exercise 6.3. Based on the portfolio studied in Example 6.4.2, investigate loss distribution in the following two cases:

- 0% correlation among sub-portfolios.
- 50% correlation among sub-portfolios.

REFERENCES

Bellini, T., 2013. Integrated bank risk modeling: a bottom-up statistical framework. European Journal of Operational Research 230, 385–398.

Bellini, T., 2016. The forward search interactive outlier detection in cointegrated VAR analysis. Advances in Data Analysis and Classification 10 (3), 351–373.

Bellini, T., 2017. Stress Testing and Risk Integration in Banks: A Statistical Framework and Practical Software Guide (in Matlab and R). Academic Press, San Diego.

Bellotti, A., 2017. Estimating unbiased expected loss, with application to consumer credit.

BIS, 2006. Basel II International Convergence of Capital Measurement and Capital Standards: A Revised Framework. BIS, Basel.

Castren, O., Dees, S., Zaher, F., 2010. Stress-testing euro area corporate default probabilities using a global macroeconomic model. Journal of Financial Stability 6, 64–74.

CreditMetrics, 1997. Creditmetrics. Technical document. www.creditmetrics.com.

CSFB, 1997. Creditrisk+: A credit risk management framework. New York, NY.

Dees, S., Di Mauro, F., Pesaran, M., Smith, L.V., 2007. Exploring the international linkages of the euro area: a global VAR analysis. Journal of Applied Econometrics 22, 1–38.

Doan, T., Litterman, R.B., Sims, A., 1984. Forecasting and conditional projections using realistic prior distributions. Econometric Reviews 3, 1–100.

Duffie, D., Singleton, K.J., 2003. Credit Risk Pricing, Measurement and Management. Princeton University Press, Princeton.

FASB, 2016. Accounting Standards Update No. 2016–13, Financial Instruments-Credit Losses (Topic 326). June 16, 2016. Financial Accounting Series. Financial Accounting Standards Board.

FRB, 2014. 2015 Supervisory Scenarios for Annual Stress Tests Required Under the Dodd–Frank Act Stress Testing Rules and the Capital Plan Rule. Board of Governors of the Federal Reserve System, Washington DC.

Gordy, M., 2003. A risk-factor foundation for risk-based capital rules. Journal of Financial Intermediation 12, 199–232.

Hamilton, J., 1994. Time Series Analysis. Princeton University Press, Princeton.

IASB, 2014. IFRS 9 Financial Instruments. Technical report, July 2014. International Accounting Standards Board.

Johansen, S., 1988. Statistical analysis of cointegration vectors. Journal of Economic Dynamics and Control 12, 231–254.

Johansen, S., 1996. Likelihood-Based Inference in Cointegrated Vector Autoregressive Models. Oxford University Press, Oxford.

Juselius, K., 2006. The Cointegrated VAR Model: Methodology and Applications. Oxford University Press, Oxford.

Koyluoglu, H., Hickman, A., 1998. Reconcilable differences. Risk 11 (10), 56–62.

LeSage, J.P., 1999. Applied Econometrics Using MATLAB. University of Toledo. http://www.spatial-econometrics.com/html/mbook.pdf.

Lutkepohl, H., 2007. New Introduction to Multiple Time Series Analysis. Springer-Verlag, Berlin.

Pesaran, M., Schuermann, T., Weiner, S., 2004. Modeling regional interdependencies using a global error-correcting macroeconometric model. Journal of Business and Economic Statistics 22, 129–162.

Pesaran, M., Smith, L.V., Smith, R.P., 2007. What if the UK or Sweden had joined the euro in 1999? An empirical evaluation using a global var. International Journal of Finance and Economics 12, 55–87.

Pfaff, B., 2008. Analysis of Integrated and Cointegrated Time Series with R. Springer, New York.

Robertson, J.C., Tallman, E.W., 1999. Vector autoregressions: forecasting and reality. Economic Review. Federal Reserve Bank of Atlanta.

Wilson, T., 1997. Portfolio credit risk (i). Risk 10, 111–117.

Index

Printed in the United States
By Bookmasters